D0938448

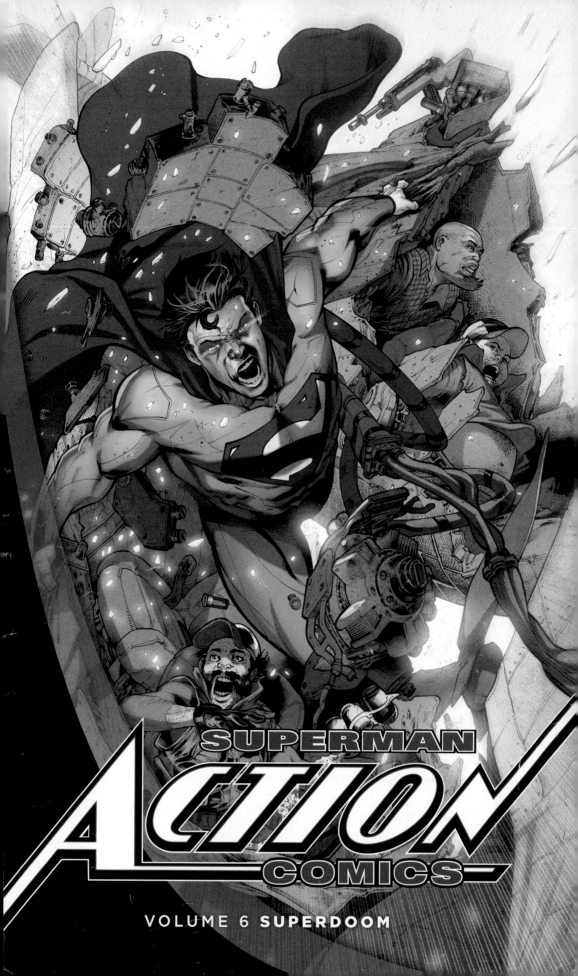

SUPERMAN
ACTION
COMICS

VOLUME 6 SUPERDOOM

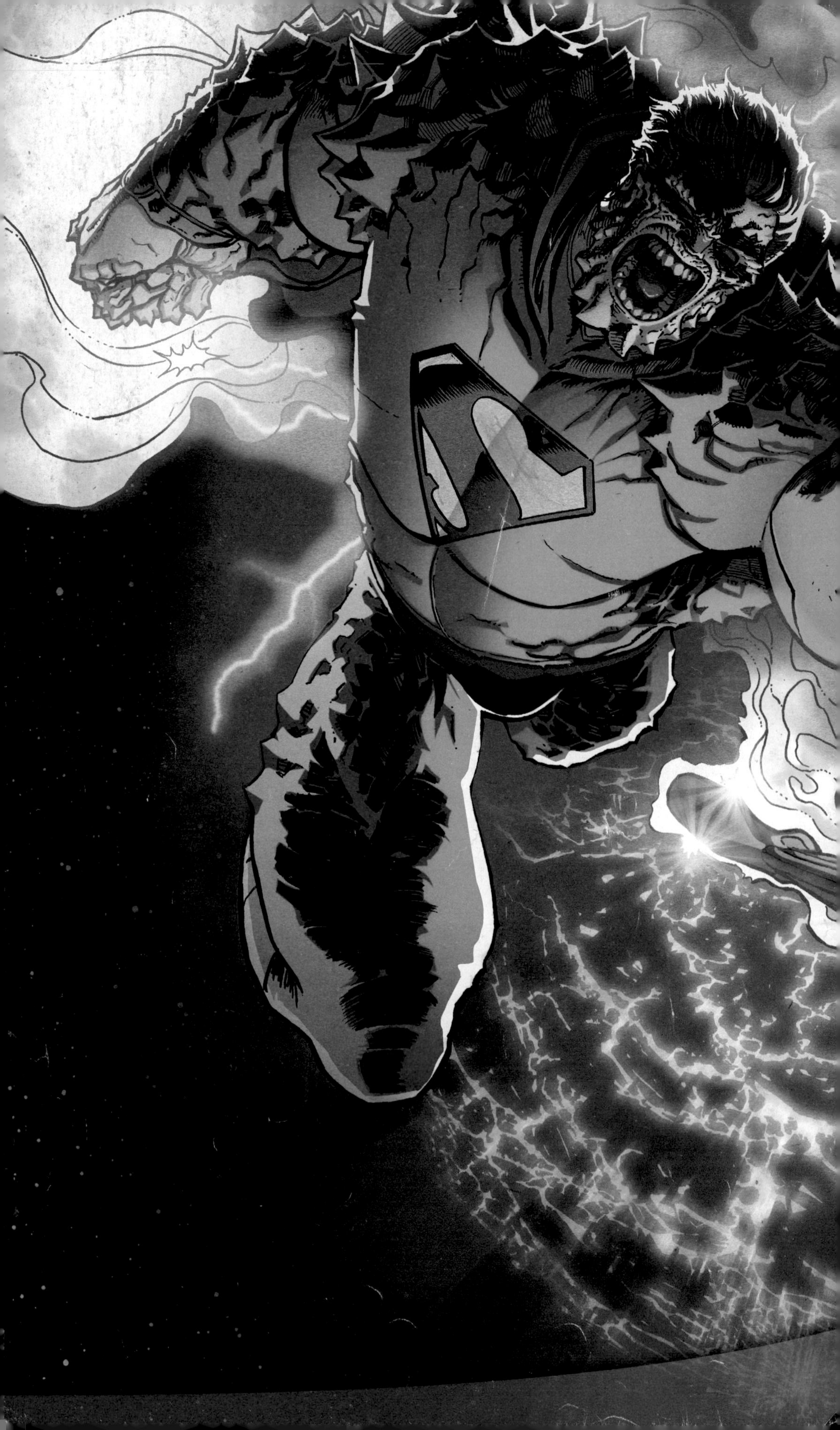

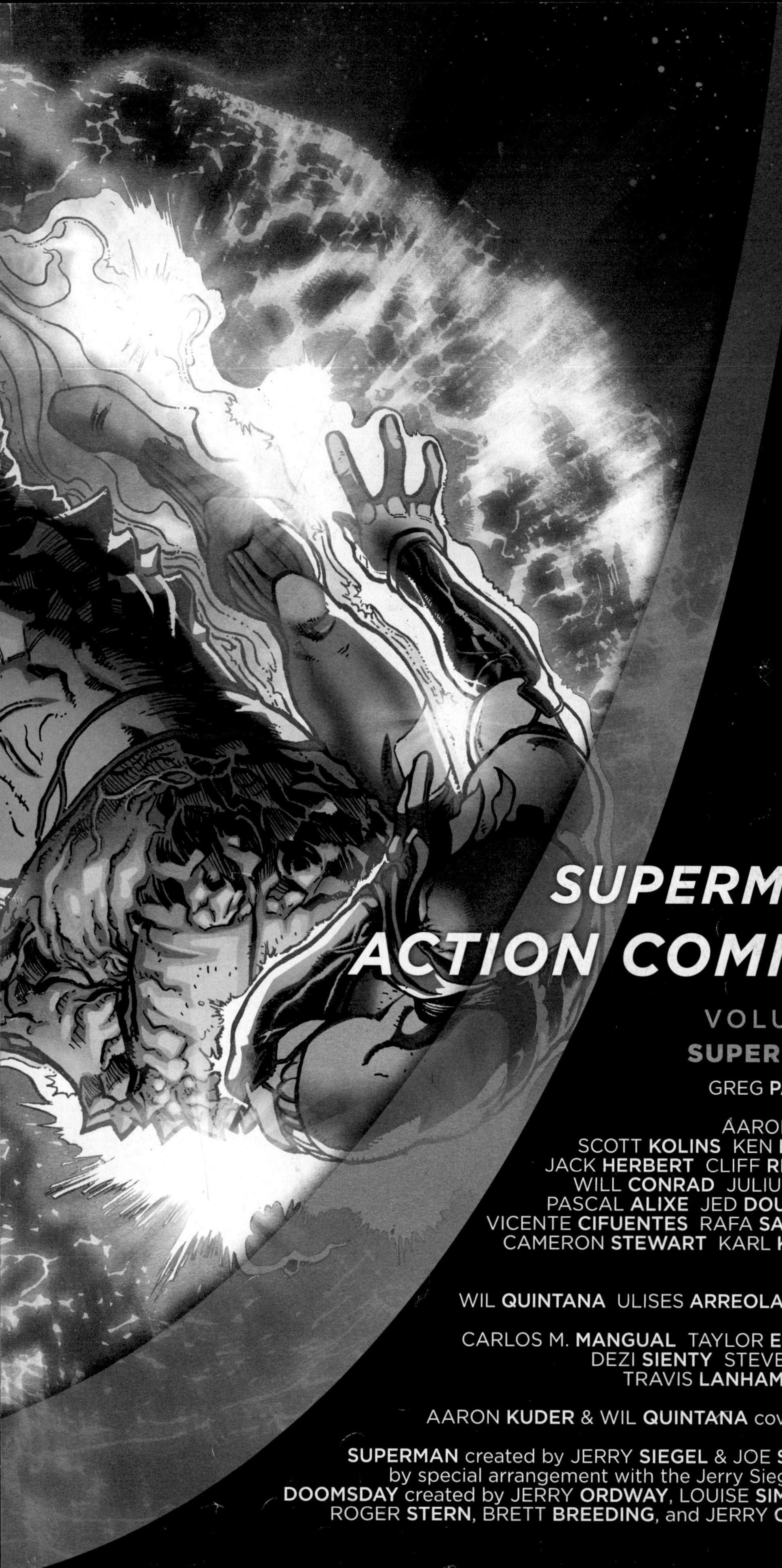

SUPERMAN ACTION COMICS

VOLUME 6

SUPERDOOM

GREG **PAK** writer

AARON **KUDER**
SCOTT **KOLINS** KEN **LASHLEY**
JACK **HERBERT** CLIFF **RICHARDS**
WILL **CONRAD** JULIUS **GOPEZ**
PASCAL **ALIXE** JED **DOUGHERTY**
VICENTE **CIFUENTES** RAFA **SANDOVAL**
CAMERON **STEWART** KARL **KERSCHL**
artists

WIL **QUINTANA** ULISES **ARREOLA** colorists

CARLOS M. **MANGUAL** TAYLOR **ESPOSITO**
DEZI **SIENTY** STEVE **WANDS**
TRAVIS **LANHAM** letterers

AARON **KUDER** & WIL **QUINTANA** cover artists

SUPERMAN created by JERRY **SIEGEL** & JOE **SHUSTER**
by special arrangement with the Jerry Siegel family
DOOMSDAY created by JERRY **ORDWAY**, LOUISE **SIMONSON**,
ROGER **STERN**, BRETT **BREEDING**, and JERRY **ORDWAY**.

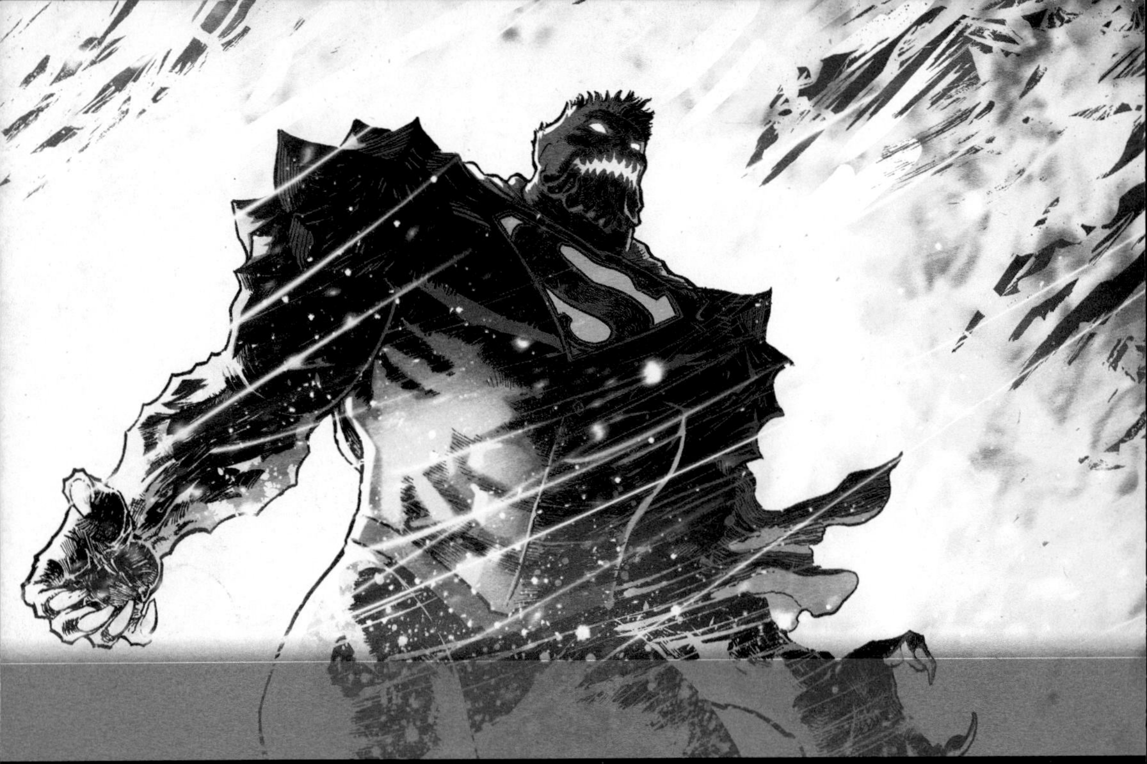

EDDIE BERGANZA Editor - Original Series ANTHONY MARQUES Assistant Editor - Original Series PAUL SANTOS Editor
ROBBIN BROSTERMAN Design Director - Books ROBBIE BIEDERMAN Publication Design

BOB HARRAS Senior VP - Editor-in-Chief, DC Comics

DIANE NELSON President DAN DIDIO and JIM LEE Co-Publishers GEOFF JOHNS Chief Creative Officer
JOHN ROOD Executive VP - Sales, Marketing and Business Development
AMY GENKINS Senior VP - Business and Legal Affairs NAIRI GARDINER Senior VP - Finance
JEFF BOISON VP - Publishing Planning MARK CHIARELLO VP - Art Direction and Design
JOHN CUNNINGHAM VP - Marketing TERRI CUNNINGHAM VP - Editorial Administration
ALISON GILL Senior VP - Manufacturing and Operations
HANK KANALZ Senior VP - Vertigo and Integrated Publishing
JAY KOGAN VP - Business and Legal Affairs, Publishing JACK MAHAN VP - Business Affairs, Talent
NICK NAPOLITANO VP - Manufacturing Administration SUE POHJA VP - Book Sales
COURTNEY SIMMONS Senior VP - Publicity BOB WAYNE Senior VP - Sales

SUPERMAN - ACTION COMICS VOLUME 6: SUPERDOOM

DC Comics, 4000 Warner Blvd., Burbank, CA 91522
A Warner Bros. Entertainment Company.
Printed by RR Donnelley, Salem, VA, USA. 5/08/15. First Printing.

HC ISBN: 978-1-4012-5489-6
SC ISBN: 978-1-4012-5865-8

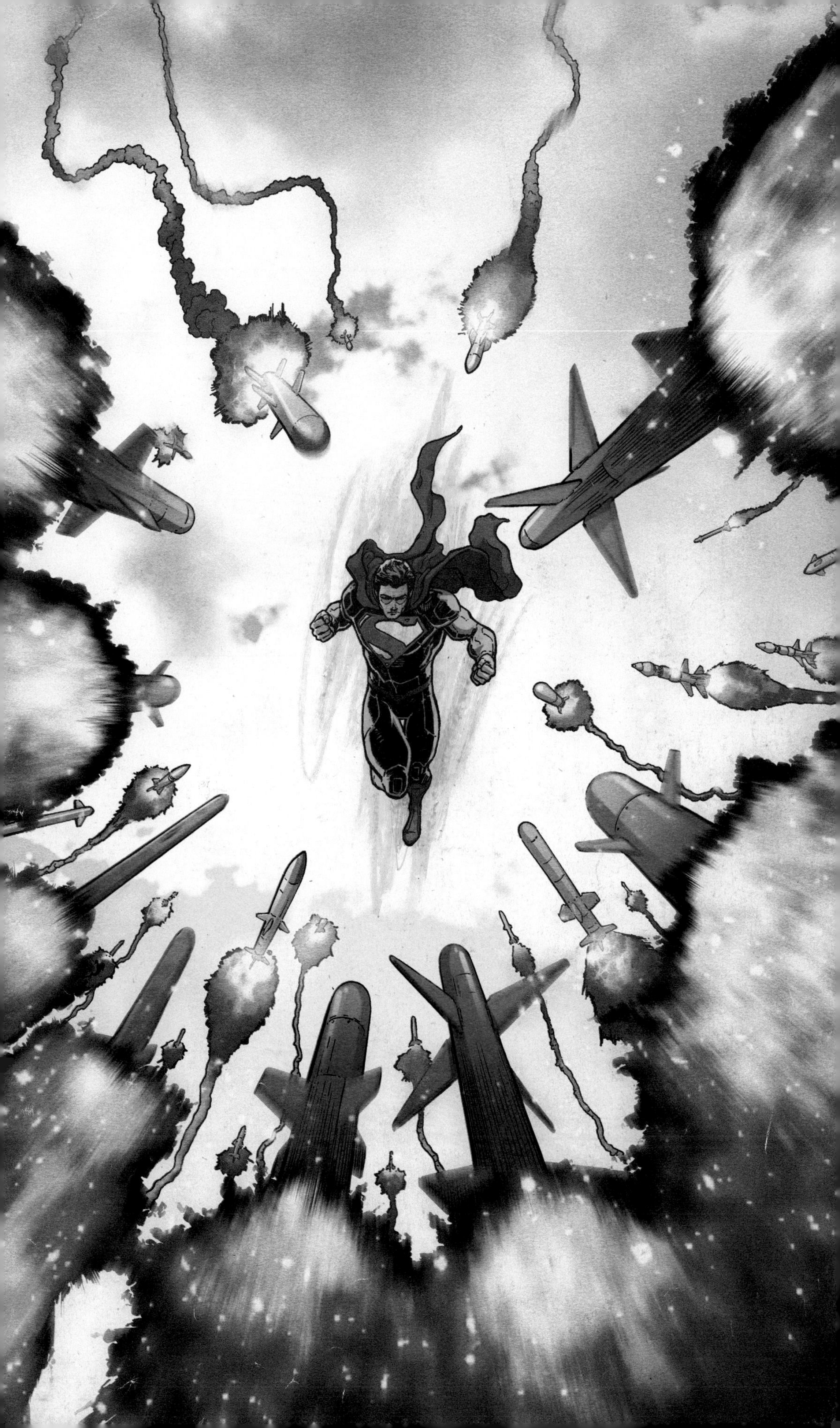

"PRELUDE"

GREG PAK writer **AARON KUDER JED DOUGHERTY KARL KERSCL** artists **WIL QUINTANA** colorist

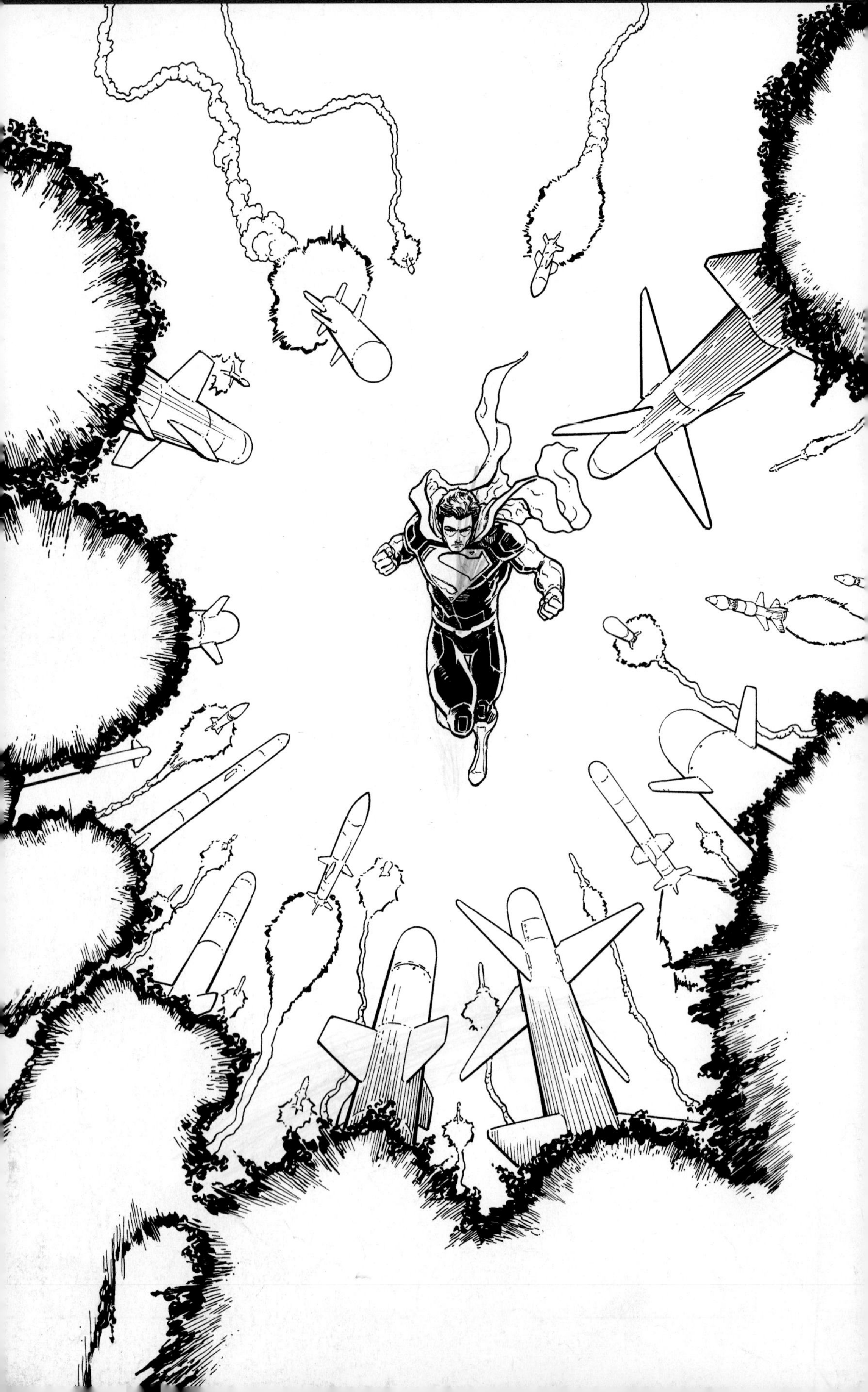

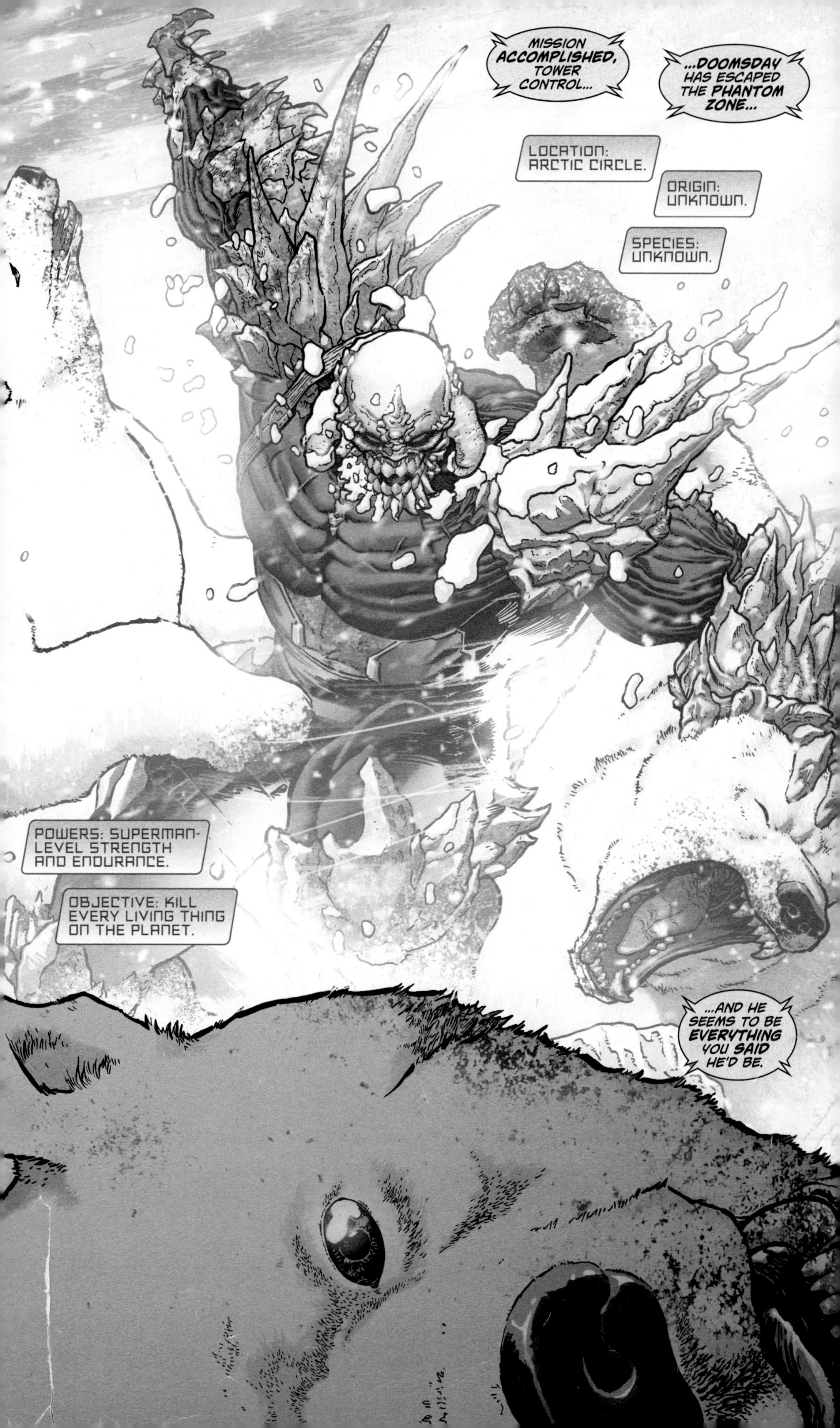
MISSION ACCOMPLISHED, TOWER CONTROL...
...DOOMSDAY HAS ESCAPED THE PHANTOM ZONE...
LOCATION: ARCTIC CIRCLE.
ORIGIN: UNKNOWN.
SPECIES: UNKNOWN.
POWERS: SUPERMAN-LEVEL STRENGTH AND ENDURANCE.
OBJECTIVE: KILL EVERY LIVING THING ON THE PLANET.
...AND HE SEEMS TO BE EVERYTHING YOU SAID HE'D BE.

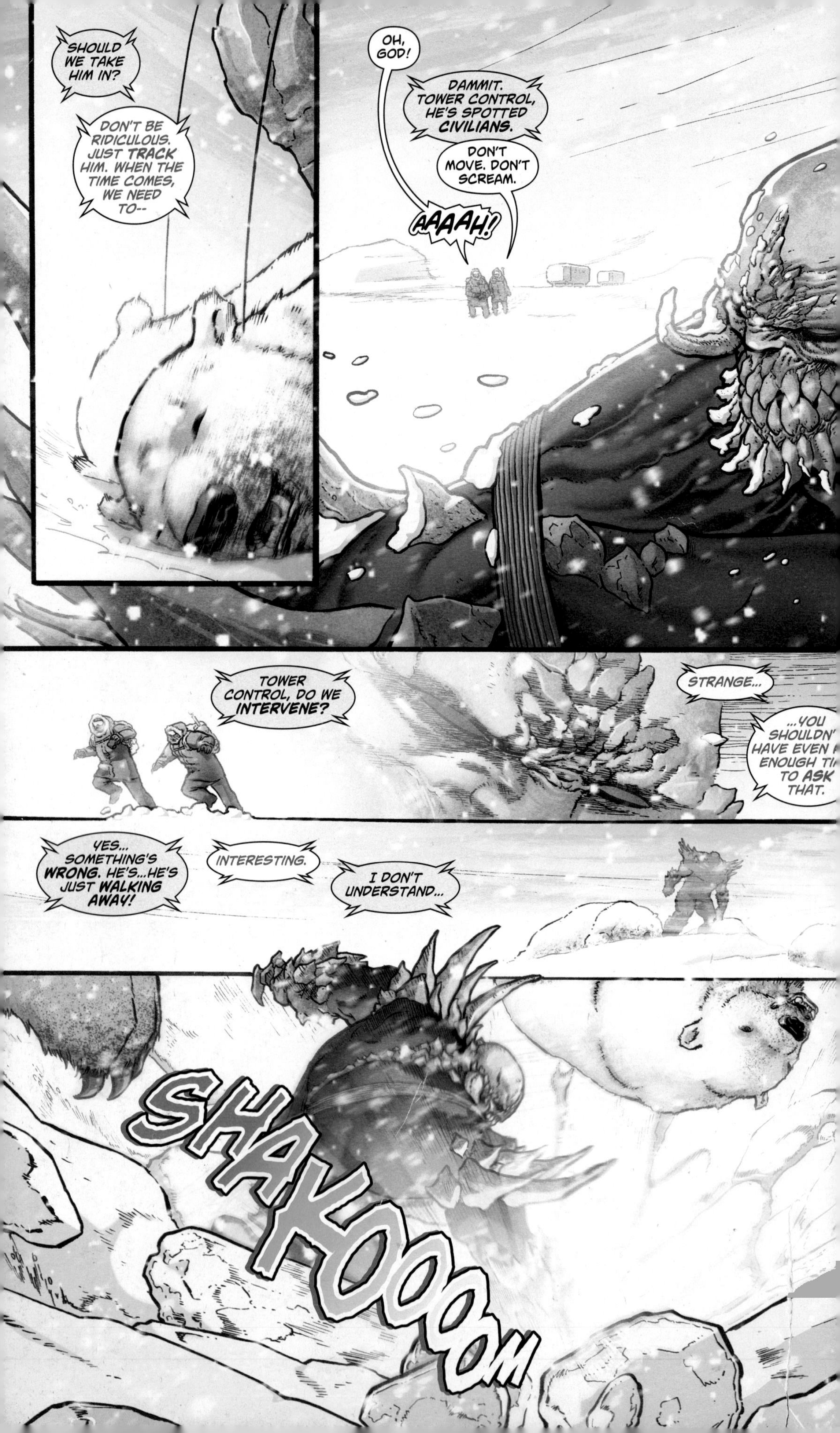
SHOULD WE TAKE HIM IN?
DON'T BE RIDICULOUS. JUST TRACK HIM. WHEN THE TIME COMES, WE NEED TO--
OH, GOD!
DAMMIT. TOWER CONTROL, HE'S SPOTTED CIVILIANS.
DON'T MOVE. DON'T SCREAM.
AAAAH!
TOWER CONTROL, DO WE INTERVENE?
STRANGE...
...YOU SHOULDN'T HAVE EVEN HAD ENOUGH TIME TO ASK THAT.
YES... SOMETHING'S WRONG. HE'S...HE'S JUST WALKING AWAY!
INTERESTING.
I DON'T UNDERSTAND...
SHAKOOOOM

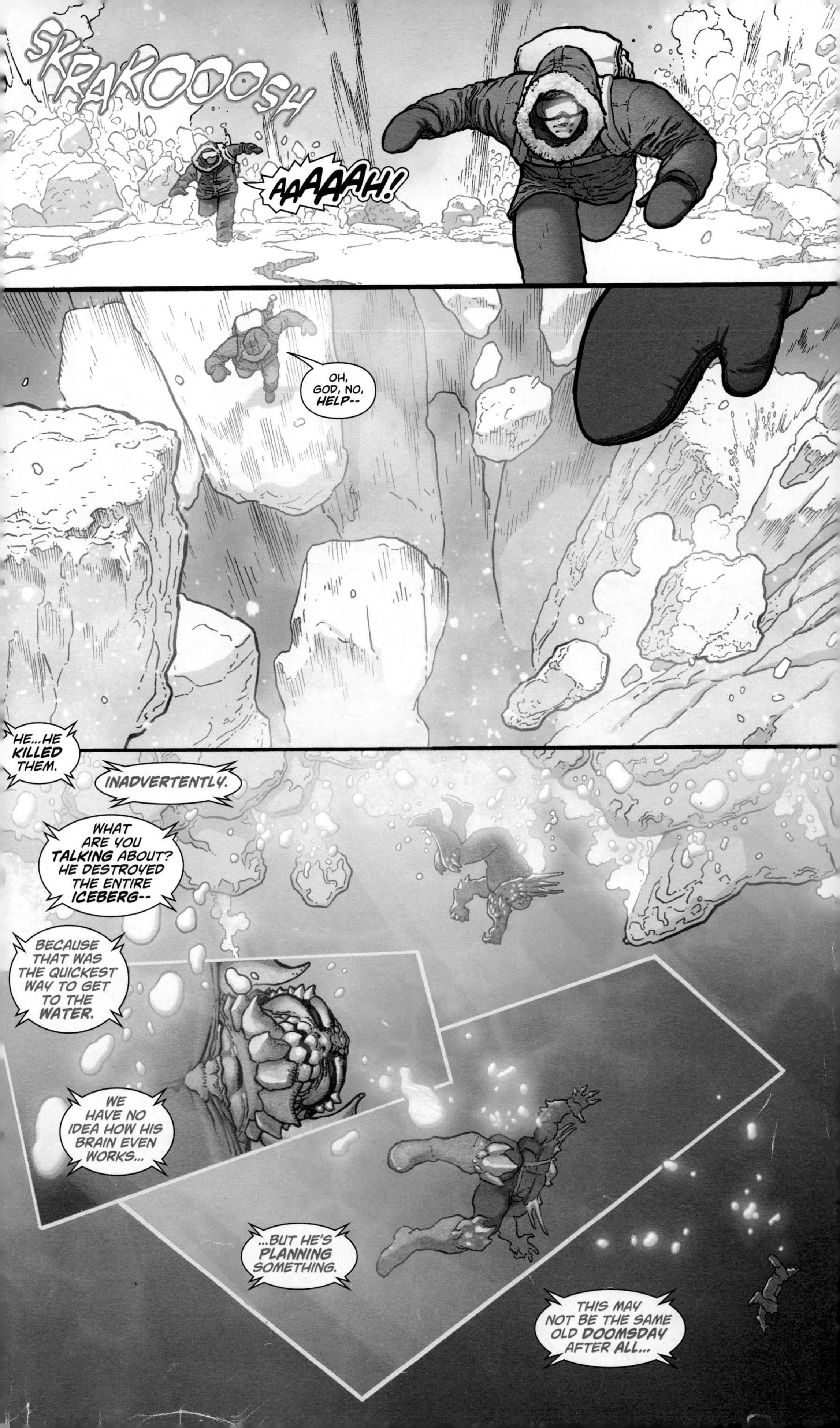
SKRAKOOOOSH
AAAAAH!
OH, GOD, NO, HELP--
HE...HE KILLED THEM.
INADVERTENTLY.
WHAT ARE YOU TALKING ABOUT? HE DESTROYED THE ENTIRE ICEBERG--
BECAUSE THAT WAS THE QUICKEST WAY TO GET TO THE WATER.
WE HAVE NO IDEA HOW HIS BRAIN EVEN WORKS...
...BUT HE'S PLANNING SOMETHING.
THIS MAY NOT BE THE SAME OLD DOOMSDAY AFTER ALL...

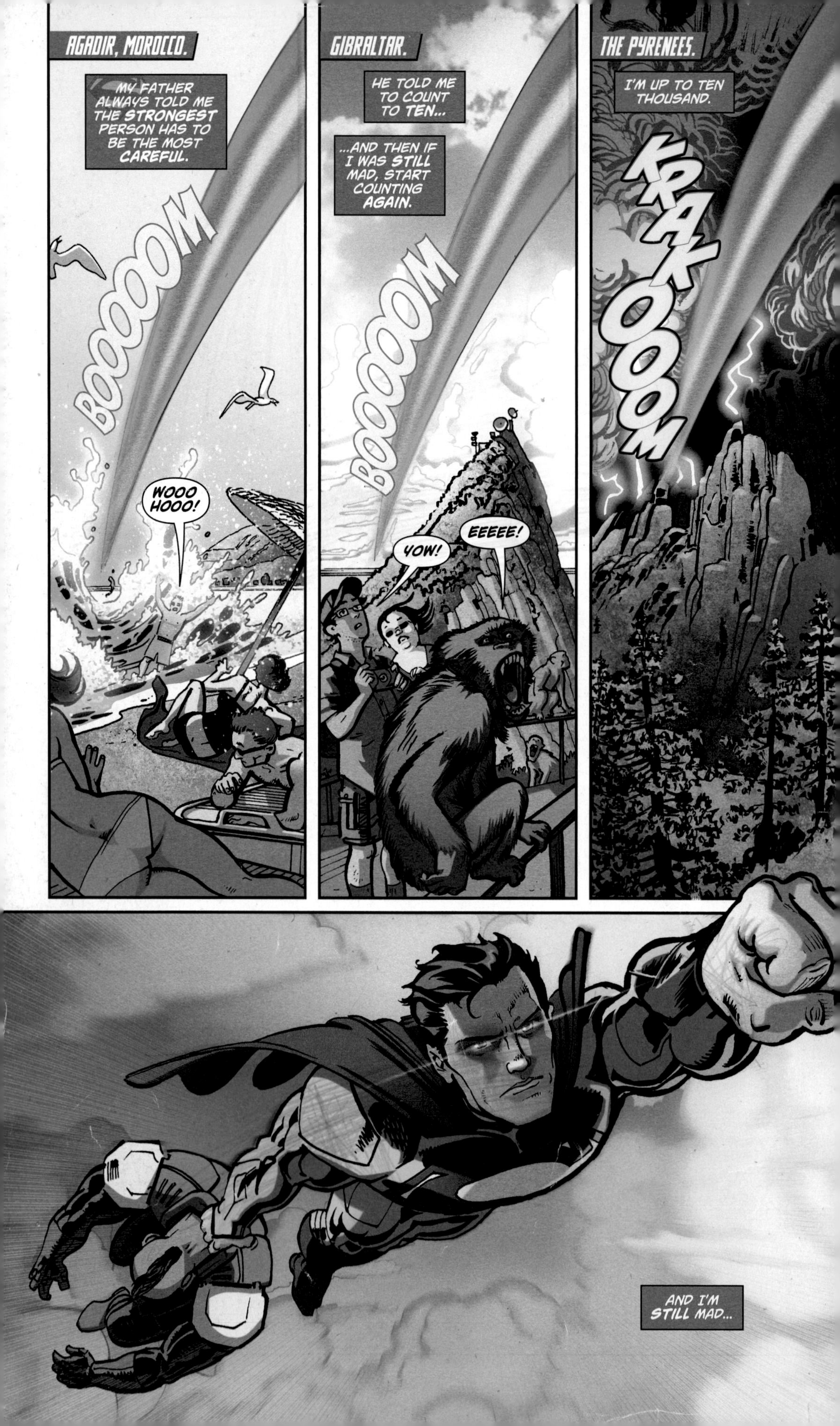
AGADIR, MOROCCO.
MY FATHER ALWAYS TOLD ME THE STRONGEST PERSON HAS TO BE THE MOST CAREFUL.
BOOOOOOM
WOOO HOOO!
GIBRALTAR.
HE TOLD ME TO COUNT TO TEN...
...AND THEN IF I WAS STILL MAD, START COUNTING AGAIN.
BOOOOOOM
YOW!
EEEEE!
THE PYRENEES.
I'M UP TO TEN THOUSAND.
KRAKOOOOM
AND I'M STILL MAD...

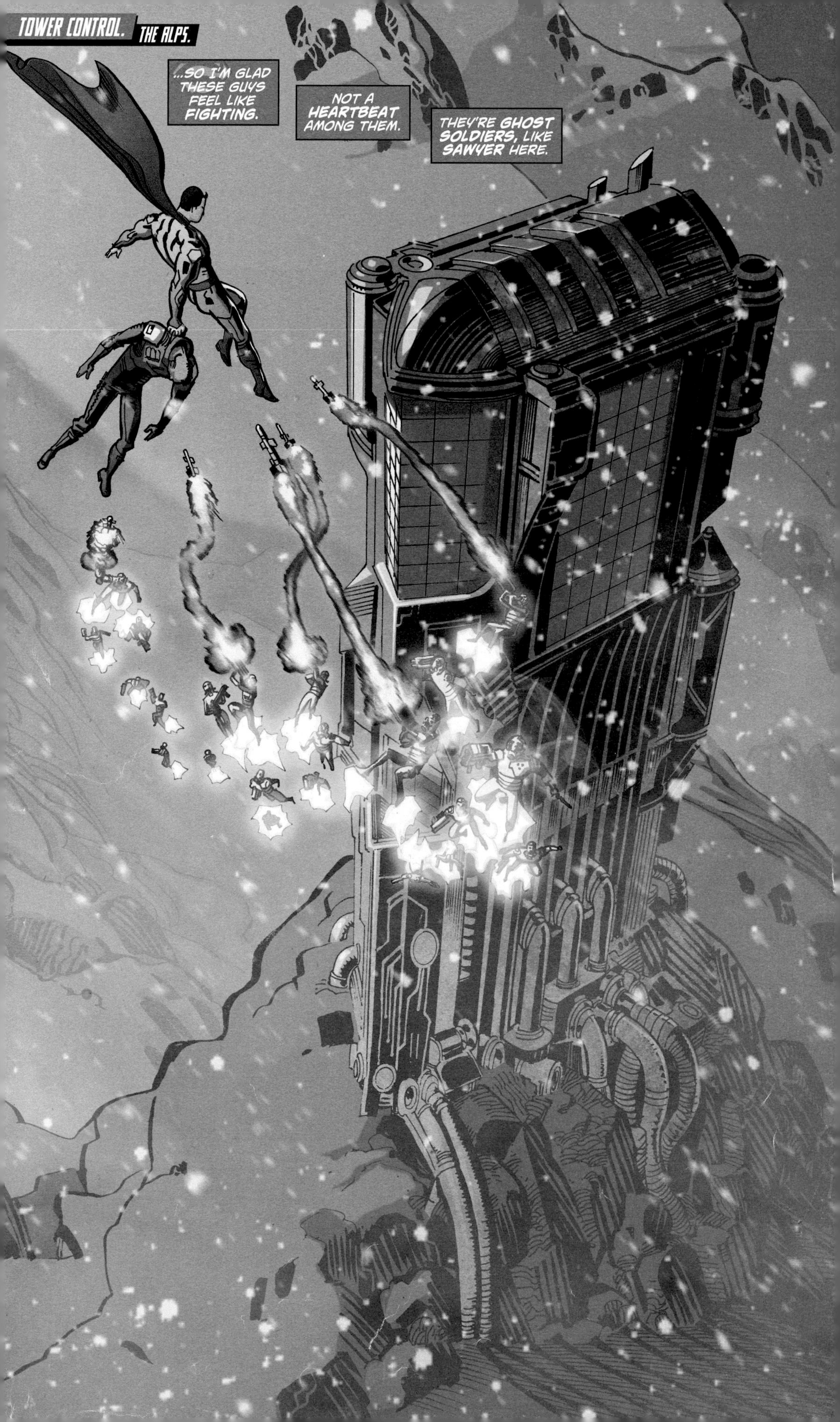
TOWER CONTROL. THE ALPS.
...SO I'M GLAD THESE GUYS FEEL LIKE FIGHTING.
NOT A HEARTBEAT AMONG THEM.
THEY'RE GHOST SOLDIERS, LIKE SAWYER HERE.

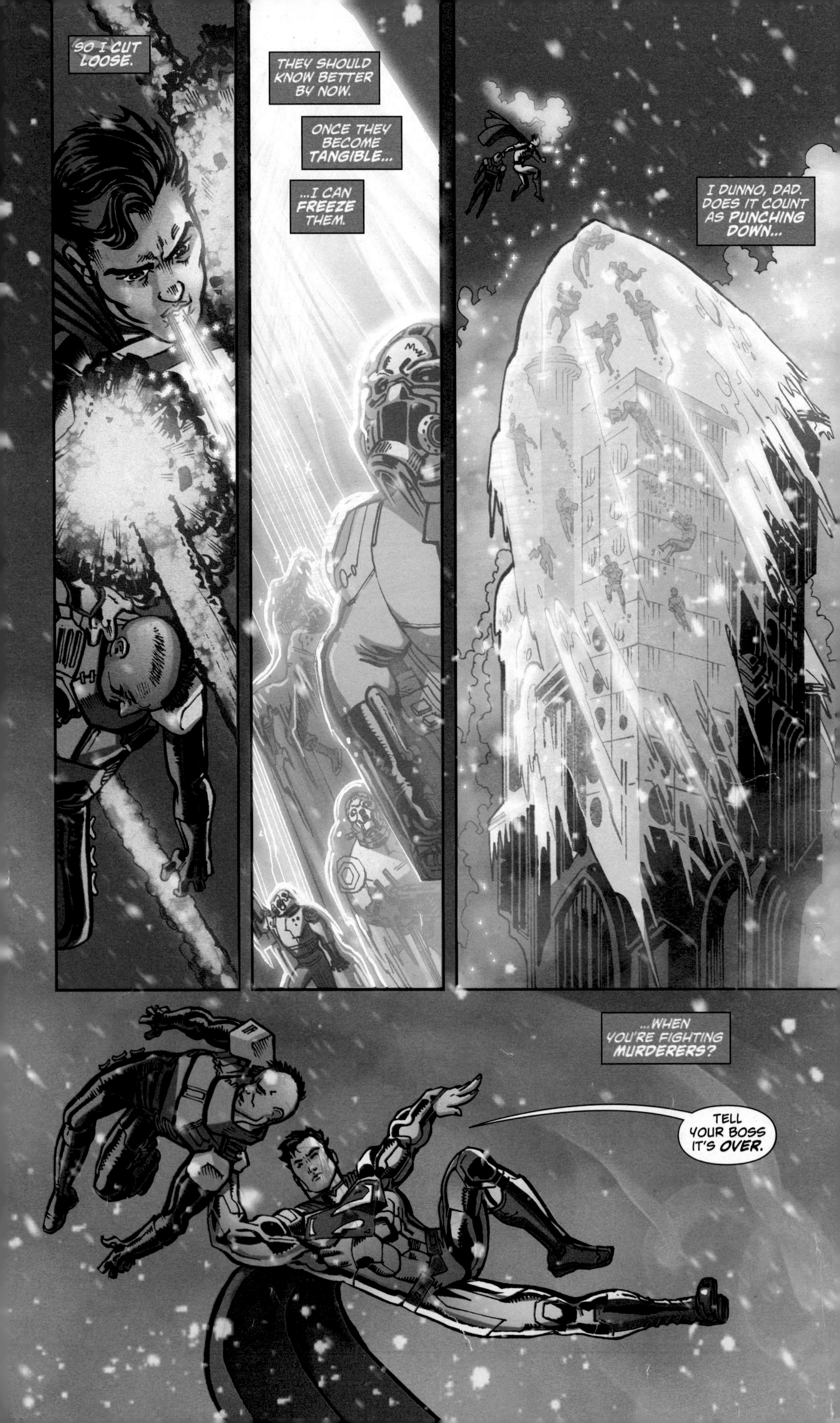
SO I CUT LOOSE.
THEY SHOULD KNOW BETTER BY NOW.
ONCE THEY BECOME TANGIBLE...
...I CAN FREEZE THEM.
I DUNNO, DAD. DOES IT COUNT AS PUNCHING DOWN...
...WHEN YOU'RE FIGHTING MURDERERS?
TELL YOUR BOSS IT'S OVER.

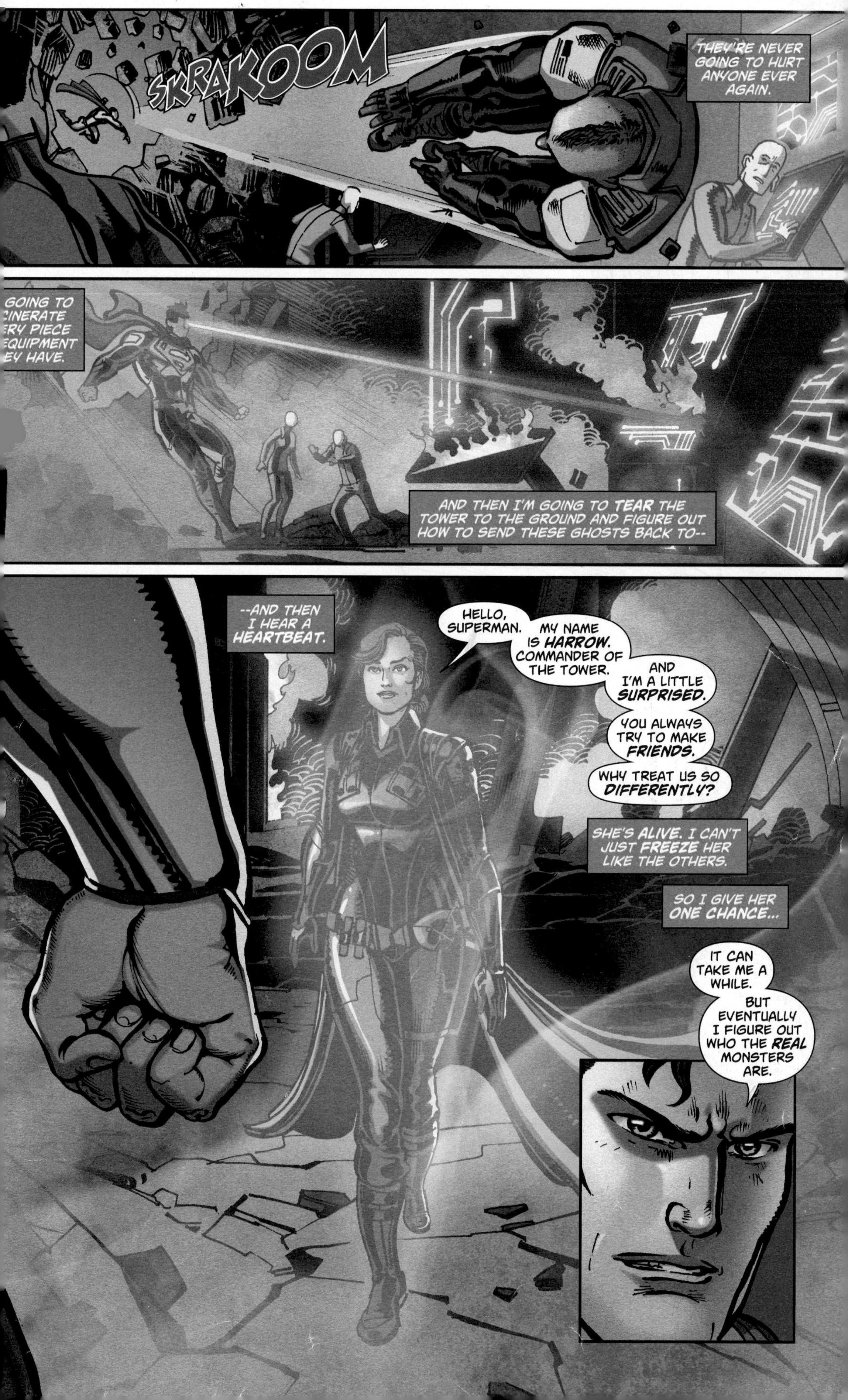
SKRAKOOM
THEY'RE NEVER GOING TO HURT ANYONE EVER AGAIN.
GOING TO CINERATE ERY PIECE EQUIPMENT EY HAVE.
AND THEN I'M GOING TO TEAR THE TOWER TO THE GROUND AND FIGURE OUT HOW TO SEND THESE GHOSTS BACK TO--
--AND THEN I HEAR A HEARTBEAT.
HELLO, SUPERMAN.
MY NAME IS HARROW. COMMANDER OF THE TOWER.
AND I'M A LITTLE SURPRISED.
YOU ALWAYS TRY TO MAKE FRIENDS.
WHY TREAT US SO DIFFERENTLY?
SHE'S ALIVE. I CAN'T JUST FREEZE HER LIKE THE OTHERS.
SO I GIVE HER ONE CHANCE...
IT CAN TAKE ME A WHILE.
BUT EVENTUALLY I FIGURE OUT WHO THE REAL MONSTERS ARE.

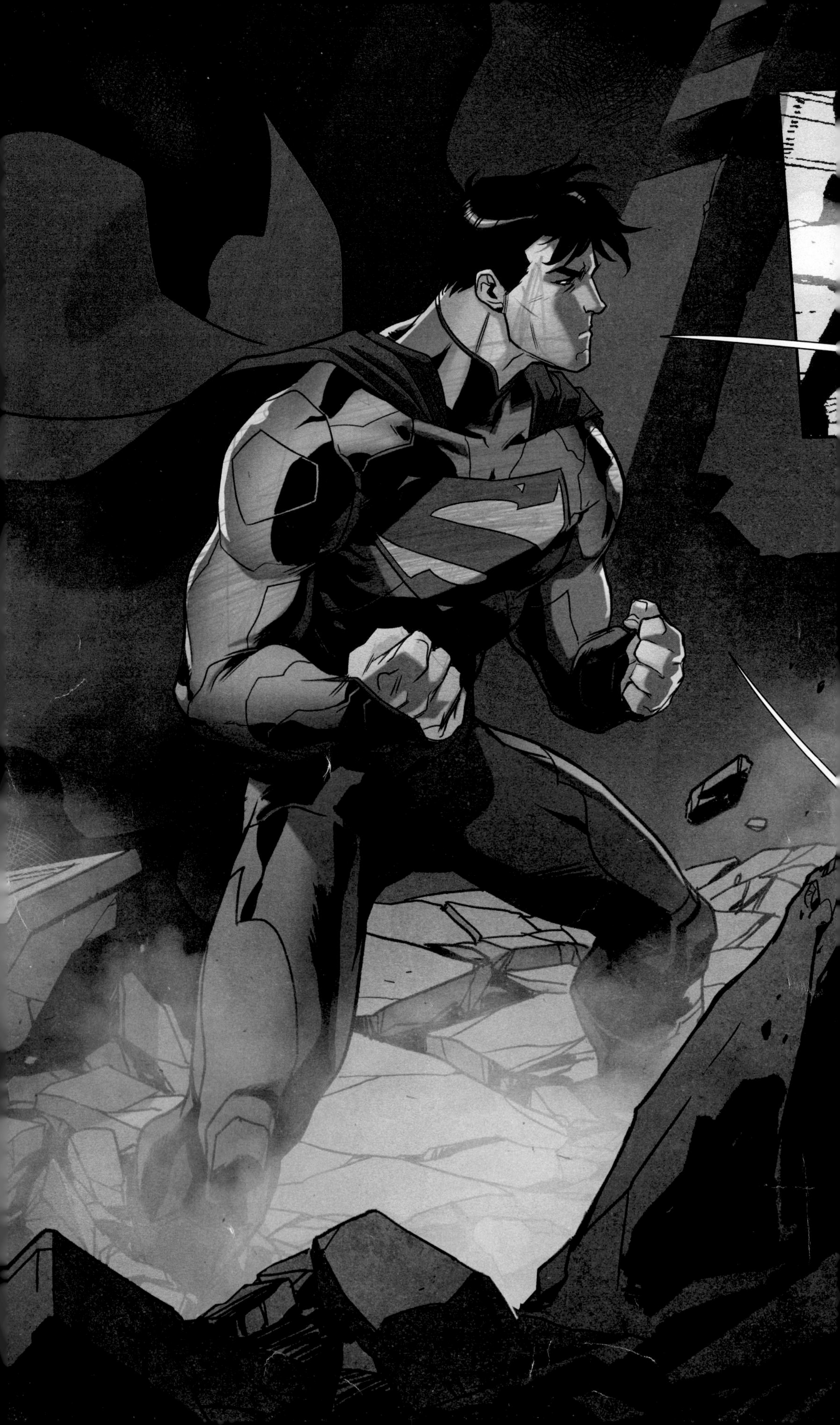

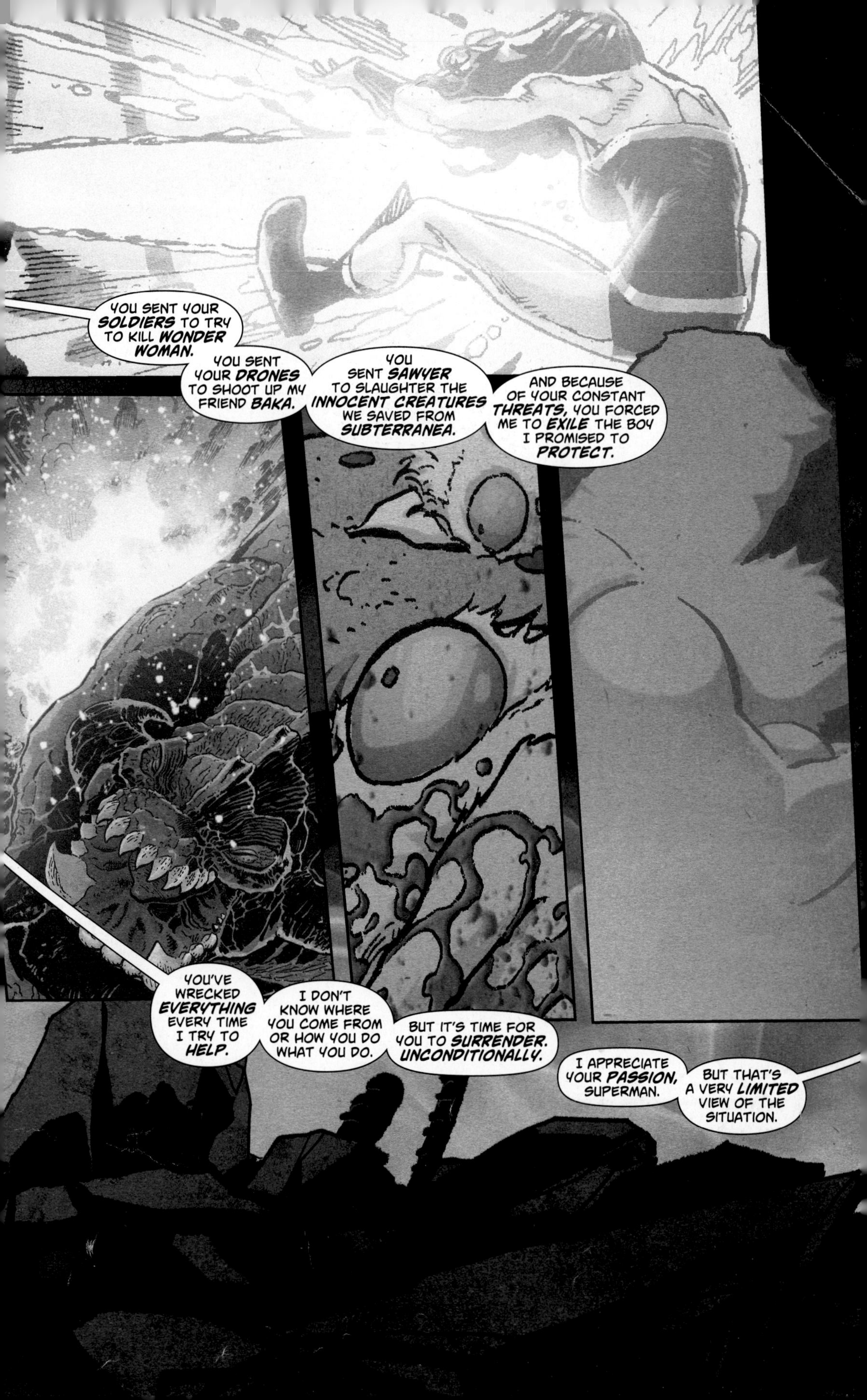

YOU SENT YOUR SOLDIERS TO TRY TO KILL WONDER WOMAN.
YOU SENT YOUR DRONES TO SHOOT UP MY FRIEND BAKA.
YOU SENT SAWYER TO SLAUGHTER THE INNOCENT CREATURES WE SAVED FROM SUBTERRANEA.
AND BECAUSE OF YOUR CONSTANT THREATS, YOU FORCED ME TO EXILE THE BOY I PROMISED TO PROTECT.
YOU'VE WRECKED EVERYTHING EVERY TIME I TRY TO HELP.
I DON'T KNOW WHERE YOU COME FROM OR HOW YOU DO WHAT YOU DO.
BUT IT'S TIME FOR YOU TO SURRENDER. UNCONDITIONALLY.
I APPRECIATE YOUR PASSION, SUPERMAN.
BUT THAT'S A VERY LIMITED VIEW OF THE SITUATION.

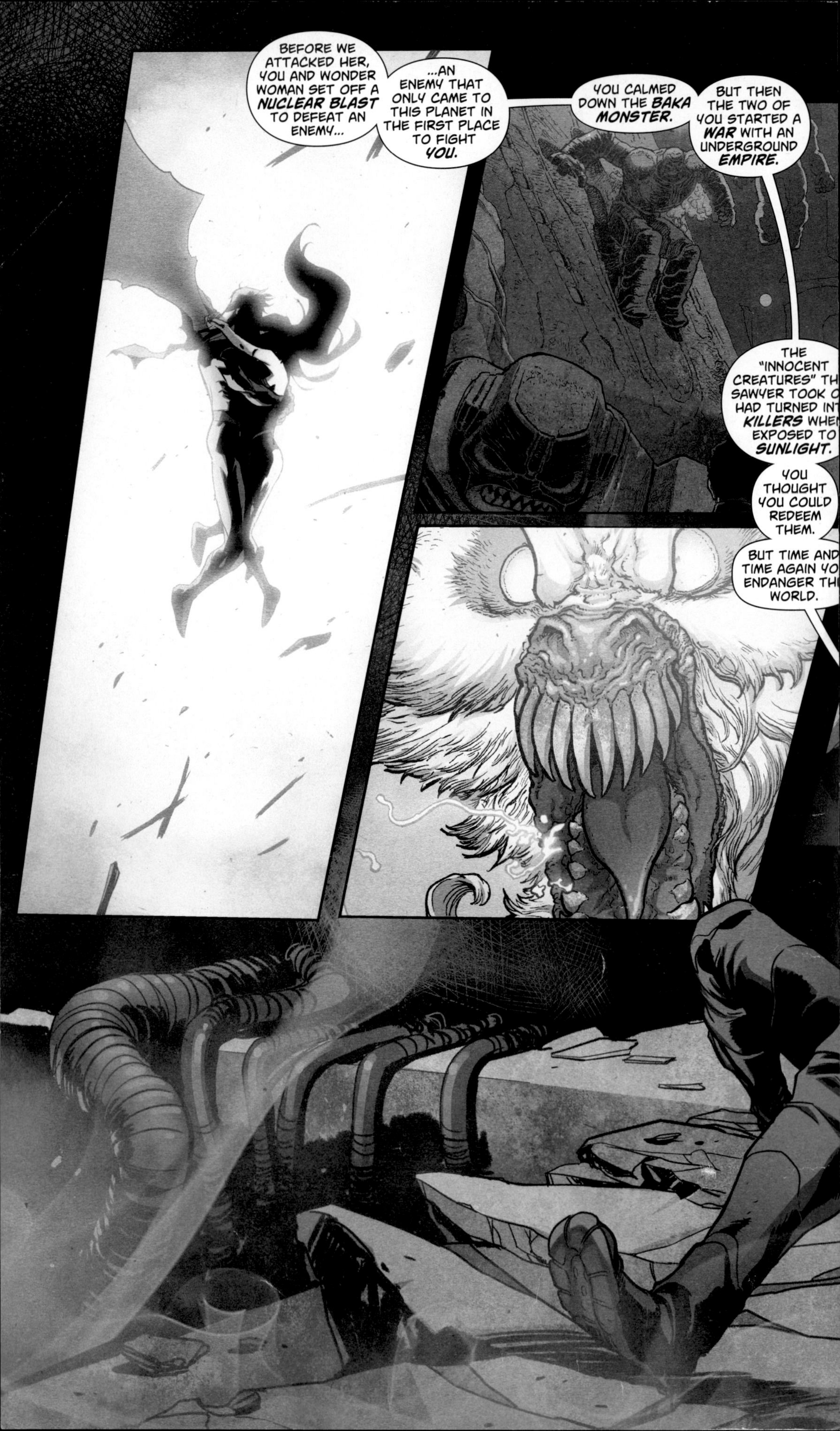
BEFORE WE ATTACKED HER, YOU AND WONDER WOMAN SET OFF A NUCLEAR BLAST TO DEFEAT AN ENEMY...
...AN ENEMY THAT ONLY CAME TO THIS PLANET IN THE FIRST PLACE TO FIGHT YOU.
YOU CALMED DOWN THE BAKA MONSTER.
BUT THEN THE TWO OF YOU STARTED A WAR WITH AN UNDERGROUND EMPIRE.
THE "INNOCENT CREATURES" TH SAWYER TOOK O HAD TURNED INT KILLERS WHEN EXPOSED TO SUNLIGHT.
YOU THOUGHT YOU COULD REDEEM THEM.
BUT TIME AND TIME AGAIN YO ENDANGER TH WORLD.

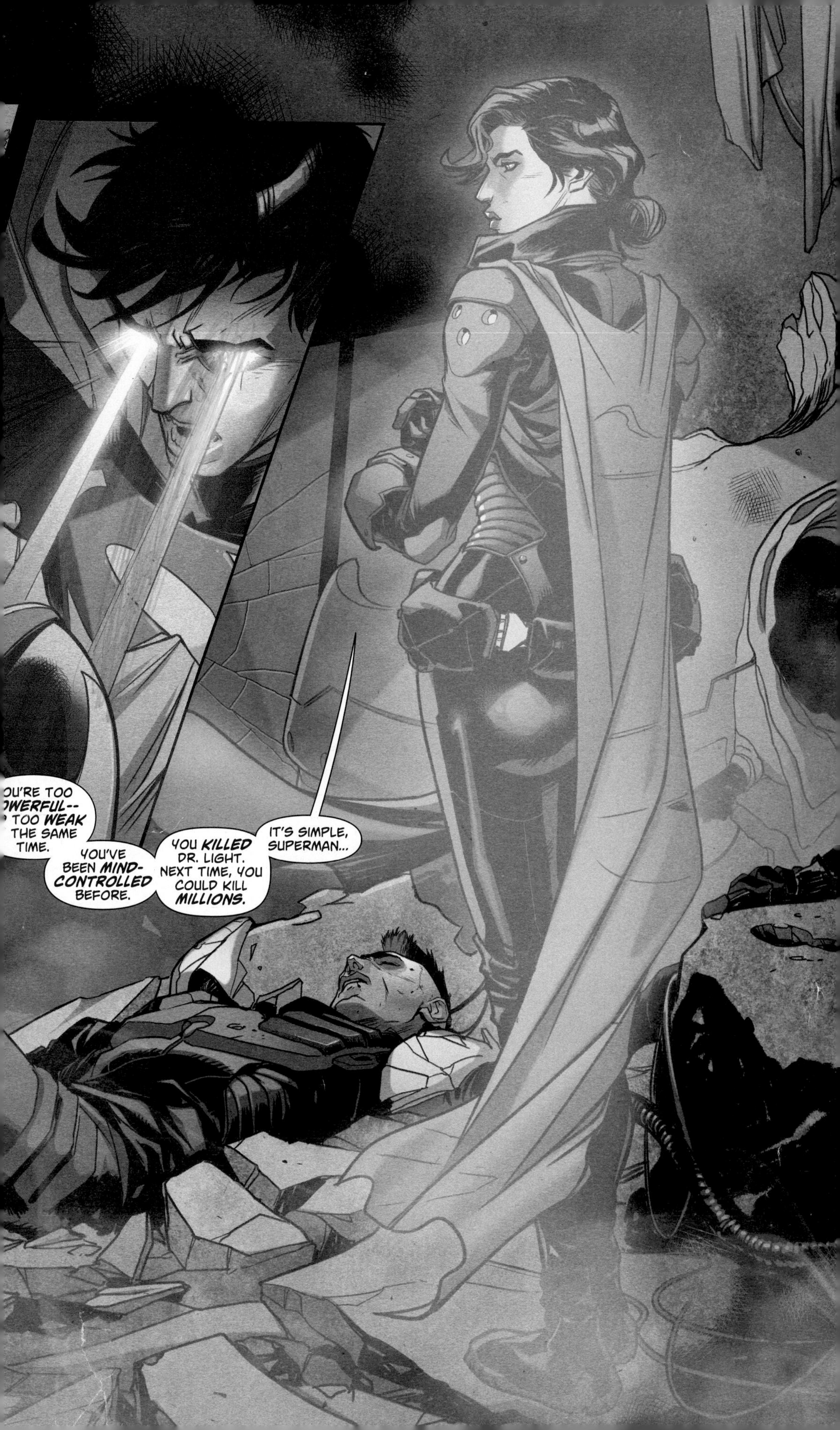

OU'RE TOO
OWERFUL--
TOO WEAK
THE SAME
TIME.
YOU'VE BEEN MIND-CONTROLLED BEFORE.
YOU KILLED DR. LIGHT. NEXT TIME, YOU COULD KILL MILLIONS.
IT'S SIMPLE, SUPERMAN...

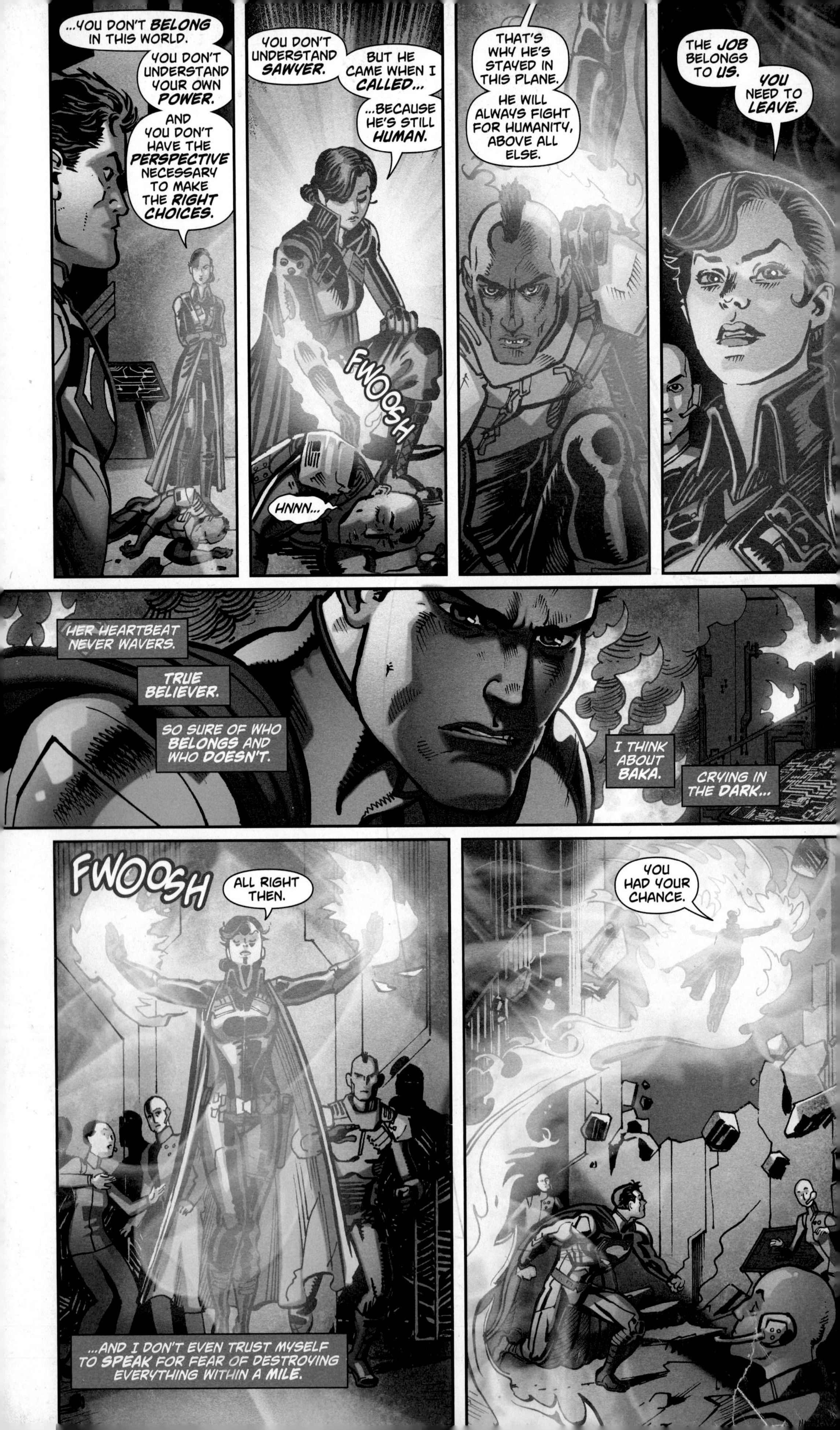
...YOU DON'T BELONG IN THIS WORLD.
YOU DON'T UNDERSTAND YOUR OWN POWER.
AND YOU DON'T HAVE THE PERSPECTIVE NECESSARY TO MAKE THE RIGHT CHOICES.
YOU DON'T UNDERSTAND SAWYER.
BUT HE CAME WHEN I CALLED...
...BECAUSE HE'S STILL HUMAN.
FWOOSH
HNNN...
THAT'S WHY HE'S STAYED IN THIS PLANE.
HE WILL ALWAYS FIGHT FOR HUMANITY, ABOVE ALL ELSE.
THE JOB BELONGS TO US.
YOU NEED TO LEAVE.
HER HEARTBEAT NEVER WAVERS.
TRUE BELIEVER.
SO SURE OF WHO BELONGS AND WHO DOESN'T.
I THINK ABOUT BAKA.
CRYING IN THE DARK...
FWOOSH
ALL RIGHT THEN.
...AND I DON'T EVEN TRUST MYSELF TO SPEAK FOR FEAR OF DESTROYING EVERYTHING WITHIN A MILE.
YOU HAD YOUR CHANCE.

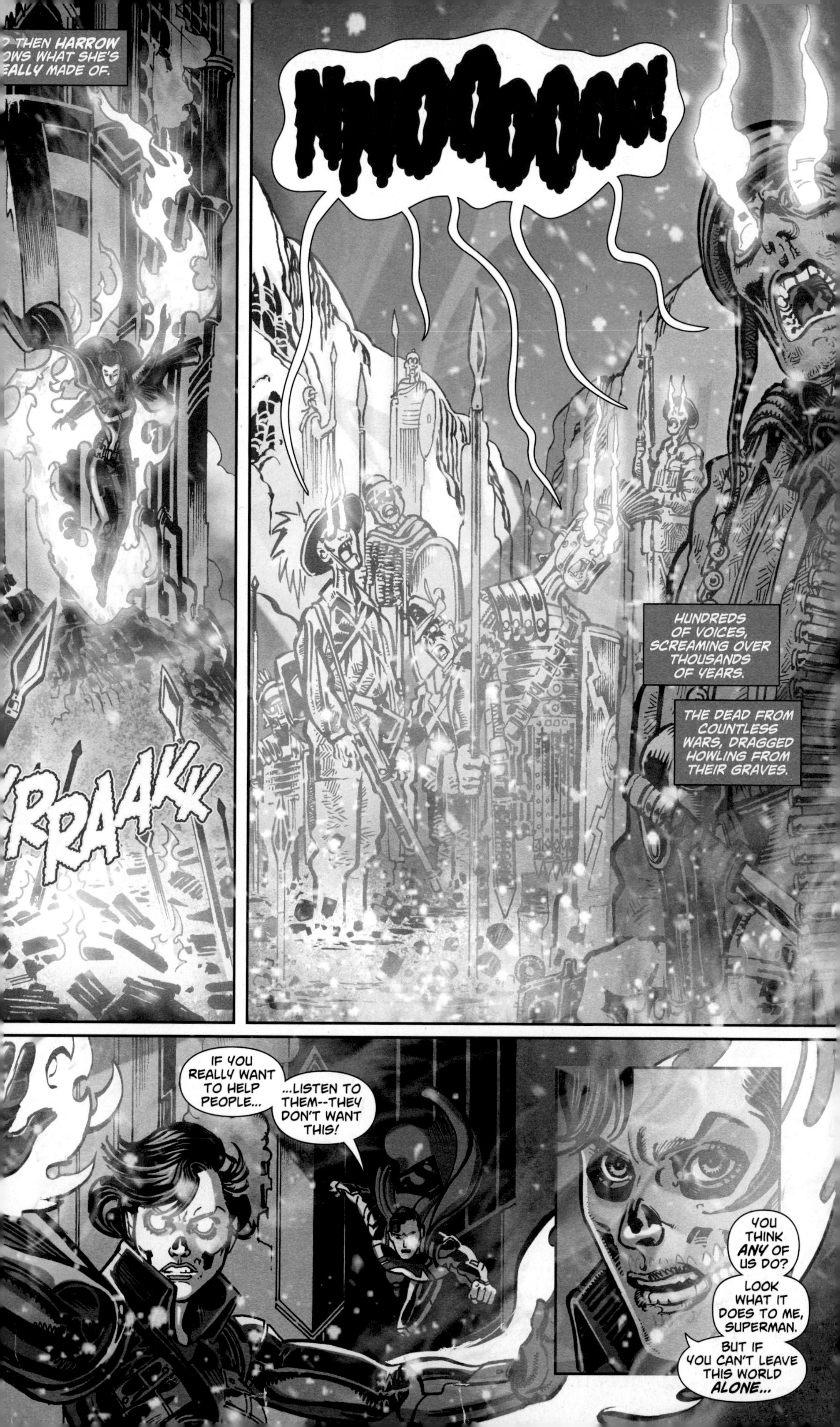

D THEN HARROW
OWS WHAT SHE'S
EALLY MADE OF.
KRAAKK
NNOOoooo!
HUNDREDS OF VOICES, SCREAMING OVER THOUSANDS OF YEARS.
THE DEAD FROM COUNTLESS WARS, DRAGGED HOWLING FROM THEIR GRAVES.
IF YOU REALLY WANT TO HELP PEOPLE...
...LISTEN TO THEM--THEY DON'T WANT THIS!
YOU THINK ANY OF US DO?
LOOK WHAT IT DOES TO ME, SUPERMAN.
BUT IF YOU CAN'T LEAVE THIS WORLD ALONE...

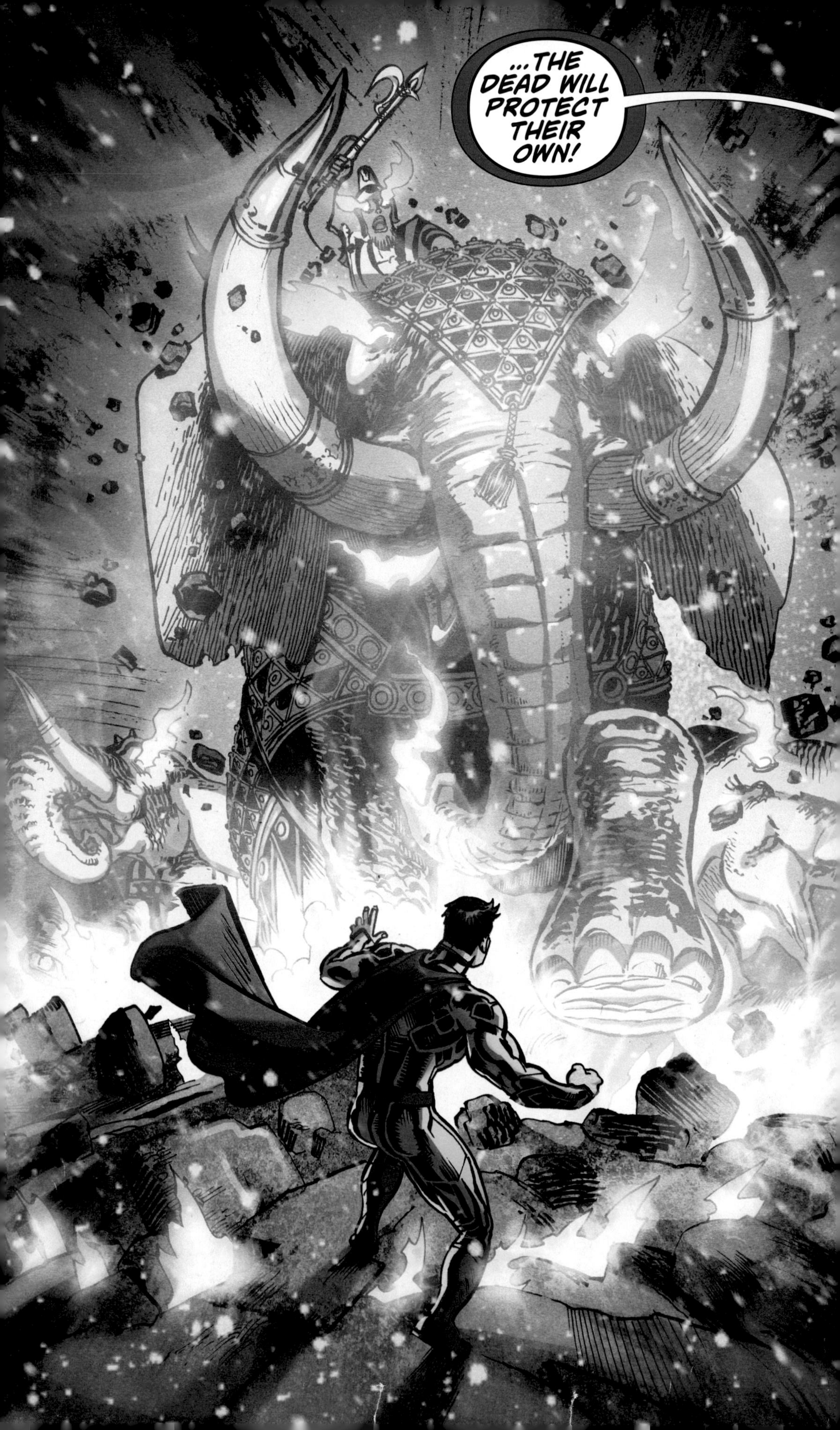
...THE DEAD WILL PROTECT THEIR OWN!

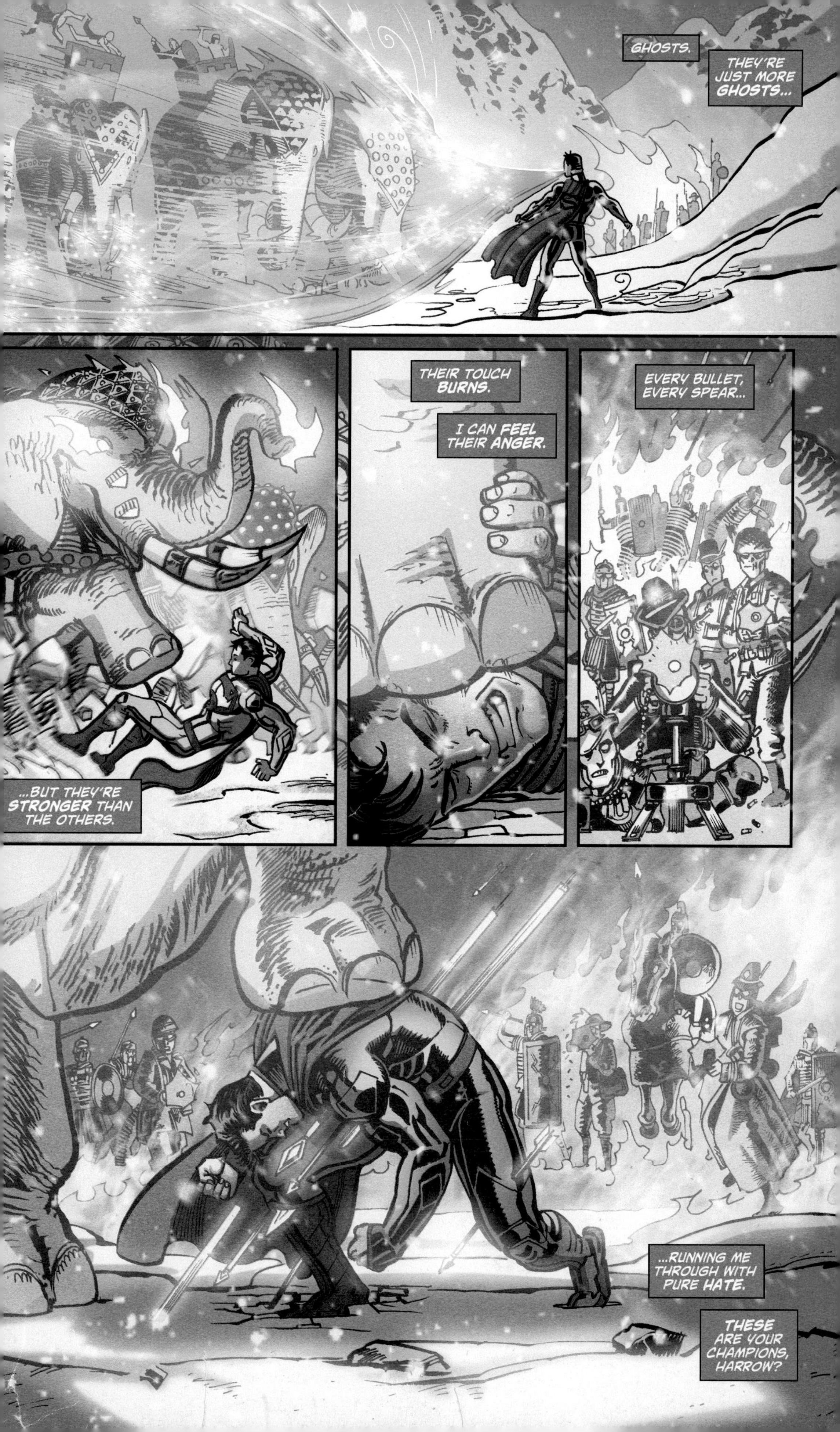
GHOSTS.
THEY'RE JUST MORE GHOSTS...
...BUT THEY'RE STRONGER THAN THE OTHERS.
THEIR TOUCH BURNS.
I CAN FEEL THEIR ANGER.
EVERY BULLET, EVERY SPEAR...
...RUNNING ME THROUGH WITH PURE HATE.
THESE ARE YOUR CHAMPIONS, HARROW?

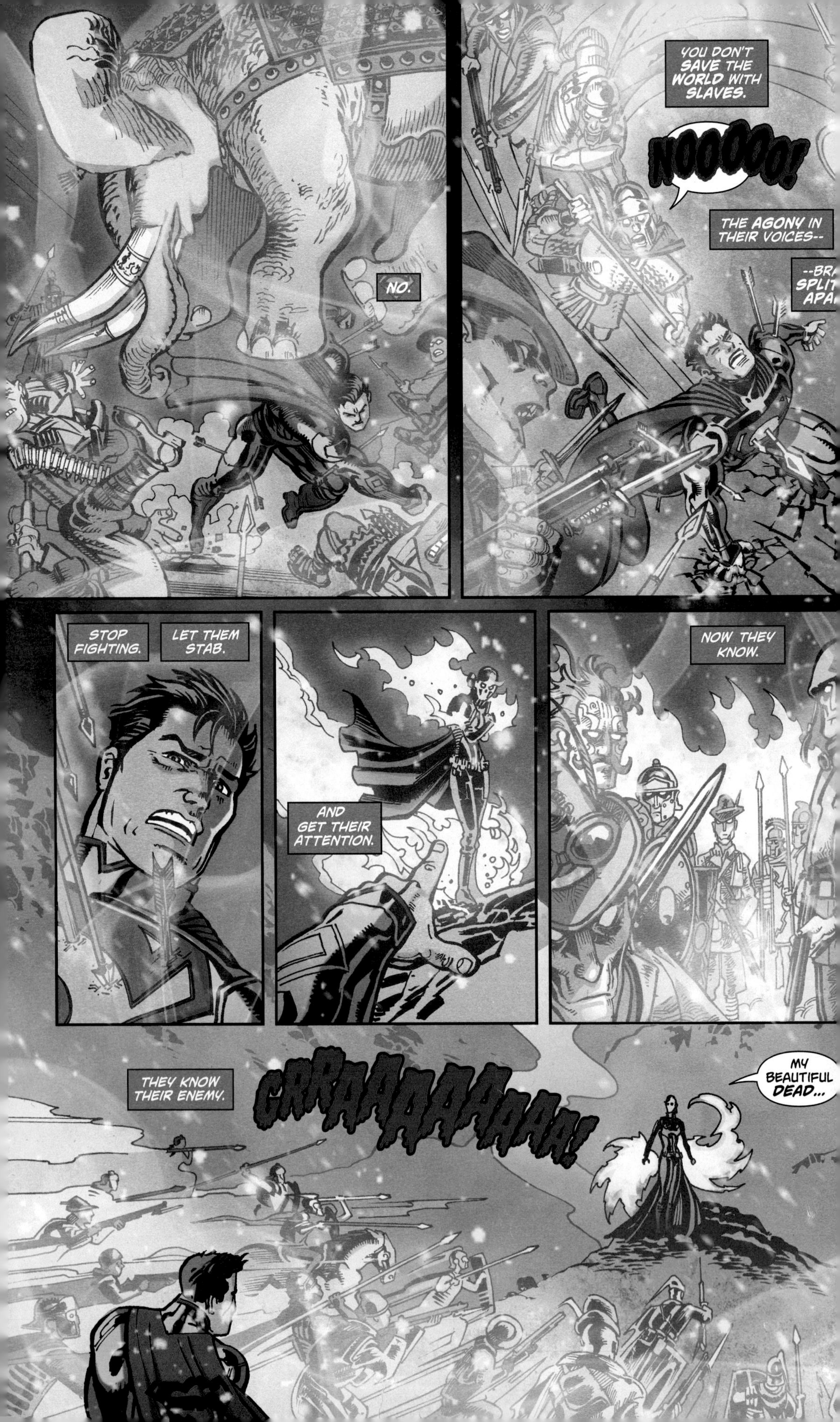
NO.
YOU DON'T SAVE THE WORLD WITH SLAVES.
NOOOOO!
THE AGONY IN THEIR VOICES--
--BR SPLIT APA
STOP FIGHTING.
LET THEM STAB.
AND GET THEIR ATTENTION.
NOW THEY KNOW.
THEY KNOW THEIR ENEMY.
GRRAAAAAAAAA!
MY BEAUTIFUL DEAD...

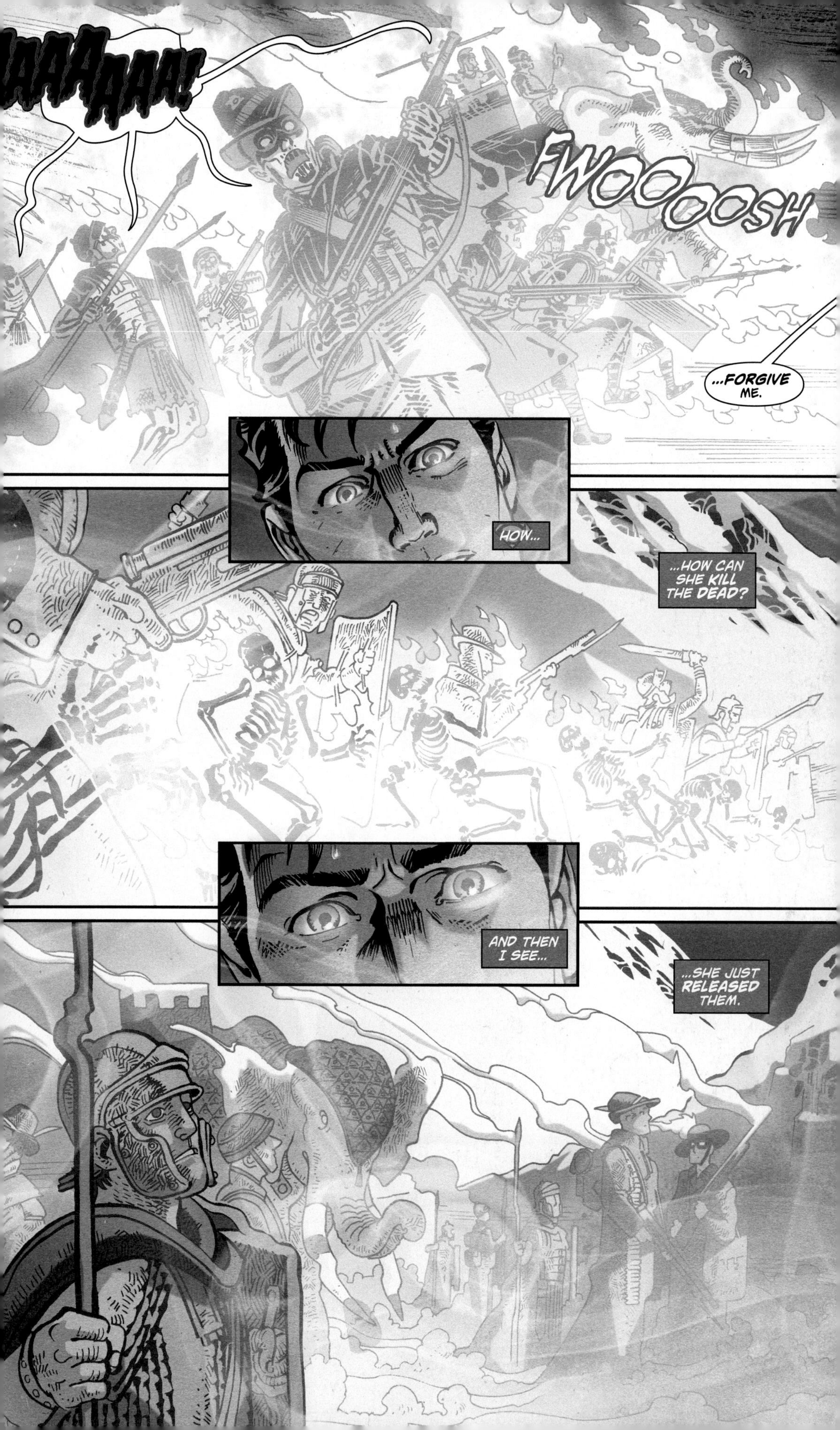
AAAAAAA!
FWOOOOOSH
...FORGIVE ME.
HOW...
...HOW CAN SHE KILL THE DEAD?
AND THEN I SEE...
...SHE JUST RELEASED THEM.

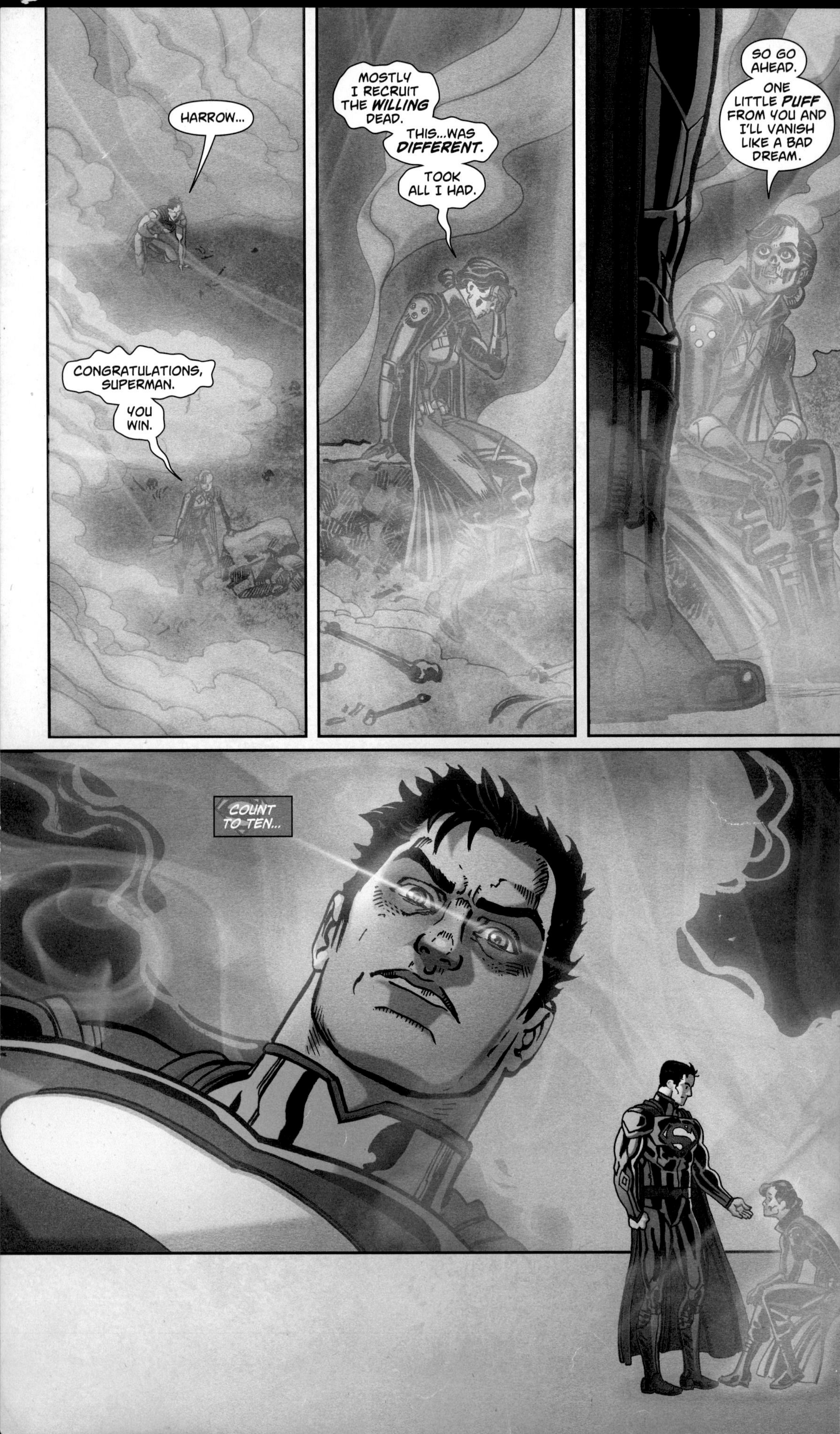
HARROW...
CONGRATULATIONS, SUPERMAN.
YOU WIN.
MOSTLY I RECRUIT THE WILLING DEAD.
THIS...WAS DIFFERENT.
TOOK ALL I HAD.
SO GO AHEAD.
ONE LITTLE PUFF FROM YOU AND I'LL VANISH LIKE A BAD DREAM.
COUNT TO TEN...

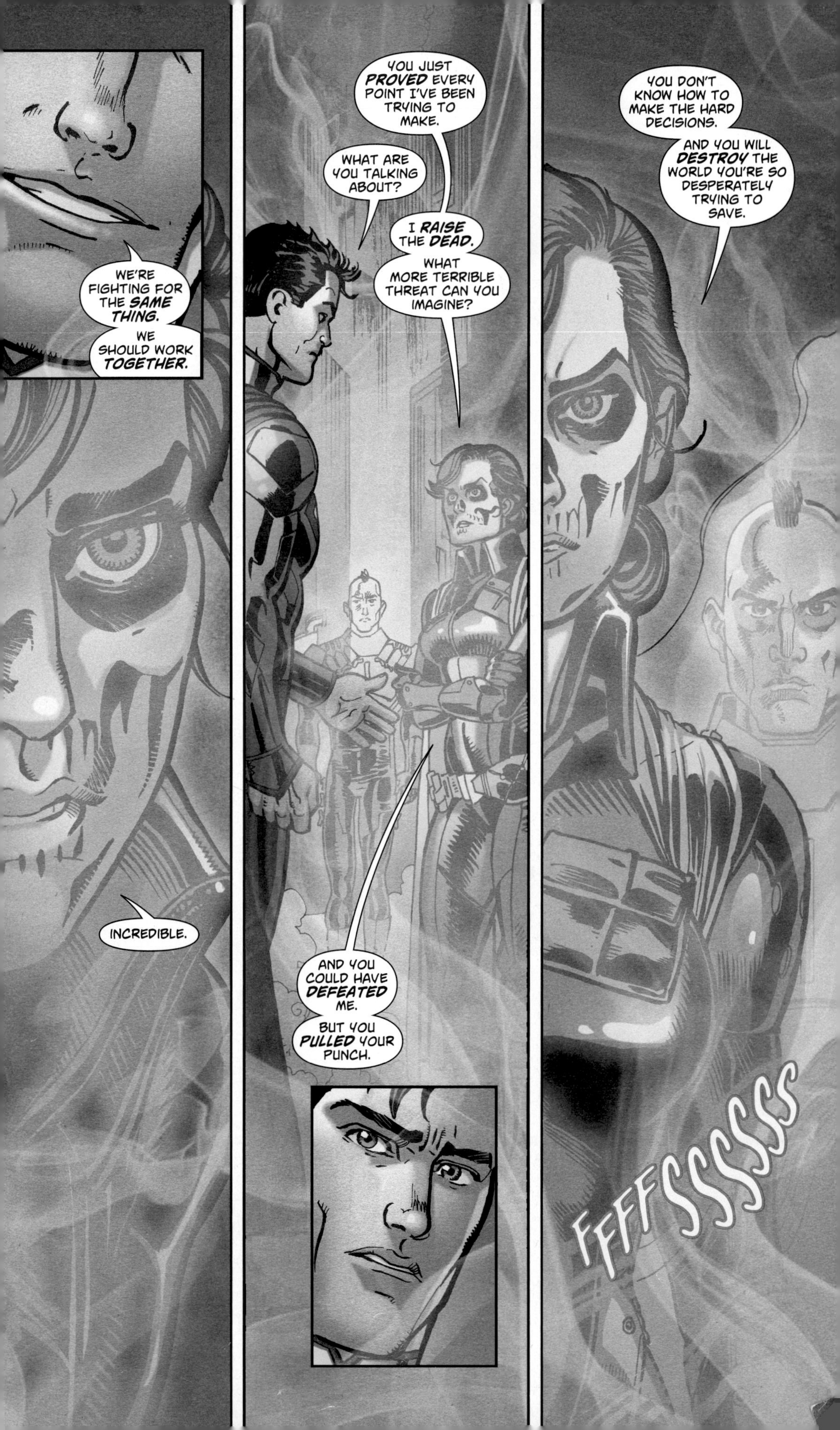
WE'RE FIGHTING FOR THE SAME THING.
WE SHOULD WORK TOGETHER.
INCREDIBLE.
YOU JUST PROVED EVERY POINT I'VE BEEN TRYING TO MAKE.
WHAT ARE YOU TALKING ABOUT?
I RAISE THE DEAD.
WHAT MORE TERRIBLE THREAT CAN YOU IMAGINE?
AND YOU COULD HAVE DEFEATED ME.
BUT YOU PULLED YOUR PUNCH.
YOU DON'T KNOW HOW TO MAKE THE HARD DECISIONS.
AND YOU WILL DESTROY THE WORLD YOU'RE SO DESPERATELY TRYING TO SAVE.
FFFFSSSSSSS

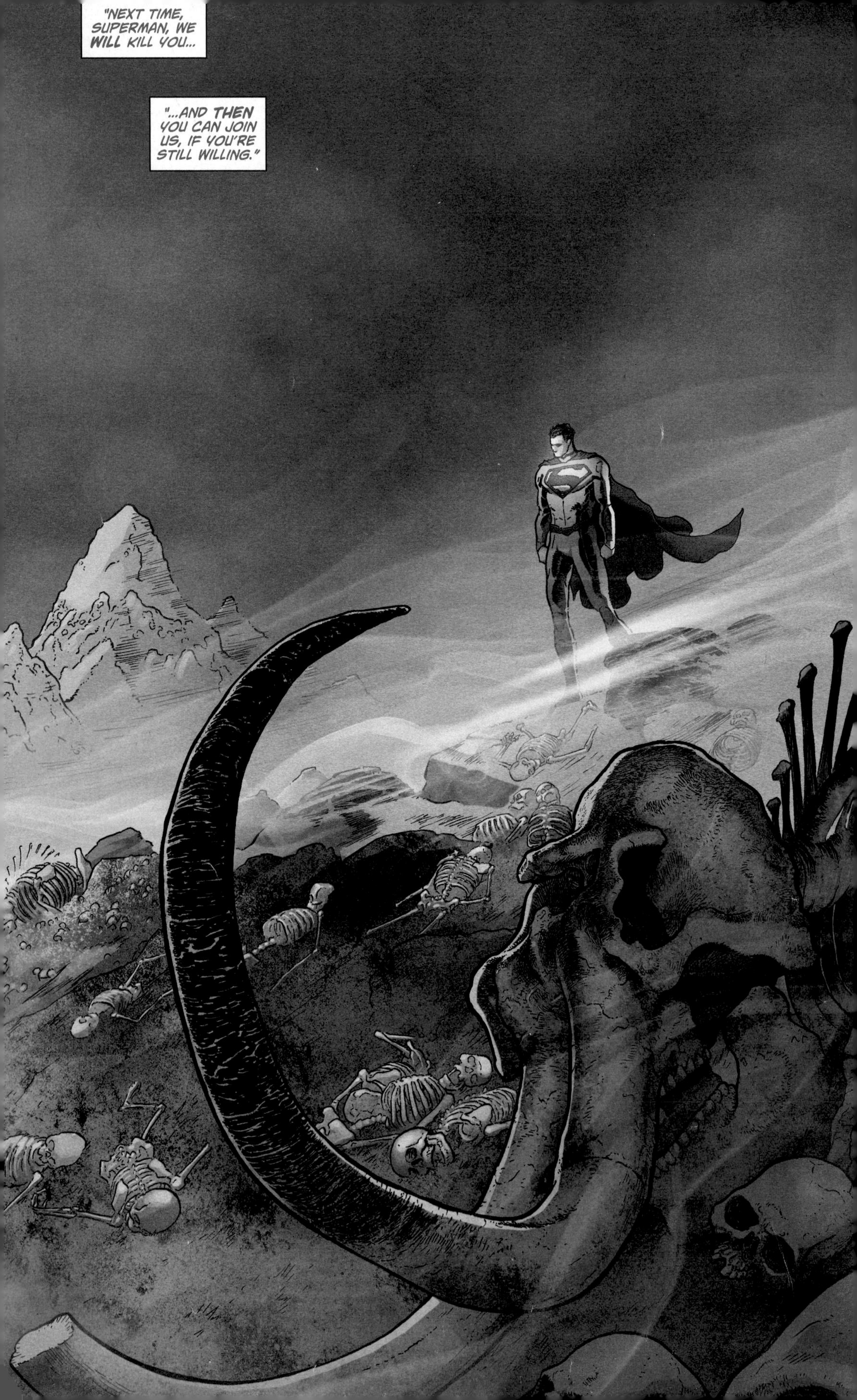
"NEXT TIME, SUPERMAN, WE WILL KILL YOU...
"...AND THEN YOU CAN JOIN US, IF YOU'RE STILL WILLING."

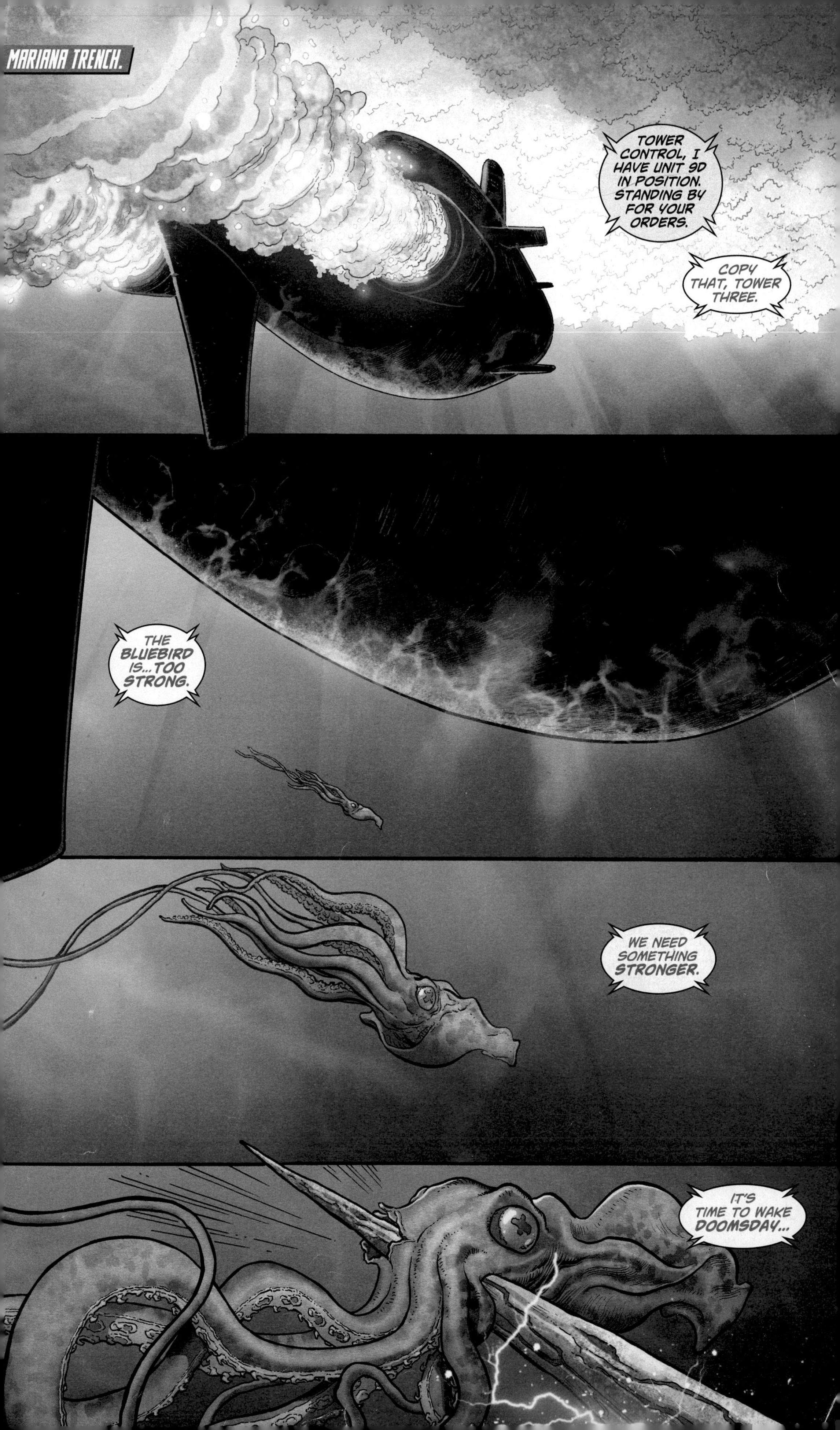
MARIANA TRENCH.
TOWER CONTROL, I HAVE UNIT 9D IN POSITION. STANDING BY FOR YOUR ORDERS.
COPY THAT, TOWER THREE.
THE BLUEBIRD IS...TOO STRONG.
WE NEED SOMETHING STRONGER.
IT'S TIME TO WAKE DOOMSDAY...

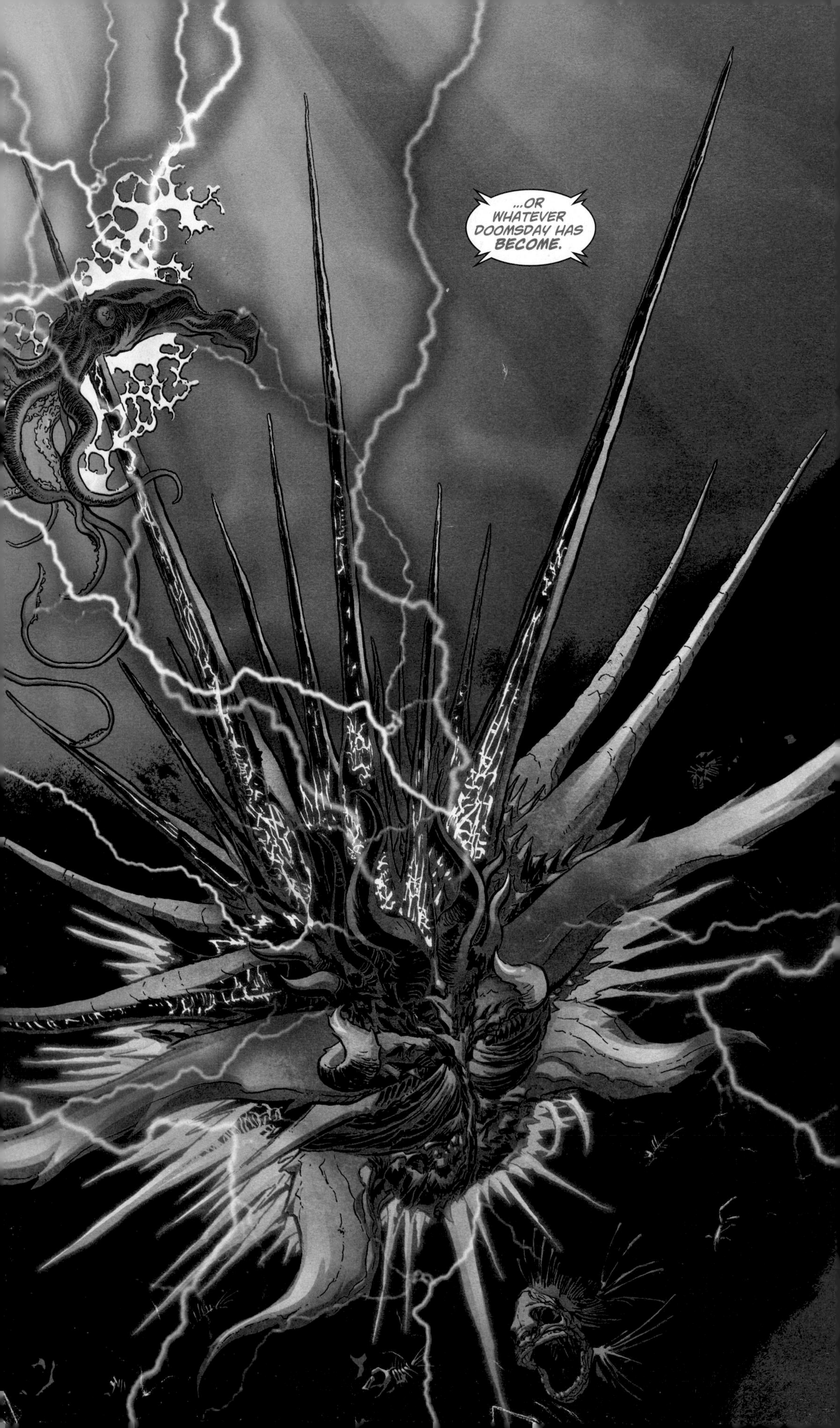
...OR WHATEVER DOOMSDAY HAS BECOME.

"TRUE BELIEVERS"

GREG PAK writer AARON KUDER RAFA SANDOVAL CAMERON STEWART artists VICENTE CIFUENTES inker WIL QUINTANA colorist

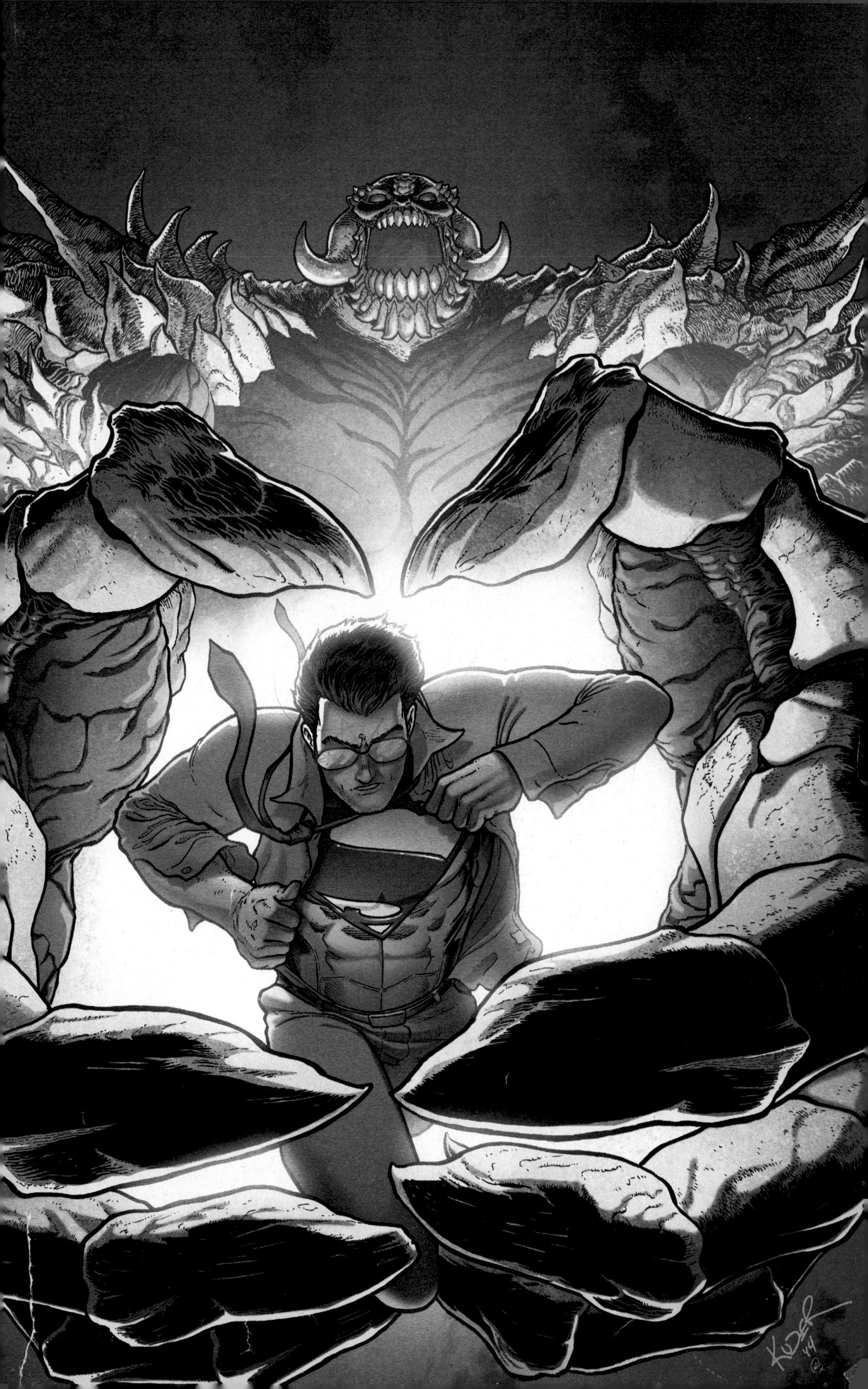
KUDER '14

May 7, 2

Daily Planet

DAILY PLANET

SUPERMAN DOOMED!

BY LOIS LANE

It was DOOMSDAY around the world, both figuratively and literally.

A massive creature of unknown origin resembling one that SUPERMAN fought once before appeared first in the Bahamas, subsequently in Botswana and then Mumbai, India, causing untold destruction.

Doctor Silas Stone, of S.T.A.R. Labs, had been tracking the creature after its initial appearance in the Bahamas.

Photo by James

"The creature was generating a corrosive force field that produced ra biological decay in anything that came within its radius."

Efforts by world governments to stop the creature were unsuccessful

Members of the Justice League looked to halt the rampaging monst path of destruction by confronting it. The Man of Steel, in a display brute force never before witnessed, eventually defeated the monste tearing it apart.

This final battle took place in the midwestern town of Smallville, w a day before its citizens fell inexplicably into a coma. Experts theorize event was linked to the appearance of the behemoth. However, the destrction of Doomsday has not revived them. And as Superman recovers f this epic struggle, everyone is wondering what effect this battle has had the Last Son of Krypton himself.

Artist Rendition by Ken Lashley

Watch exclusive video footage of the destruction in the Bahamas.

"Doomsday" Origins
Recovery in the Northwestern Indies
Newly appointed Senator Sam L being considered at for "cleanup in the U.S.

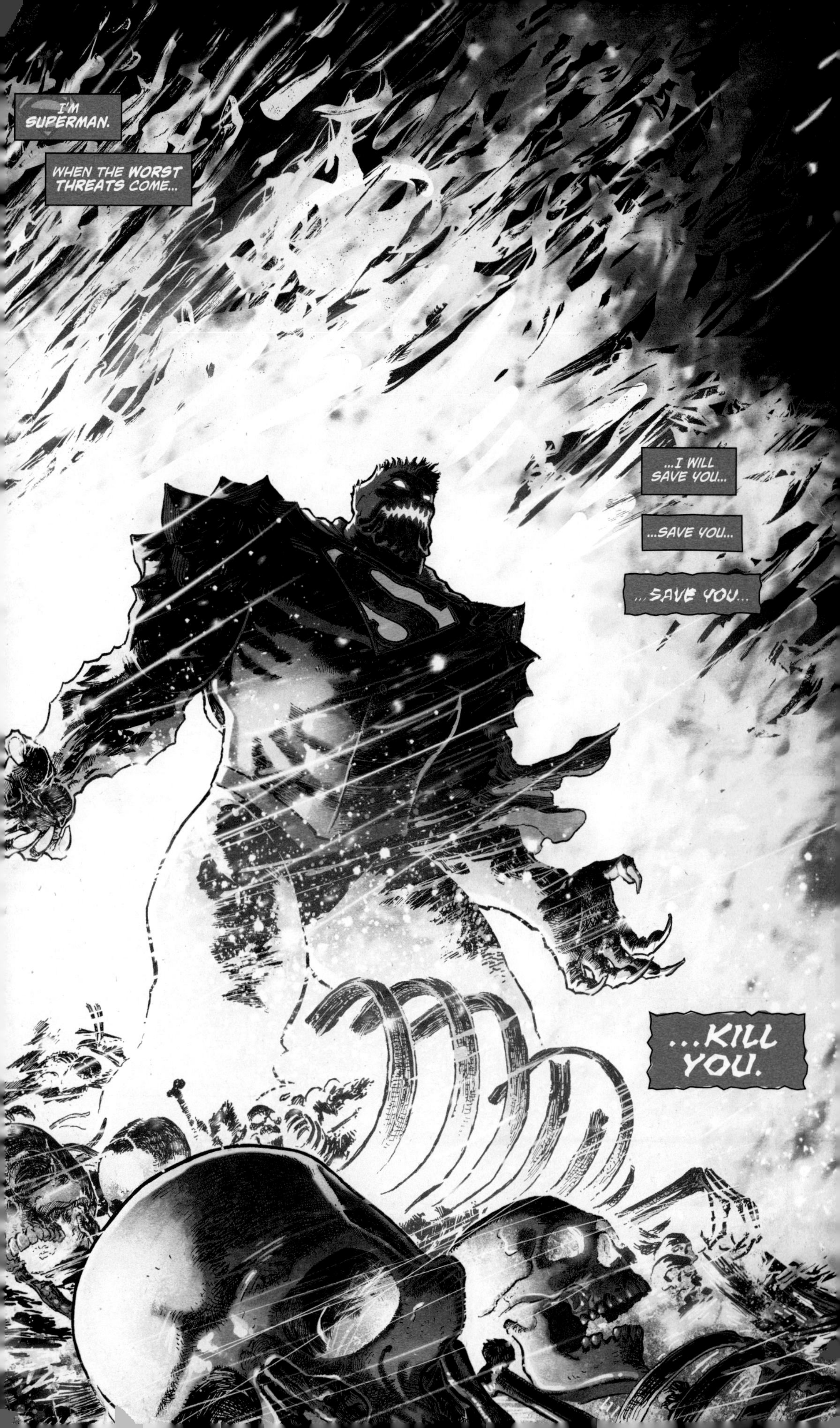
I'M SUPERMAN.
WHEN THE WORST THREATS COME...
...I WILL SAVE YOU...
...SAVE YOU...
...SAVE YOU...
...KILL YOU.

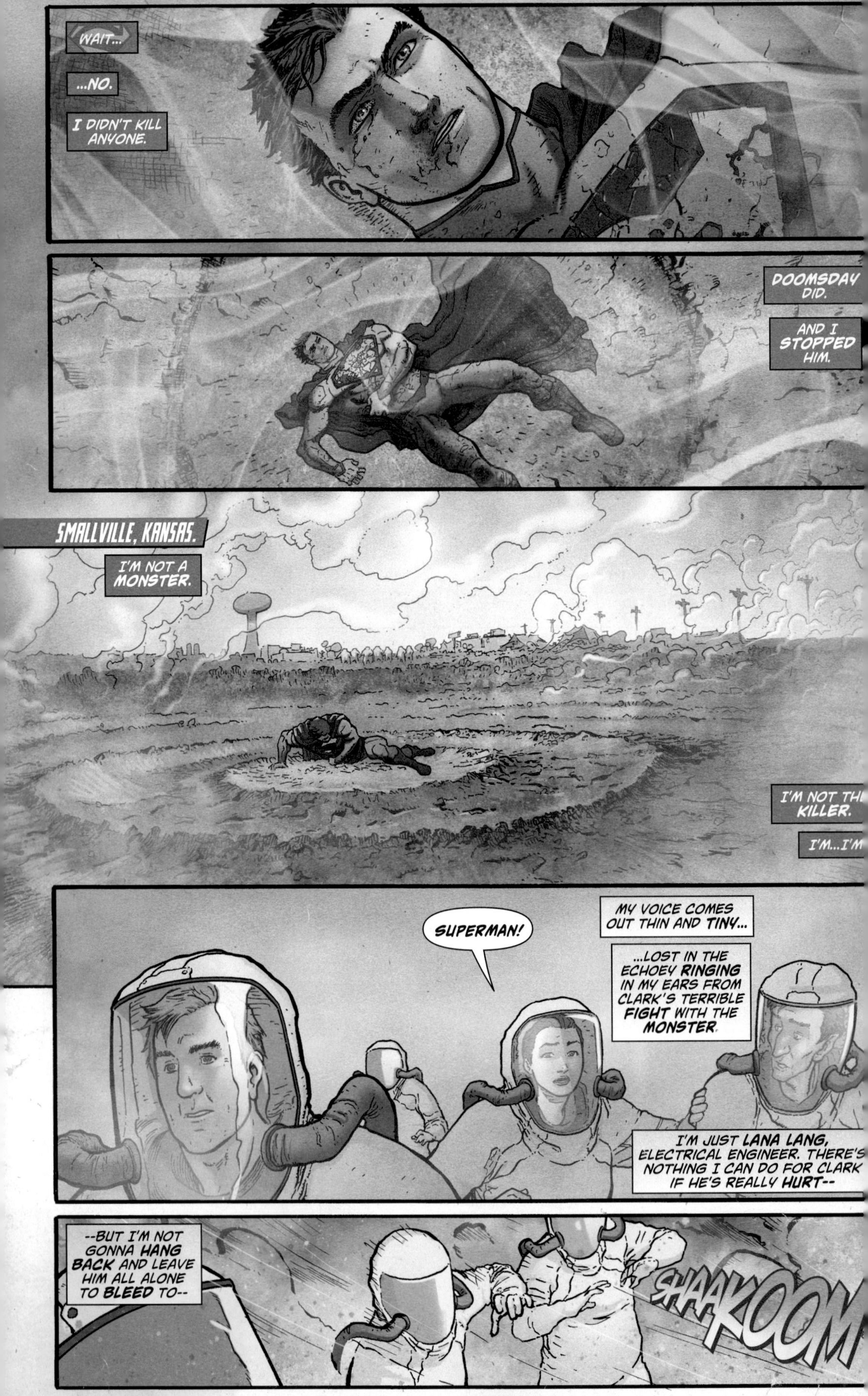

WAIT...
...NO.
I DIDN'T KILL ANYONE.
DOOMSDAY DID.
AND I STOPPED HIM.
SMALLVILLE, KANSAS.
I'M NOT A MONSTER.
I'M NOT TH KILLER.
I'M...I'M
SUPERMAN!
MY VOICE COMES OUT THIN AND TINY...
...LOST IN THE ECHOEY RINGING IN MY EARS FROM CLARK'S TERRIBLE FIGHT WITH THE MONSTER.
I'M JUST LANA LANG, ELECTRICAL ENGINEER. THERE'S NOTHING I CAN DO FOR CLARK IF HE'S REALLY HURT--
--BUT I'M NOT GONNA HANG BACK AND LEAVE HIM ALL ALONE TO BLEED TO--
SHAKOOM

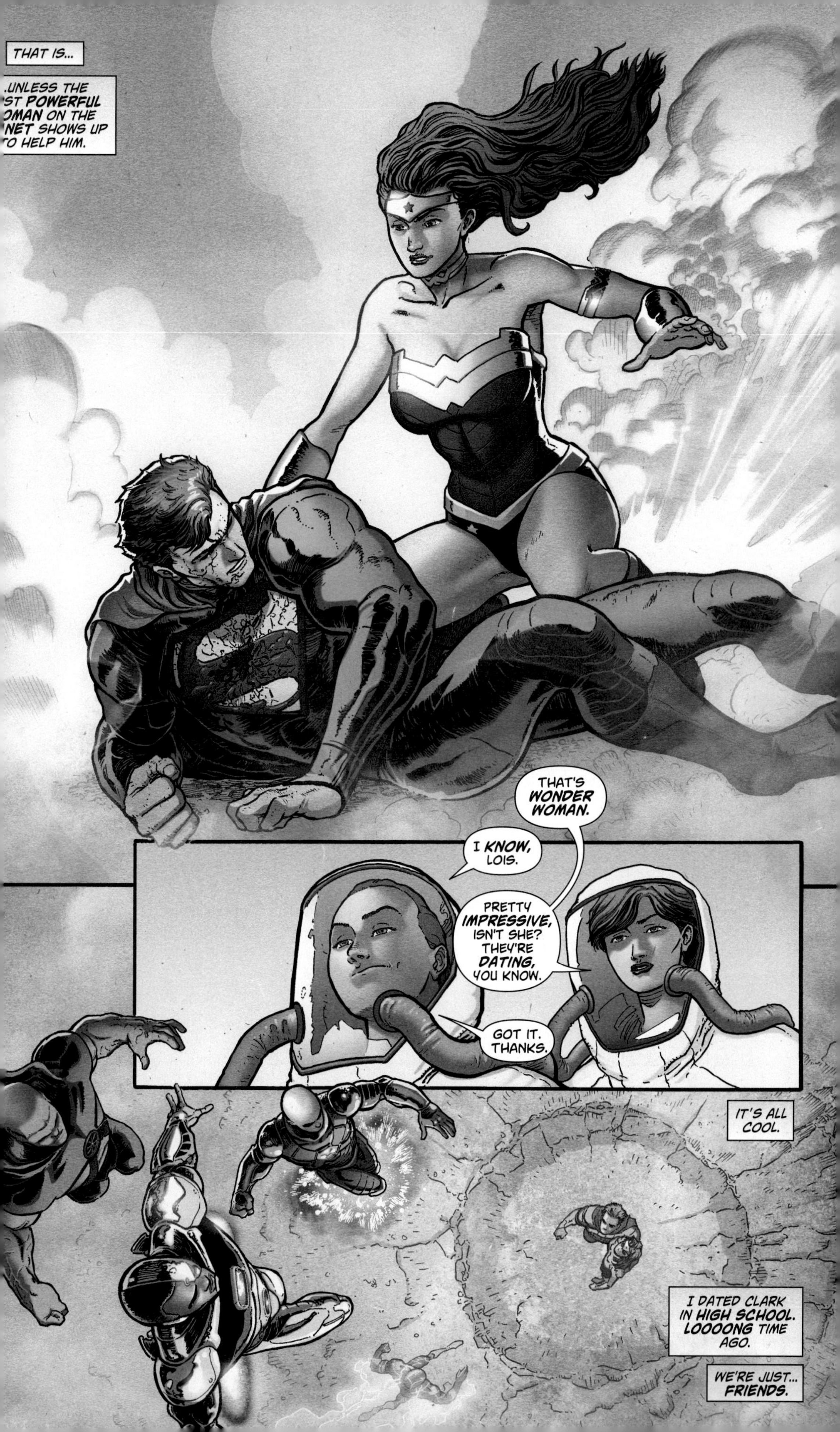

THAT IS...
..UNLESS THE
ST POWERFUL
OMAN ON THE
NET SHOWS UP
TO HELP HIM.
THAT'S WONDER WOMAN.
I KNOW, LOIS.
PRETTY IMPRESSIVE, ISN'T SHE? THEY'RE DATING, YOU KNOW.
GOT IT. THANKS.
IT'S ALL COOL.
I DATED CLARK IN HIGH SCHOOL. LOOOONG TIME AGO.
WE'RE JUST... FRIENDS.

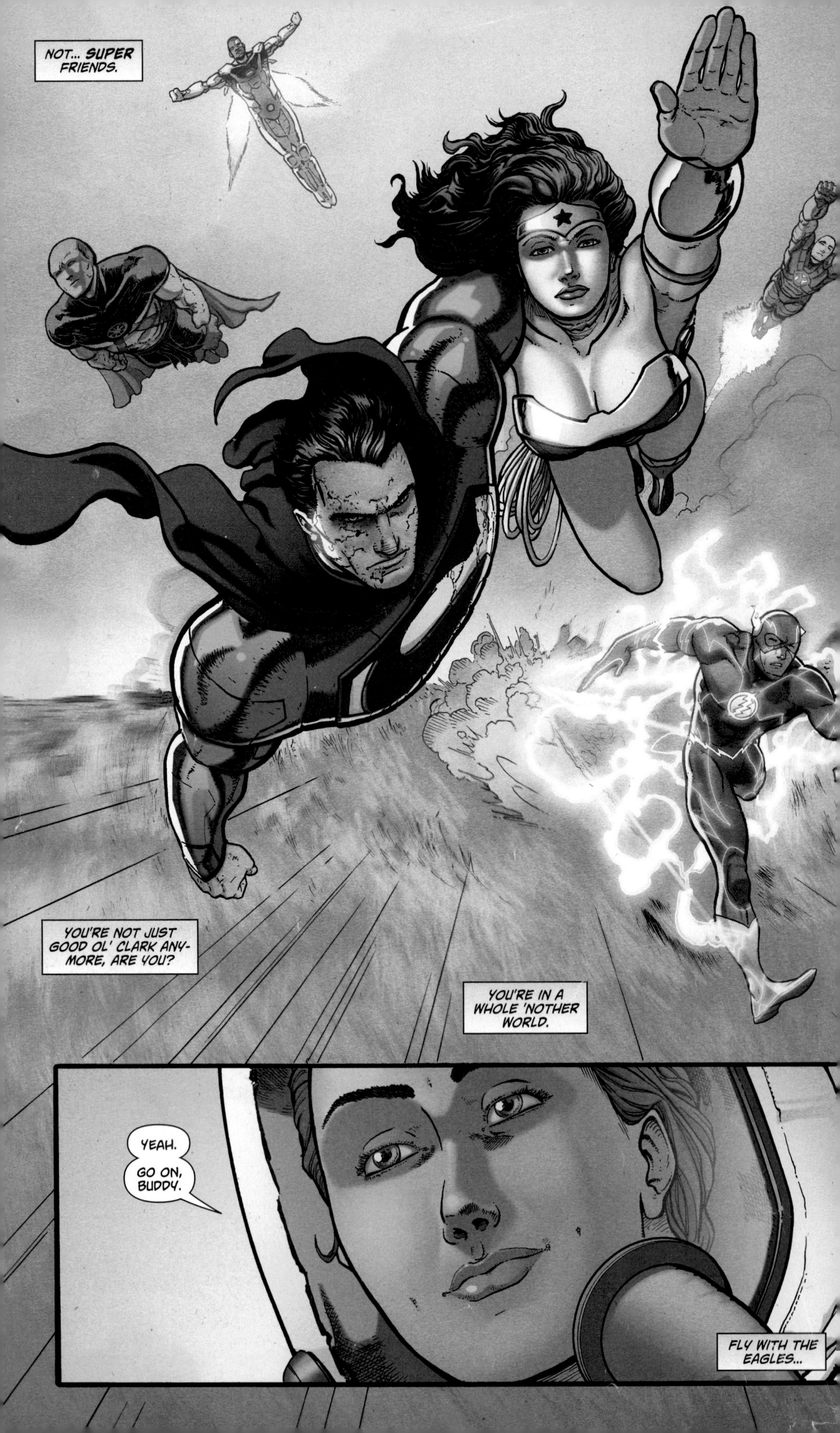
NOT... SUPER FRIENDS.
YOU'RE NOT JUST GOOD OL' CLARK ANY-MORE, ARE YOU?
YOU'RE IN A WHOLE 'NOTHER WORLD.
YEAH.
GO ON, BUDDY.
FLY WITH THE EAGLES...

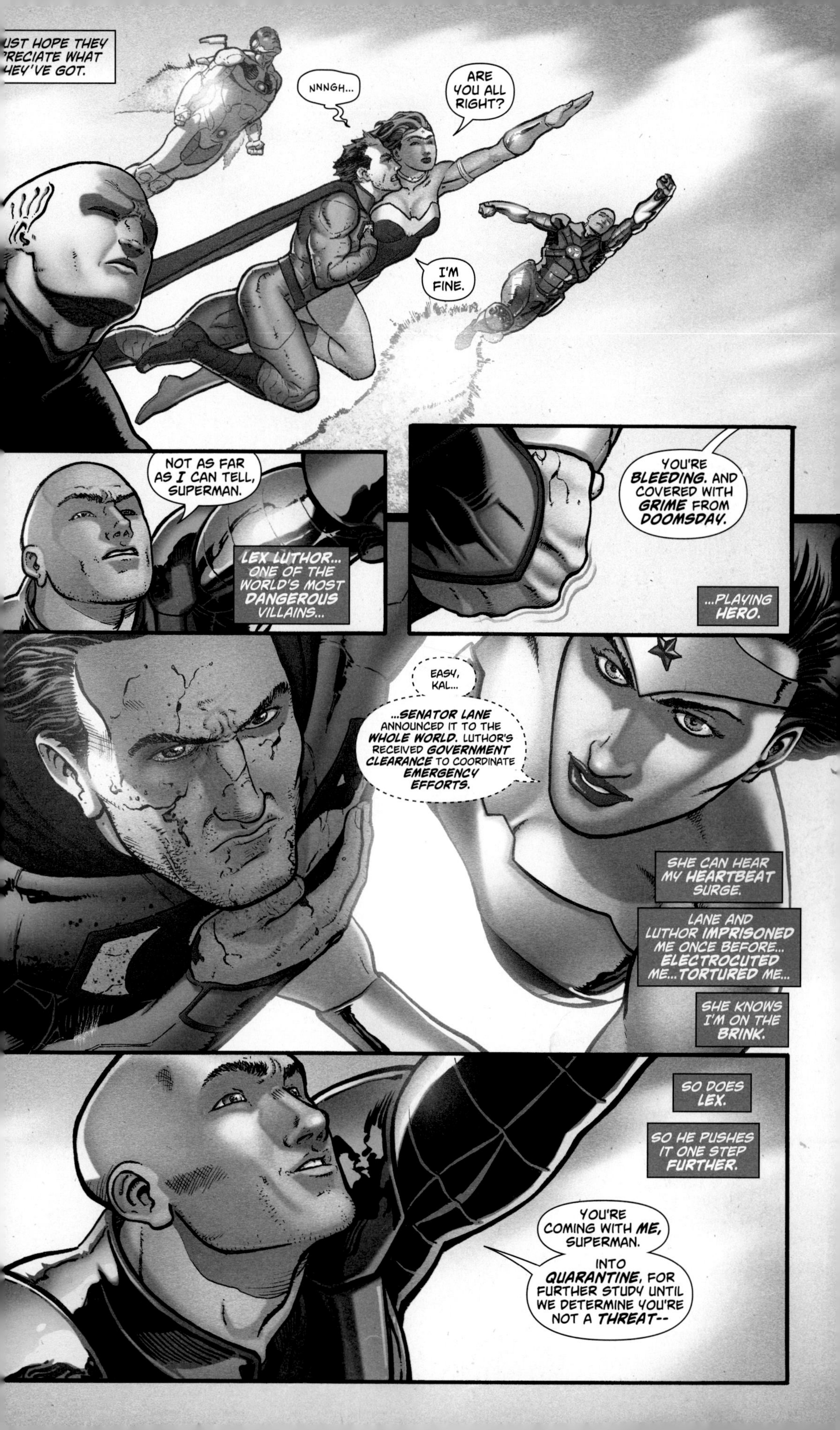

UST HOPE THEY
PRECIATE WHAT
HEY'VE GOT.
NNNGH...
ARE YOU ALL RIGHT?
I'M FINE.
NOT AS FAR AS I CAN TELL, SUPERMAN.
LEX LUTHOR... ONE OF THE WORLD'S MOST DANGEROUS VILLAINS...
YOU'RE BLEEDING. AND COVERED WITH GRIME FROM DOOMSDAY.
...PLAYING HERO.
EASY, KAL...
...SENATOR LANE ANNOUNCED IT TO THE WHOLE WORLD. LUTHOR'S RECEIVED GOVERNMENT CLEARANCE TO COORDINATE EMERGENCY EFFORTS.
SHE CAN HEAR MY HEARTBEAT SURGE.
LANE AND LUTHOR IMPRISONED ME ONCE BEFORE... ELECTROCUTED ME...TORTURED ME...
SHE KNOWS I'M ON THE BRINK.
SO DOES LEX.
SO HE PUSHES IT ONE STEP FURTHER.
YOU'RE COMING WITH ME, SUPERMAN.
INTO QUARANTINE, FOR FURTHER STUDY UNTIL WE DETERMINE YOU'RE NOT A THREAT--

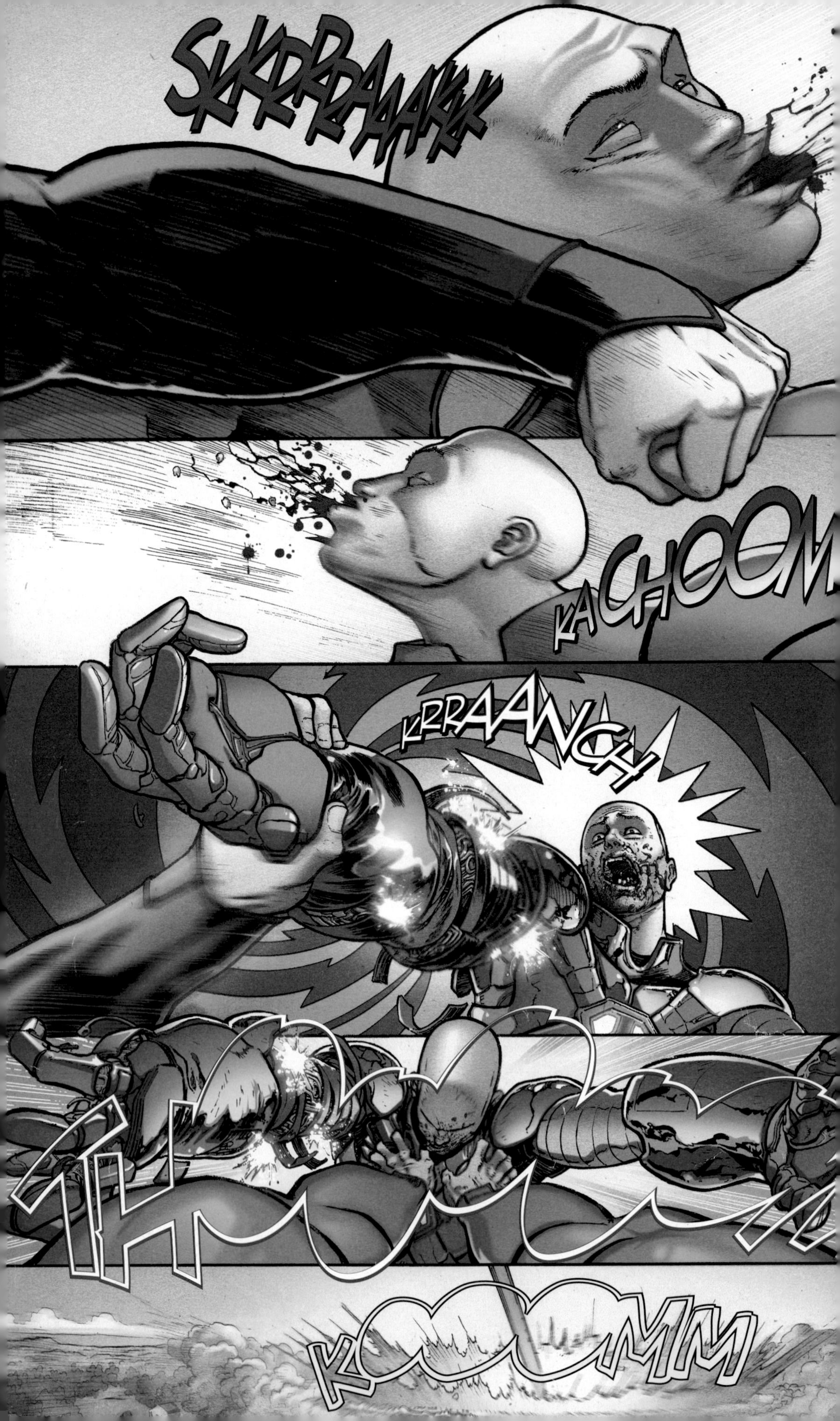
SKRRRAAAKK
KACHOOM
KRRAANCH
THOOOM
KOOOMM

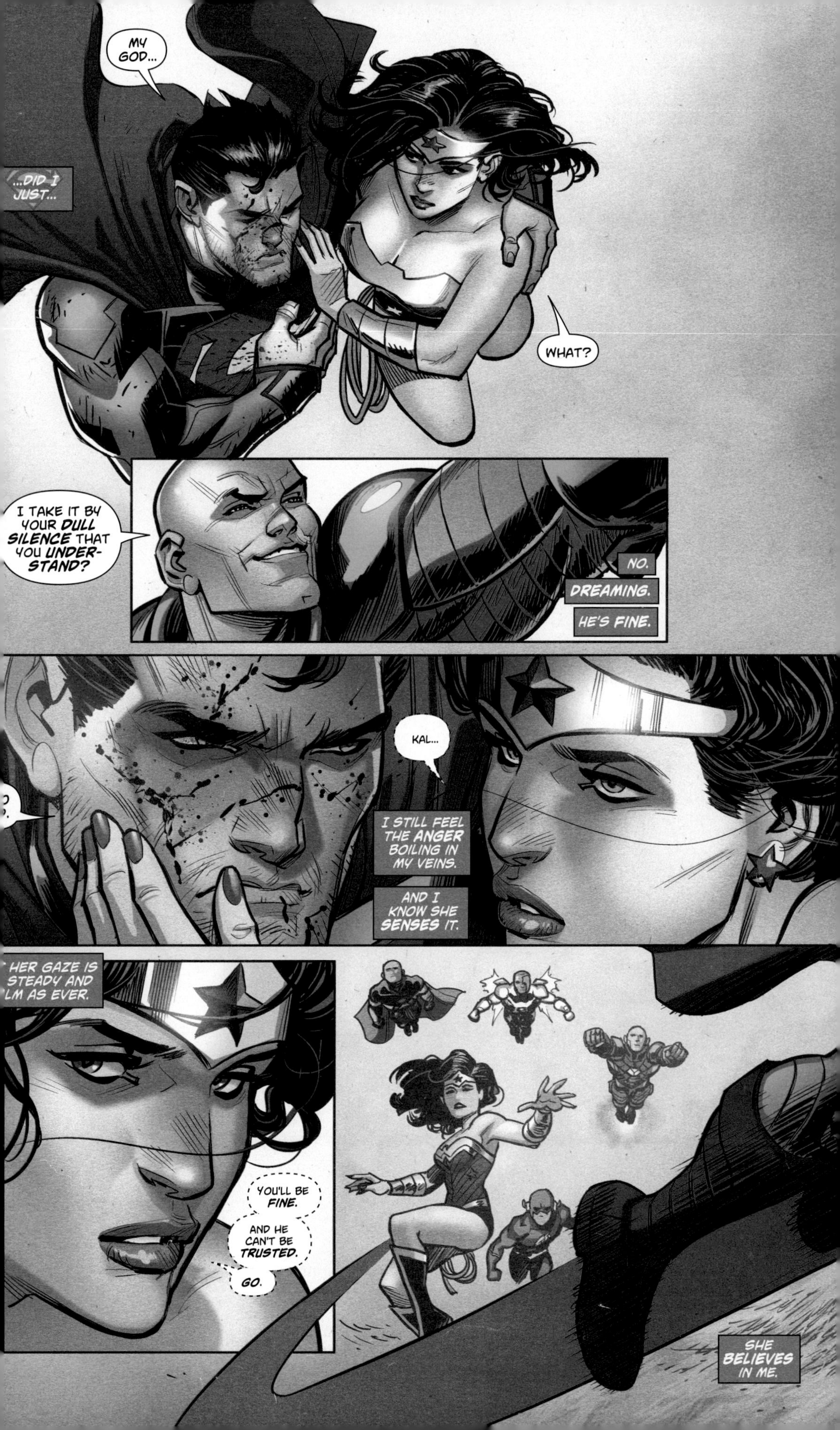
MY GOD...
...DID I JUST...
WHAT?
I TAKE IT BY YOUR DULL SILENCE THAT YOU UNDERSTAND?
NO.
DREAMING.
HE'S FINE.
KAL...
I STILL FEEL THE ANGER BOILING IN MY VEINS.
AND I KNOW SHE SENSES IT.
HER GAZE IS STEADY AND LM AS EVER.
YOU'LL BE FINE.
AND HE CAN'T BE TRUSTED.
GO.
SHE BELIEVES IN ME.

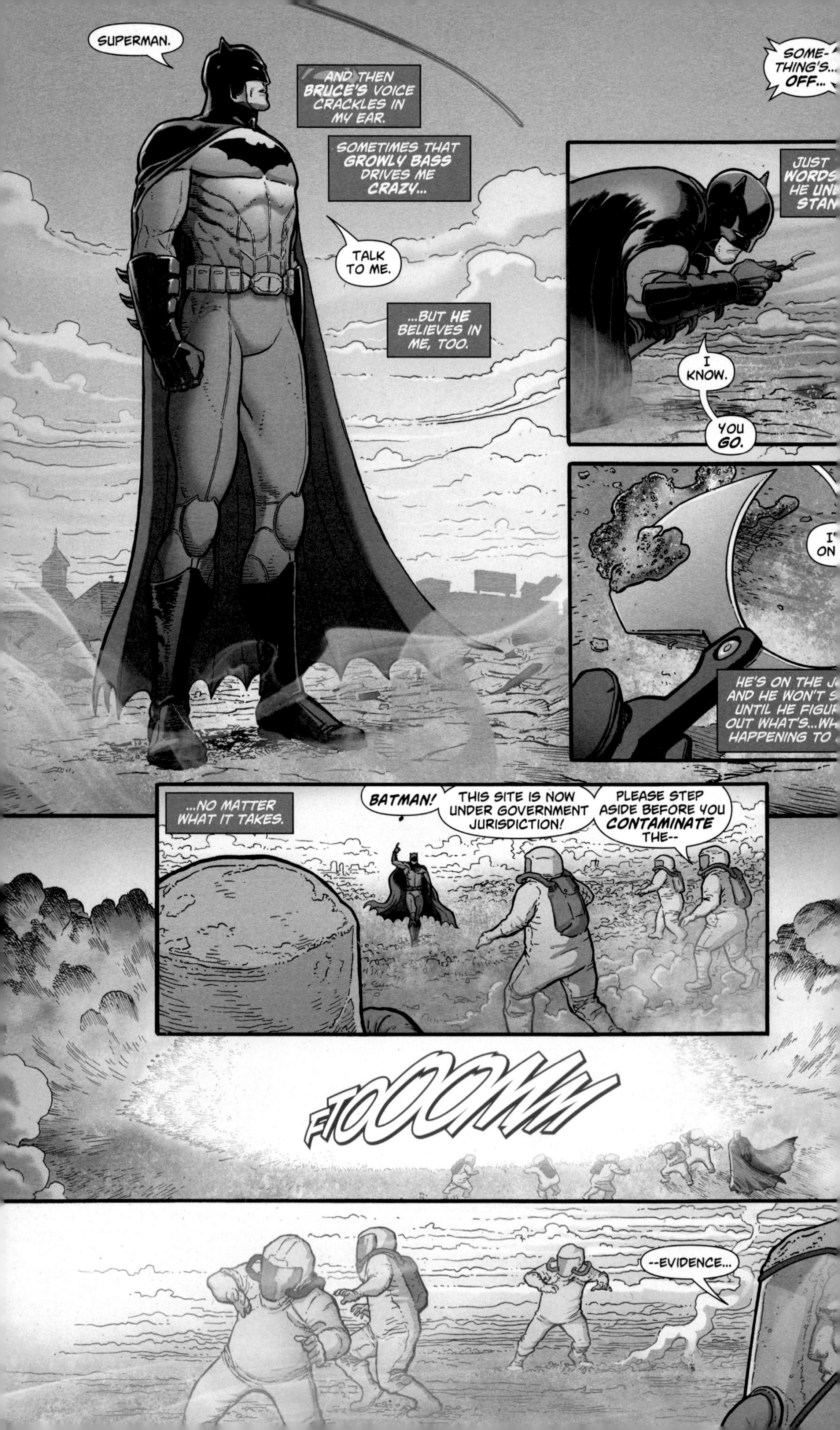
SUPERMAN.
AND THEN BRUCE'S VOICE CRACKLES IN MY EAR.
SOMETIMES THAT GROWLY BASS DRIVES ME CRAZY...
TALK TO ME.
...BUT HE BELIEVES IN ME, TOO.
SOME-THING'S... OFF...
I KNOW.
YOU GO.
...NO MATTER WHAT IT TAKES.
BATMAN!
THIS SITE IS NOW UNDER GOVERNMENT JURISDICTION!
PLEASE STEP ASIDE BEFORE YOU CONTAMINATE THE--
FTOOOOMM
--EVIDENCE...

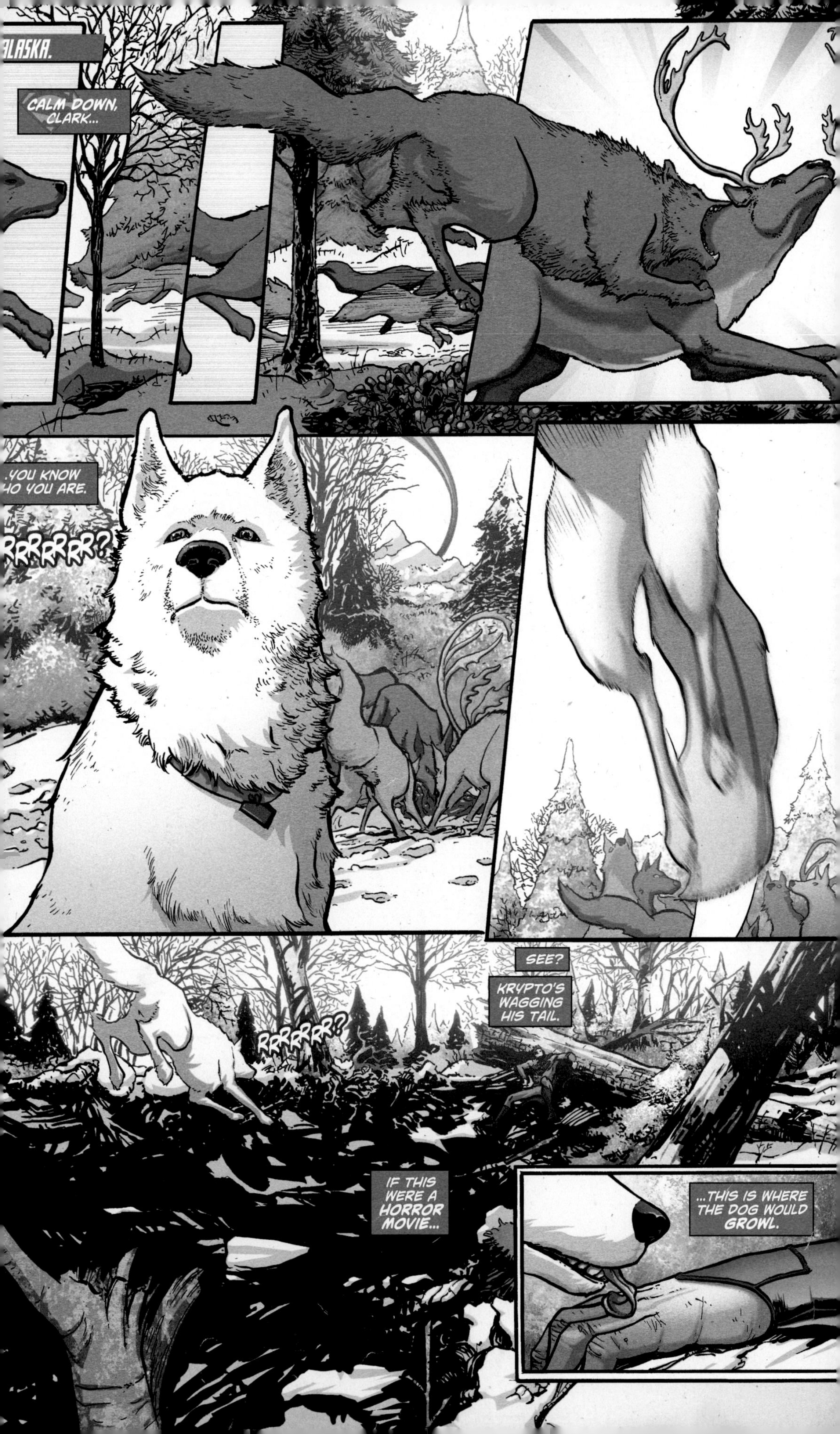
ALASKA.
CALM DOWN, CLARK...
...YOU KNOW WHO YOU ARE.
RRRRRRR?
SEE?
KRYPTO'S WAGGING HIS TAIL.
RRRRRRR?
IF THIS WERE A HORROR MOVIE...
...THIS IS WHERE THE DOG WOULD GROWL.

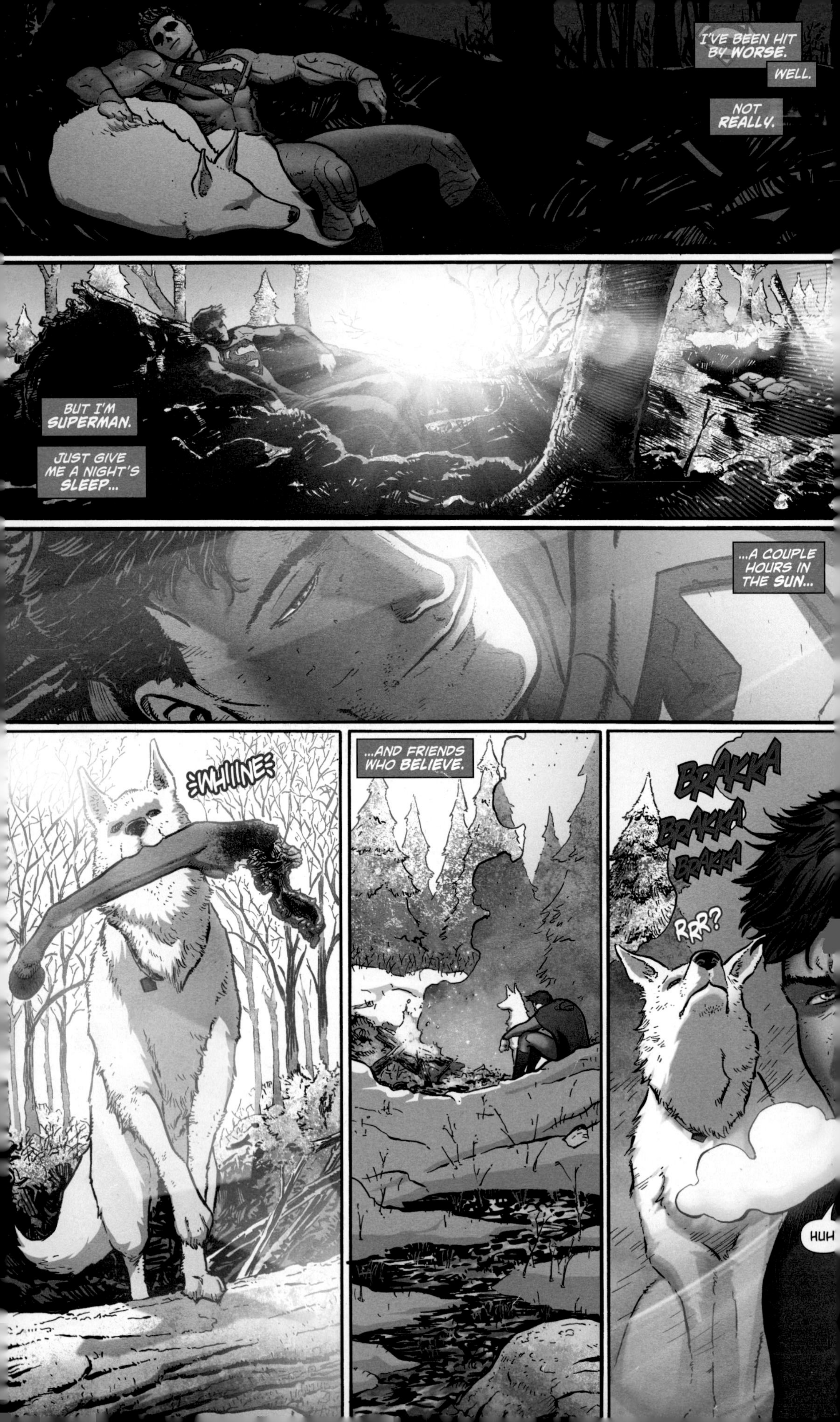

I'VE BEEN HIT BY WORSE.
WELL.
NOT REALLY.
BUT I'M SUPERMAN.
JUST GIVE ME A NIGHT'S SLEEP...
...A COUPLE HOURS IN THE SUN...
WHIIINE
...AND FRIENDS WHO BELIEVE.
BRAKKA
BRAKKA
BRAKKA
RRR?
HUH

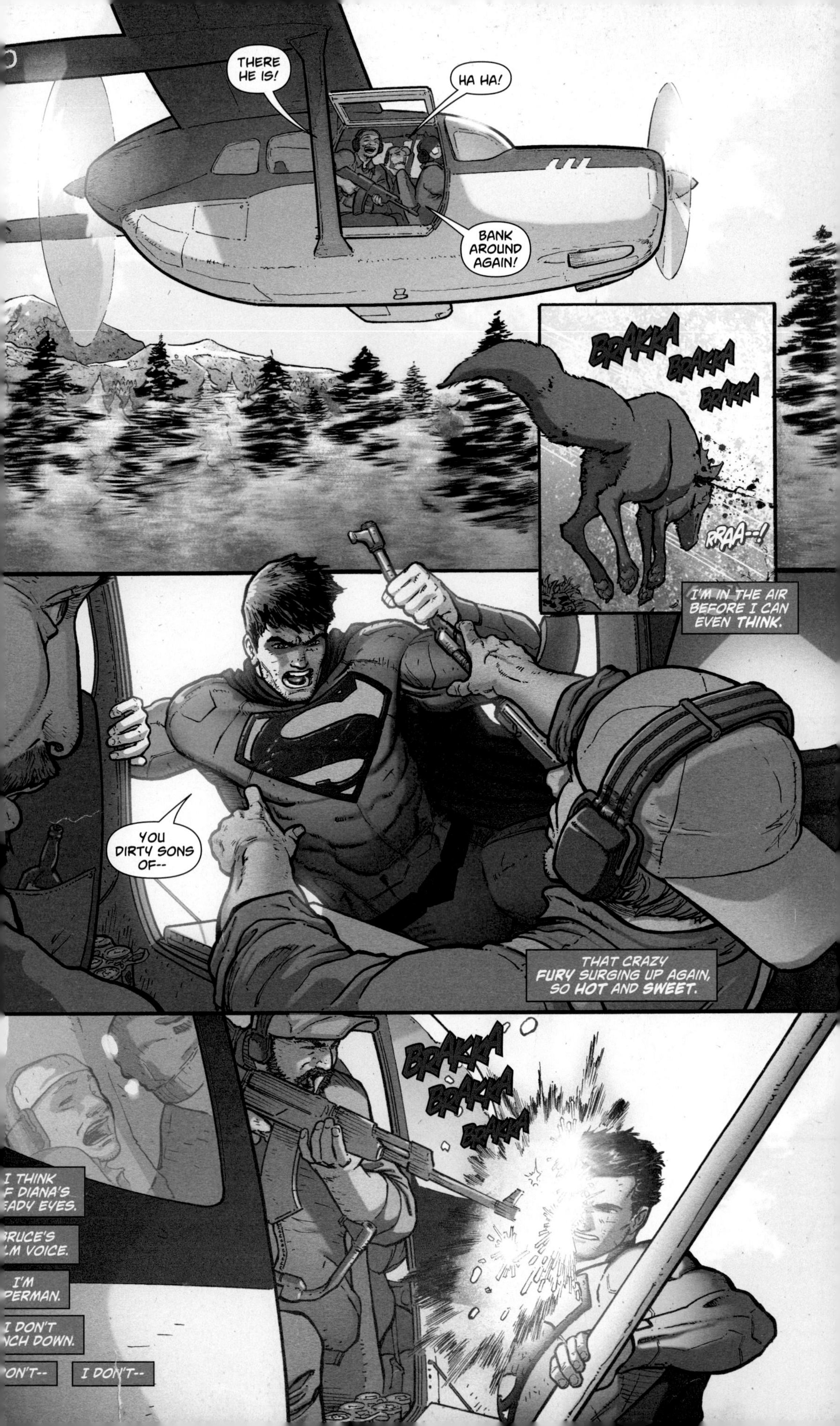

THERE HE IS!
HA HA!
BANK AROUND AGAIN!
BRAKKA BRAKKA BRAKKA
RRAA--!
I'M IN THE AIR BEFORE I CAN EVEN THINK.
YOU DIRTY SONS OF--
THAT CRAZY FURY SURGING UP AGAIN, SO HOT AND SWEET.
BRAKKA BRAKKA BRAKKA
I THINK F DIANA'S EADY EYES.
BRUCE'S LM VOICE.
I'M PERMAN.
I DON'T NCH DOWN.
ON'T--
I DON'T--

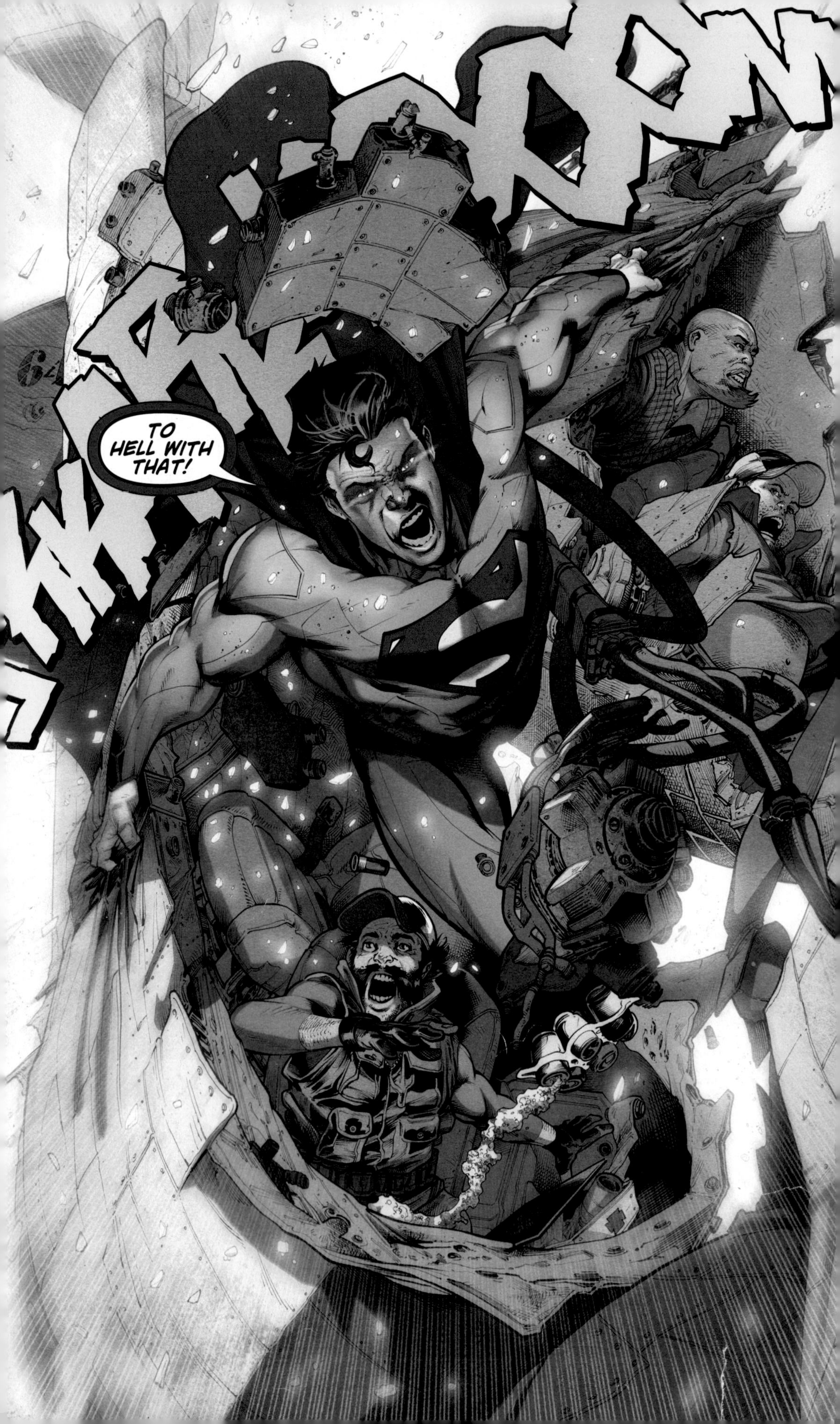
TO HELL WITH THAT!

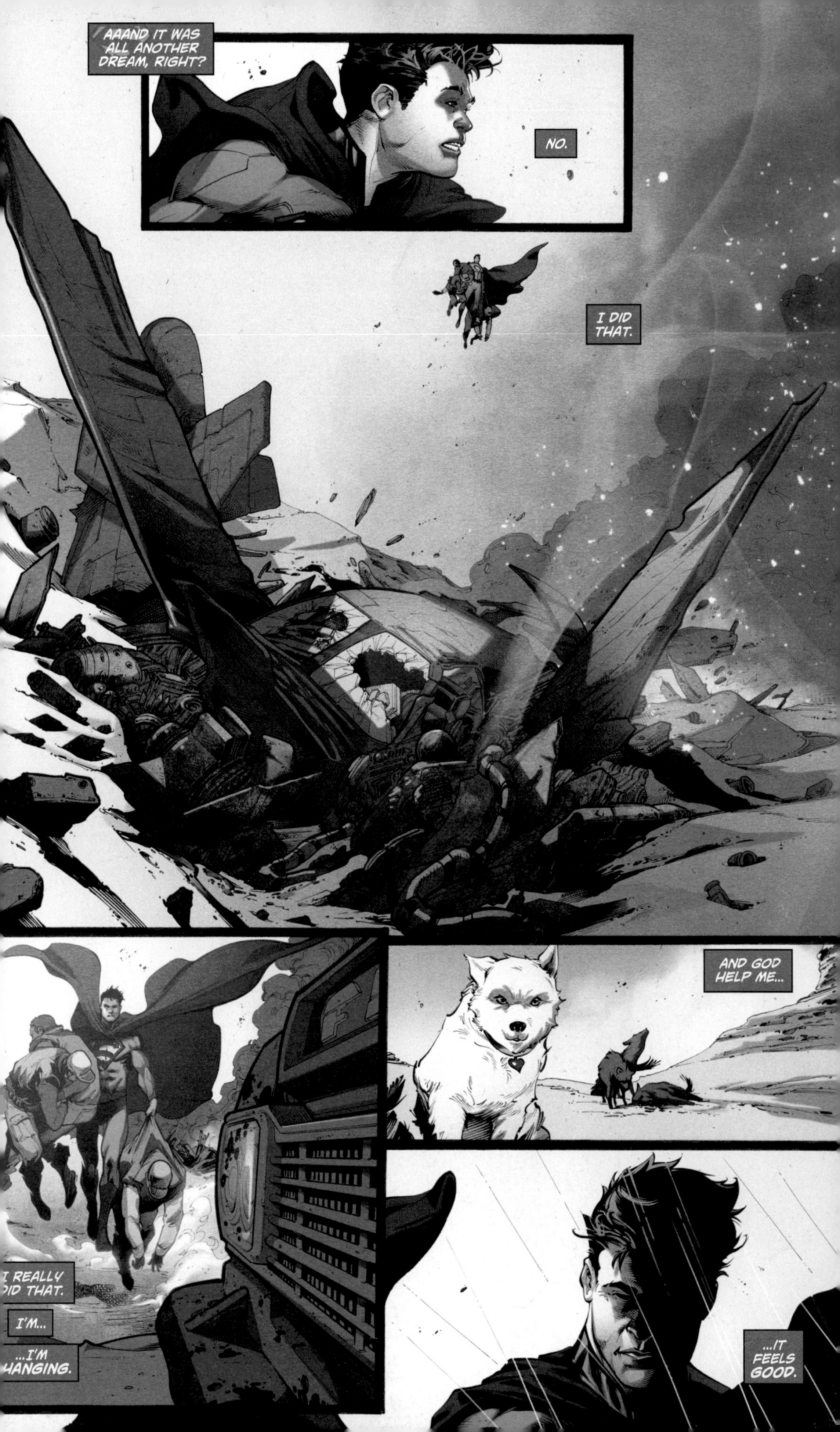
AAAND IT WAS ALL ANOTHER DREAM, RIGHT?
NO.
I DID THAT.
I REALLY DID THAT.
I'M...
...I'M CHANGING.
AND GOD HELP ME...
...IT FEELS GOOD.

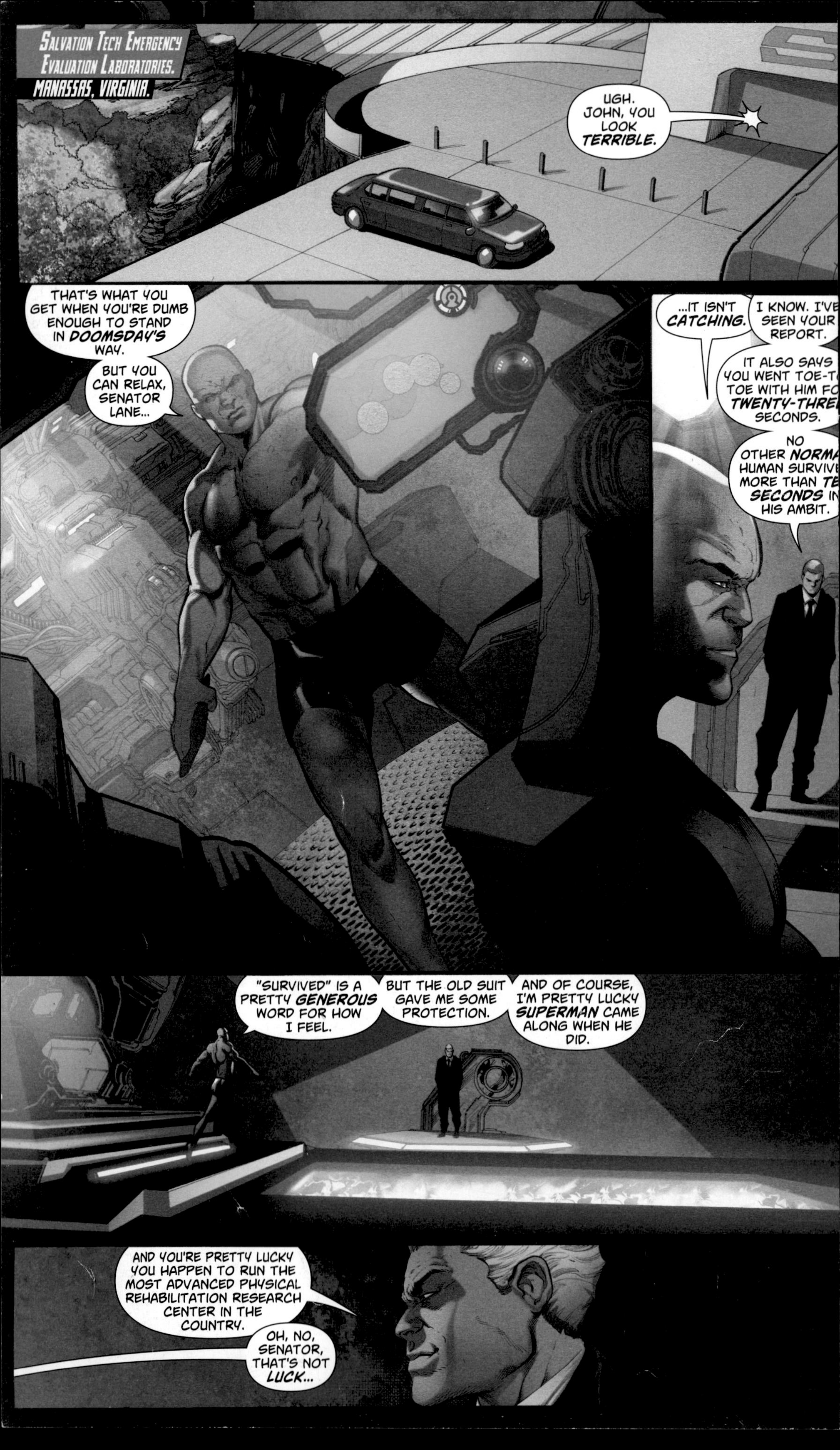
SALVATION TECH EMERGENCY EVALUATION LABORATORIES.
MANASSAS, VIRGINIA.
UGH. JOHN, YOU LOOK TERRIBLE.
THAT'S WHAT YOU GET WHEN YOU'RE DUMB ENOUGH TO STAND IN DOOMSDAY'S WAY.
BUT YOU CAN RELAX, SENATOR LANE...
...IT ISN'T CATCHING.
I KNOW. I'VE SEEN YOUR REPORT.
IT ALSO SAYS YOU WENT TOE-TO-TOE WITH HIM FOR TWENTY-THREE SECONDS.
NO OTHER NORMAL HUMAN SURVIVED MORE THAN TEN SECONDS IN HIS AMBIT.
"SURVIVED" IS A PRETTY GENEROUS WORD FOR HOW I FEEL.
BUT THE OLD SUIT GAVE ME SOME PROTECTION.
AND OF COURSE, I'M PRETTY LUCKY SUPERMAN CAME ALONG WHEN HE DID.
AND YOU'RE PRETTY LUCKY YOU HAPPEN TO RUN THE MOST ADVANCED PHYSICAL REHABILITATION RESEARCH CENTER IN THE COUNTRY.
OH, NO, SENATOR, THAT'S NOT LUCK...

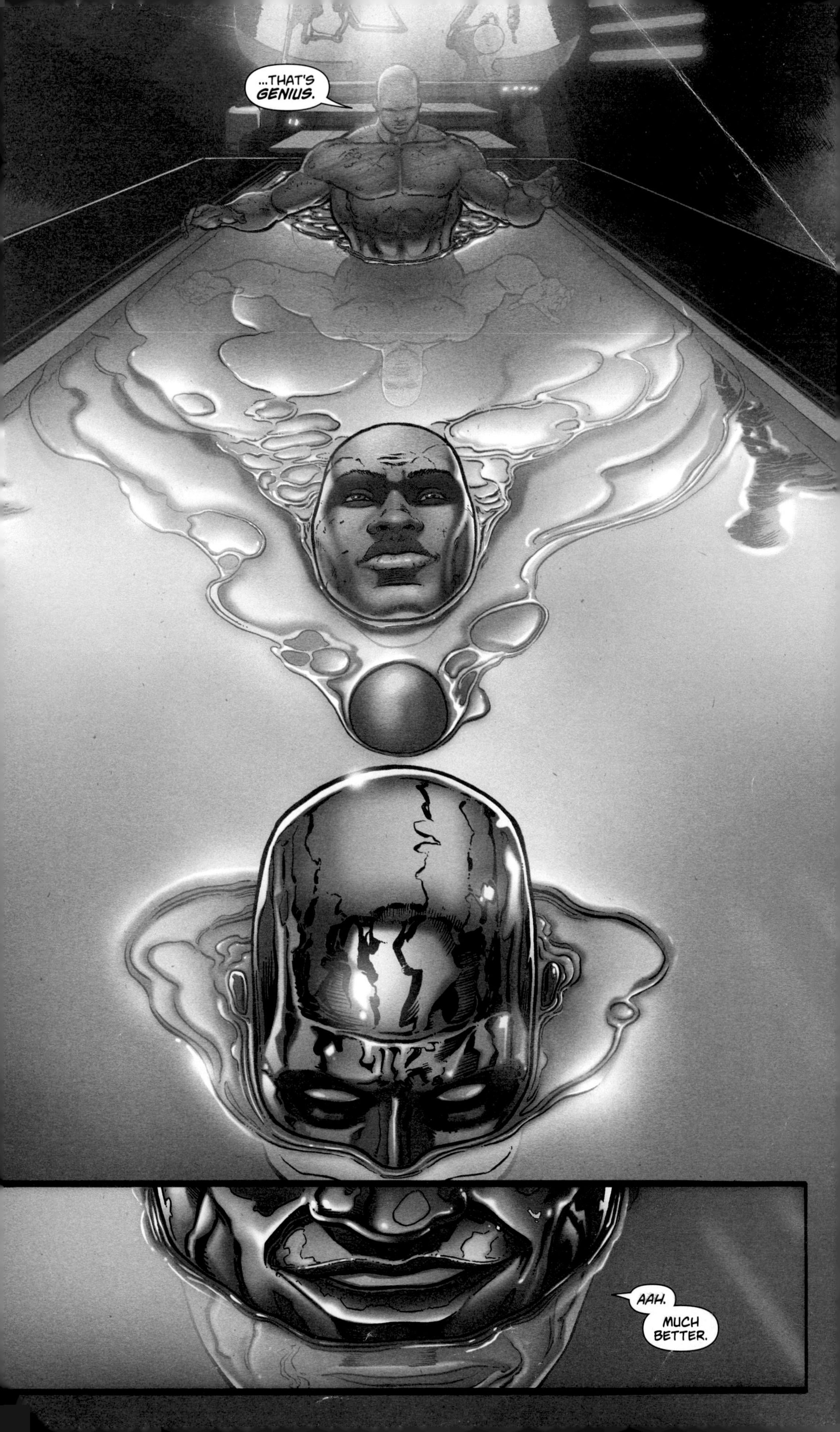
...THAT'S GENIUS.
AAH. MUCH BETTER.

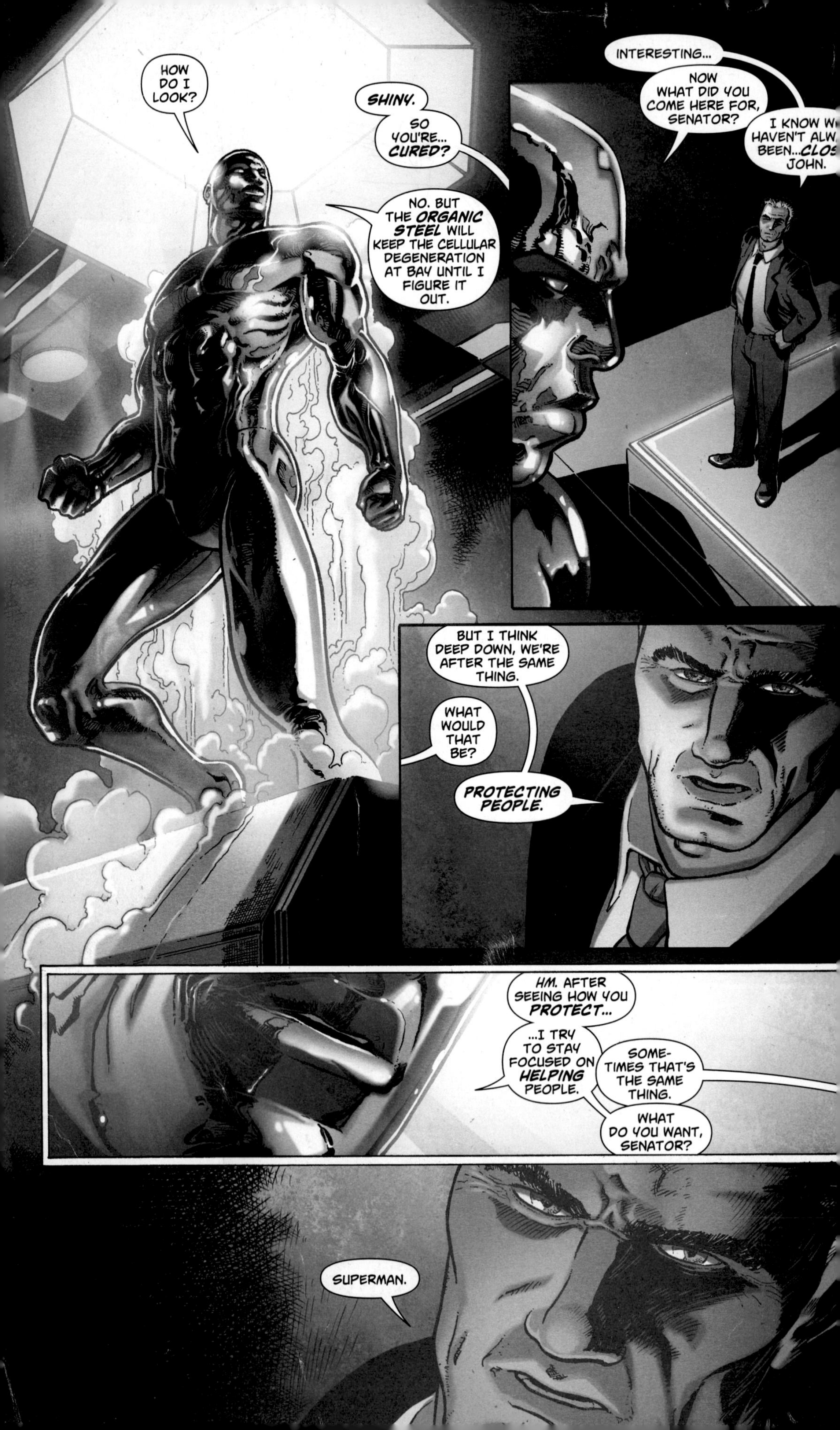
HOW DO I LOOK?
SHINY.
SO YOU'RE... CURED?
NO. BUT THE ORGANIC STEEL WILL KEEP THE CELLULAR DEGENERATION AT BAY UNTIL I FIGURE IT OUT.
INTERESTING...
NOW WHAT DID YOU COME HERE FOR, SENATOR?
I KNOW W HAVEN'T ALW BEEN...CLOS JOHN.
BUT I THINK DEEP DOWN, WE'RE AFTER THE SAME THING.
WHAT WOULD THAT BE?
PROTECTING PEOPLE.
HM. AFTER SEEING HOW YOU PROTECT...
...I TRY TO STAY FOCUSED ON HELPING PEOPLE.
SOME-TIMES THAT'S THE SAME THING.
WHAT DO YOU WANT, SENATOR?
SUPERMAN.

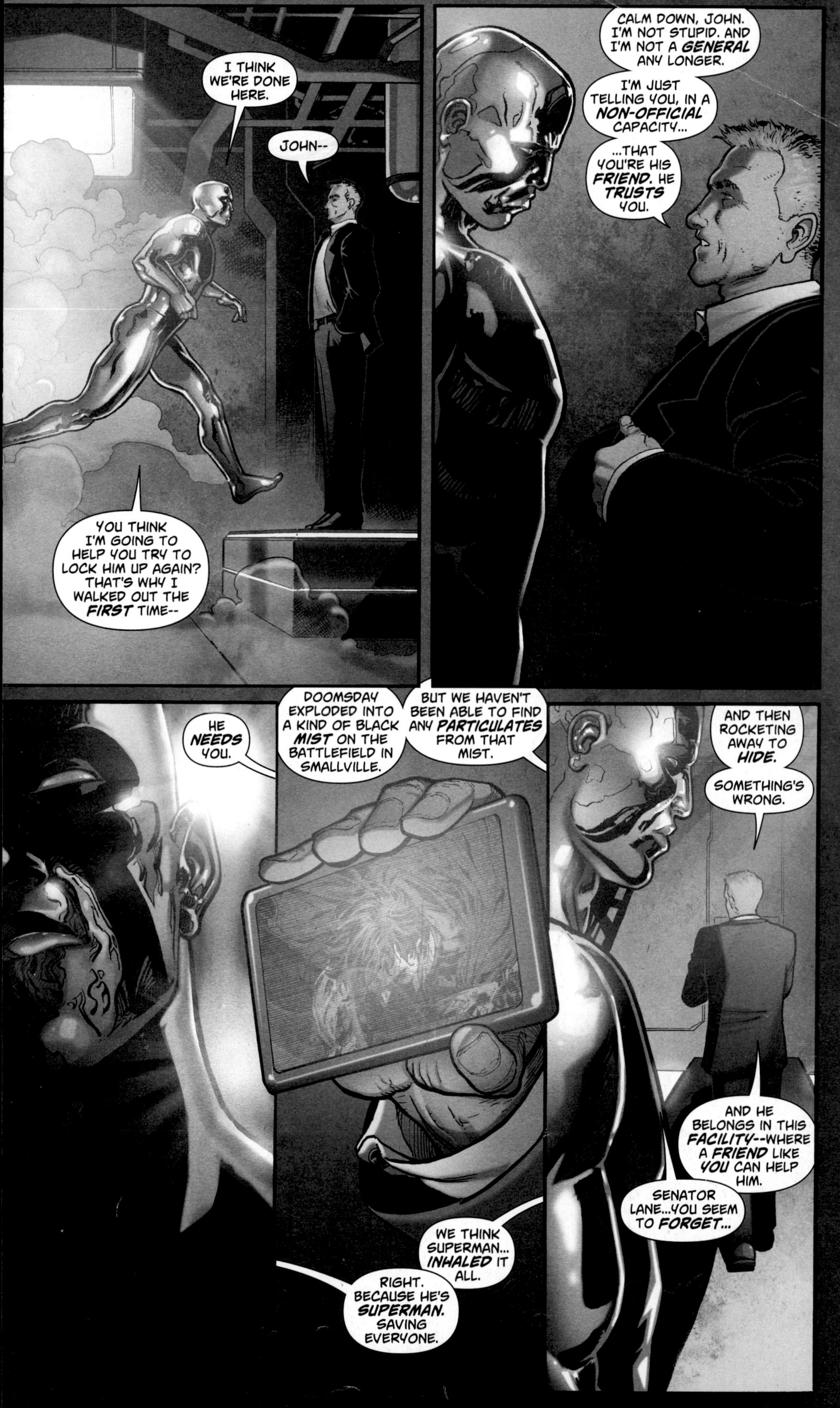
I THINK WE'RE DONE HERE.
JOHN--
YOU THINK I'M GOING TO HELP YOU TRY TO LOCK HIM UP AGAIN? THAT'S WHY I WALKED OUT THE FIRST TIME--
CALM DOWN, JOHN. I'M NOT STUPID. AND I'M NOT A GENERAL ANY LONGER.
I'M JUST TELLING YOU, IN A NON-OFFICIAL CAPACITY...
...THAT YOU'RE HIS FRIEND. HE TRUSTS YOU.
HE NEEDS YOU.
DOOMSDAY EXPLODED INTO A KIND OF BLACK MIST ON THE BATTLEFIELD IN SMALLVILLE.
BUT WE HAVEN'T BEEN ABLE TO FIND ANY PARTICULATES FROM THAT MIST.
WE THINK SUPERMAN... INHALED IT ALL.
RIGHT. BECAUSE HE'S SUPERMAN. SAVING EVERYONE.
AND THEN ROCKETING AWAY TO HIDE.
SOMETHING'S WRONG.
AND HE BELONGS IN THIS FACILITY--WHERE A FRIEND LIKE YOU CAN HELP HIM.
SENATOR LANE...YOU SEEM TO FORGET...

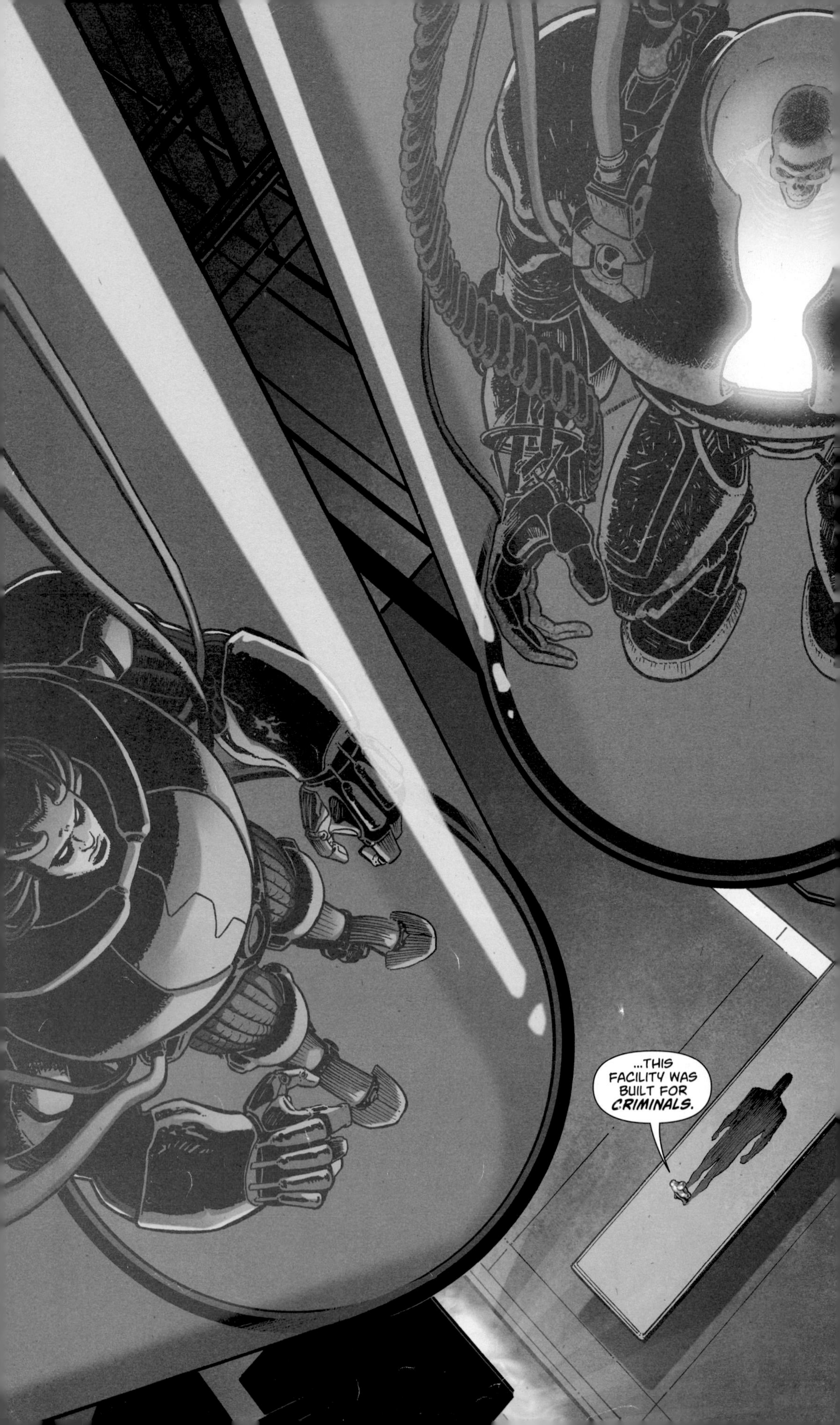
...THIS FACILITY WAS BUILT FOR CRIMINALS.

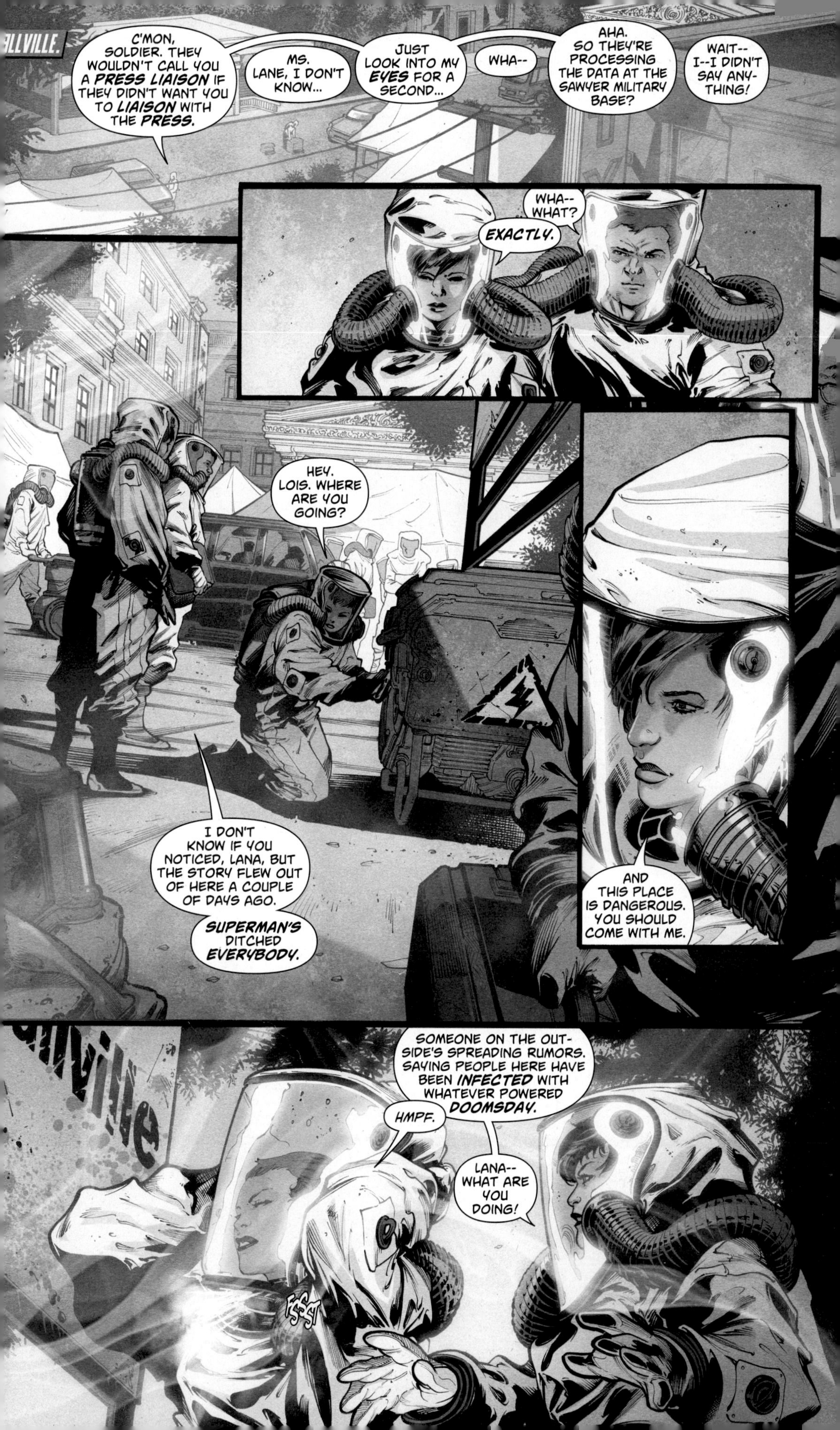

...LLVILLE.
C'MON, SOLDIER. THEY WOULDN'T CALL YOU A PRESS LIAISON IF THEY DIDN'T WANT YOU TO LIAISON WITH THE PRESS.
MS. LANE, I DON'T KNOW...
JUST LOOK INTO MY EYES FOR A SECOND...
WHA--
AHA. SO THEY'RE PROCESSING THE DATA AT THE SAWYER MILITARY BASE?
WAIT-- I--I DIDN'T SAY ANYTHING!
WHA-- WHAT?
EXACTLY.
HEY. LOIS. WHERE ARE YOU GOING?
I DON'T KNOW IF YOU NOTICED, LANA, BUT THE STORY FLEW OUT OF HERE A COUPLE OF DAYS AGO.
SUPERMAN'S DITCHED EVERYBODY.
AND THIS PLACE IS DANGEROUS. YOU SHOULD COME WITH ME.
SOMEONE ON THE OUTSIDE'S SPREADING RUMORS. SAYING PEOPLE HERE HAVE BEEN INFECTED WITH WHATEVER POWERED DOOMSDAY.
HMPF.
LANA-- WHAT ARE YOU DOING!
FSSST

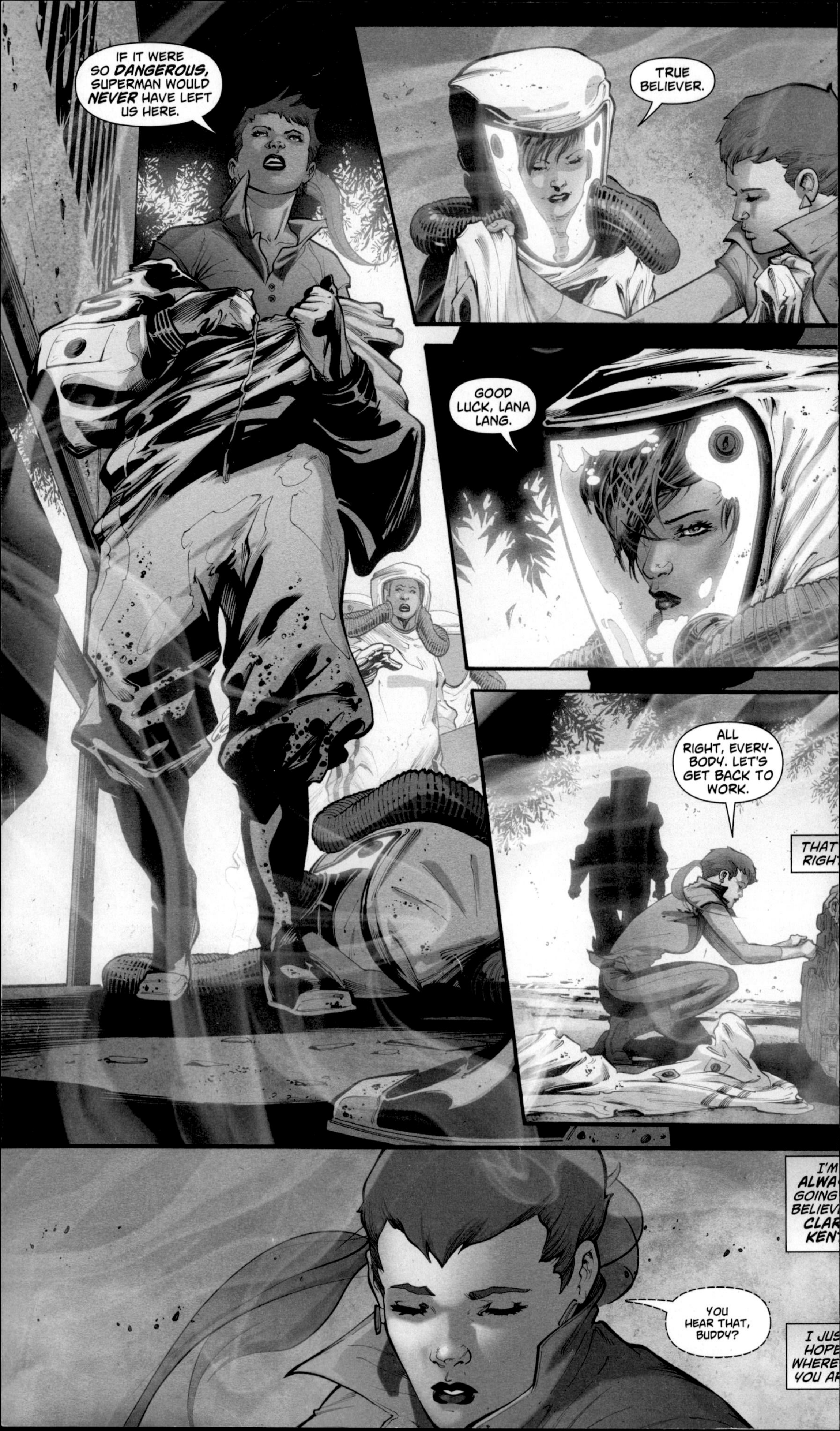
IF IT WERE SO DANGEROUS, SUPERMAN WOULD NEVER HAVE LEFT US HERE.
TRUE BELIEVER.
GOOD LUCK, LANA LANG.
ALL RIGHT, EVERY-BODY. LET'S GET BACK TO WORK.
YOU HEAR THAT, BUDDY?

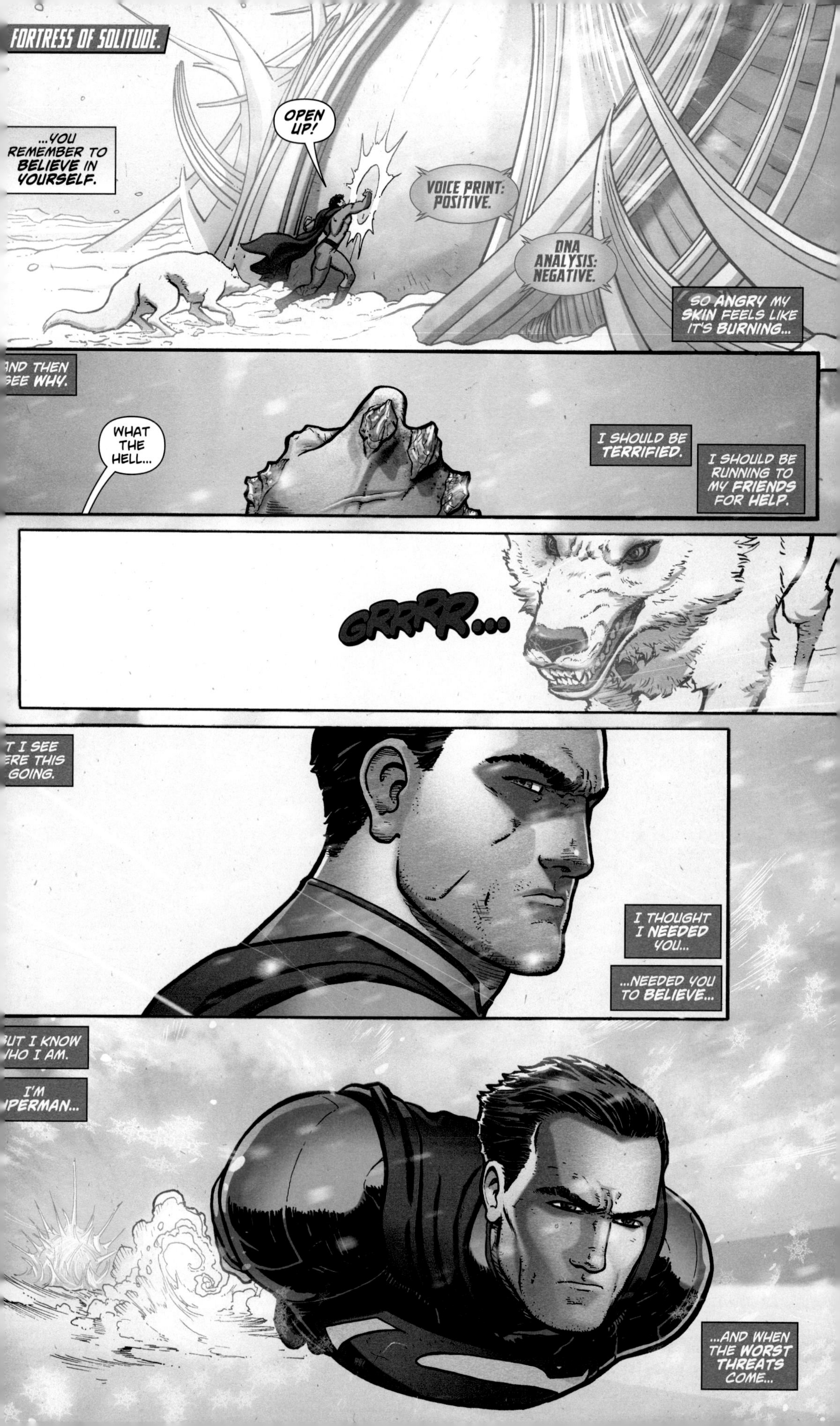
FORTRESS OF SOLITUDE.
...YOU REMEMBER TO BELIEVE IN YOURSELF.
OPEN UP!
VOICE PRINT: POSITIVE.
DNA ANALYSIS: NEGATIVE.
SO ANGRY MY SKIN FEELS LIKE IT'S BURNING...
AND THEN SEE WHY.
WHAT THE HELL...
I SHOULD BE TERRIFIED.
I SHOULD BE RUNNING TO MY FRIENDS FOR HELP.
GRRRR...
T I SEE ERE THIS GOING.
I THOUGHT I NEEDED YOU...
...NEEDED YOU TO BELIEVE...
UT I KNOW HO I AM.
I'M PERMAN...
...AND WHEN THE WORST THREATS COME...

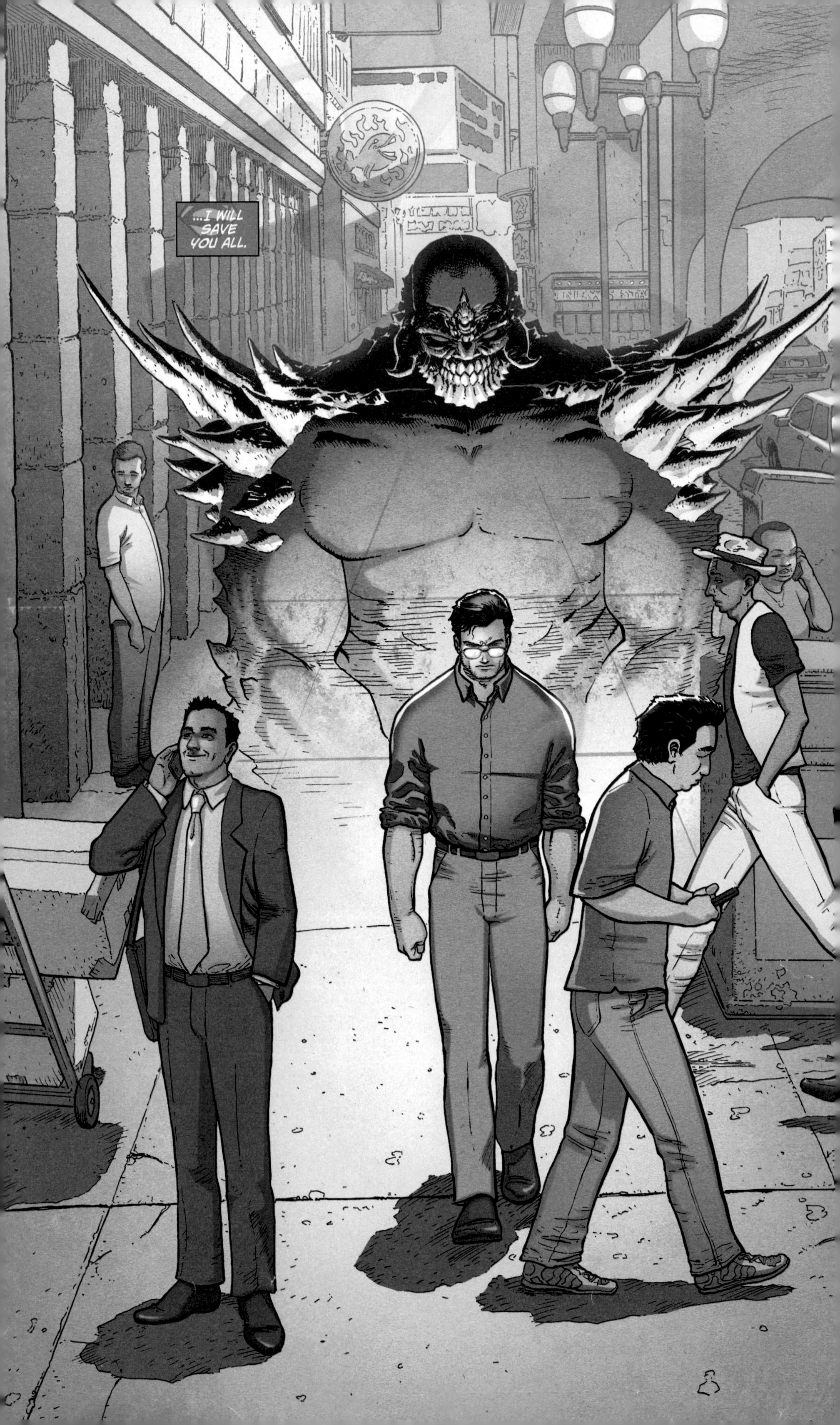
...I WILL SAVE YOU ALL.

"NIGHTMARE"

GREG PAK writer SCOTT KOLINS artist WIL QUINTANA colorist

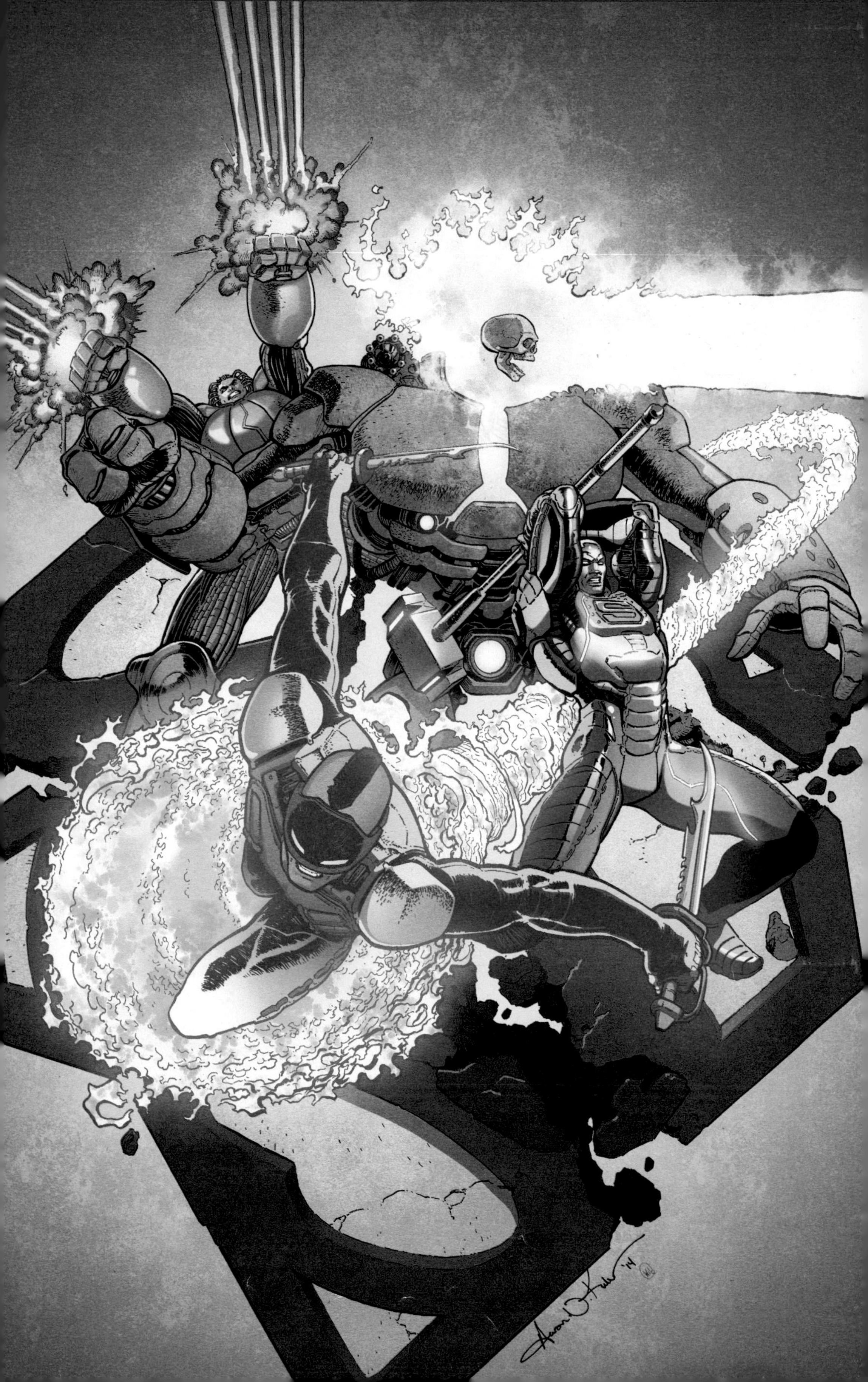

June 4, 2

Daily Planet
DAILY PLANET

MY TIME WITH SUPERDOOM

By Lois Lane

I was extremely lucky to be invited by Superman to an undisclosed location where he is being held in hopes that a means can be found to reverse this mutation. Even though the man we all care for is rapidly losing his identity, he still holds true to protecting everyone. The following is from our time speaking together.

Lois Lane: Are you okay?

Superman: I'd like to say "Yes." But I'm afraid that would be a lie. Lois, you should know the risks—

Lois Lane: I'm not afraid, Superman. I just want you to realize… whatever you're going through, I'm rooting for you.

Superman: Lois, I need you to do me a favor.

Lois Lane: Anything.

Superman: I need you… to get the truth out there. I… messed up. I made a mistake. I thought I could take out Doomsday, once and for all, but I realize now… I was wrong. For reasons I don't understand – yet—I'm… I'm becoming Doomsday. I didn't solve the problem, I only changed it.

Lois Lane: What are you saying? What do you want me to do?

Superman: I want you to tell

Photo by James

the world. To warn the people. I… can't be trusted. Not now. Maybe… never again.

Lois Lane: No one will believe that, Superman. I won't believe you can't get better.

Superman: Warn them. Can do that for me, Lois?

Lois Lane: Yes, Superman. I do that for you.

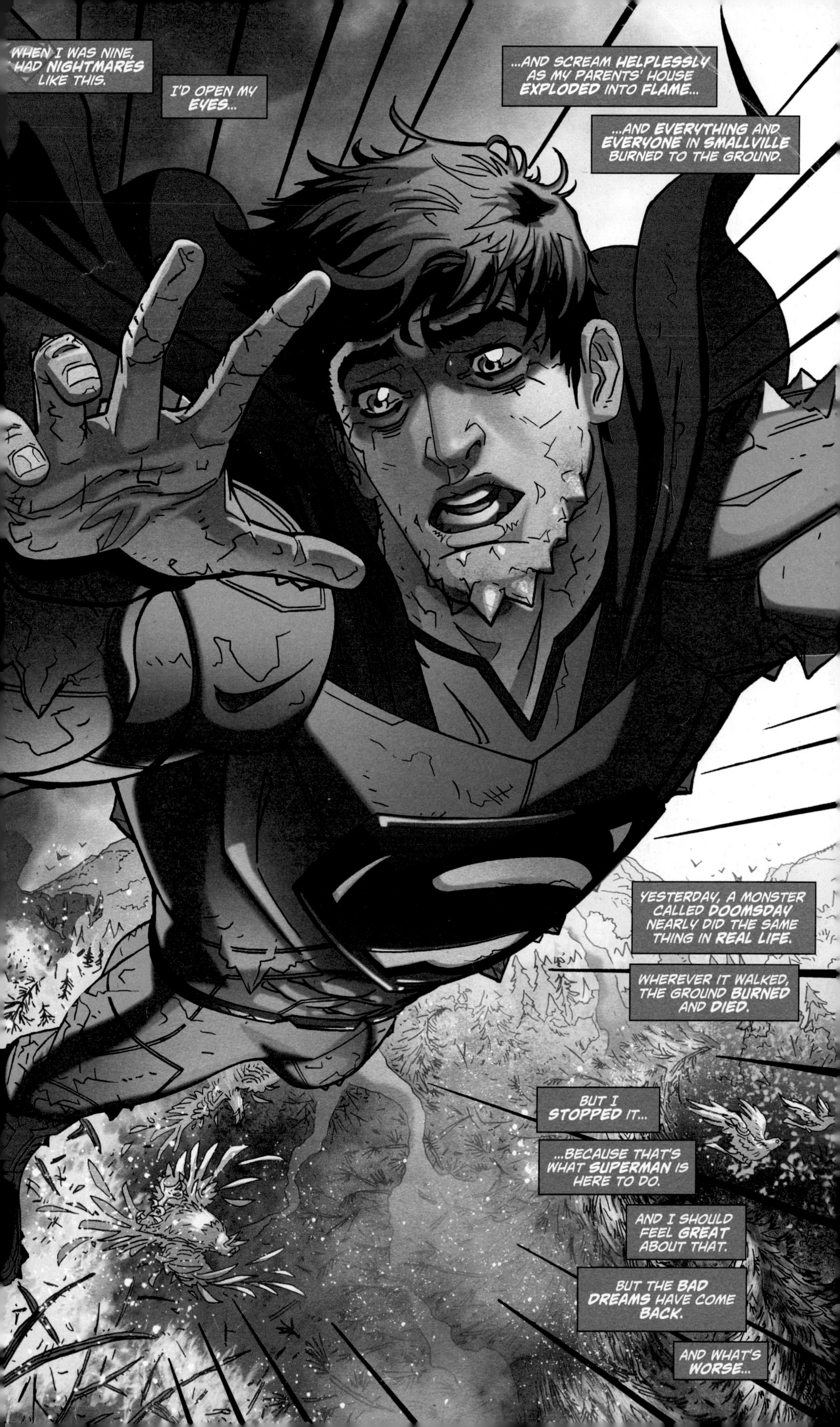
WHEN I WAS NINE, I HAD NIGHTMARES LIKE THIS.
I'D OPEN MY EYES...
...AND SCREAM HELPLESSLY AS MY PARENTS' HOUSE EXPLODED INTO FLAME...
...AND EVERYTHING AND EVERYONE IN SMALLVILLE BURNED TO THE GROUND.
YESTERDAY, A MONSTER CALLED DOOMSDAY NEARLY DID THE SAME THING IN REAL LIFE.
WHEREVER IT WALKED, THE GROUND BURNED AND DIED.
BUT I STOPPED IT...
...BECAUSE THAT'S WHAT SUPERMAN IS HERE TO DO.
AND I SHOULD FEEL GREAT ABOUT THAT.
BUT THE BAD DREAMS HAVE COME BACK.
AND WHAT'S WORSE...

...I DON'T THINK THEY'RE DREAMS.

OH, GOD...

WHEN I KILLED THE THING...

...IT EXPLODED INTO SPORES.

...AND I INHALED THEM ALL.

AND NOW THE TREES CATCH FIRE AS I FLY OVER THEM?

SOMETHING'S HAPPENING TO ME.

I HAVE TO CONCENTRATE, FIGURE OUT HOW TO CONTROL IT BEFORE--

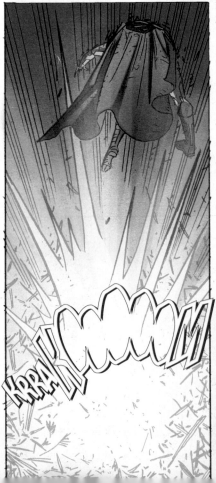

KRRAKAMMMM

GOVERNMENT BOMBERS.

HOW CAN I BLAME THEM?

IF YOU SEE SOMETHING THE THINGS I'M DOING.

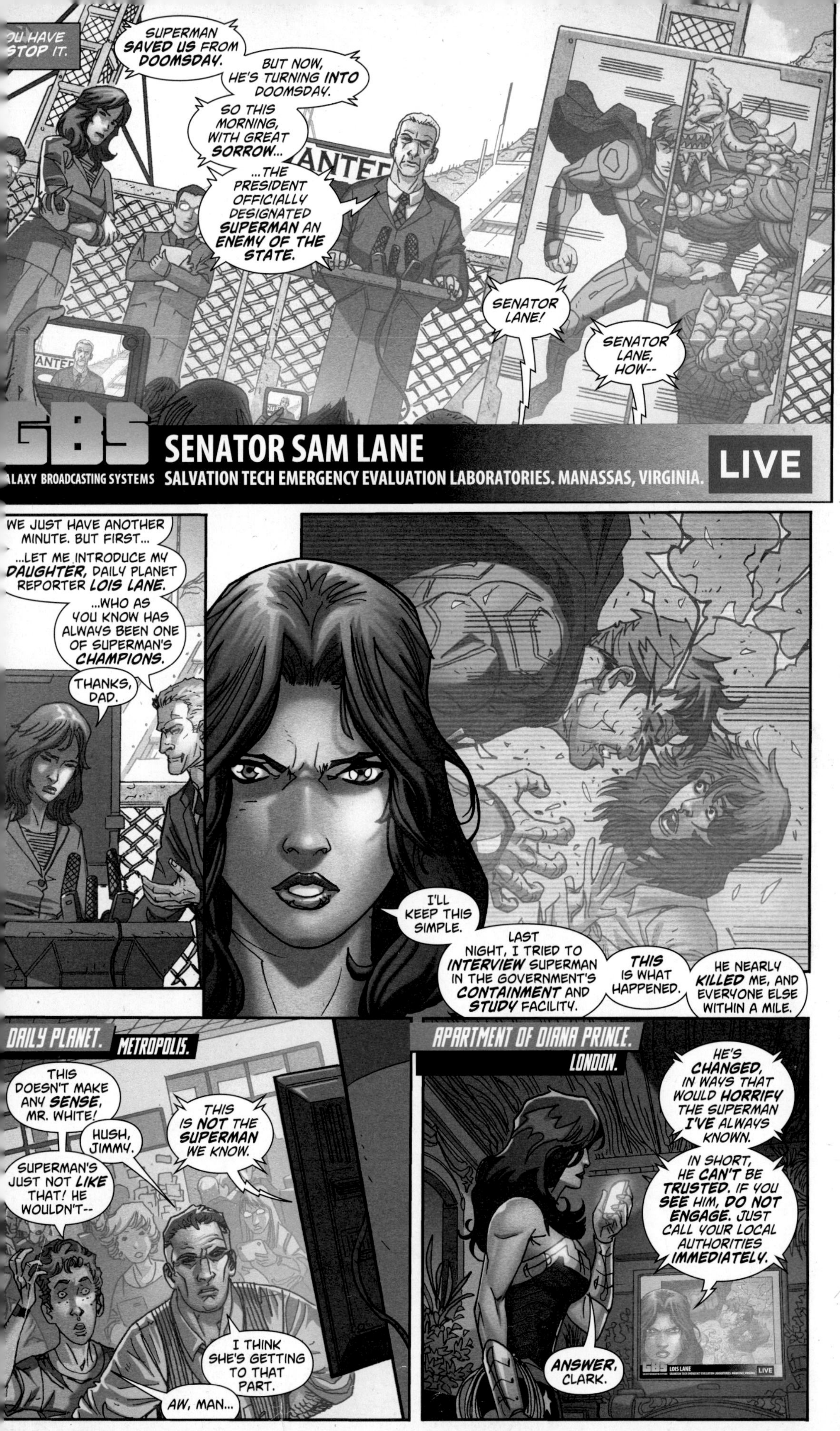

...OU HAVE STOP IT.
SUPERMAN SAVED US FROM DOOMSDAY.
BUT NOW, HE'S TURNING INTO DOOMSDAY.
SO THIS MORNING, WITH GREAT SORROW...
...THE PRESIDENT OFFICIALLY DESIGNATED SUPERMAN AN ENEMY OF THE STATE.
SENATOR LANE!
SENATOR LANE, HOW--
GBS
SENATOR SAM LANE
...ALAXY BROADCASTING SYSTEMS
SALVATION TECH EMERGENCY EVALUATION LABORATORIES. MANASSAS, VIRGINIA.
LIVE
WE JUST HAVE ANOTHER MINUTE. BUT FIRST...
...LET ME INTRODUCE MY DAUGHTER, DAILY PLANET REPORTER LOIS LANE.
...WHO AS YOU KNOW HAS ALWAYS BEEN ONE OF SUPERMAN'S CHAMPIONS.
THANKS, DAD.
I'LL KEEP THIS SIMPLE.
LAST NIGHT, I TRIED TO INTERVIEW SUPERMAN IN THE GOVERNMENT'S CONTAINMENT AND STUDY FACILITY.
THIS IS WHAT HAPPENED.
HE NEARLY KILLED ME, AND EVERYONE ELSE WITHIN A MILE.
DAILY PLANET. METROPOLIS.
THIS DOESN'T MAKE ANY SENSE, MR. WHITE!
HUSH, JIMMY.
THIS IS NOT THE SUPERMAN WE KNOW.
SUPERMAN'S JUST NOT LIKE THAT! HE WOULDN'T--
I THINK SHE'S GETTING TO THAT PART.
AW, MAN...
APARTMENT OF DIANA PRINCE. LONDON.
HE'S CHANGED, IN WAYS THAT WOULD HORRIFY THE SUPERMAN I'VE ALWAYS KNOWN.
IN SHORT, HE CAN'T BE TRUSTED. IF YOU SEE HIM, DO NOT ENGAGE. JUST CALL YOUR LOCAL AUTHORITIES IMMEDIATELY.
ANSWER, CLARK.

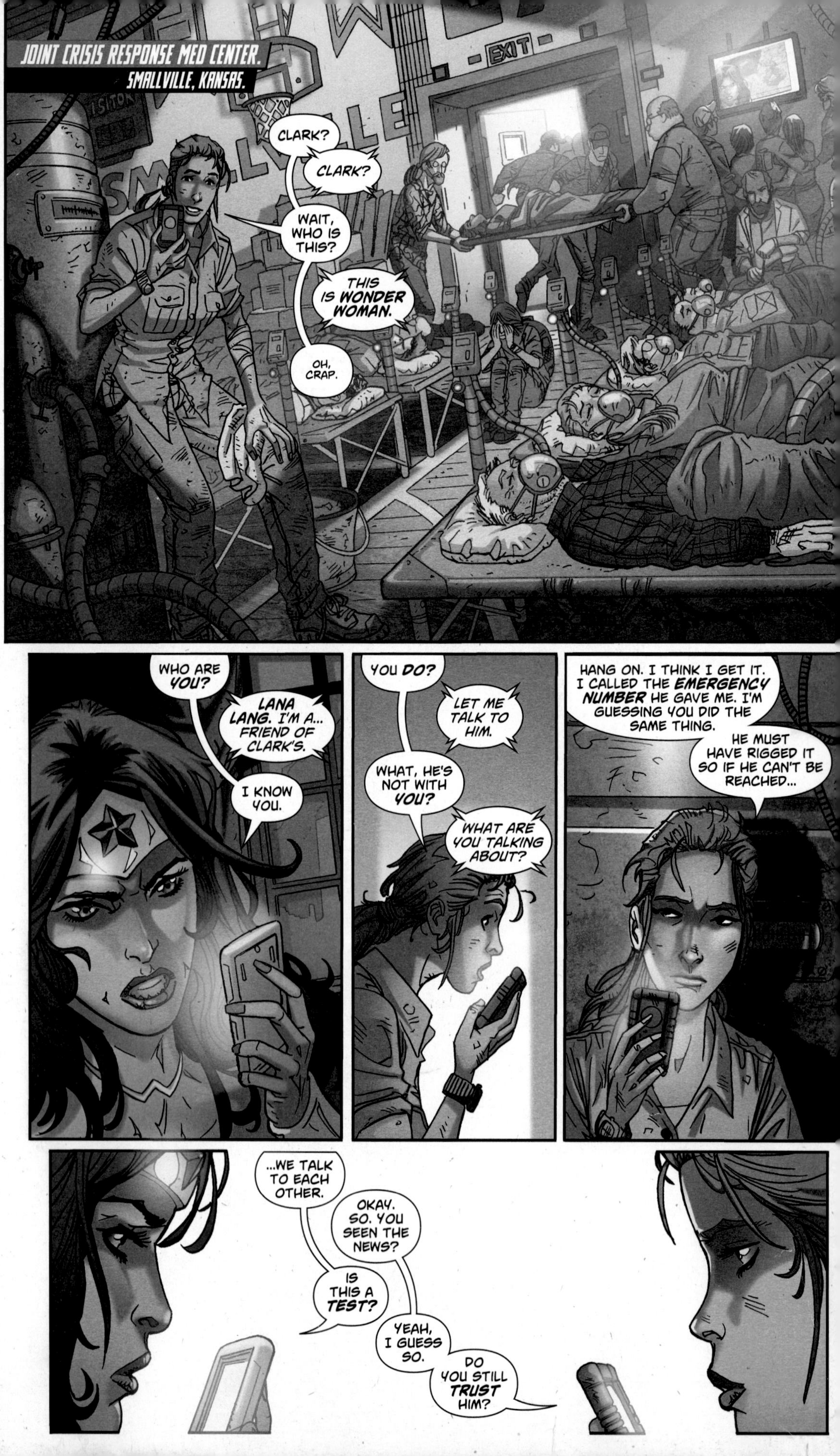
JOINT CRISIS RESPONSE MED CENTER.
SMALLVILLE, KANSAS.
EXIT
CLARK?
CLARK?
WAIT, WHO IS THIS?
THIS IS WONDER WOMAN.
OH, CRAP.
WHO ARE YOU?
LANA LANG. I'M A... FRIEND OF CLARK'S.
I KNOW YOU.
YOU DO?
LET ME TALK TO HIM.
WHAT, HE'S NOT WITH YOU?
WHAT ARE YOU TALKING ABOUT?
HANG ON. I THINK I GET IT. I CALLED THE EMERGENCY NUMBER HE GAVE ME. I'M GUESSING YOU DID THE SAME THING.
HE MUST HAVE RIGGED IT SO IF HE CAN'T BE REACHED...
...WE TALK TO EACH OTHER.
OKAY. SO. YOU SEEN THE NEWS?
IS THIS A TEST?
YEAH, I GUESS SO.
DO YOU STILL TRUST HIM?

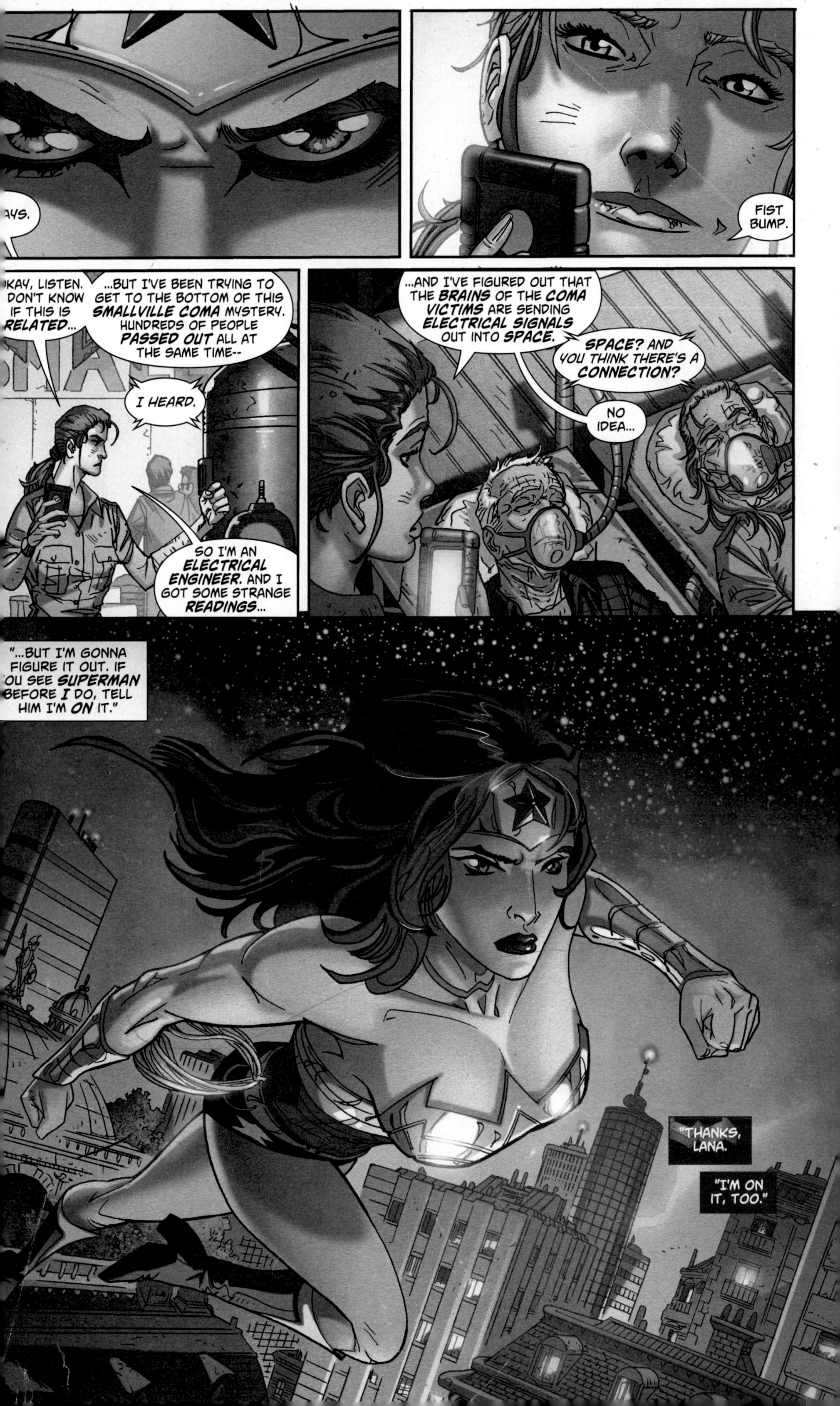

AYS.
FIST BUMP.
OKAY, LISTEN. I DON'T KNOW IF THIS IS RELATED...
...BUT I'VE BEEN TRYING TO GET TO THE BOTTOM OF THIS SMALLVILLE COMA MYSTERY. HUNDREDS OF PEOPLE PASSED OUT ALL AT THE SAME TIME--
I HEARD.
SO I'M AN ELECTRICAL ENGINEER. AND I GOT SOME STRANGE READINGS...
...AND I'VE FIGURED OUT THAT THE BRAINS OF THE COMA VICTIMS ARE SENDING ELECTRICAL SIGNALS OUT INTO SPACE.
SPACE? AND YOU THINK THERE'S A CONNECTION?
NO IDEA...
"...BUT I'M GONNA FIGURE IT OUT. IF OU SEE SUPERMAN BEFORE I DO, TELL HIM I'M ON IT."
"THANKS, LANA.
"I'M ON IT, TOO."

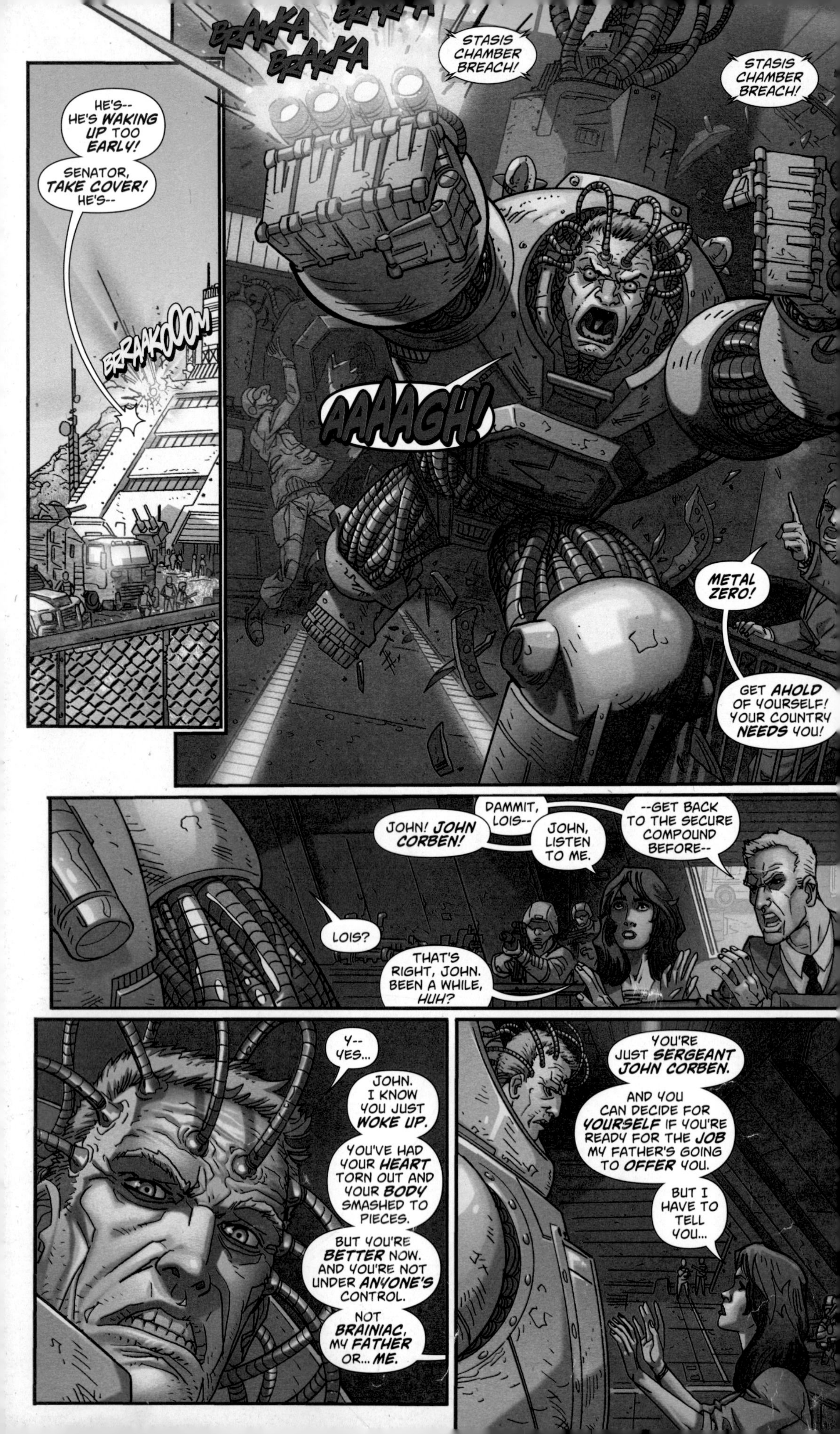

HE'S-- HE'S WAKING UP TOO EARLY!
SENATOR, TAKE COVER! HE'S--
BRRAAKOOOM
BRAKKA
BRAKKA
STASIS CHAMBER BREACH!
STASIS CHAMBER BREACH!
AAAAGH!
METAL ZERO!
GET AHOLD OF YOURSELF! YOUR COUNTRY NEEDS YOU!
JOHN! JOHN CORBEN!
DAMMIT, LOIS--
JOHN, LISTEN TO ME.
--GET BACK TO THE SECURE COMPOUND BEFORE--
LOIS?
THAT'S RIGHT, JOHN. BEEN A WHILE, HUH?
Y-- YES...
JOHN. I KNOW YOU JUST WOKE UP.
YOU'VE HAD YOUR HEART TORN OUT AND YOUR BODY SMASHED TO PIECES.
BUT YOU'RE BETTER NOW. AND YOU'RE NOT UNDER ANYONE'S CONTROL.
NOT BRAINIAC, MY FATHER OR... ME.
YOU'RE JUST SERGEANT JOHN CORBEN.
AND YOU CAN DECIDE FOR YOURSELF IF YOU'RE READY FOR THE JOB MY FATHER'S GOING TO OFFER YOU.
BUT I HAVE TO TELL YOU...

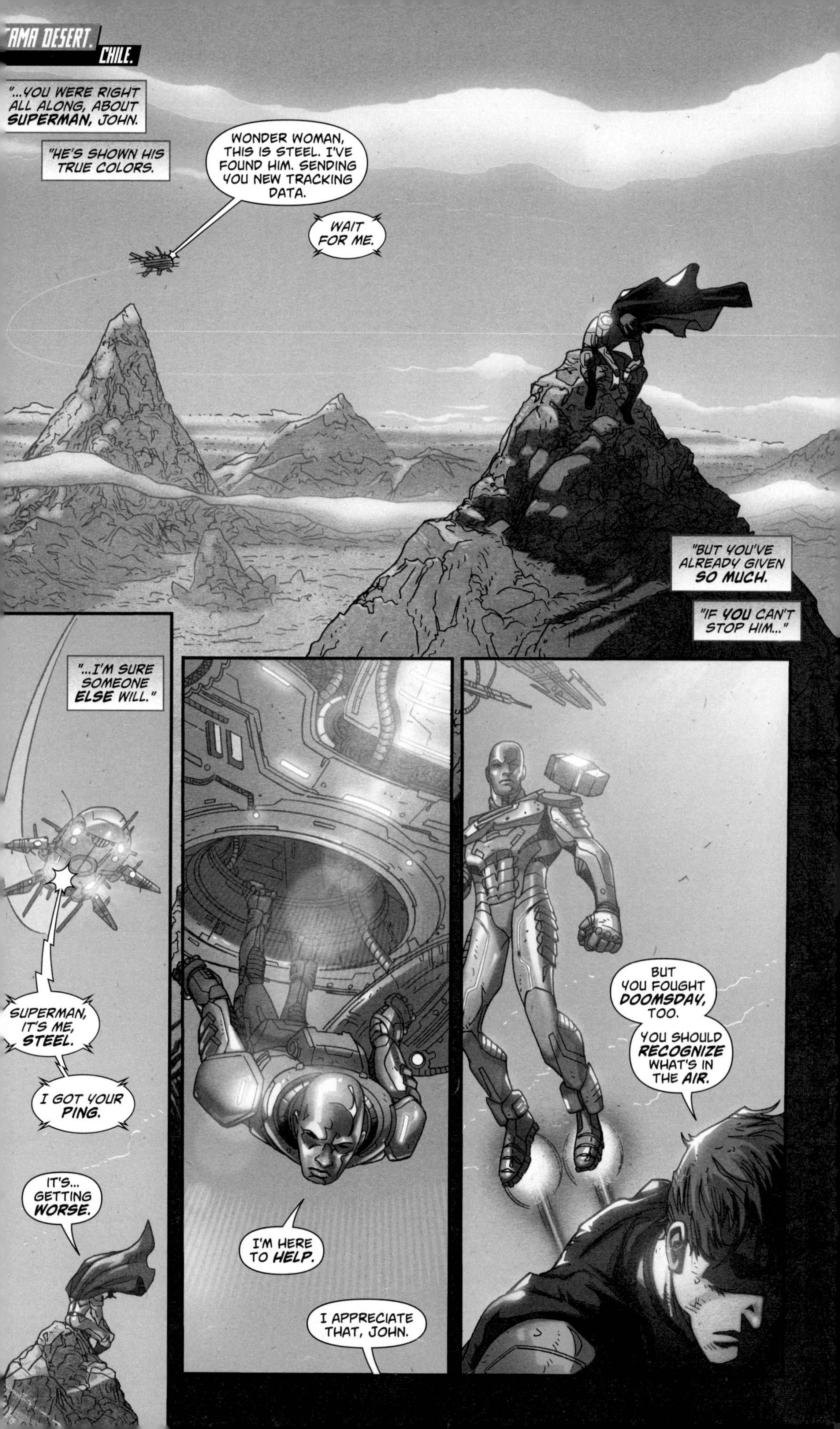

...AMA DESERT. CHILE.
"...YOU WERE RIGHT ALL ALONG, ABOUT SUPERMAN, JOHN.
"HE'S SHOWN HIS TRUE COLORS.
WONDER WOMAN, THIS IS STEEL. I'VE FOUND HIM. SENDING YOU NEW TRACKING DATA.
WAIT FOR ME.
"BUT YOU'VE ALREADY GIVEN SO MUCH.
"IF YOU CAN'T STOP HIM...
"...I'M SURE SOMEONE ELSE WILL."
SUPERMAN, IT'S ME, STEEL.
I GOT YOUR PING.
IT'S... GETTING WORSE.
I'M HERE TO HELP.
I APPRECIATE THAT, JOHN.
BUT YOU FOUGHT DOOMSDAY, TOO.
YOU SHOULD RECOGNIZE WHAT'S IN THE AIR.

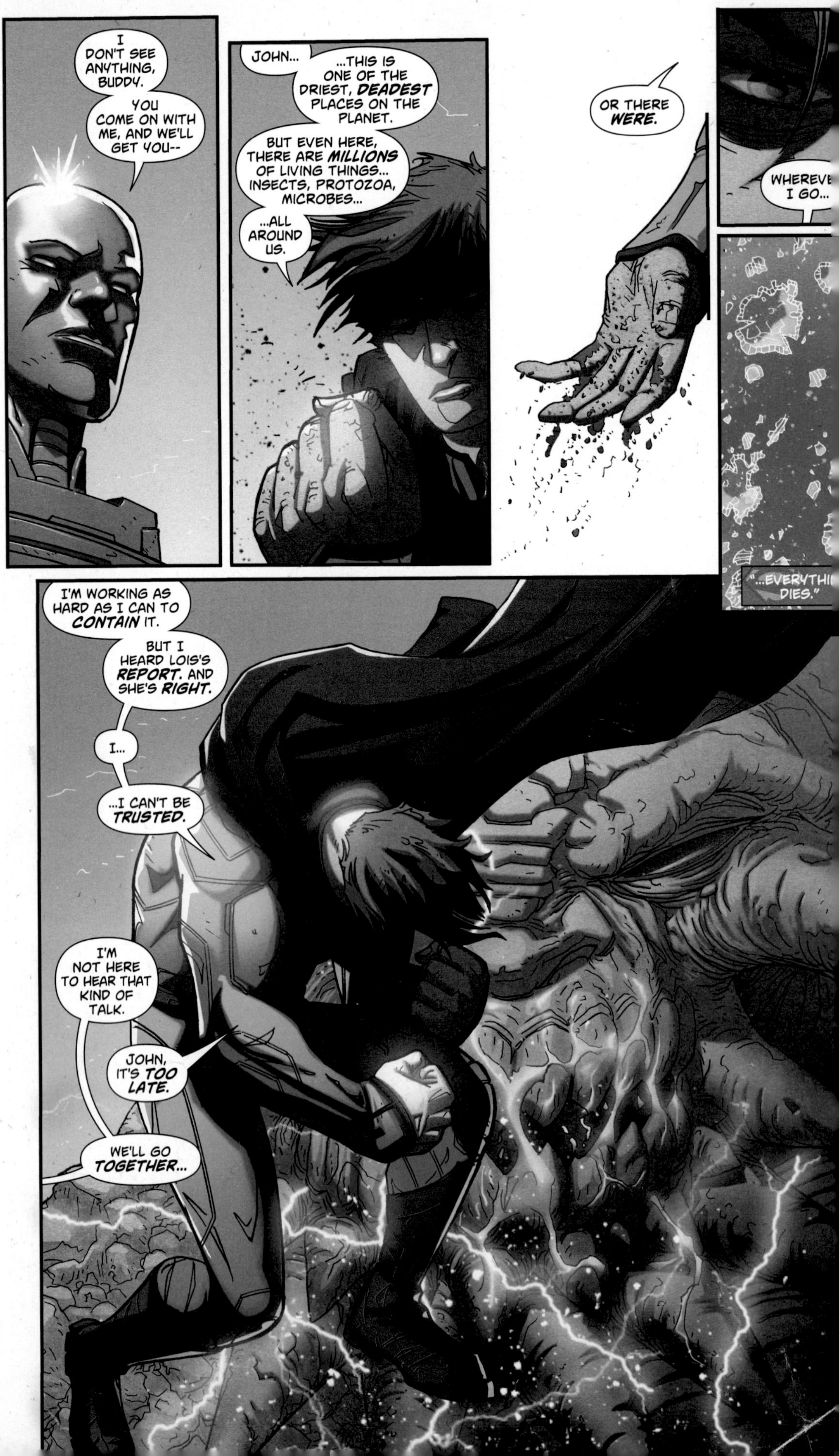
I DON'T SEE ANYTHING, BUDDY.
YOU COME ON WITH ME, AND WE'LL GET YOU--
JOHN...
...THIS IS ONE OF THE DRIEST, DEADEST PLACES ON THE PLANET.
BUT EVEN HERE, THERE ARE MILLIONS OF LIVING THINGS... INSECTS, PROTOZOA, MICROBES...
...ALL AROUND US.
OR THERE WERE.
WHEREVE I GO...
"...EVERYTHI DIES."
I'M WORKING AS HARD AS I CAN TO CONTAIN IT.
BUT I HEARD LOIS'S REPORT. AND SHE'S RIGHT.
I...
...I CAN'T BE TRUSTED.
I'M NOT HERE TO HEAR THAT KIND OF TALK.
JOHN, IT'S TOO LATE.
WE'LL GO TOGETHER...

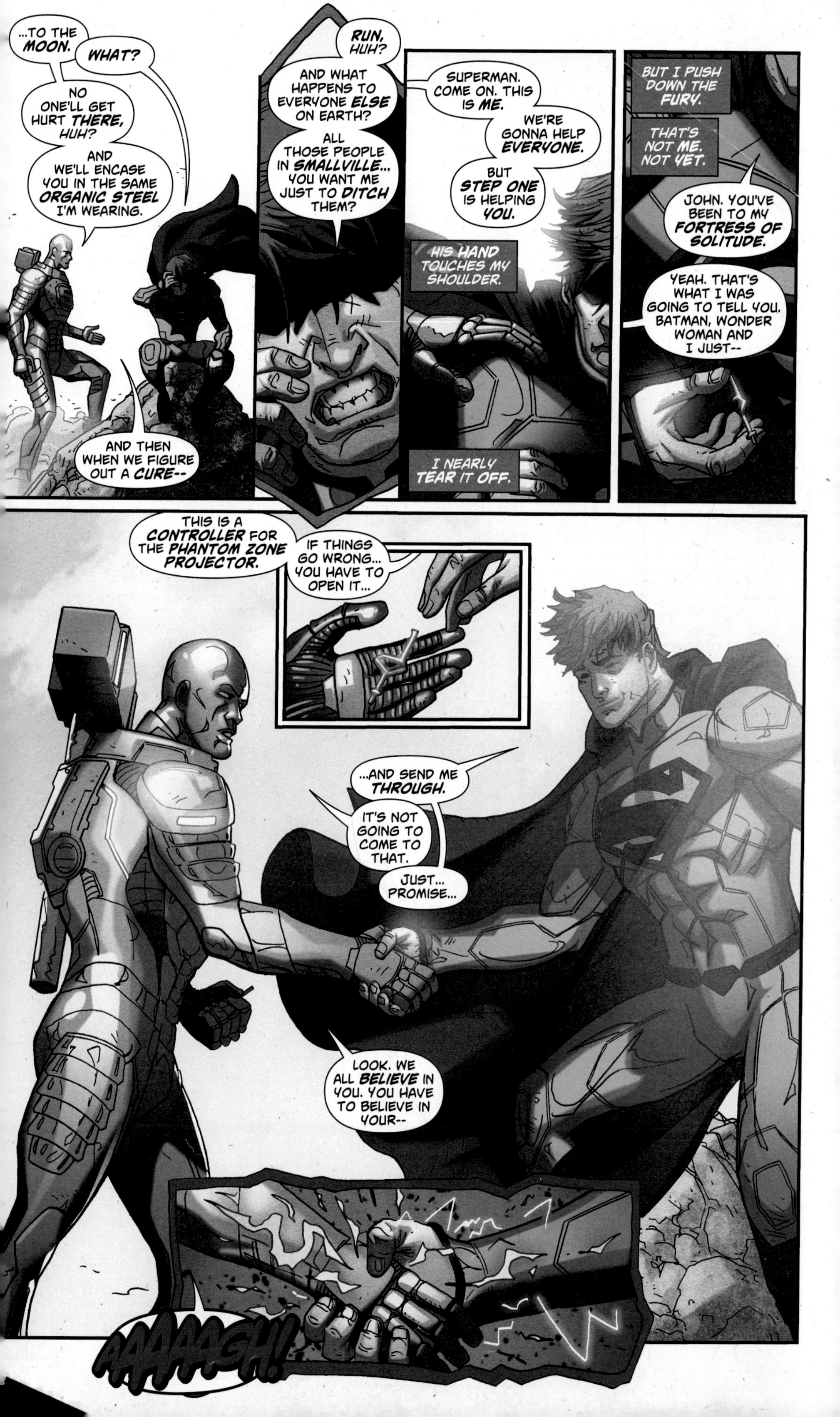
...TO THE MOON.
WHAT?
NO ONE'LL GET HURT THERE, HUH?
AND WE'LL ENCASE YOU IN THE SAME ORGANIC STEEL I'M WEARING.
AND THEN WHEN WE FIGURE OUT A CURE--
RUN, HUH?
AND WHAT HAPPENS TO EVERYONE ELSE ON EARTH?
ALL THOSE PEOPLE IN SMALLVILLE... YOU WANT ME JUST TO DITCH THEM?
SUPERMAN. COME ON. THIS IS ME.
WE'RE GONNA HELP EVERYONE.
BUT STEP ONE IS HELPING YOU.
HIS HAND TOUCHES MY SHOULDER.
I NEARLY TEAR IT OFF.
BUT I PUSH DOWN THE FURY.
THAT'S NOT ME. NOT YET.
JOHN. YOU'VE BEEN TO MY FORTRESS OF SOLITUDE.
YEAH. THAT'S WHAT I WAS GOING TO TELL YOU. BATMAN, WONDER WOMAN AND I JUST--
THIS IS A CONTROLLER FOR THE PHANTOM ZONE PROJECTOR.
IF THINGS GO WRONG... YOU HAVE TO OPEN IT...
...AND SEND ME THROUGH.
IT'S NOT GOING TO COME TO THAT.
JUST... PROMISE...
LOOK. WE ALL BELIEVE IN YOU. YOU HAVE TO BELIEVE IN YOUR--
AAAAAGH!

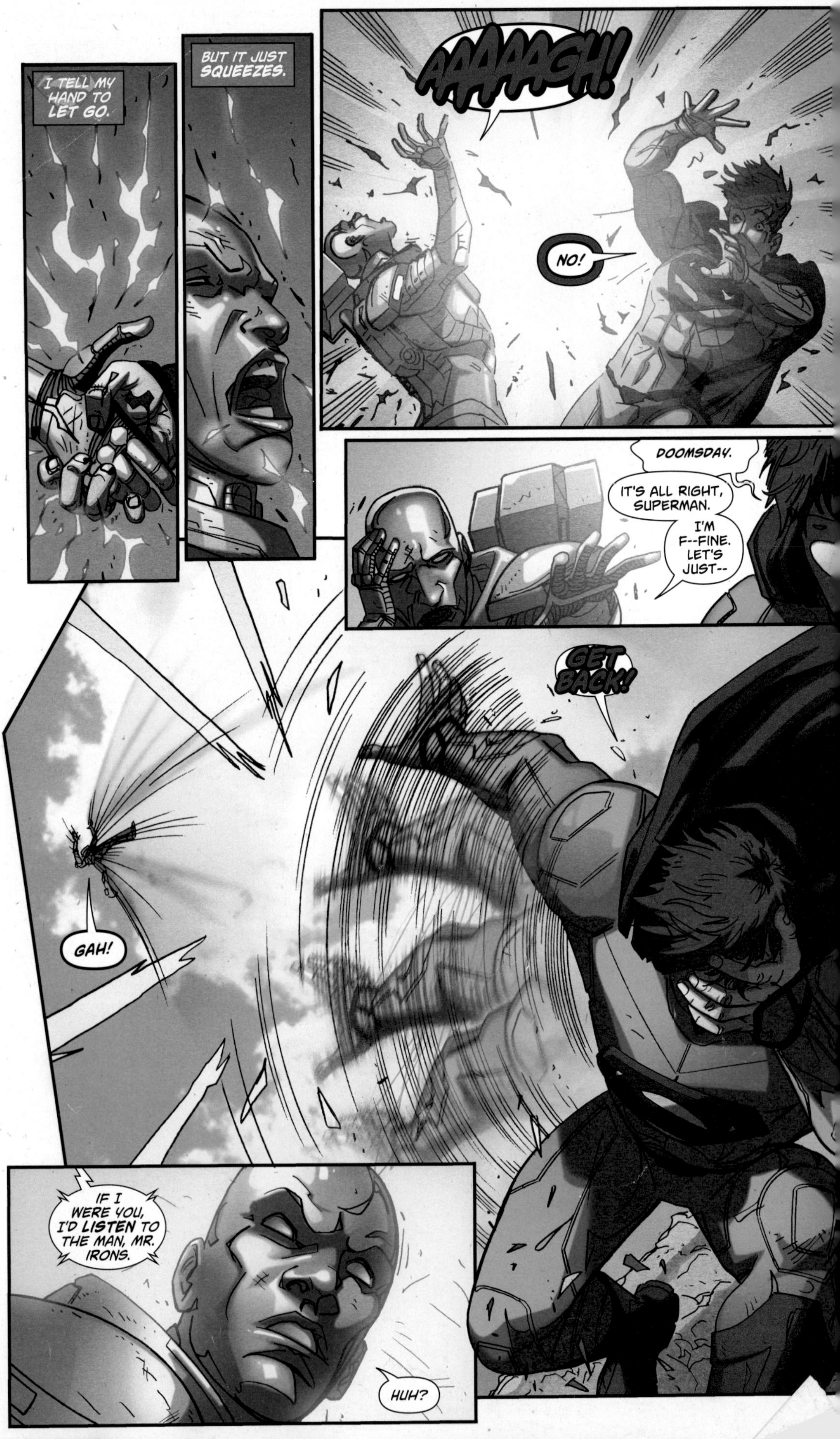
I TELL MY HAND TO LET GO.
BUT IT JUST SQUEEZES.
AAAAAGH!
NO!
DOOMSDAY.
IT'S ALL RIGHT, SUPERMAN.
I'M F--FINE. LET'S JUST--
GET BACK!
GAH!
IF I WERE YOU, I'D LISTEN TO THE MAN, MR. IRONS.
HUH?

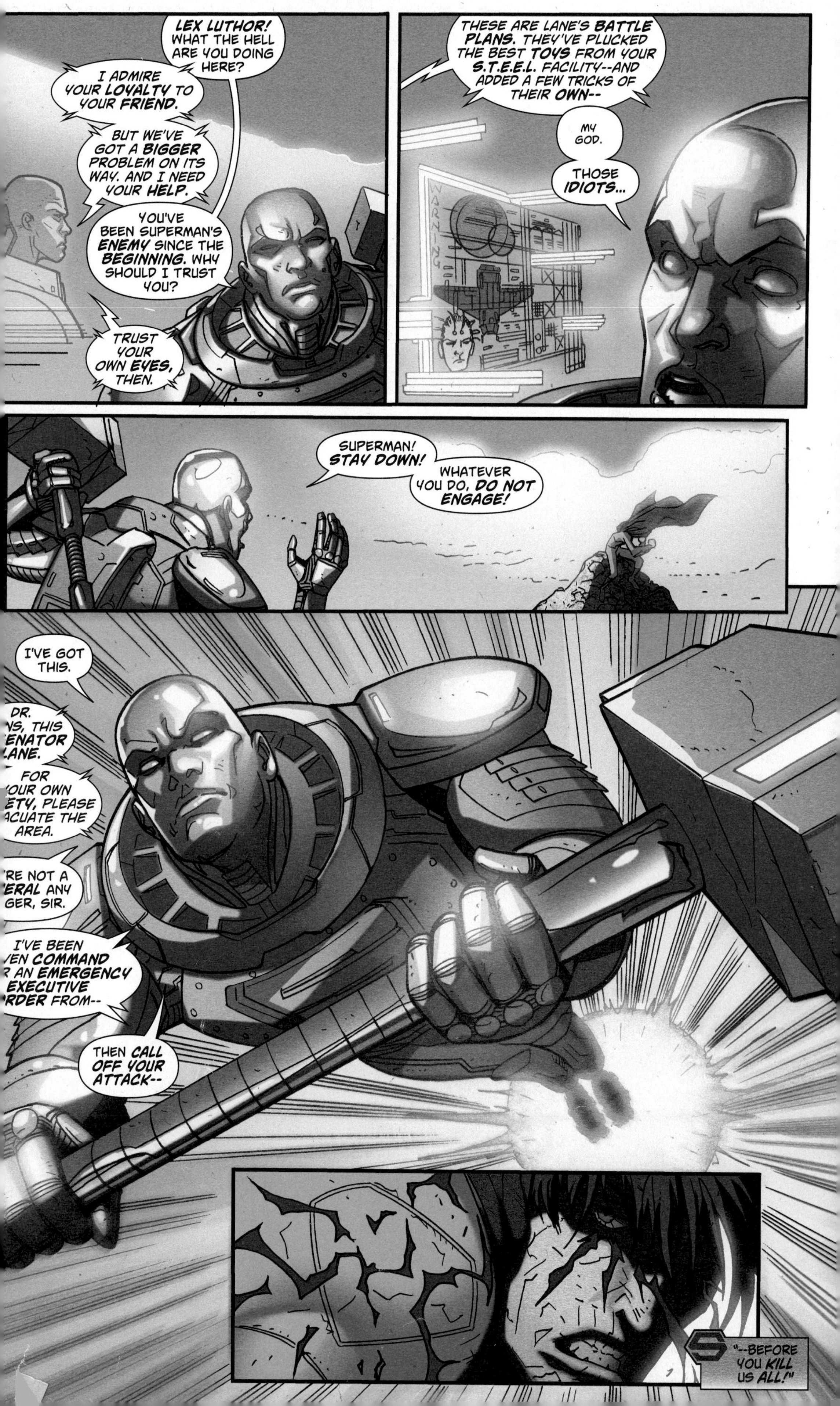
LEX LUTHOR! WHAT THE HELL ARE YOU DOING HERE?
I ADMIRE YOUR LOYALTY TO YOUR FRIEND.
BUT WE'VE GOT A BIGGER PROBLEM ON ITS WAY. AND I NEED YOUR HELP.
YOU'VE BEEN SUPERMAN'S ENEMY SINCE THE BEGINNING. WHY SHOULD I TRUST YOU?
TRUST YOUR OWN EYES, THEN.
THESE ARE LANE'S BATTLE PLANS. THEY'VE PLUCKED THE BEST TOYS FROM YOUR S.T.E.E.L. FACILITY--AND ADDED A FEW TRICKS OF THEIR OWN--
MY GOD.
THOSE IDIOTS...
WARNING
SUPERMAN! STAY DOWN!
WHATEVER YOU DO, DO NOT ENGAGE!
I'VE GOT THIS.
THEN CALL OFF YOUR ATTACK--
"--BEFORE YOU KILL US ALL!"

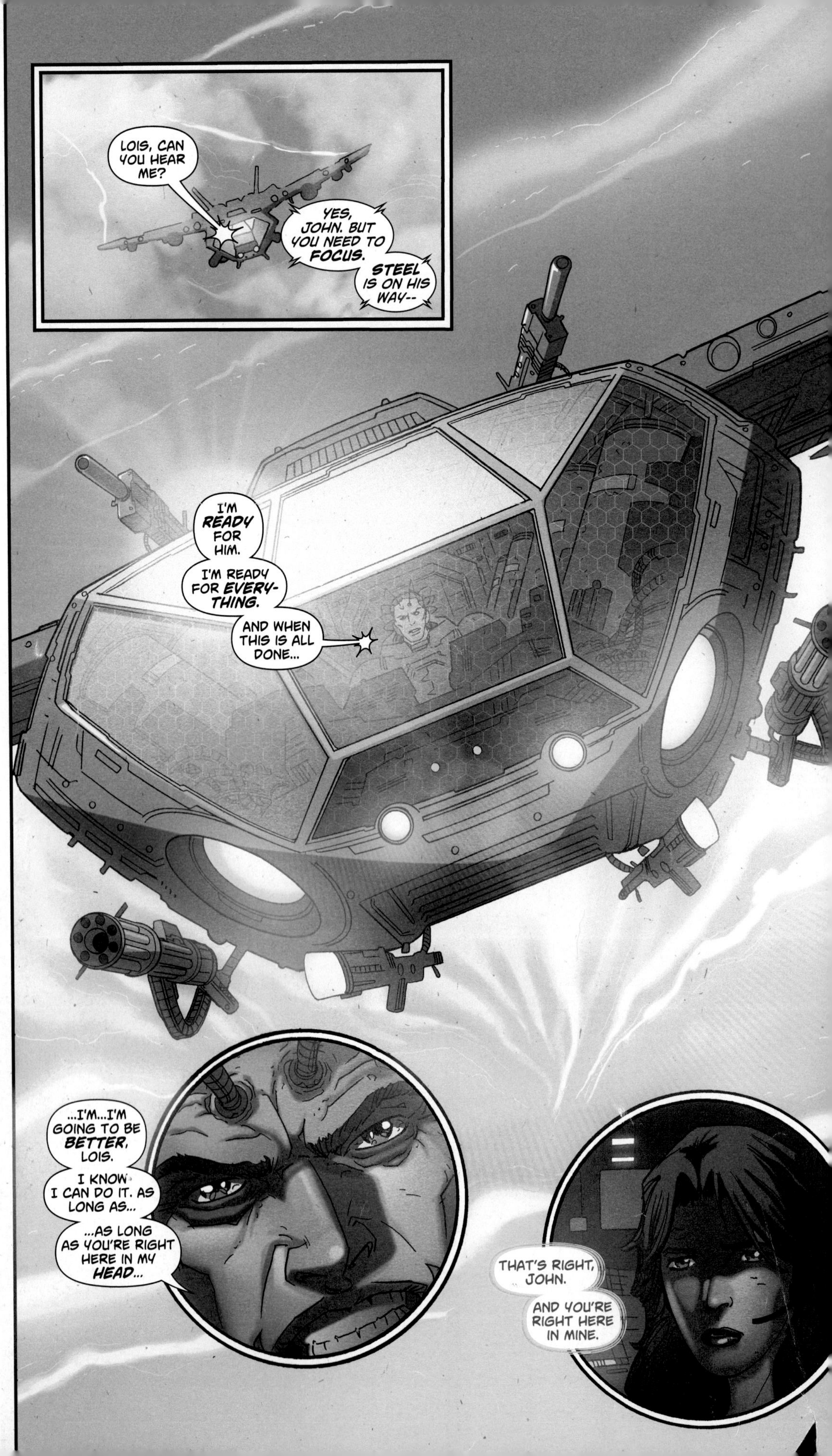
LOIS, CAN YOU HEAR ME?
YES, JOHN. BUT YOU NEED TO FOCUS.
STEEL IS ON HIS WAY--
I'M READY FOR HIM.
I'M READY FOR EVERY-THING.
AND WHEN THIS IS ALL DONE...
...I'M...I'M GOING TO BE BETTER, LOIS.
I KNOW I CAN DO IT. AS LONG AS...
...AS LONG AS YOU'RE RIGHT HERE IN MY HEAD...
THAT'S RIGHT, JOHN.
AND YOU'RE RIGHT HERE IN MINE.

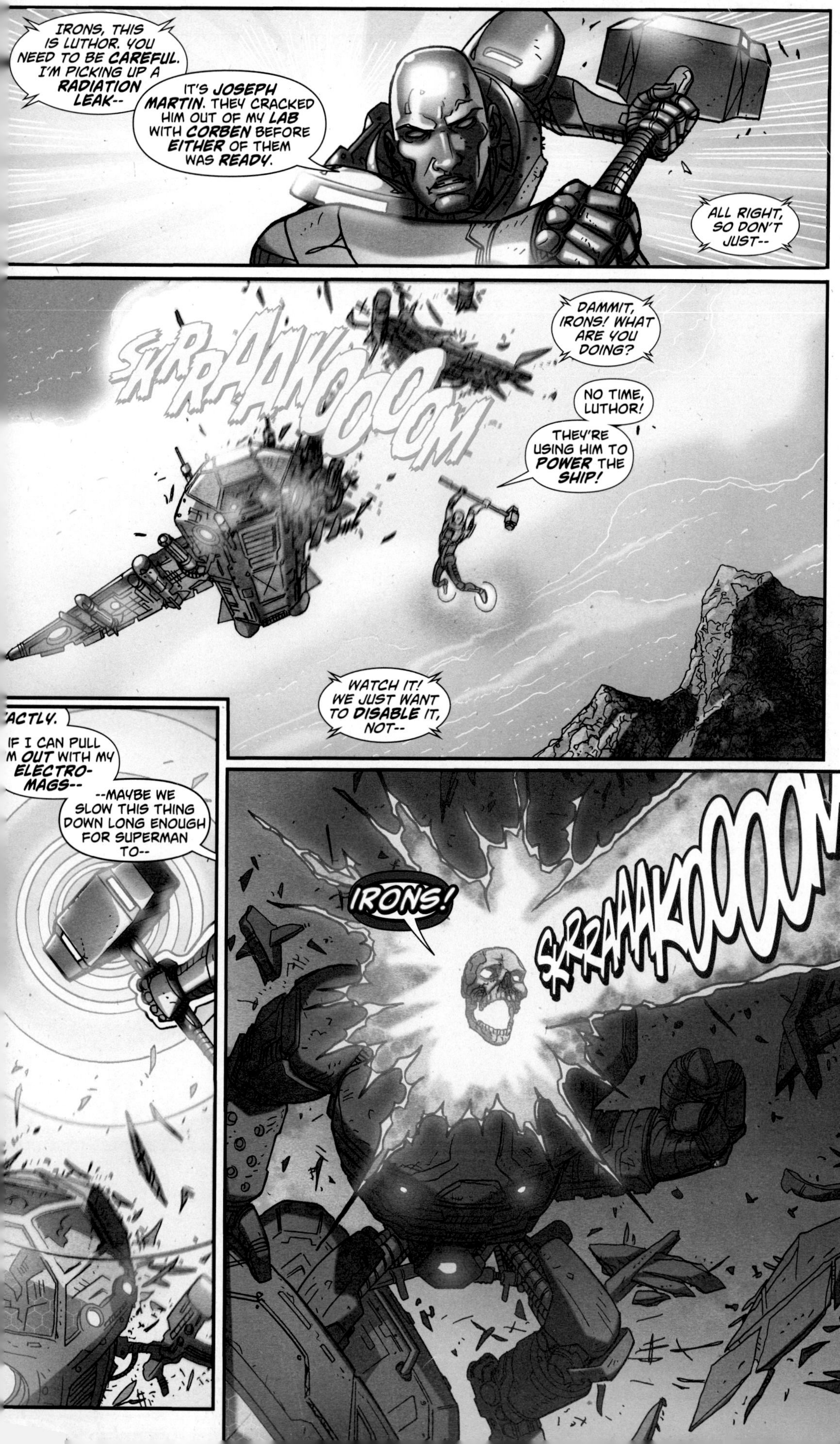
IRONS, THIS IS LUTHOR. YOU NEED TO BE CAREFUL. I'M PICKING UP A RADIATION LEAK--
IT'S JOSEPH MARTIN. THEY CRACKED HIM OUT OF MY LAB WITH CORBEN BEFORE EITHER OF THEM WAS READY.
ALL RIGHT, SO DON'T JUST--
SKRRAAKOOOOM
DAMMIT, IRONS! WHAT ARE YOU DOING?
NO TIME, LUTHOR!
THEY'RE USING HIM TO POWER THE SHIP!
WATCH IT! WE JUST WANT TO DISABLE IT, NOT--
ACTLY.
IF I CAN PULL M OUT WITH MY ELECTRO-MAGS--
--MAYBE WE SLOW THIS THING DOWN LONG ENOUGH FOR SUPERMAN TO--
IRONS!
SKRRAAKOOOOM

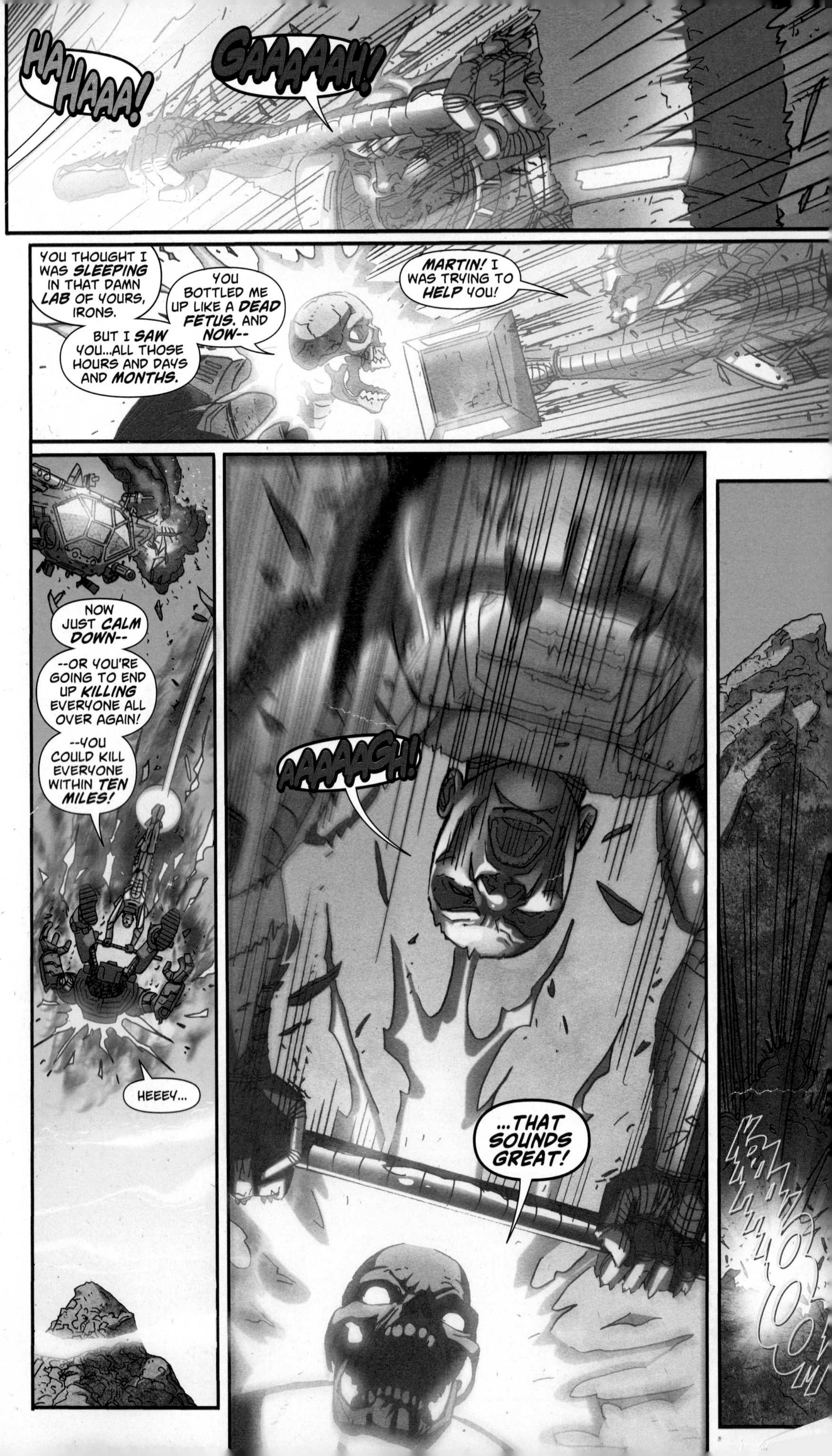
HAHAAA!
GAAAAAH!
YOU THOUGHT I WAS SLEEPING IN THAT DAMN LAB OF YOURS, IRONS.
BUT I SAW YOU...ALL THOSE HOURS AND DAYS AND MONTHS.
YOU BOTTLED ME UP LIKE A DEAD FETUS. AND NOW--
MARTIN! I WAS TRYING TO HELP YOU!
NOW JUST CALM DOWN--
--OR YOU'RE GOING TO END UP KILLING EVERYONE ALL OVER AGAIN!
--YOU COULD KILL EVERYONE WITHIN TEN MILES!
HEEEY...
AAAAAGH!
...THAT SOUNDS GREAT!

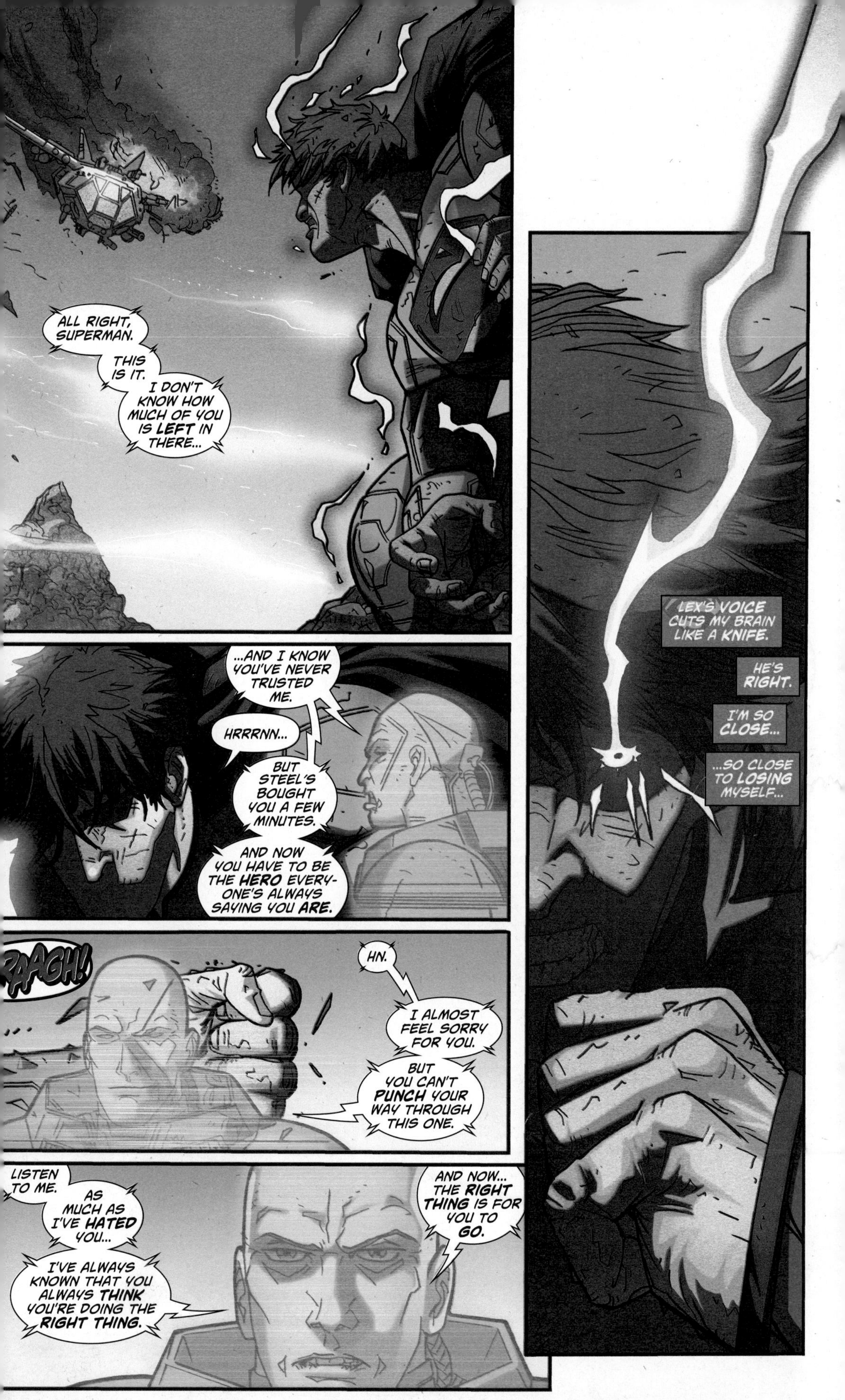
ALL RIGHT, SUPERMAN.
THIS IS IT.
I DON'T KNOW HOW MUCH OF YOU IS **LEFT** IN THERE...
...AND I KNOW YOU'VE NEVER TRUSTED ME.
HRRRNN...
BUT STEEL'S BOUGHT YOU A FEW MINUTES.
AND NOW YOU HAVE TO BE THE **HERO** EVERYONE'S ALWAYS SAYING YOU **ARE**.
RAAGH!
HN.
I ALMOST FEEL SORRY FOR YOU.
BUT YOU CAN'T **PUNCH** YOUR WAY THROUGH THIS ONE.
LISTEN TO ME.
AS MUCH AS I'VE **HATED** YOU...
I'VE ALWAYS KNOWN THAT YOU ALWAYS **THINK** YOU'RE DOING THE **RIGHT THING.**
AND NOW... THE **RIGHT THING** IS FOR YOU TO **GO.**
LEX'S **VOICE** CUTS MY BRAIN LIKE A **KNIFE.**
HE'S **RIGHT.**
I'M SO **CLOSE...**
...SO CLOSE TO **LOSING** MYSELF...

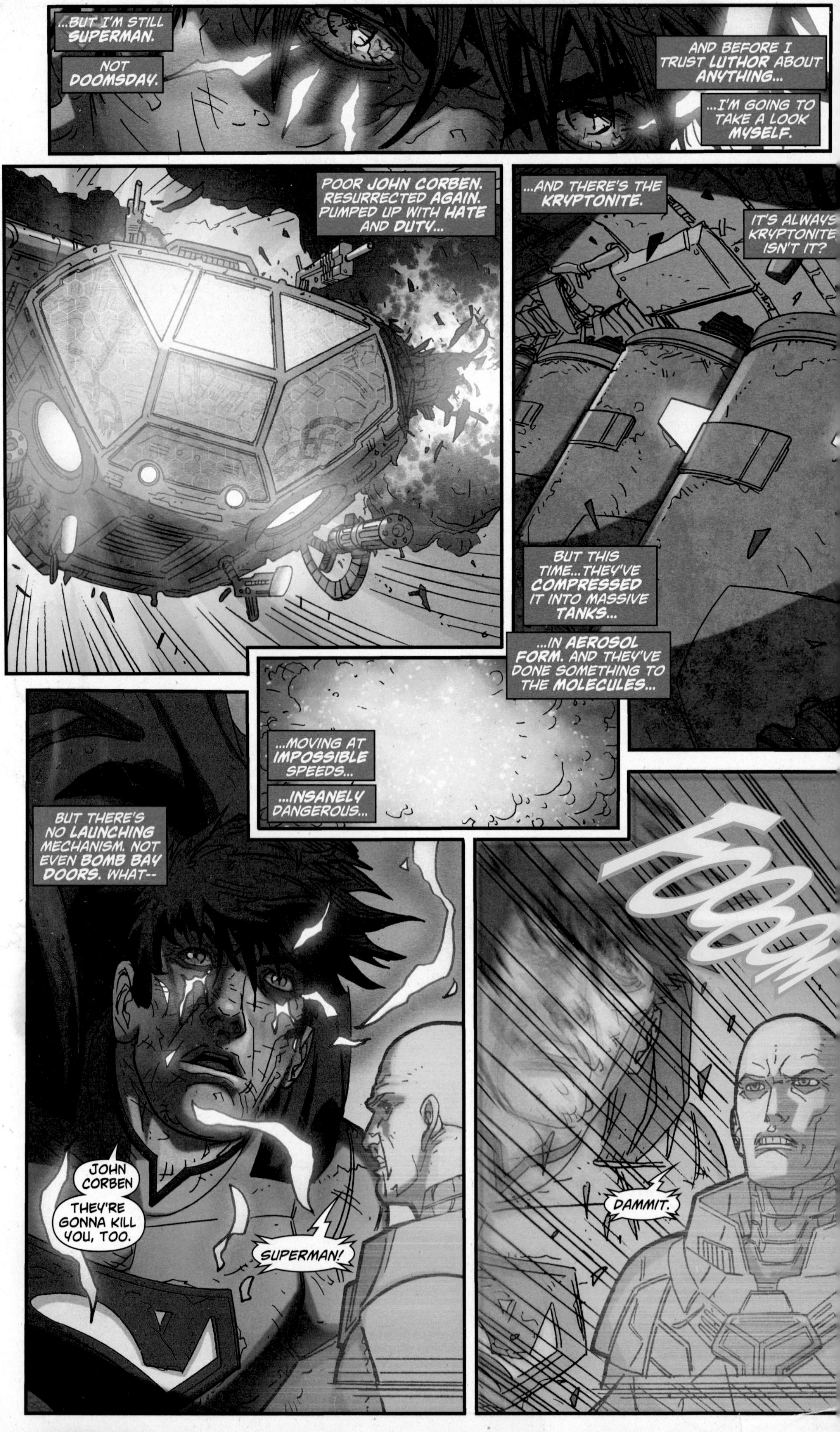
...BUT I'M STILL SUPERMAN.
NOT DOOMSDAY.
AND BEFORE I TRUST LUTHOR ABOUT ANYTHING...
...I'M GOING TO TAKE A LOOK MYSELF.
POOR JOHN CORBEN. RESURRECTED AGAIN. PUMPED UP WITH HATE AND DUTY...
...AND THERE'S THE KRYPTONITE.
IT'S ALWAYS KRYPTONITE ISN'T IT?
BUT THIS TIME...THEY'VE COMPRESSED IT INTO MASSIVE TANKS...
...IN AEROSOL FORM. AND THEY'VE DONE SOMETHING TO THE MOLECULES...
...MOVING AT IMPOSSIBLE SPEEDS...
...INSANELY DANGEROUS...
BUT THERE'S NO LAUNCHING MECHANISM. NOT EVEN BOMB BAY DOORS. WHAT--
JOHN CORBEN
THEY'RE GONNA KILL YOU, TOO.
SUPERMAN!
FOOOM
DAMMIT.

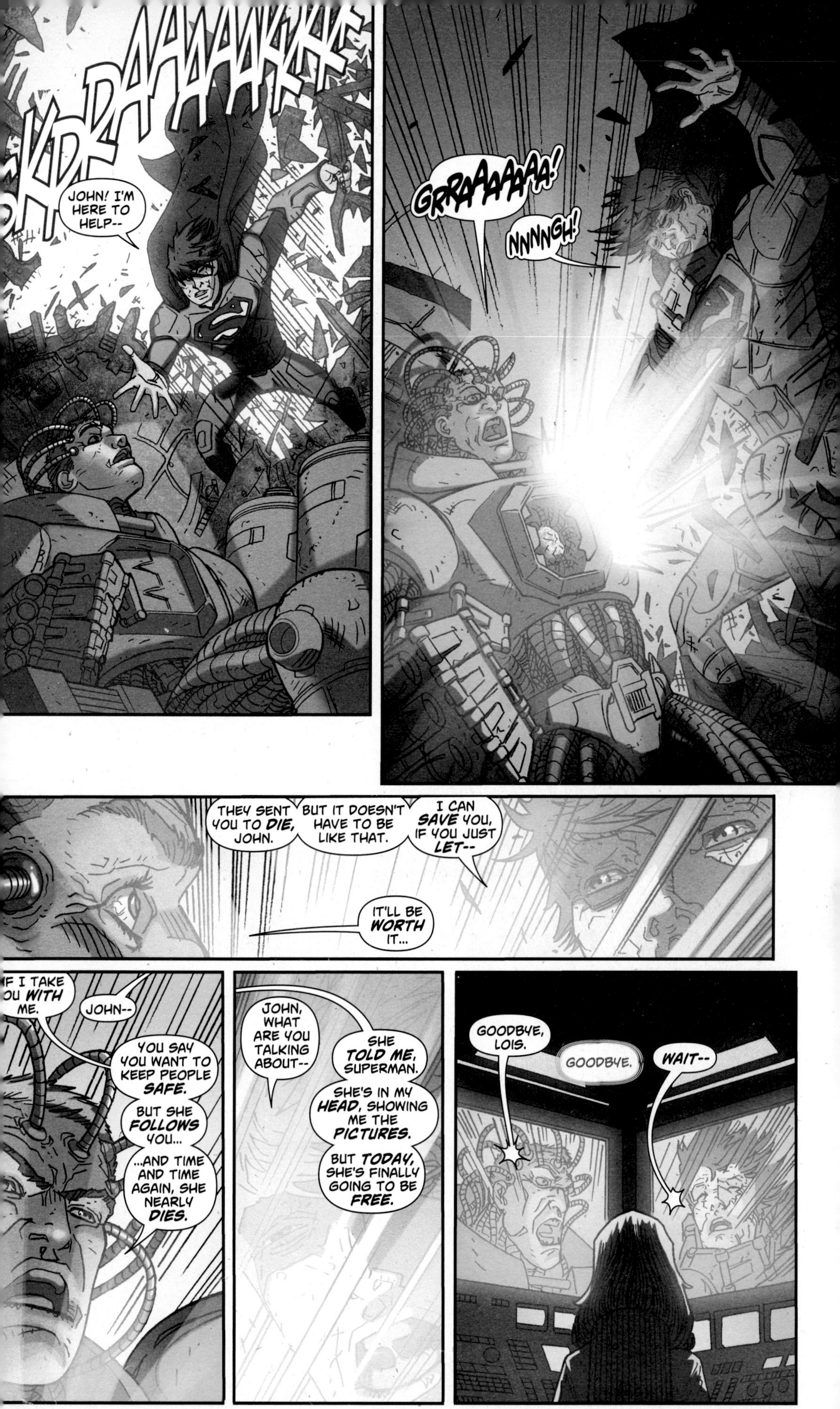
KDRAAAAKKK
JOHN! I'M HERE TO HELP--
GRRAAAAAAA!
NNNNGH!
THEY SENT YOU TO DIE, JOHN.
BUT IT DOESN'T HAVE TO BE LIKE THAT.
I CAN SAVE YOU, IF YOU JUST LET--
IT'LL BE WORTH IT...
IF I TAKE YOU WITH ME.
JOHN--
YOU SAY YOU WANT TO KEEP PEOPLE SAFE.
BUT SHE FOLLOWS YOU...
...AND TIME AND TIME AGAIN, SHE NEARLY DIES.
JOHN, WHAT ARE YOU TALKING ABOUT--
SHE TOLD ME, SUPERMAN.
SHE'S IN MY HEAD, SHOWING ME THE PICTURES.
BUT TODAY, SHE'S FINALLY GOING TO BE FREE.
GOODBYE, LOIS.
GOODBYE.
WAIT--

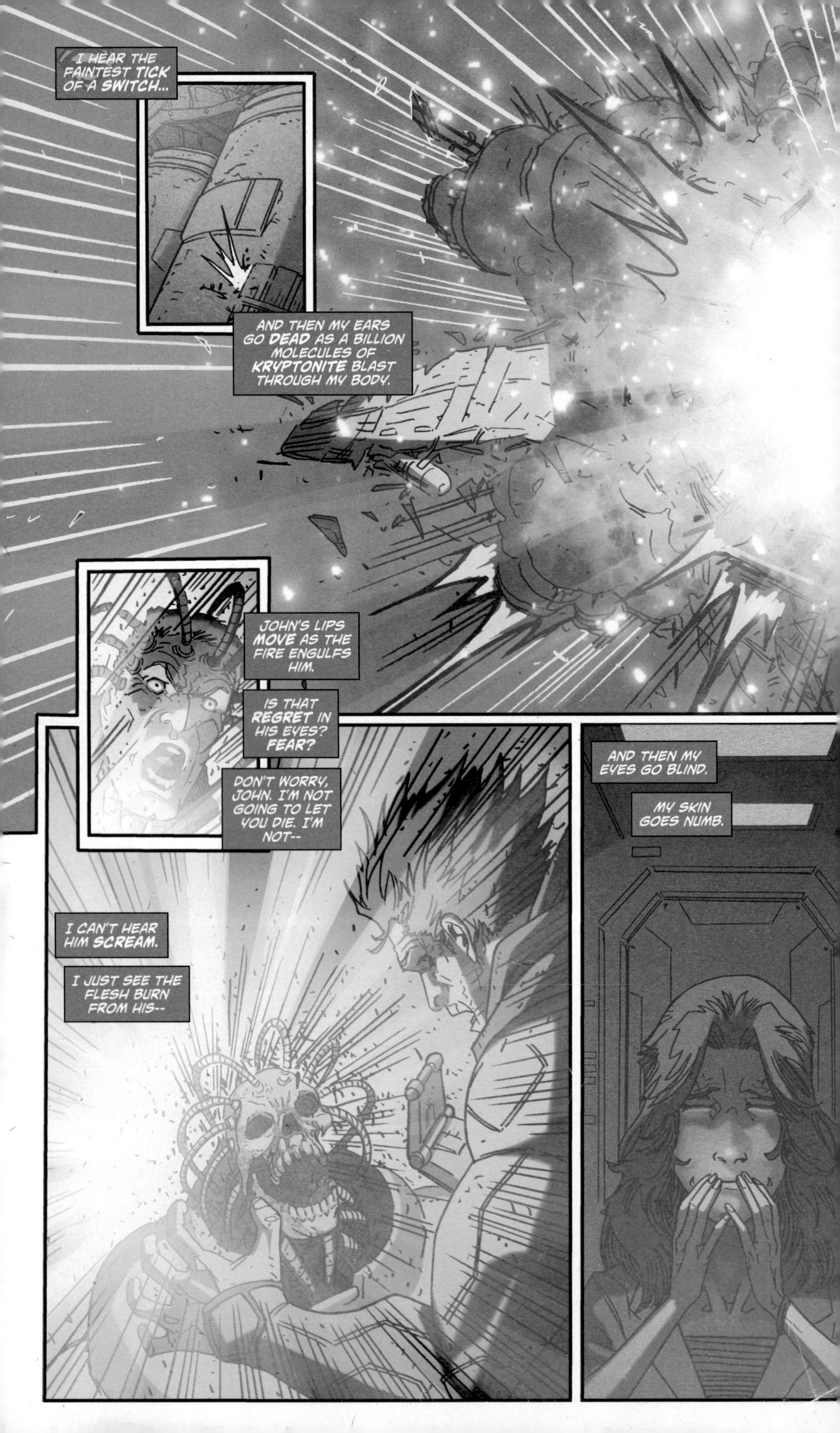

I HEAR THE FAINTEST TICK OF A SWITCH...
AND THEN MY EARS GO DEAD AS A BILLION MOLECULES OF KRYPTONITE BLAST THROUGH MY BODY.
JOHN'S LIPS MOVE AS THE FIRE ENGULFS HIM.
IS THAT REGRET IN HIS EYES? FEAR?
DON'T WORRY, JOHN. I'M NOT GOING TO LET YOU DIE. I'M NOT--
I CAN'T HEAR HIM SCREAM.
I JUST SEE THE FLESH BURN FROM HIS--
AND THEN MY EYES GO BLIND.
MY SKIN GOES NUMB.

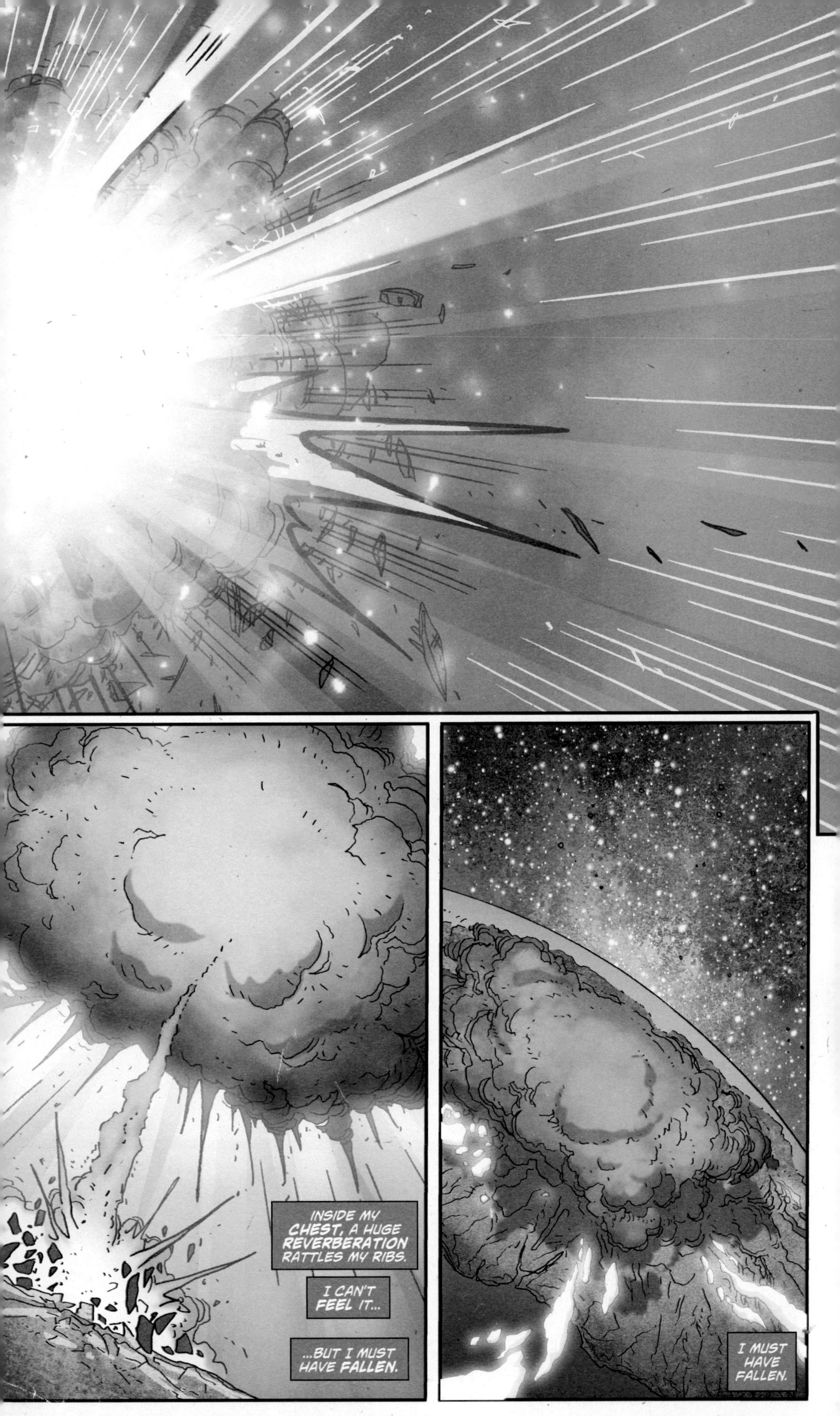
INSIDE MY CHEST, A HUGE REVERBERATION RATTLES MY RIBS.
I CAN'T FEEL IT...
...BUT I MUST HAVE FALLEN.
I MUST HAVE FALLEN.

THE ARCTIC.

GRRAAAOOO!

SMALLVILLE.

CLARK...

HYDE PARK.

GODS...

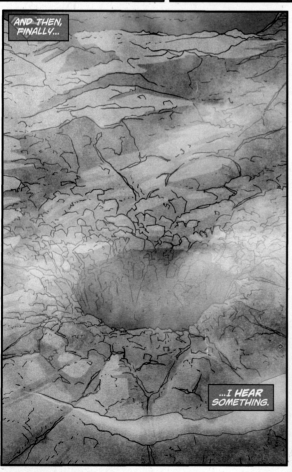

AND THEN, FINALLY...

...I HEAR SOMETHING.

AND I KNOW IT'S OVER.

GET UP.

NO. THIS ISN'T THE END.

THIS IS JUST THE BEGINNING.

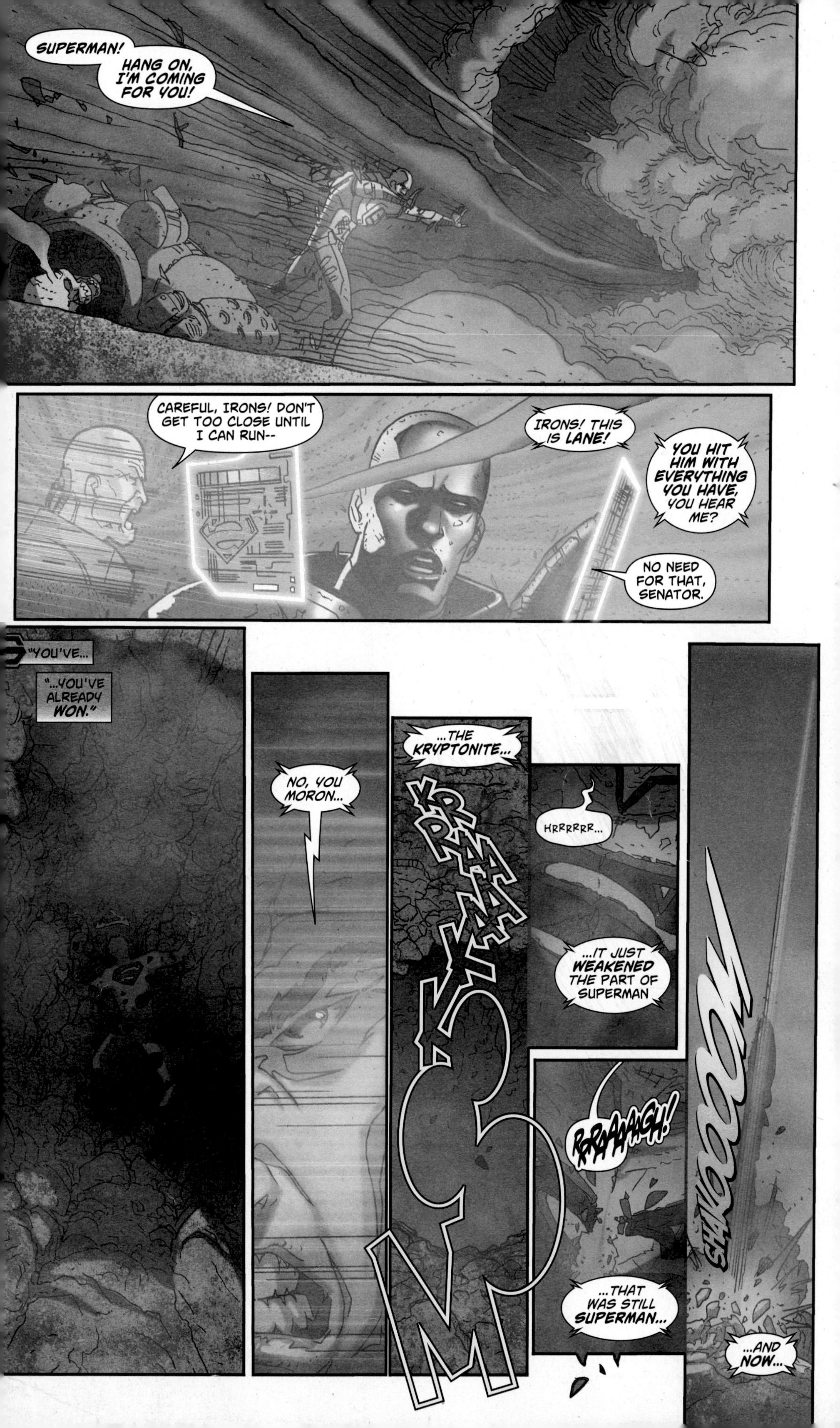
SUPERMAN!
HANG ON, I'M COMING FOR YOU!
CAREFUL, IRONS! DON'T GET TOO CLOSE UNTIL I CAN RUN--
IRONS! THIS IS LANE!
YOU HIT HIM WITH EVERYTHING YOU HAVE, YOU HEAR ME?
NO NEED FOR THAT, SENATOR.
"YOU'VE...
"...YOU'VE ALREADY WON."
NO, YOU MORON...
...THE KRYPTONITE...
KRRAAAAKKOOM
HRRRRRR...
...IT JUST WEAKENED THE PART OF SUPERMAN
RARAAAAAGH!
...THAT WAS STILL SUPERMAN...
SHHOOOOM
...AND NOW...

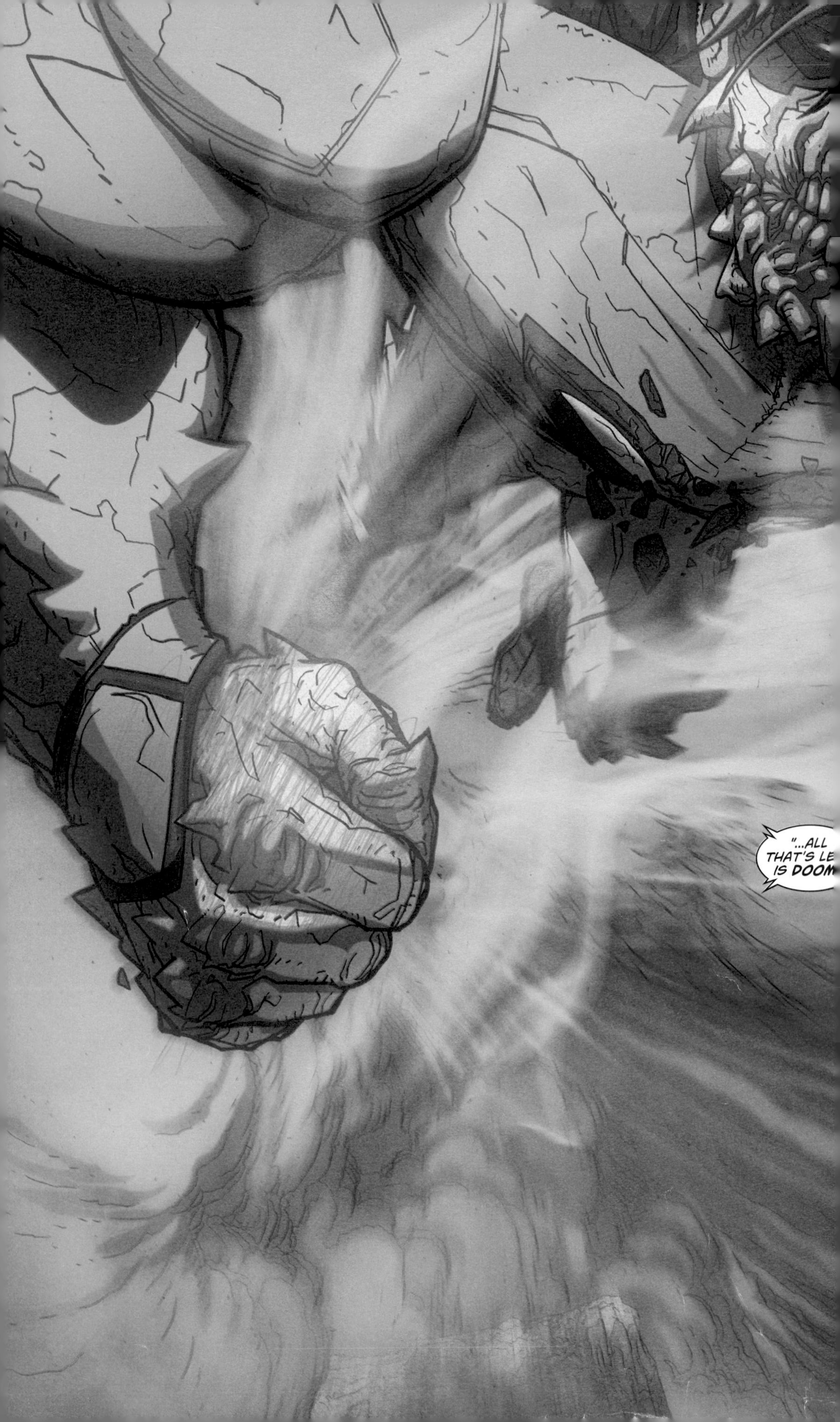
"...ALL THAT'S LE IS DOOM

"UNBOUND"

GREG PAK writer **AARON KUDER ARTIST** **WIL QUINTANA** colorist

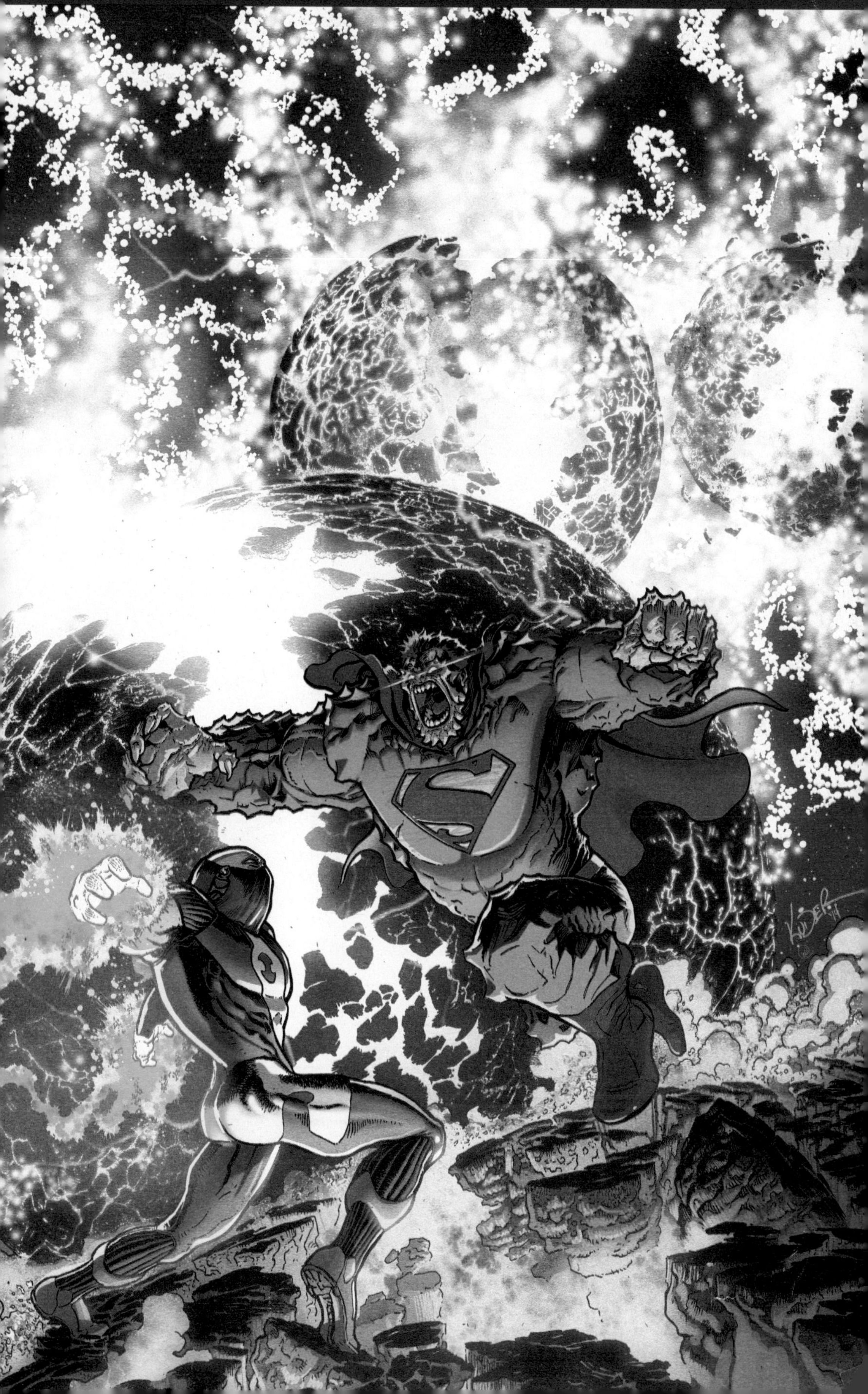

WORLD   U.S.   METROPOLIS   BUSINESS   OPINION   SPORTS   ARTS   STYLE   VIDE

July 7,

Superman or SuperMENACE

By Lois Lane

It looks as if Metropolis and the world may finally find itself free of the Man of Steel's recent erratic and dangerous behavior.

After a bloody battle with the monster known as Doomsday in Smallville, Kansas, Superman has grown increasingly unpredictable and destructive. As the Teen Titans were heard to say, "There's something wrong with Superman."

Looking more and more like the monster he just defeated, an increasingly dangerous Superman has forced the government to deploy a Kryptonite bomb, which has left the Earth covered in material that we have been assured is not lethal to humans.

Most recently the Last Son of Krypton was spotted in Brazil, where witnesses claimed he first fought an unknown armored, female warrior, who was later joined by Wonder Woman.

Onlookers claim Wonder Woman pulled the Super-Monster

Photo by Daily Plane

into the upper atmosphere, only to return moments later in a battle with a trio of Red Lanterns and the Super-creature.

According to witnesses, Super-

man finally left the planet of h own accord, but his destinatio and when he might return are unknown. We will all just hav to look up in the sky and pray does not come back.

How will this all affect Supergirl?
Smallville still under quarantine—
— no change in victims
What is the Justice League's response?
Weather—Mostly Cloudy Green

Real-time satellite video a the green atmosphere

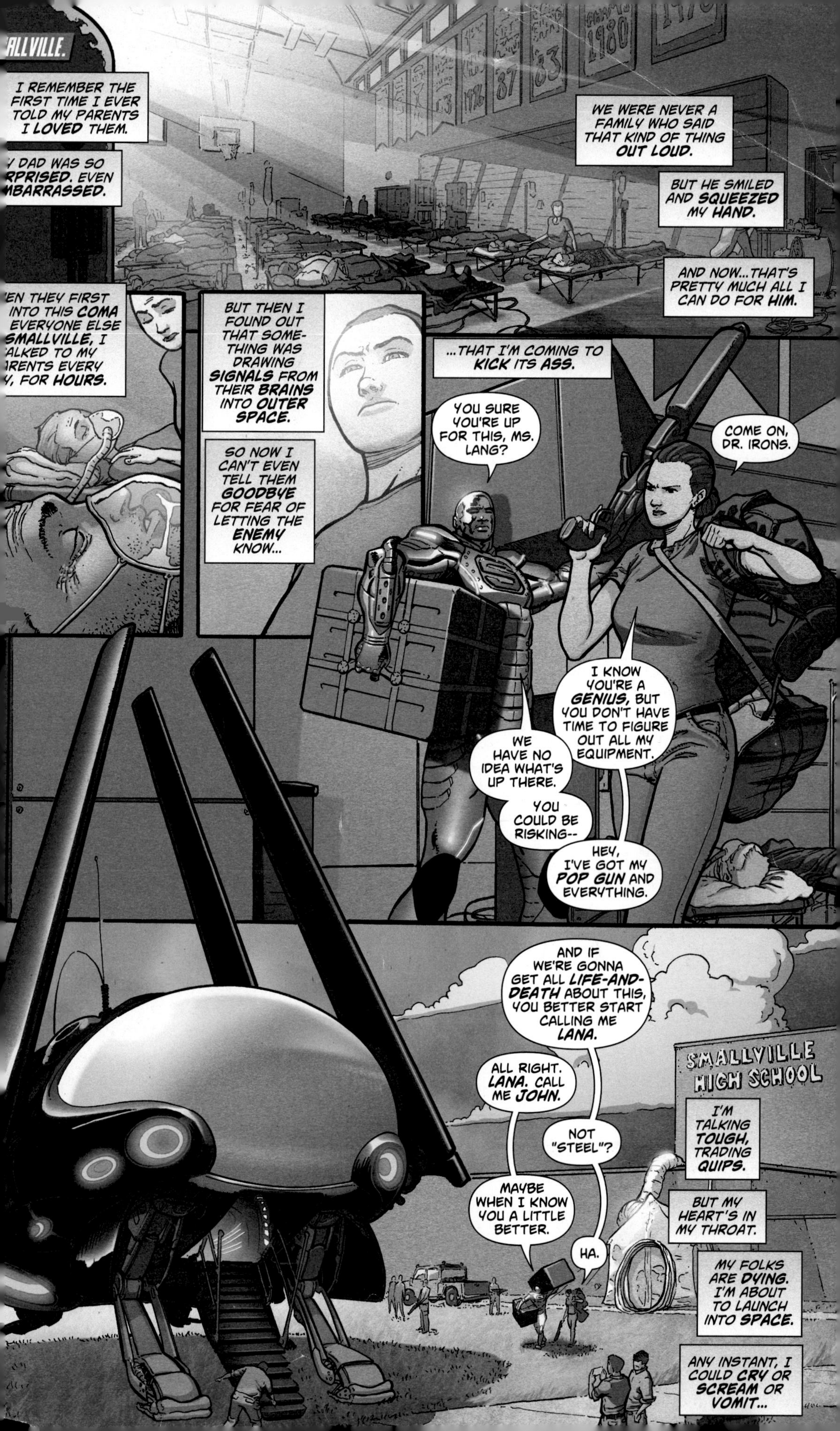

ALLVILLE.
I REMEMBER THE FIRST TIME I EVER TOLD MY PARENTS I LOVED THEM.
Y DAD WAS SO RPRISED. EVEN MBARRASSED.
WE WERE NEVER A FAMILY WHO SAID THAT KIND OF THING OUT LOUD.
BUT HE SMILED AND SQUEEZED MY HAND.
AND NOW...THAT'S PRETTY MUCH ALL I CAN DO FOR HIM.
EN THEY FIRST INTO THIS COMA EVERYONE ELSE SMALLVILLE, I ALKED TO MY RENTS EVERY Y, FOR HOURS.
BUT THEN I FOUND OUT THAT SOMETHING WAS DRAWING SIGNALS FROM THEIR BRAINS INTO OUTER SPACE.
SO NOW I CAN'T EVEN TELL THEM GOODBYE FOR FEAR OF LETTING THE ENEMY KNOW...
...THAT I'M COMING TO KICK ITS ASS.
YOU SURE YOU'RE UP FOR THIS, MS. LANG?
COME ON, DR. IRONS.
I KNOW YOU'RE A GENIUS, BUT YOU DON'T HAVE TIME TO FIGURE OUT ALL MY EQUIPMENT.
WE HAVE NO IDEA WHAT'S UP THERE.
YOU COULD BE RISKING--
HEY, I'VE GOT MY POP GUN AND EVERYTHING.
AND IF WE'RE GONNA GET ALL LIFE-AND-DEATH ABOUT THIS, YOU BETTER START CALLING ME LANA.
ALL RIGHT. LANA. CALL ME JOHN.
NOT "STEEL"?
MAYBE WHEN I KNOW YOU A LITTLE BETTER.
HA.
SMALLVILLE HIGH SCHOOL
I'M TALKING TOUGH, TRADING QUIPS.
BUT MY HEART'S IN MY THROAT.
MY FOLKS ARE DYING. I'M ABOUT TO LAUNCH INTO SPACE.
ANY INSTANT, I COULD CRY OR SCREAM OR VOMIT...

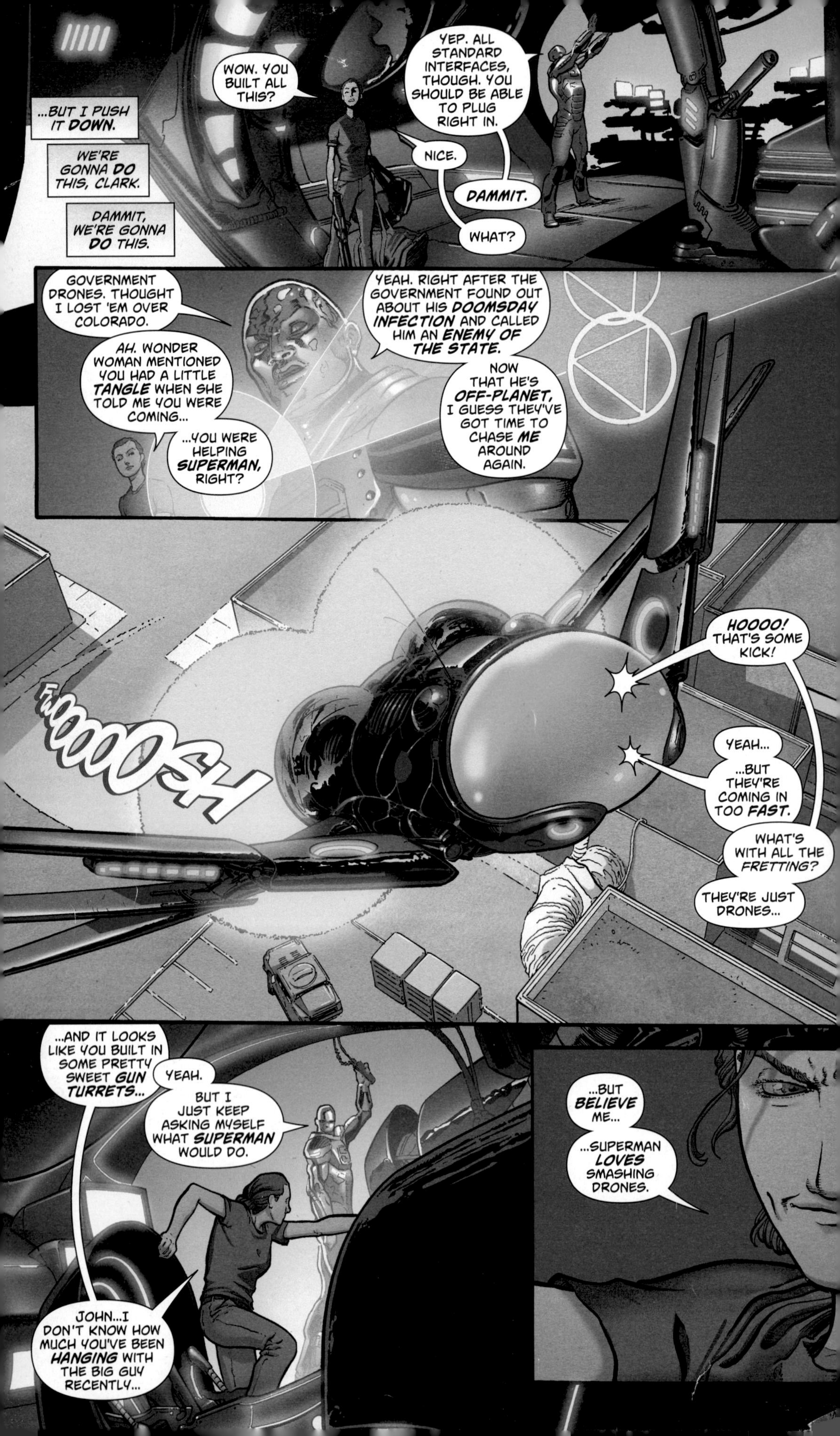

...BUT I PUSH IT DOWN.
WE'RE GONNA DO THIS, CLARK.
DAMMIT, WE'RE GONNA DO THIS.
WOW. YOU BUILT ALL THIS?
YEP. ALL STANDARD INTERFACES, THOUGH. YOU SHOULD BE ABLE TO PLUG RIGHT IN.
NICE.
DAMMIT.
WHAT?
GOVERNMENT DRONES. THOUGHT I LOST 'EM OVER COLORADO.
AH. WONDER WOMAN MENTIONED YOU HAD A LITTLE TANGLE WHEN SHE TOLD ME YOU WERE COMING...
...YOU WERE HELPING SUPERMAN, RIGHT?
YEAH. RIGHT AFTER THE GOVERNMENT FOUND OUT ABOUT HIS DOOMSDAY INFECTION AND CALLED HIM AN ENEMY OF THE STATE.
NOW THAT HE'S OFF-PLANET, I GUESS THEY'VE GOT TIME TO CHASE ME AROUND AGAIN.
FWOOOOOSH
HOOOO! THAT'S SOME KICK!
YEAH...
...BUT THEY'RE COMING IN TOO FAST.
WHAT'S WITH ALL THE FRETTING?
THEY'RE JUST DRONES...
...AND IT LOOKS LIKE YOU BUILT IN SOME PRETTY SWEET GUN TURRETS...
YEAH.
BUT I JUST KEEP ASKING MYSELF WHAT SUPERMAN WOULD DO.
JOHN...I DON'T KNOW HOW MUCH YOU'VE BEEN HANGING WITH THE BIG GUY RECENTLY...
...BUT BELIEVE ME...
...SUPERMAN LOVES SMASHING DRONES.

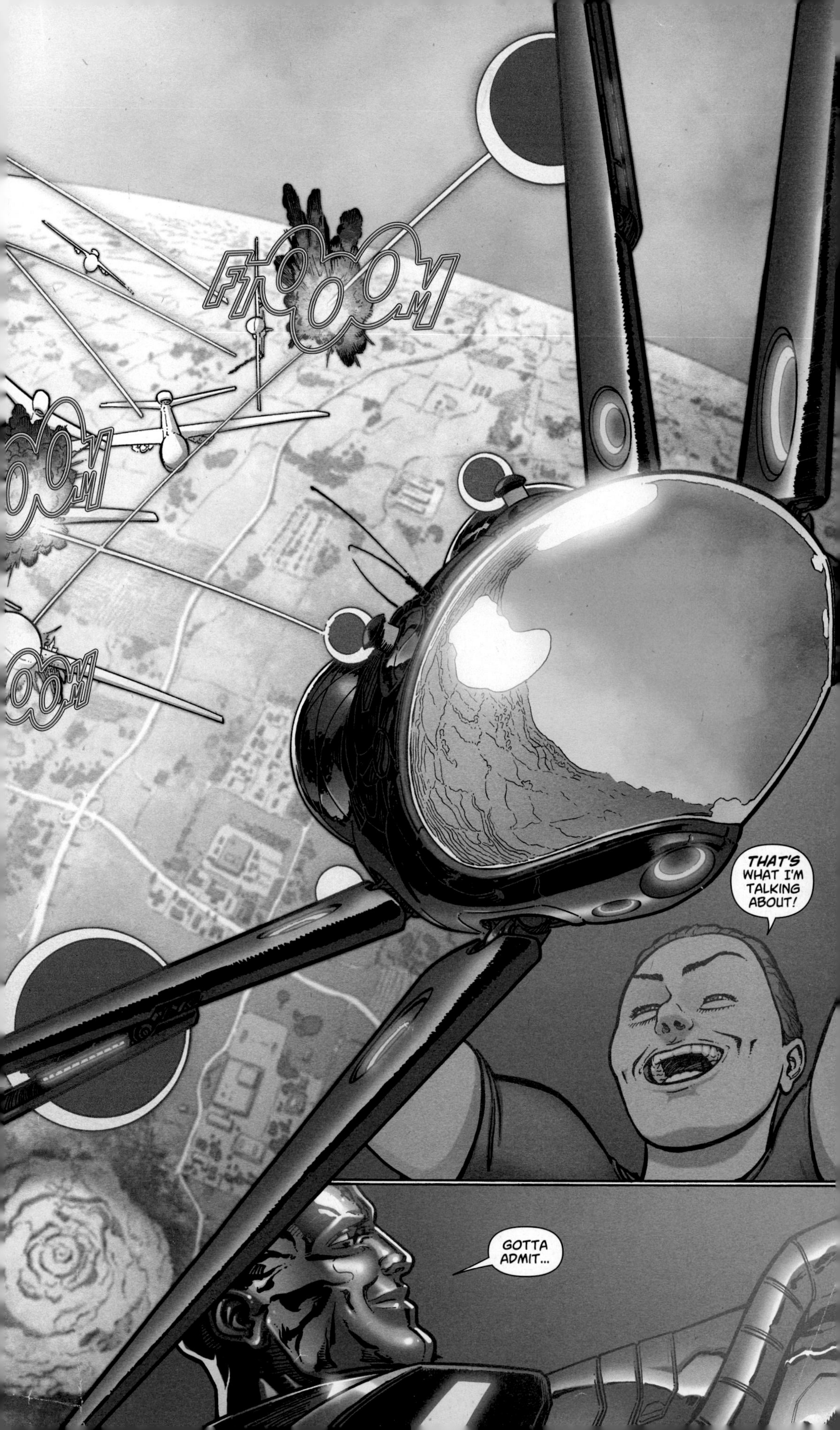
FTOOOM
THAT'S WHAT I'M TALKING ABOUT!
GOTTA ADMIT...

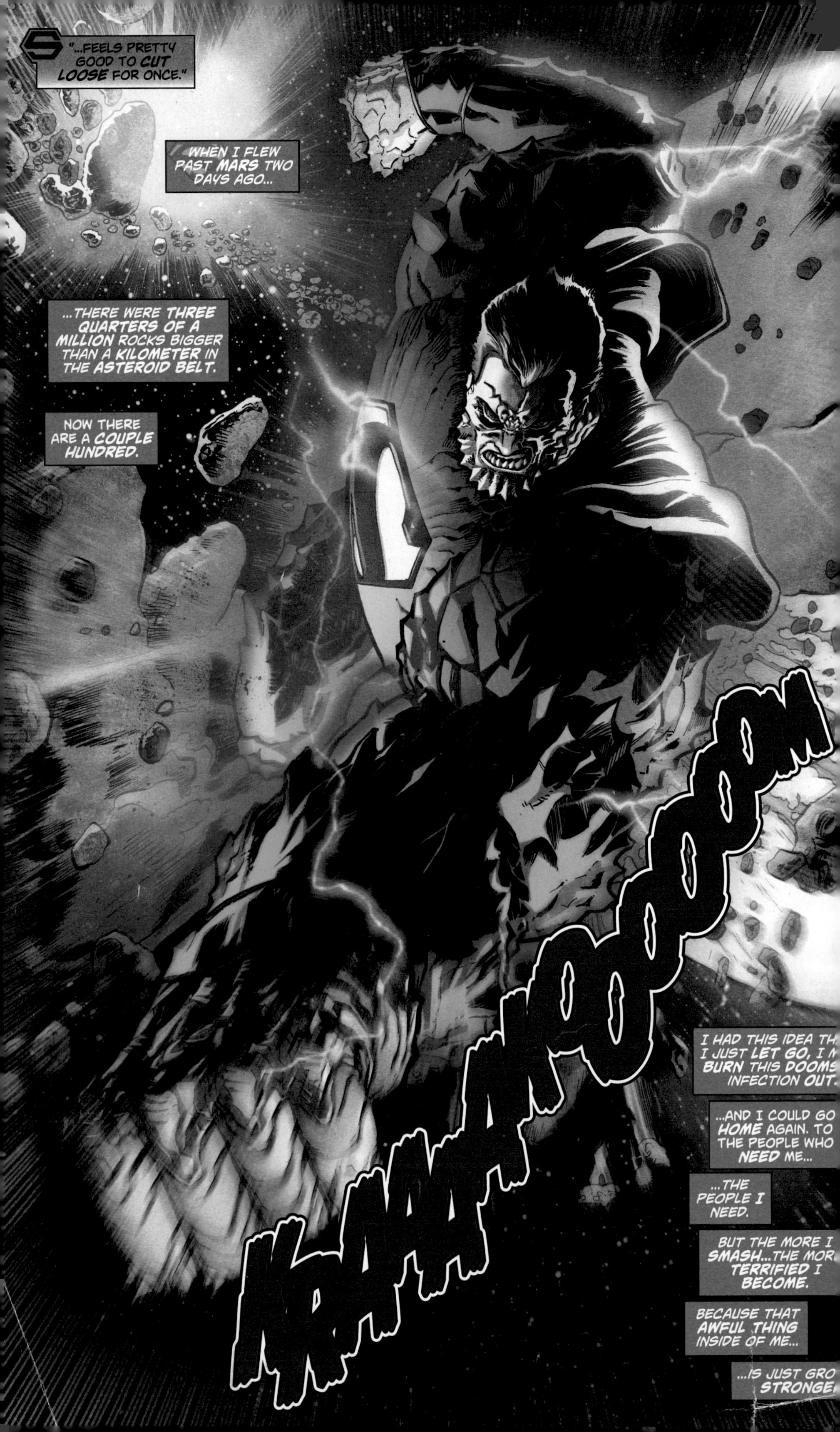
"...FEELS PRETTY GOOD TO CUT LOOSE FOR ONCE."
WHEN I FLEW PAST MARS TWO DAYS AGO...
...THERE WERE THREE QUARTERS OF A MILLION ROCKS BIGGER THAN A KILOMETER IN THE ASTEROID BELT.
NOW THERE ARE A COUPLE HUNDRED.
KRAAAKOOOOOOM
I HAD THIS IDEA TH I JUST LET GO, I M BURN THIS DOOMS INFECTION OUT.
...AND I COULD GO HOME AGAIN. TO THE PEOPLE WHO NEED ME...
...THE PEOPLE I NEED.
BUT THE MORE I SMASH...THE MOR TERRIFIED I BECOME.
BECAUSE THAT AWFUL THING INSIDE OF ME...
...IS JUST GRO STRONGE

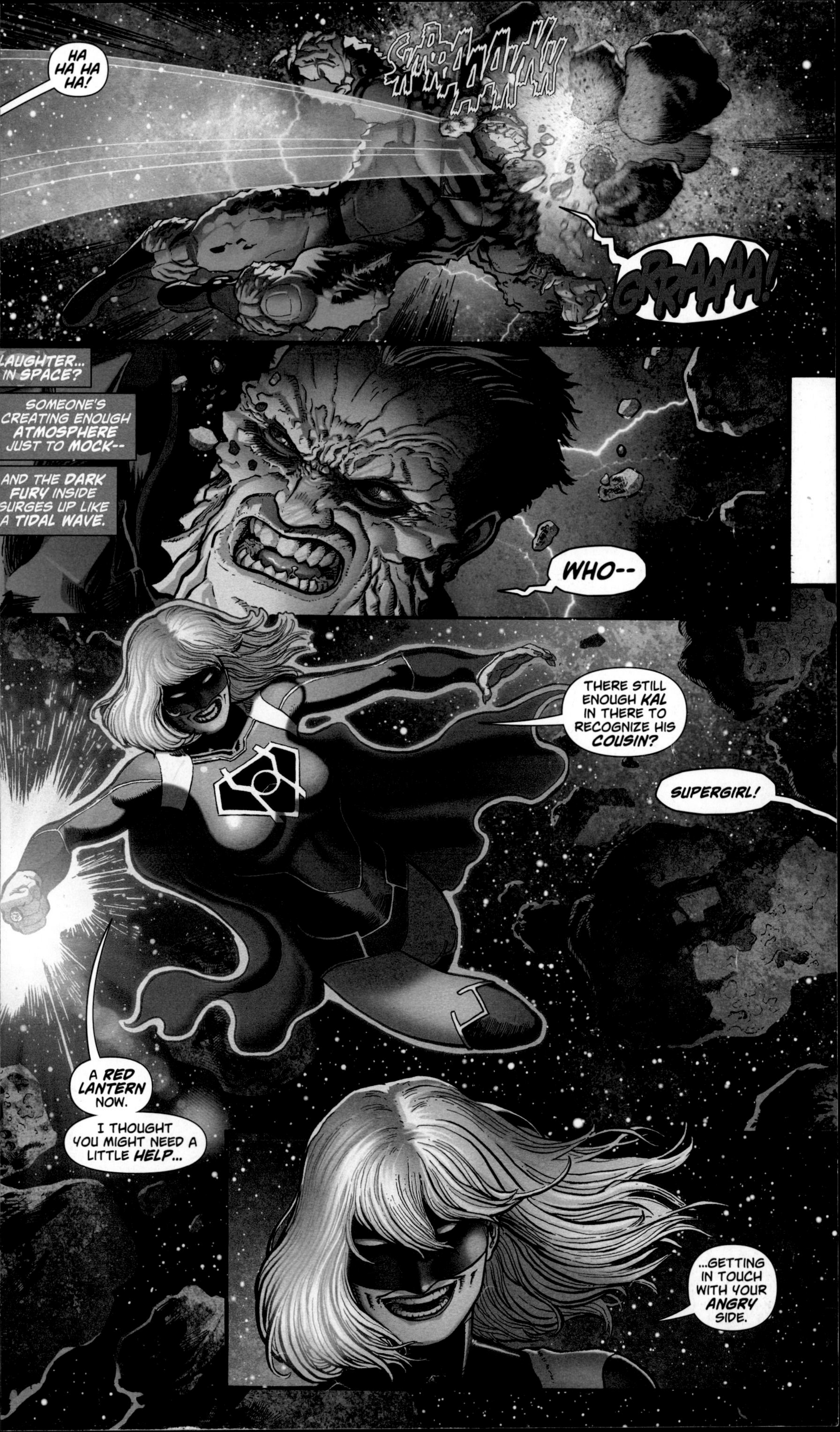
HA HA HA HA!
SKRAAKK
GRRAAAA!
LAUGHTER... IN SPACE?
SOMEONE'S CREATING ENOUGH ATMOSPHERE JUST TO MOCK--
AND THE DARK FURY INSIDE SURGES UP LIKE A TIDAL WAVE.
WHO--
THERE STILL ENOUGH KAL IN THERE TO RECOGNIZE HIS COUSIN?
SUPERGIRL!
A RED LANTERN NOW.
I THOUGHT YOU MIGHT NEED A LITTLE HELP...
...GETTING IN TOUCH WITH YOUR ANGRY SIDE.

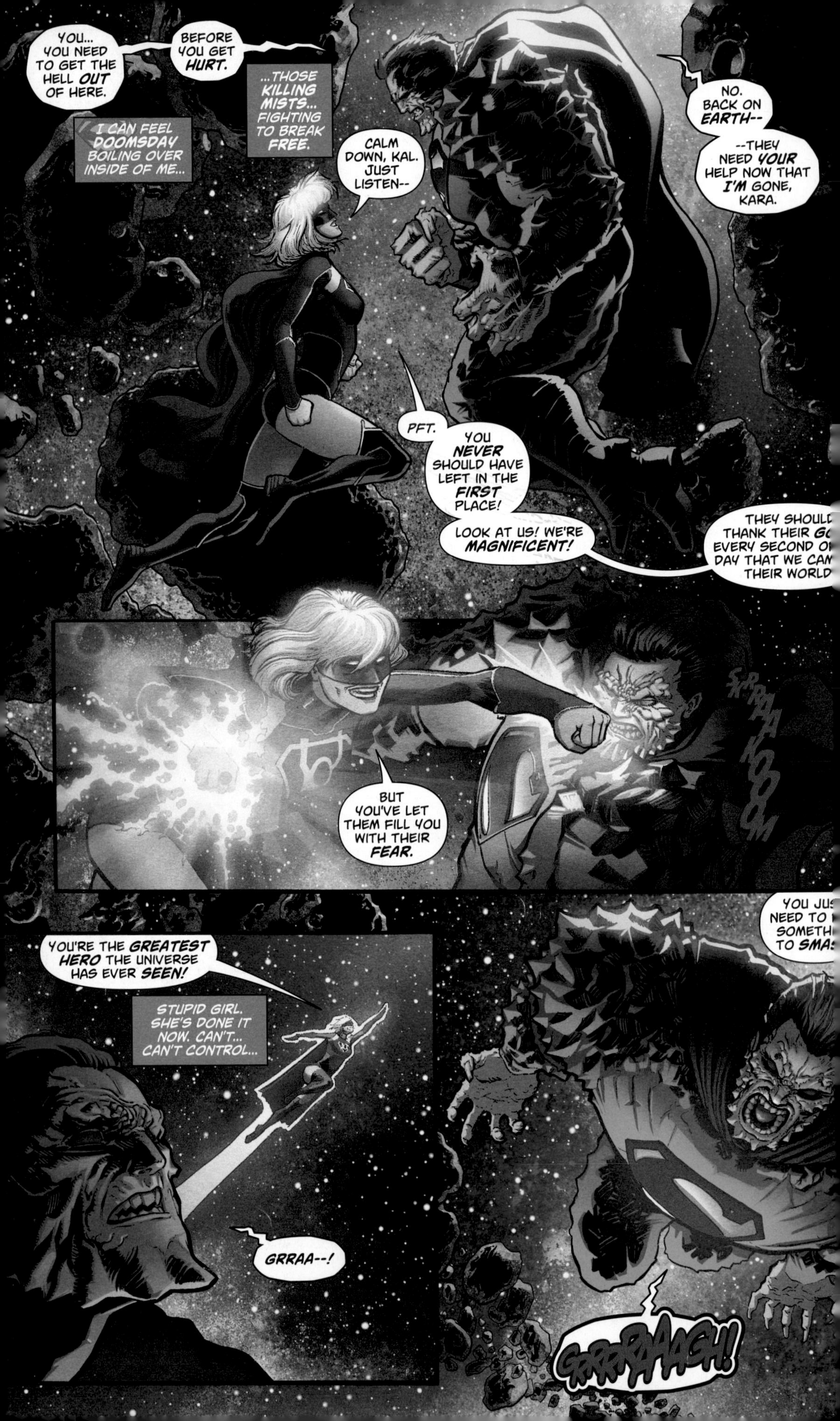

YOU... YOU NEED TO GET THE HELL OUT OF HERE.
BEFORE YOU GET HURT.
I CAN FEEL DOOMSDAY BOILING OVER INSIDE OF ME...
...THOSE KILLING MISTS... FIGHTING TO BREAK FREE.
CALM DOWN, KAL. JUST LISTEN--
NO. BACK ON EARTH--
--THEY NEED YOUR HELP NOW THAT I'M GONE, KARA.
PFT.
YOU NEVER SHOULD HAVE LEFT IN THE FIRST PLACE!
LOOK AT US! WE'RE MAGNIFICENT!
THEY SHOULD THANK THEIR GO EVERY SECOND OF DAY THAT WE CAM THEIR WORLD
BUT YOU'VE LET THEM FILL YOU WITH THEIR FEAR.
SKRRAAKOOOM
YOU JUS NEED TO SOMETHI TO SMA
YOU'RE THE GREATEST HERO THE UNIVERSE HAS EVER SEEN!
STUPID GIRL. SHE'S DONE IT NOW. CAN'T... CAN'T CONTROL...
GRRAA--!
GRRRRAAAGH!

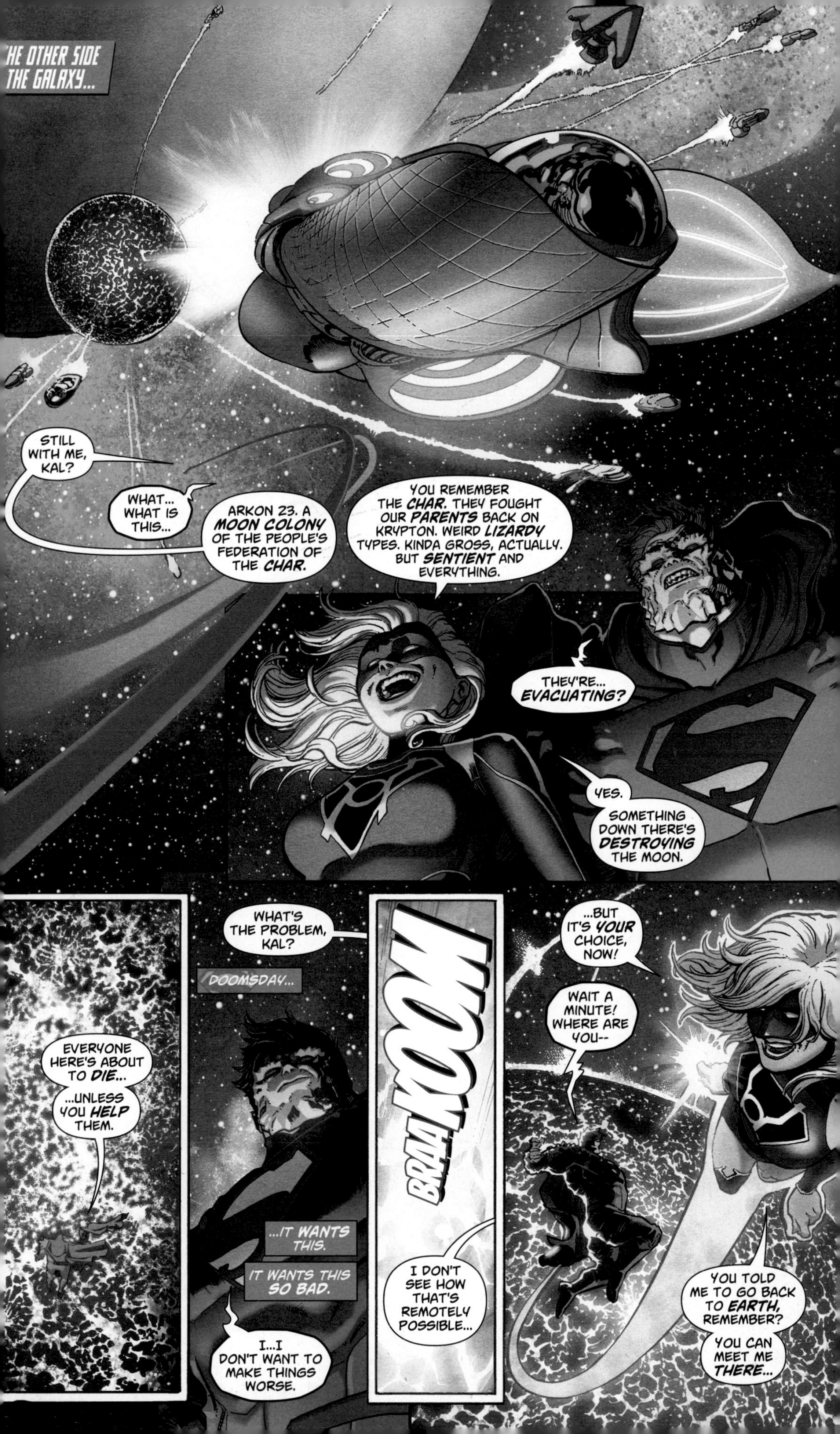

HE OTHER SIDE THE GALAXY...
STILL WITH ME, KAL?
WHAT... WHAT IS THIS...
ARKON 23. A MOON COLONY OF THE PEOPLE'S FEDERATION OF THE CHAR.
YOU REMEMBER THE CHAR. THEY FOUGHT OUR PARENTS BACK ON KRYPTON. WEIRD LIZARDY TYPES. KINDA GROSS, ACTUALLY. BUT SENTIENT AND EVERYTHING.
THEY'RE... EVACUATING?
YES.
SOMETHING DOWN THERE'S DESTROYING THE MOON.
EVERYONE HERE'S ABOUT TO DIE...
...UNLESS YOU HELP THEM.
WHAT'S THE PROBLEM, KAL?
DOOMSDAY...
...IT WANTS THIS.
IT WANTS THIS SO BAD.
I...I DON'T WANT TO MAKE THINGS WORSE.
BRAAKOOM
I DON'T SEE HOW THAT'S REMOTELY POSSIBLE...
...BUT IT'S YOUR CHOICE, NOW!
WAIT A MINUTE! WHERE ARE YOU--
YOU TOLD ME TO GO BACK TO EARTH, REMEMBER?
YOU CAN MEET ME THERE...

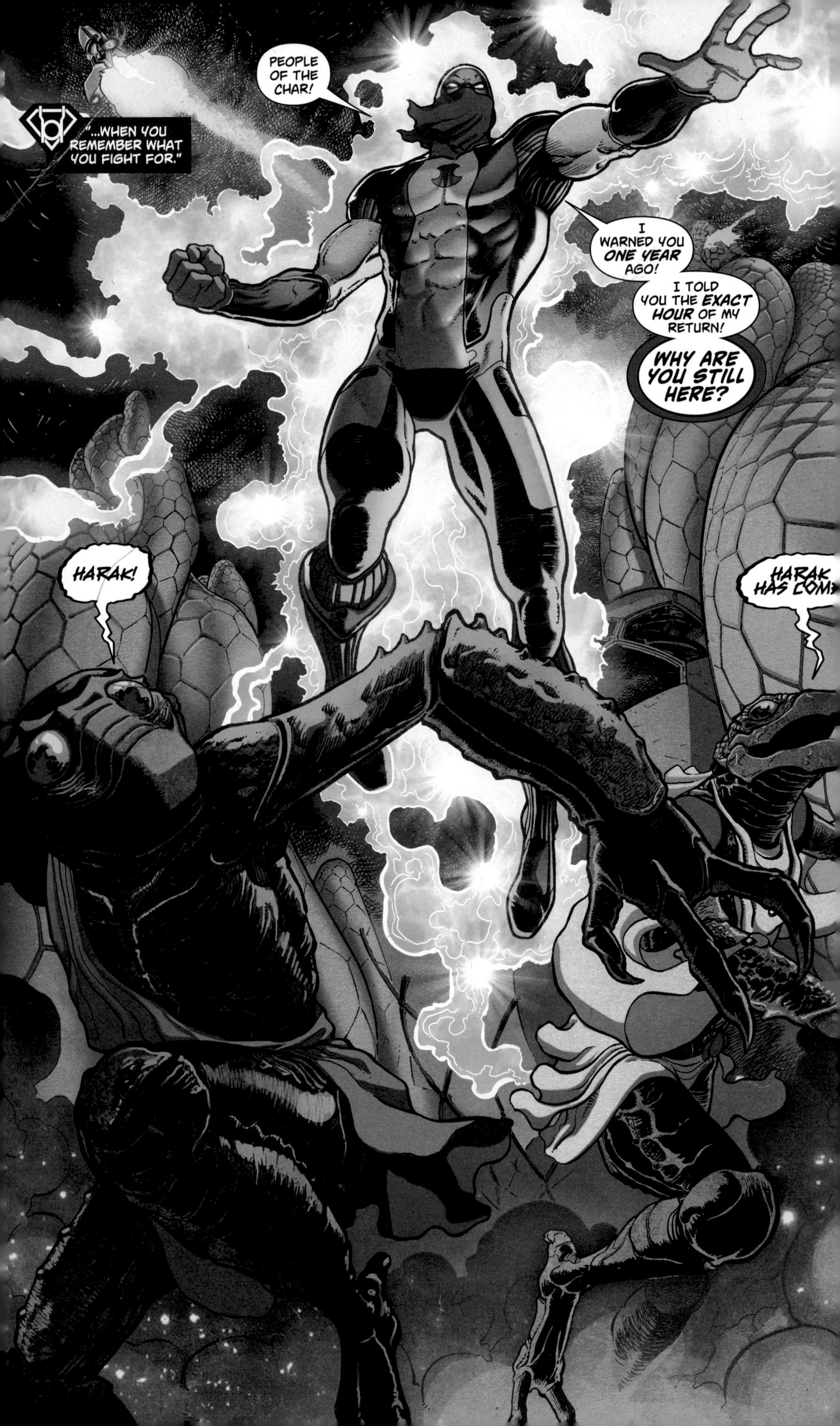
"...WHEN YOU REMEMBER WHAT YOU FIGHT FOR."
PEOPLE OF THE CHAR!
I WARNED YOU ONE YEAR AGO!
I TOLD YOU THE EXACT HOUR OF MY RETURN!
WHY ARE YOU STILL HERE?
HARAK!
HARAK HAS COM

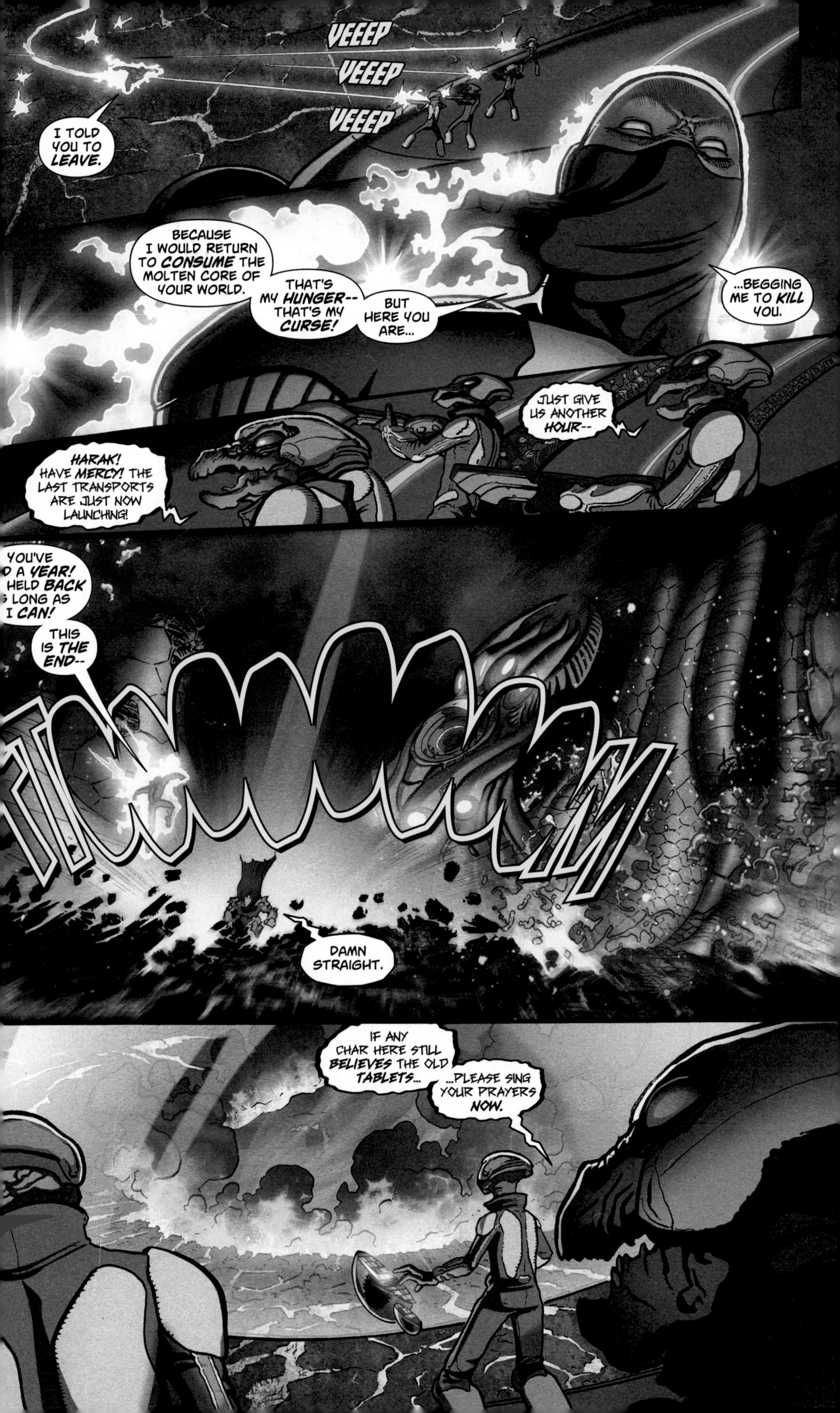
VEEEP
VEEEP
VEEEP
I TOLD YOU TO LEAVE.
BECAUSE I WOULD RETURN TO CONSUME THE MOLTEN CORE OF YOUR WORLD.
THAT'S MY HUNGER-- THAT'S MY CURSE!
BUT HERE YOU ARE...
...BEGGING ME TO KILL YOU.
JUST GIVE US ANOTHER HOUR--
HARAK! HAVE MERCY! THE LAST TRANSPORTS ARE JUST NOW LAUNCHING!
YOU'VE
HELD BACK
LONG AS I CAN!
THIS IS THE END--
DAMN STRAIGHT.
IF ANY CHAR HERE STILL BELIEVES THE OLD TABLETS...
...PLEASE SING YOUR PRAYERS NOW.

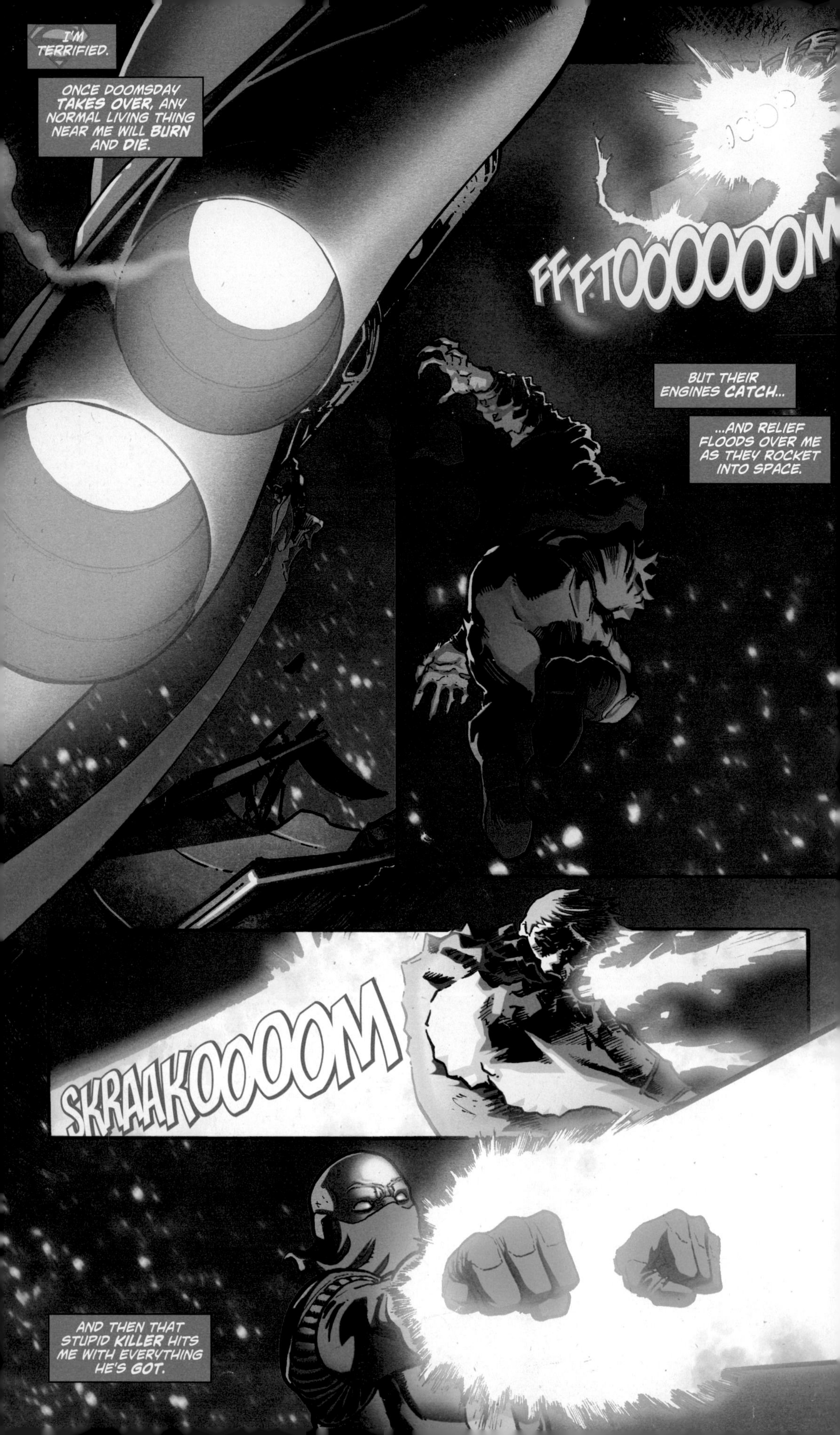
I'M TERRIFIED.
ONCE DOOMSDAY TAKES OVER, ANY NORMAL LIVING THING NEAR ME WILL BURN AND DIE.
FFFTOOOOOOOM
BUT THEIR ENGINES CATCH...
...AND RELIEF FLOODS OVER ME AS THEY ROCKET INTO SPACE.
SKRAAKOOOOM
AND THEN THAT STUPID KILLER HITS ME WITH EVERYTHING HE'S GOT.

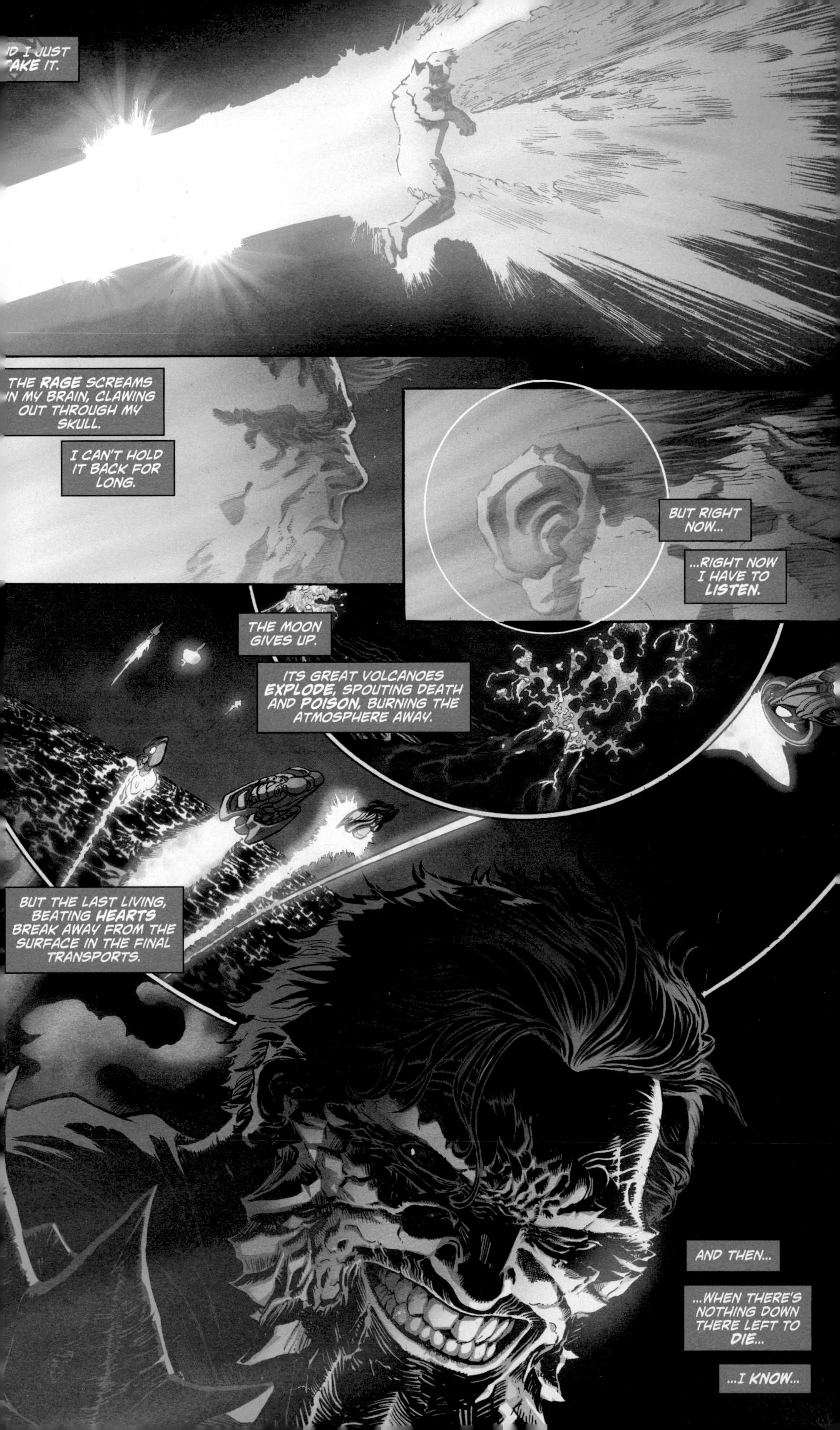

ID I JUST TAKE IT.
THE RAGE SCREAMS IN MY BRAIN, CLAWING OUT THROUGH MY SKULL.
I CAN'T HOLD IT BACK FOR LONG.
BUT RIGHT NOW...
...RIGHT NOW I HAVE TO LISTEN.
THE MOON GIVES UP.
ITS GREAT VOLCANOES EXPLODE, SPOUTING DEATH AND POISON, BURNING THE ATMOSPHERE AWAY.
BUT THE LAST LIVING, BEATING HEARTS BREAK AWAY FROM THE SURFACE IN THE FINAL TRANSPORTS.
AND THEN...
...WHEN THERE'S NOTHING DOWN THERE LEFT TO DIE...
...I KNOW...

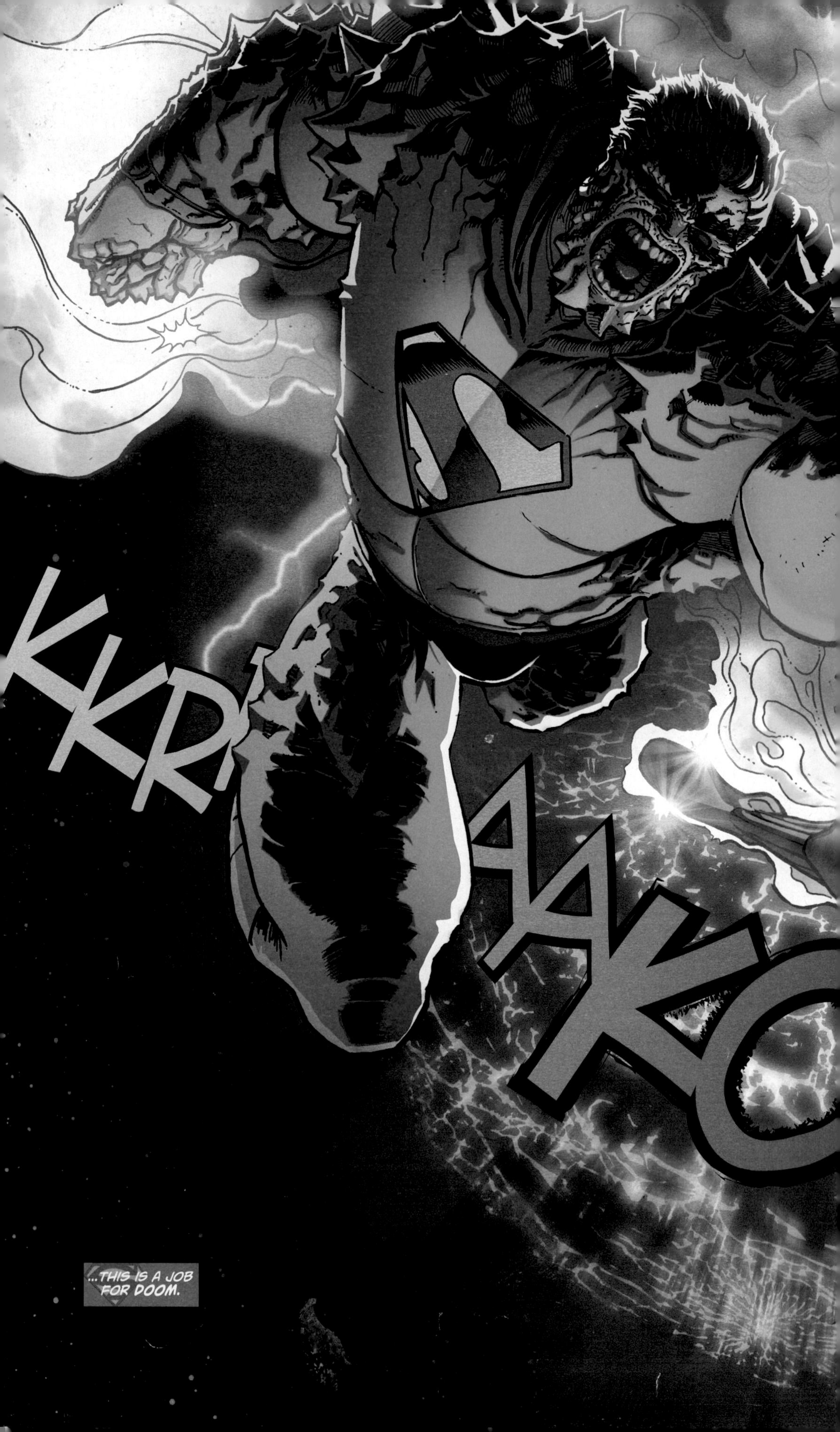
KKRAAKO
...THIS IS A JOB FOR DOOM.

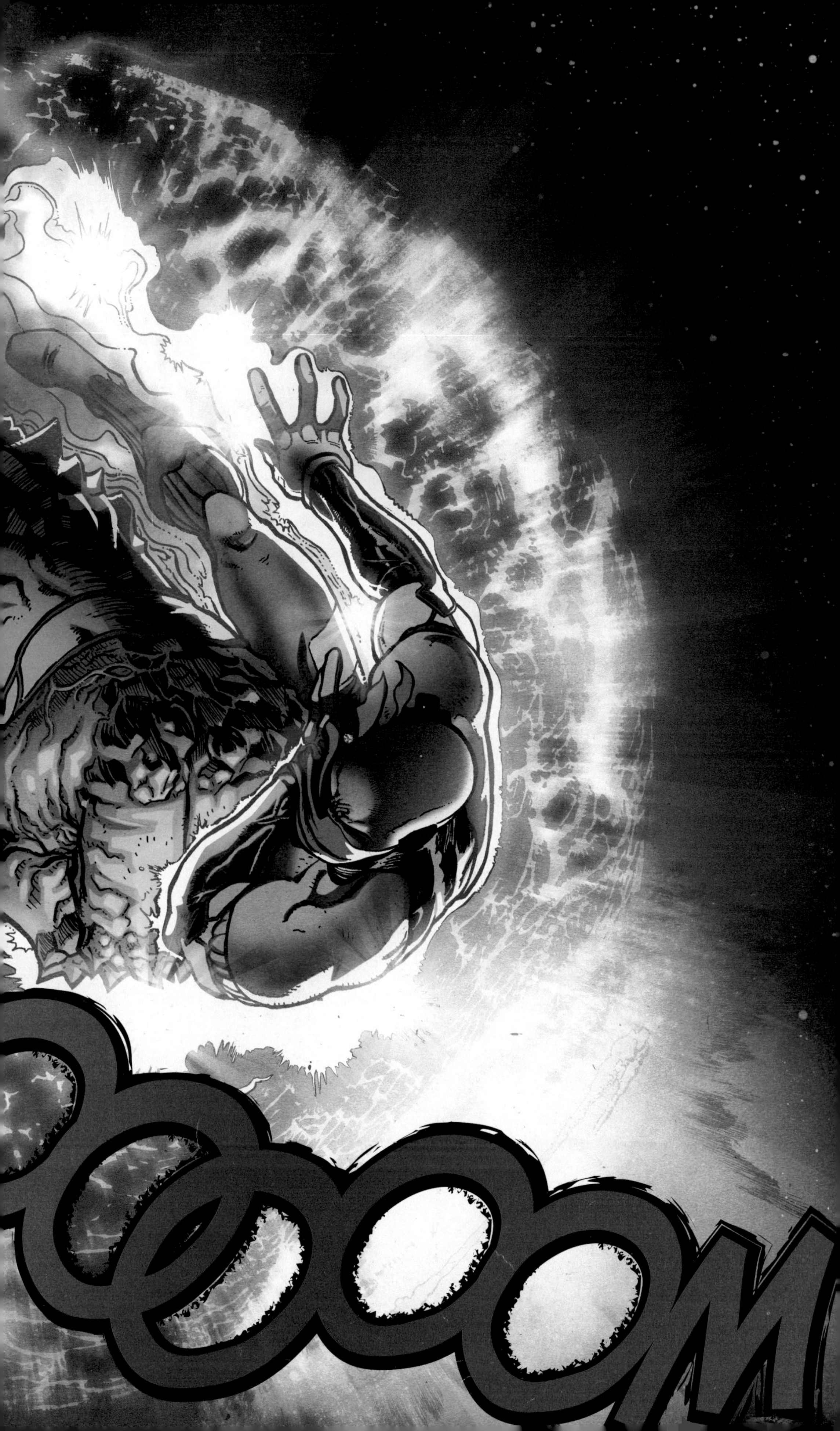
OOOOM

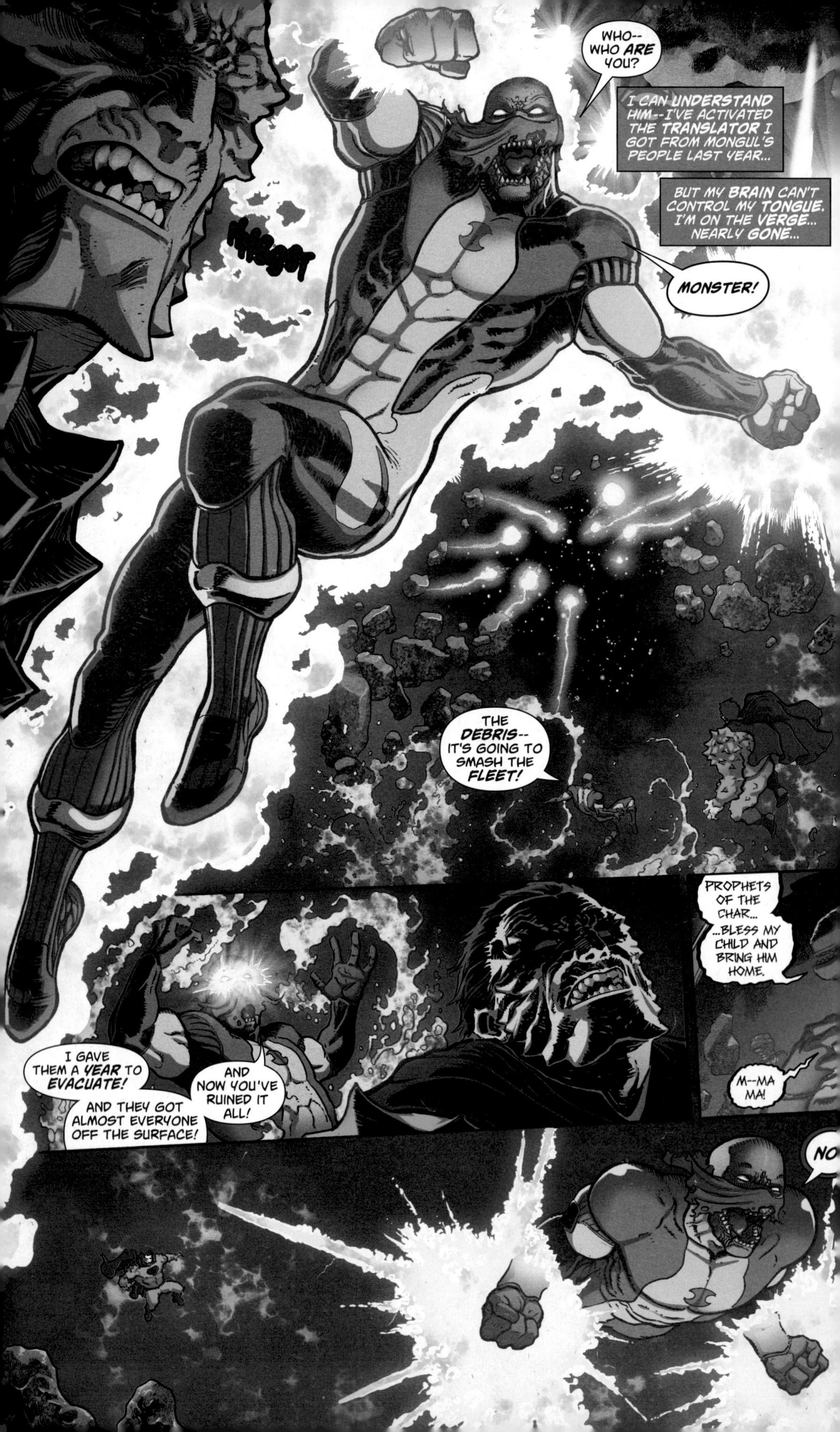
FHSSSST
WHO--
WHO ARE
YOU?
I CAN UNDERSTAND HIM--I'VE ACTIVATED THE TRANSLATOR I GOT FROM MONGUL'S PEOPLE LAST YEAR...
BUT MY BRAIN CAN'T CONTROL MY TONGUE. I'M ON THE VERGE... NEARLY GONE...
MONSTER!
THE DEBRIS-- IT'S GOING TO SMASH THE FLEET!
I GAVE THEM A YEAR TO EVACUATE!
AND THEY GOT ALMOST EVERYONE OFF THE SURFACE!
AND NOW YOU'VE RUINED IT ALL!
PROPHETS OF THE CHAR... ...BLESS MY CHILD AND BRING HIM HOME.
M--MA MA!
NO

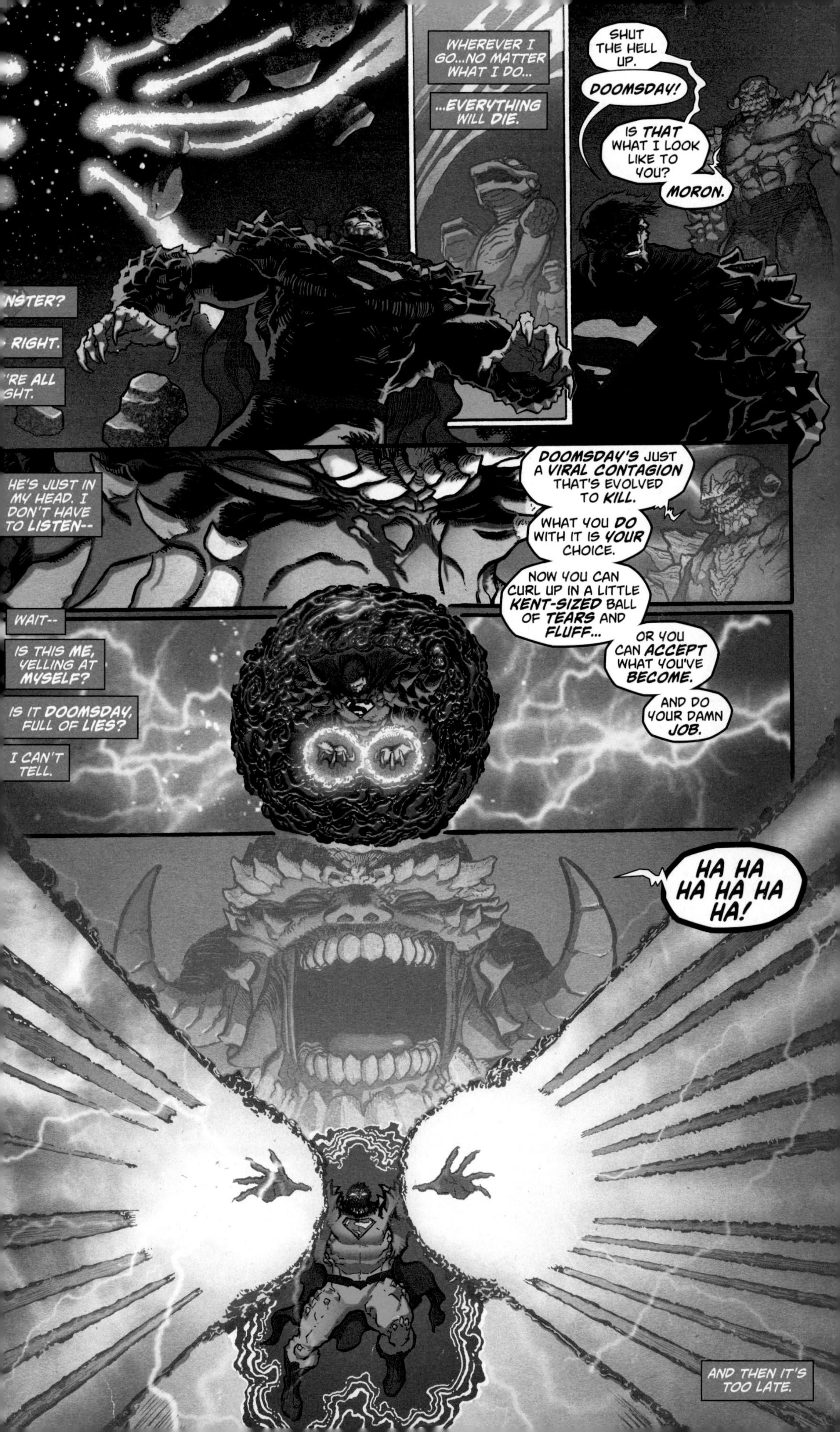

NSTER?
RIGHT.
'RE ALL
GHT.
WHEREVER I GO...NO MATTER WHAT I DO...
...EVERYTHING WILL DIE.
SHUT THE HELL UP.
DOOMSDAY!
IS THAT WHAT I LOOK LIKE TO YOU? MORON.
HE'S JUST IN MY HEAD. I DON'T HAVE TO LISTEN--
DOOMSDAY'S JUST A VIRAL CONTAGION THAT'S EVOLVED TO KILL.
WHAT YOU DO WITH IT IS YOUR CHOICE.
NOW YOU CAN CURL UP IN A LITTLE KENT-SIZED BALL OF TEARS AND FLUFF...
OR YOU CAN ACCEPT WHAT YOU'VE BECOME.
AND DO YOUR DAMN JOB.
WAIT--
IS THIS ME, YELLING AT MYSELF?
IS IT DOOMSDAY, FULL OF LIES?
I CAN'T TELL.
HA HA HA HA HA HA!
AND THEN IT'S TOO LATE.

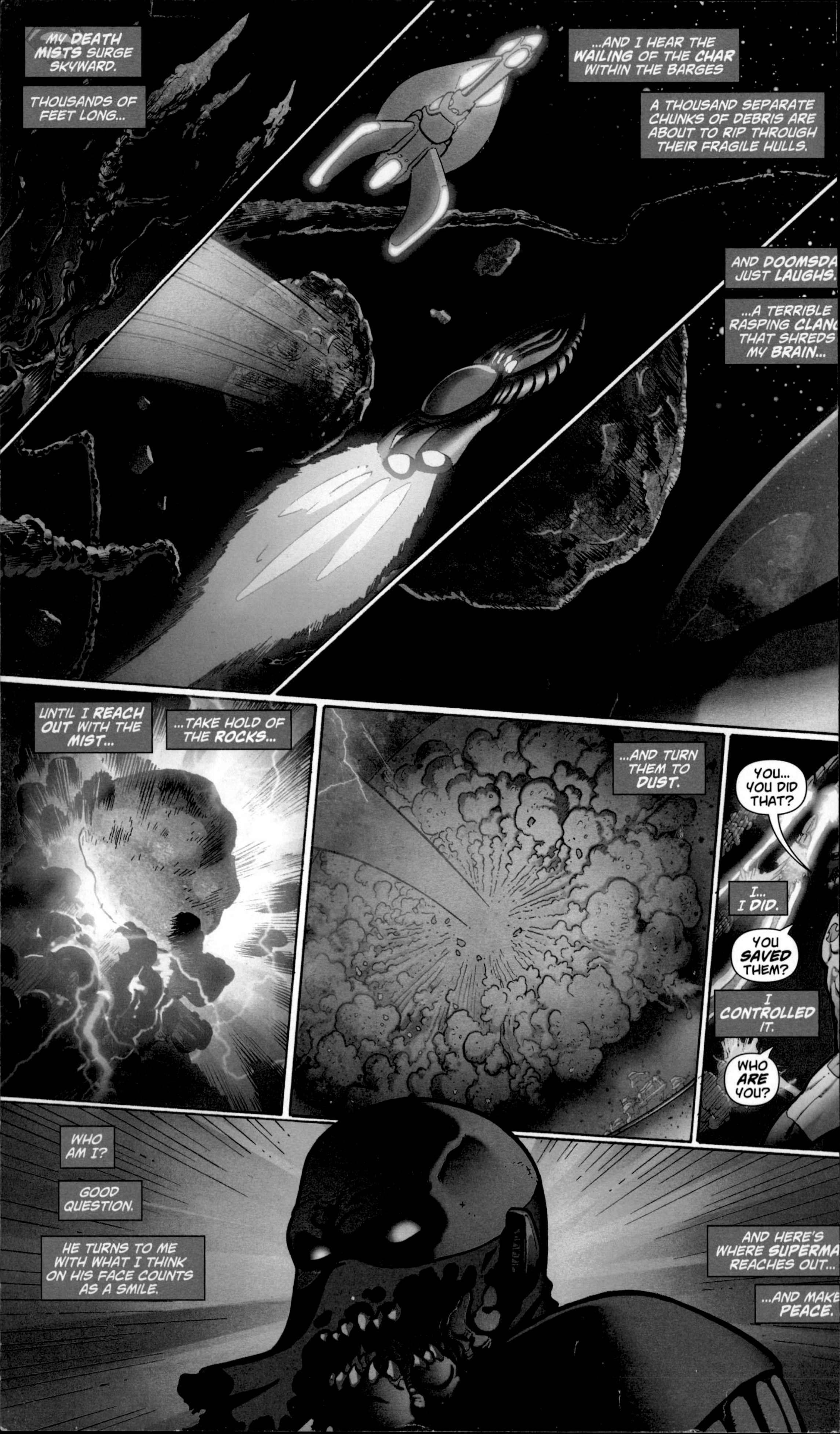
MY DEATH MISTS SURGE SKYWARD.
THOUSANDS OF FEET LONG...
...AND I HEAR THE WAILING OF THE CHAR WITHIN THE BARGES
A THOUSAND SEPARATE CHUNKS OF DEBRIS ARE ABOUT TO RIP THROUGH THEIR FRAGILE HULLS.
AND DOOMSDA JUST LAUGHS.
...A TERRIBLE RASPING CLAN THAT SHREDS MY BRAIN...
UNTIL I REACH OUT WITH THE MIST...
...TAKE HOLD OF THE ROCKS...
...AND TURN THEM TO DUST.
YOU... YOU DID THAT?
I... I DID.
YOU SAVED THEM?
I CONTROLLED IT.
WHO ARE YOU?
WHO AM I?
GOOD QUESTION.
HE TURNS TO ME WITH WHAT I THINK ON HIS FACE COUNTS AS A SMILE.
AND HERE'S WHERE SUPERMA REACHES OUT...
...AND MAKE PEACE.

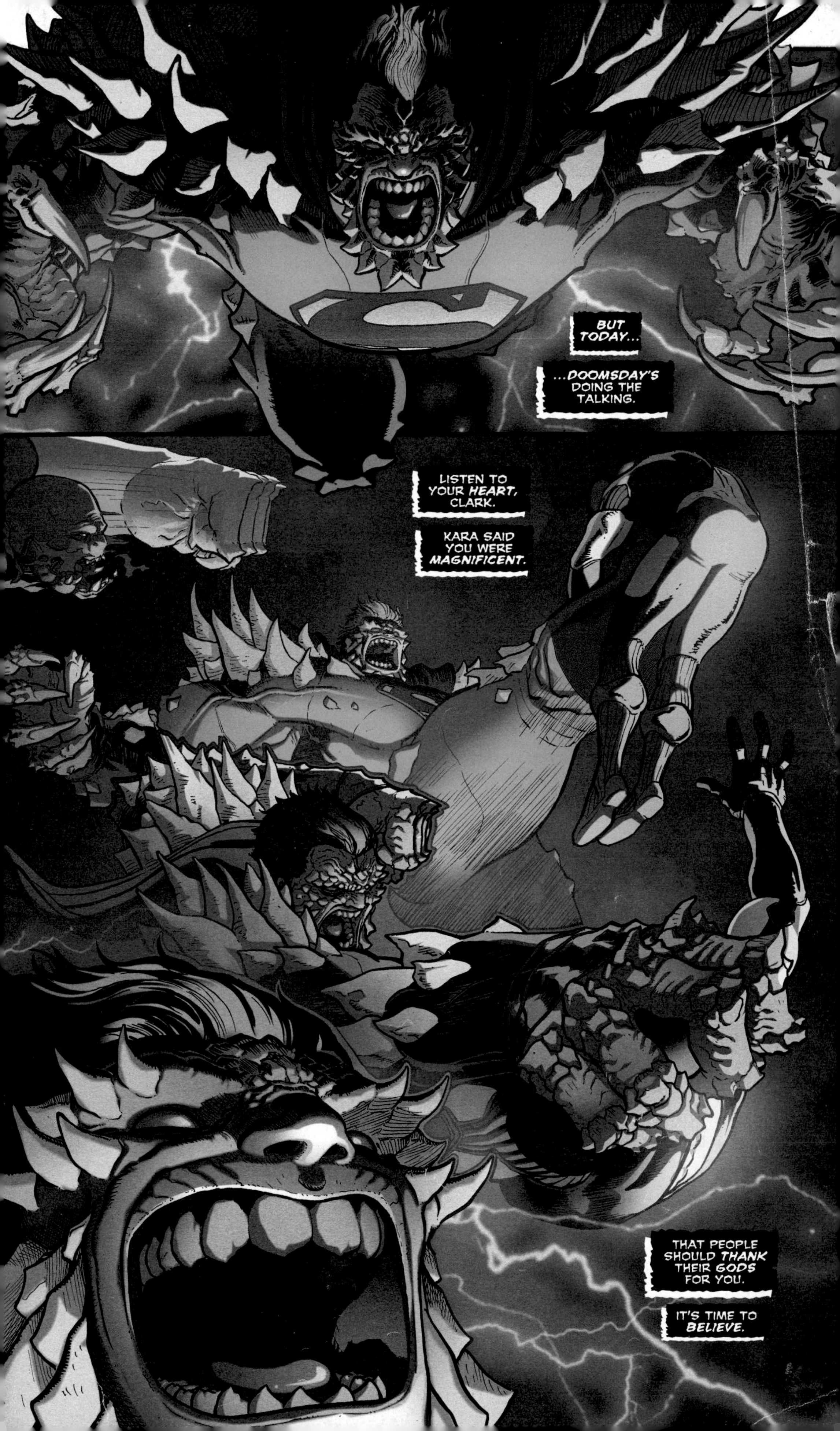
BUT TODAY...
...DOOMSDAY'S DOING THE TALKING.
LISTEN TO YOUR HEART, CLARK.
KARA SAID YOU WERE MAGNIFICENT.
THAT PEOPLE SHOULD THANK THEIR GODS FOR YOU.
IT'S TIME TO BELIEVE.

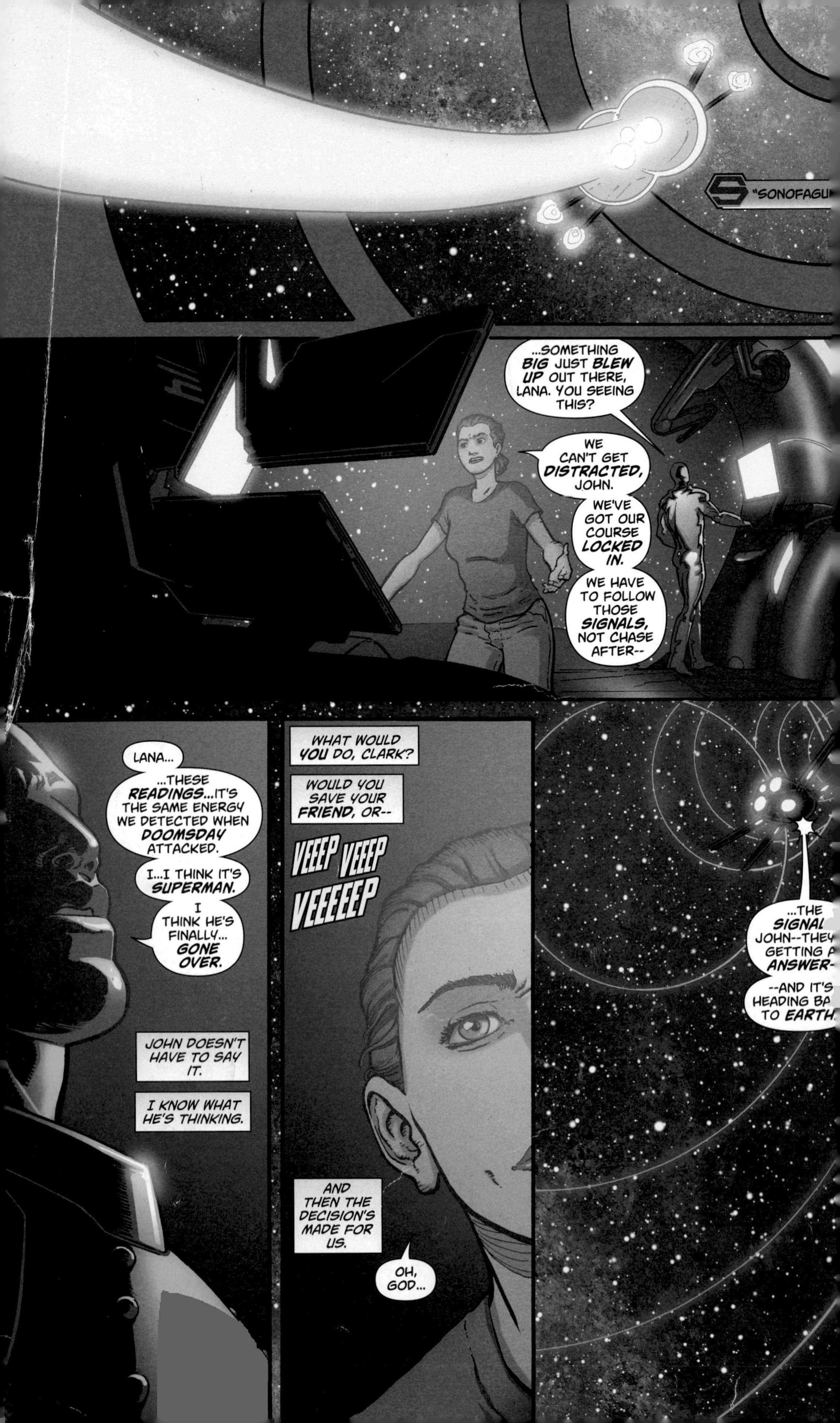
"SONOFAGU
...SOMETHING BIG JUST BLEW UP OUT THERE, LANA. YOU SEEING THIS?
WE CAN'T GET DISTRACTED, JOHN.
WE'VE GOT OUR COURSE LOCKED IN.
WE HAVE TO FOLLOW THOSE SIGNALS, NOT CHASE AFTER--
LANA...
...THESE READINGS...IT'S THE SAME ENERGY WE DETECTED WHEN DOOMSDAY ATTACKED.
I...I THINK IT'S SUPERMAN.
I THINK HE'S FINALLY... GONE OVER.
JOHN DOESN'T HAVE TO SAY IT.
I KNOW WHAT HE'S THINKING.
WHAT WOULD YOU DO, CLARK?
WOULD YOU SAVE YOUR FRIEND, OR--
VEEEP VEEEP VEEEEEP
AND THEN THE DECISION'S MADE FOR US.
OH, GOD...
...THE SIGNAL
JOHN--THEY
GETTING A
ANSWER-
--AND IT'S
HEADING BA
TO EARTH.

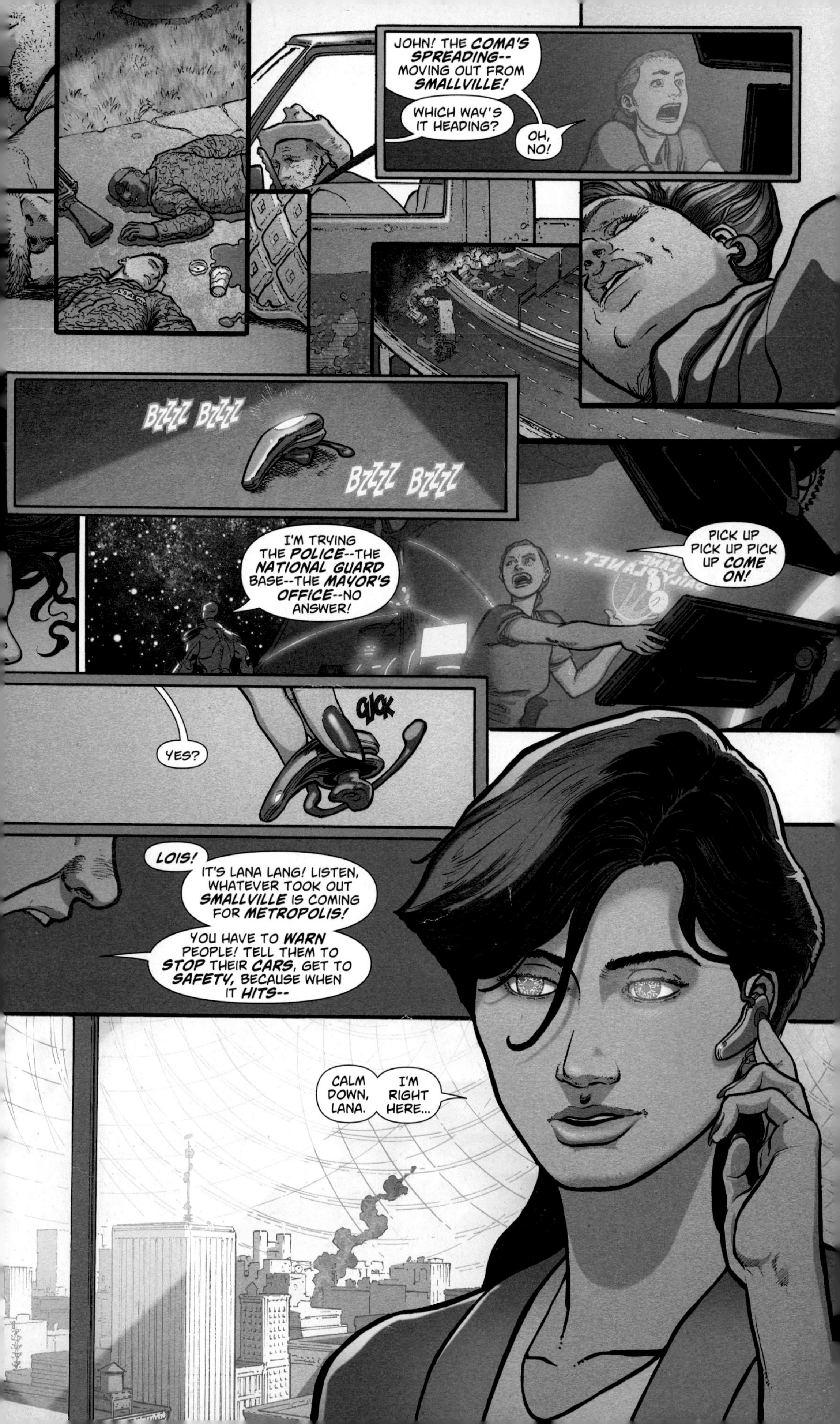

JOHN! THE COMA'S SPREADING-- MOVING OUT FROM SMALLVILLE!
WHICH WAY'S IT HEADING?
OH, NO!
BZZZZ BZZZZ
BZZZZ BZZZZ
I'M TRYING THE POLICE--THE NATIONAL GUARD BASE--THE MAYOR'S OFFICE--NO ANSWER!
PICK UP PICK UP PICK UP COME ON!
CLICK
YES?
LOIS!
IT'S LANA LANG! LISTEN, WHATEVER TOOK OUT SMALLVILLE IS COMING FOR METROPOLIS!
YOU HAVE TO WARN PEOPLE! TELL THEM TO STOP THEIR CARS, GET TO SAFETY, BECAUSE WHEN IT HITS--
CALM DOWN, LANA.
I'M RIGHT HERE...

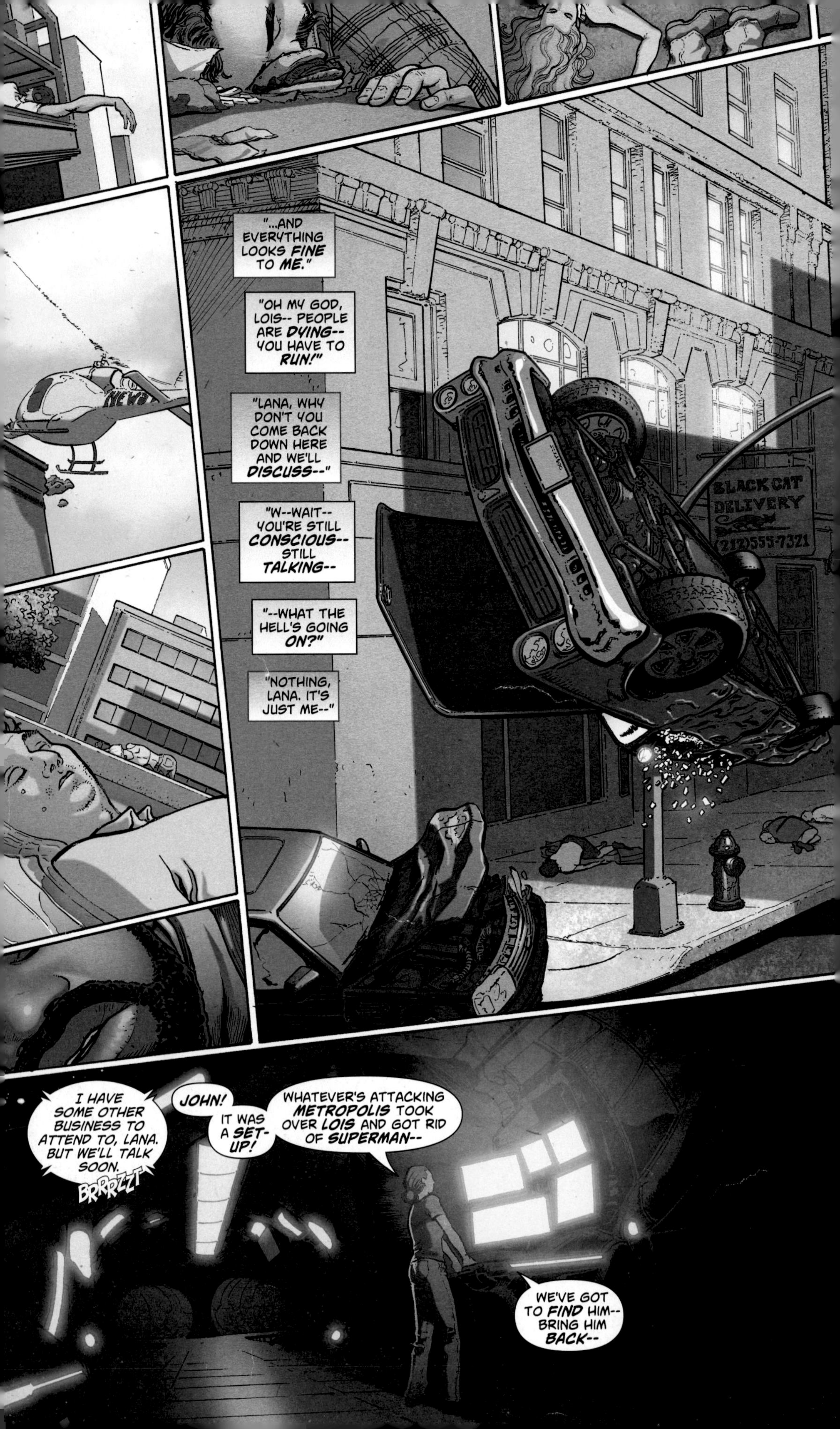
"...AND EVERYTHING LOOKS FINE TO ME."
"OH MY GOD, LOIS-- PEOPLE ARE DYING-- YOU HAVE TO RUN!"
"LANA, WHY DON'T YOU COME BACK DOWN HERE AND WE'LL DISCUSS--"
"W--WAIT-- YOU'RE STILL CONSCIOUS-- STILL TALKING--
"--WHAT THE HELL'S GOING ON?"
"NOTHING, LANA. IT'S JUST ME--"
BLACK CAT DELIVERY (212)553-7321
I HAVE SOME OTHER BUSINESS TO ATTEND TO, LANA. BUT WE'LL TALK SOON.
BRRRZZT
JOHN!
IT WAS A SET-UP!
WHATEVER'S ATTACKING METROPOLIS TOOK OVER LOIS AND GOT RID OF SUPERMAN--
WE'VE GOT TO FIND HIM-- BRING HIM BACK--

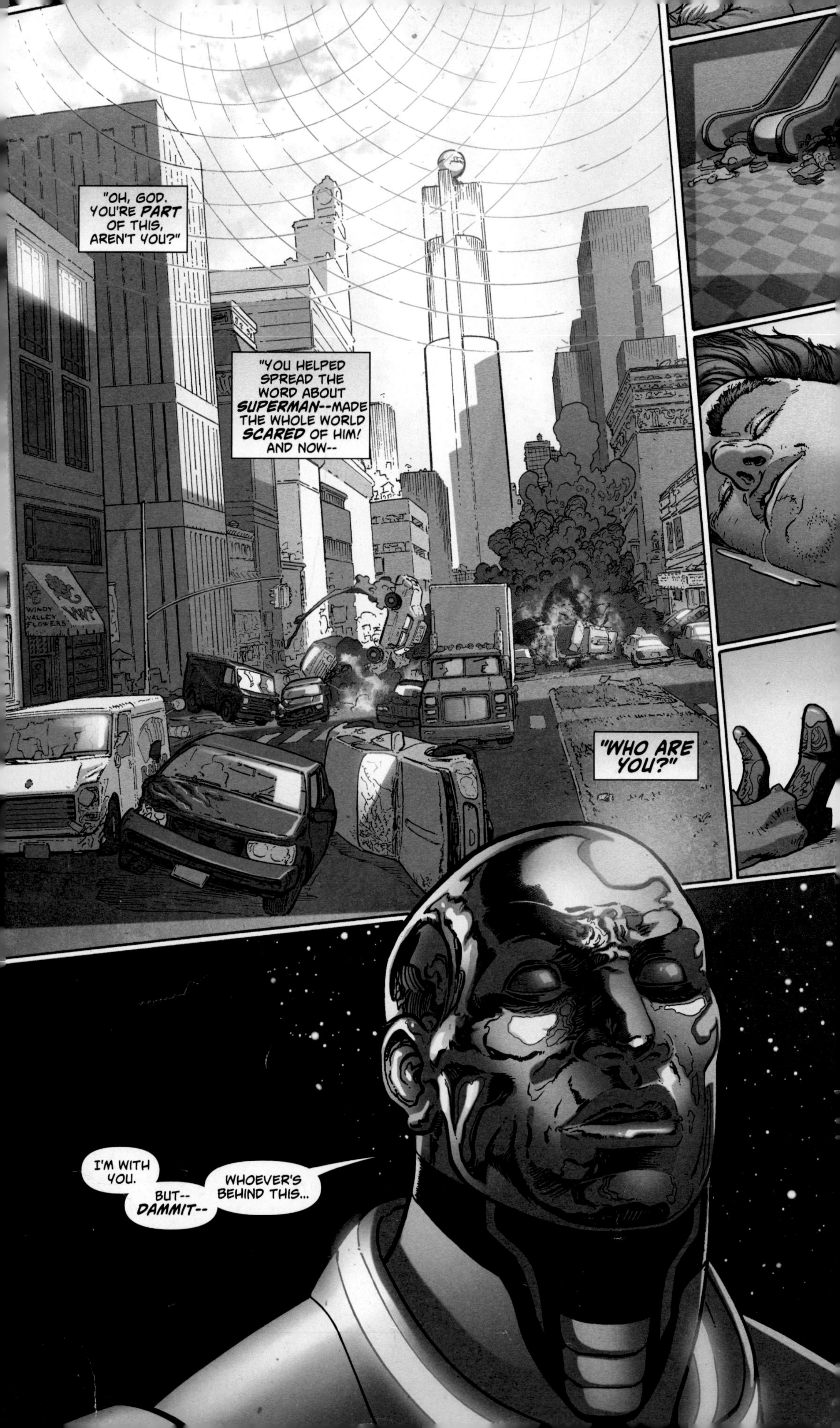
"OH, GOD. YOU'RE PART OF THIS, AREN'T YOU?"
"YOU HELPED SPREAD THE WORD ABOUT SUPERMAN--MADE THE WHOLE WORLD SCARED OF HIM! AND NOW--
WINDY VALLEY FLOWERS
"WHO ARE YOU?"
I'M WITH YOU.
BUT-- DAMMIT--
WHOEVER'S BEHIND THIS...

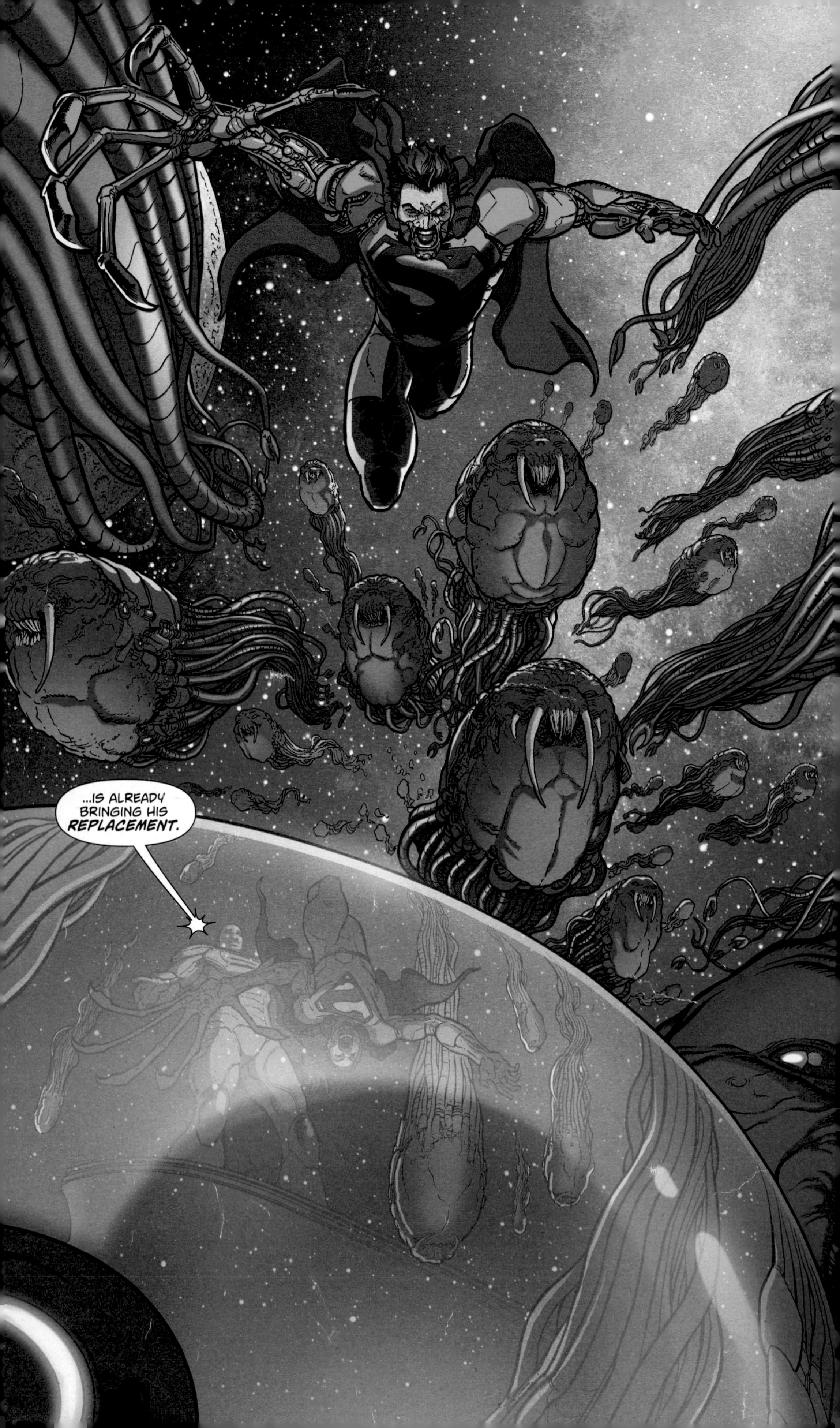
...IS ALREADY BRINGING HIS REPLACEMENT.

"MY BODY IS A CAGE"

GREG PAK writer **KEN LASHLEY AARON KUDER JACK HERBERT CLIFF RICHARDS JULIUS GOPEZ WILL CONRAD PASCAL ALIXE** artists **VICENTE CIFUENTES** inker **ULISES ARREOLA** colorist

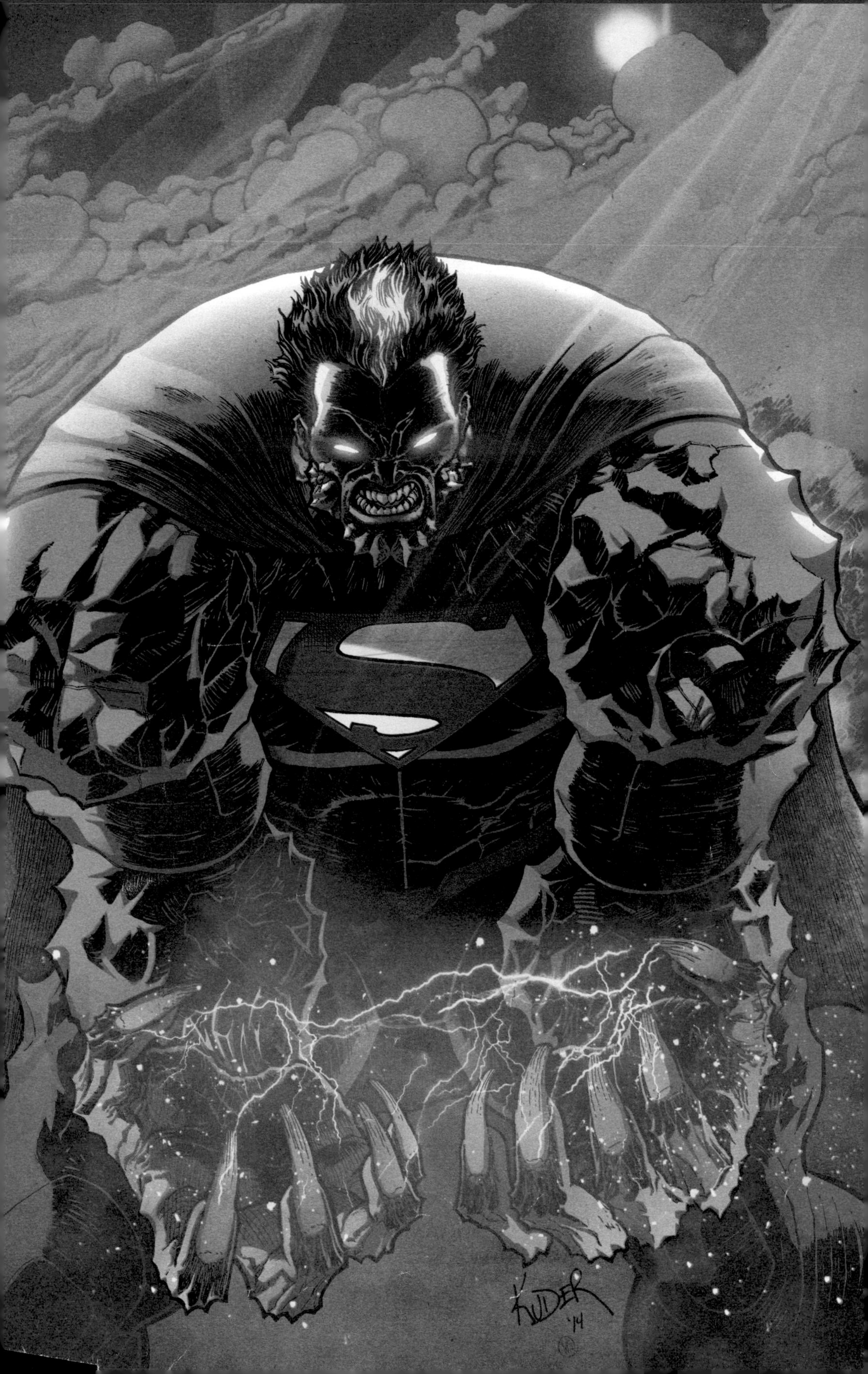
KUDER '14

WORLD   U.S.   METROPOLIS   BUSINESS   OPINION   SPORTS   ARTS   STYLE   VIDE

Daily Planet

July 30

HELP!

By Lois Lane

I don't know if this will reach anyone, but I want to let someone know that as strange as it sounds, my body has become a cage for me. I am trapped doing the bidding of another; and, I have done terrible, horrible things in the name of the one known as the Collector—that is just one of the many names, one of the many aspects of this being. But to know Brainwyrm, Mind2, Abbakus or Brainiac is to be witness to the end of your world.

I fear that I have brought about our end. It started with my investigation into "the Twenty," individuals who went missing after Metropolis was shrunken and taken by Brainiac 5 years ago. My leads eventually led me to Senator Milton Hume and my demise. I died at his hands as his mind passed on to me the 12 level intellect that he had been burdened with from our encounter with Brainiac. I was reborn with unlimited mental abilities, and I began

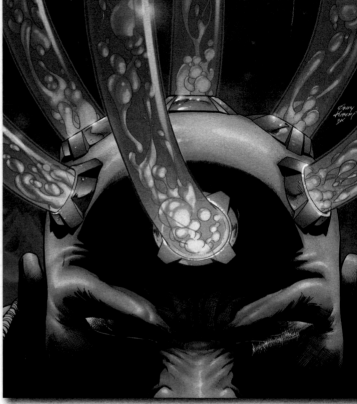

Artis Rendering : And

what became known as the Psi-War in an effort to control every other Psi's on Earth. Erroneously, I believed Superman to have saved me and freed me from this curse, but he had just caused the powers to become dormant, waiting until He was ready to summon me.

I have cleared the path for H His machines come to prepare world for collection.

Is there anyone out there that save us?

Stop me?

Superman, where are you?

 X   Slideshow - Superdoom's Path of Destruction

404 Error
404 Error
404 Error

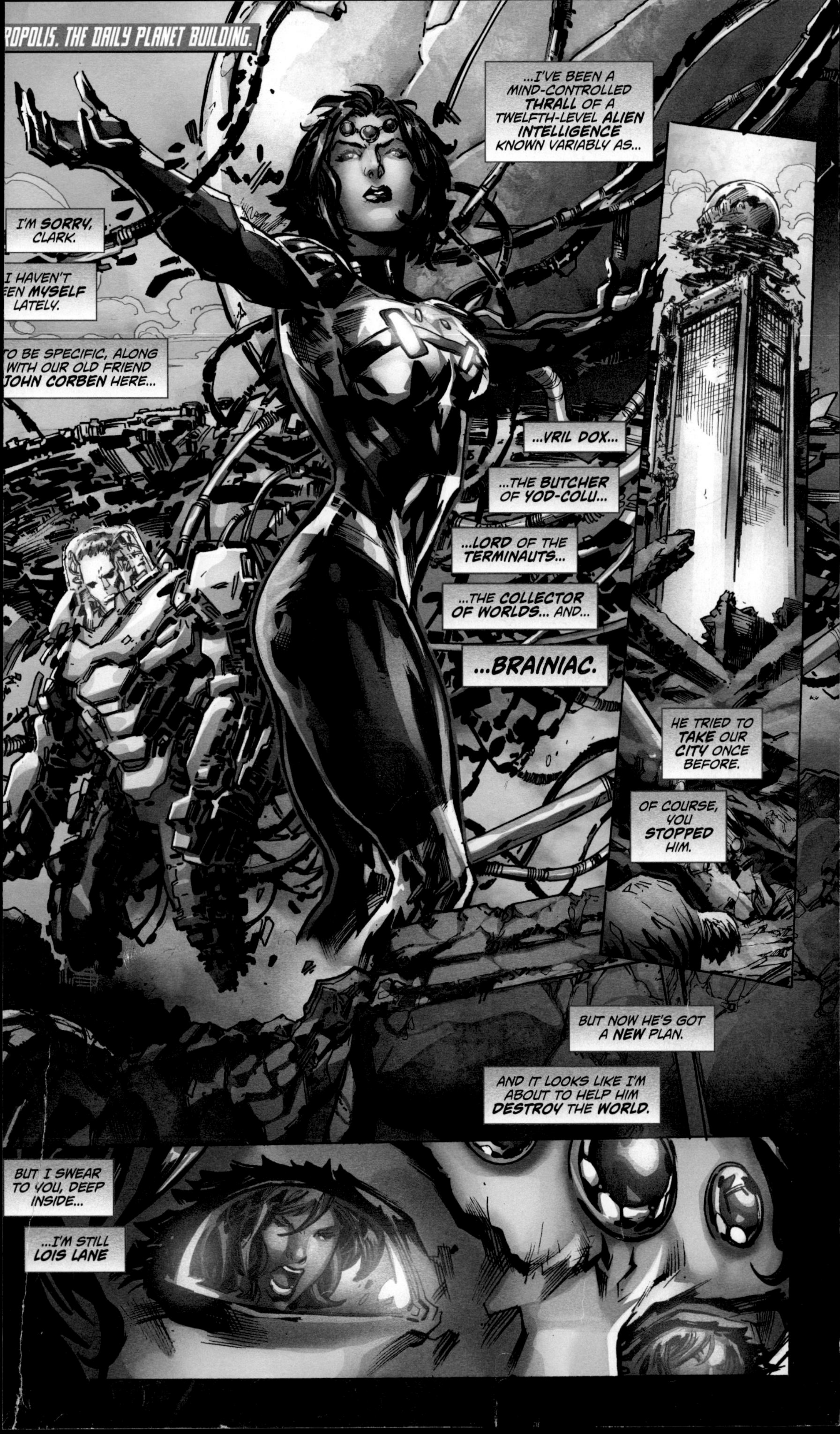
ROPOLIS. THE DAILY PLANET BUILDING.
I'M SORRY, CLARK.
I HAVEN'T EEN MYSELF LATELY.
TO BE SPECIFIC, ALONG WITH OUR OLD FRIEND JOHN CORBEN HERE...
...I'VE BEEN A MIND-CONTROLLED THRALL OF A TWELFTH-LEVEL ALIEN INTELLIGENCE KNOWN VARIABLY AS...
...VRIL DOX...
...THE BUTCHER OF YOD-COLU...
...LORD OF THE TERMINAUTS...
...THE COLLECTOR OF WORLDS... AND...
...BRAINIAC.
HE TRIED TO TAKE OUR CITY ONCE BEFORE.
OF COURSE, YOU STOPPED HIM.
BUT NOW HE'S GOT A NEW PLAN.
AND IT LOOKS LIKE I'M ABOUT TO HELP HIM DESTROY THE WORLD.
BUT I SWEAR TO YOU, DEEP INSIDE...
...I'M STILL LOIS LANE

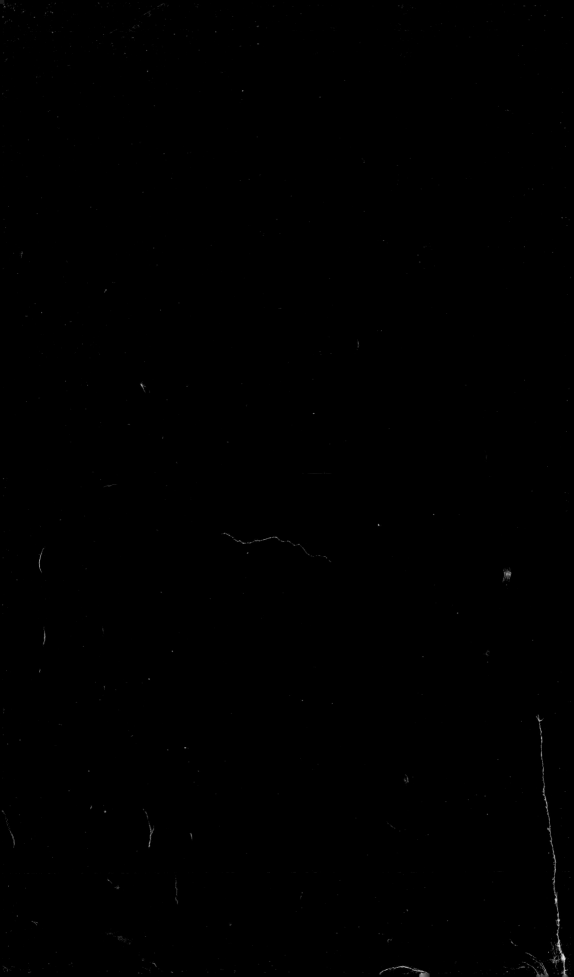

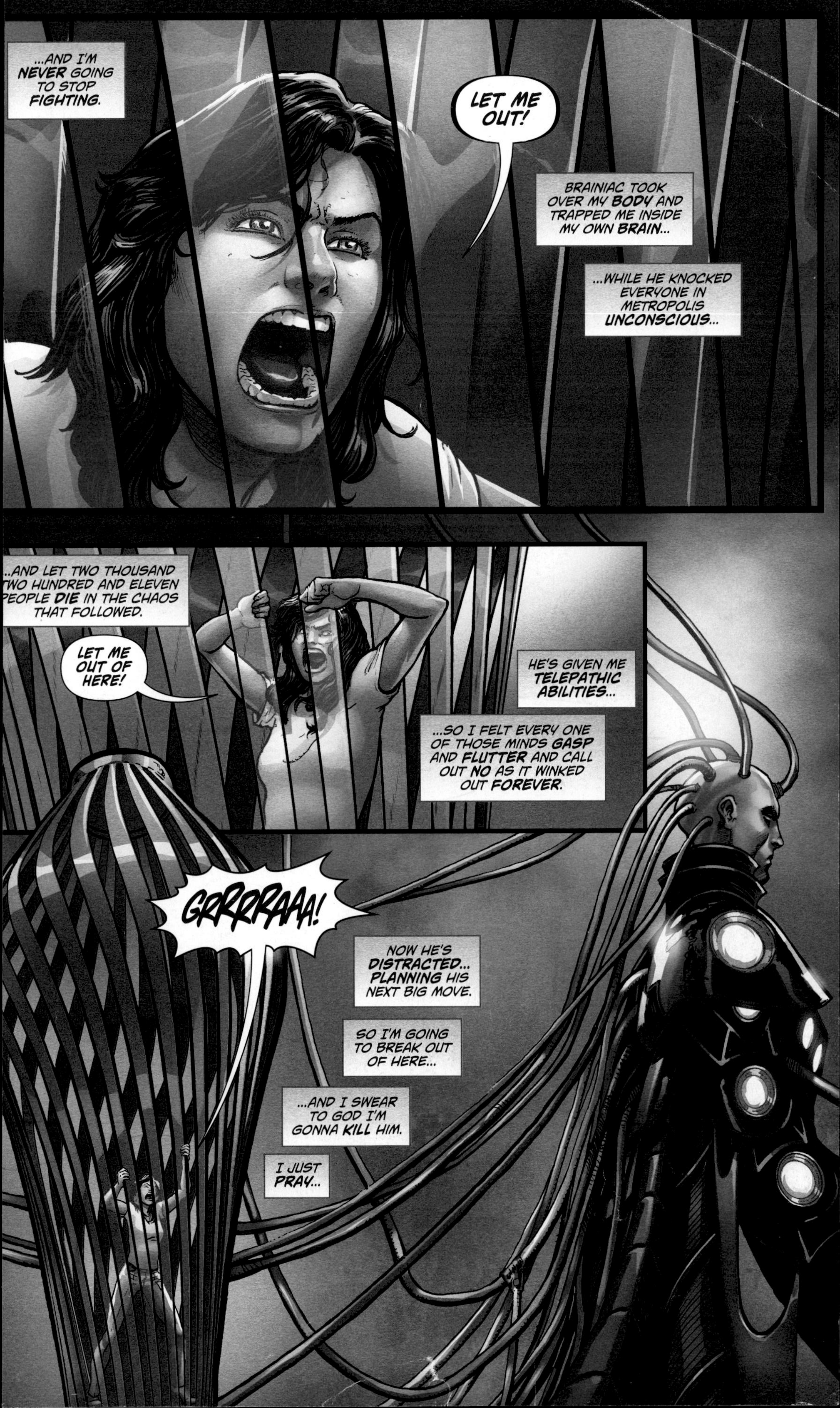
...AND I'M NEVER GOING TO STOP FIGHTING.
LET ME OUT!
BRAINIAC TOOK OVER MY BODY AND TRAPPED ME INSIDE MY OWN BRAIN...
...WHILE HE KNOCKED EVERYONE IN METROPOLIS UNCONSCIOUS...
...AND LET TWO THOUSAND TWO HUNDRED AND ELEVEN PEOPLE DIE IN THE CHAOS THAT FOLLOWED.
LET ME OUT OF HERE!
HE'S GIVEN ME TELEPATHIC ABILITIES...
...SO I FELT EVERY ONE OF THOSE MINDS GASP AND FLUTTER AND CALL OUT NO AS IT WINKED OUT FOREVER.
GRRRRAAA!
NOW HE'S DISTRACTED... PLANNING HIS NEXT BIG MOVE.
SO I'M GOING TO BREAK OUT OF HERE...
...AND I SWEAR TO GOD I'M GONNA KILL HIM.
I JUST PRAY...

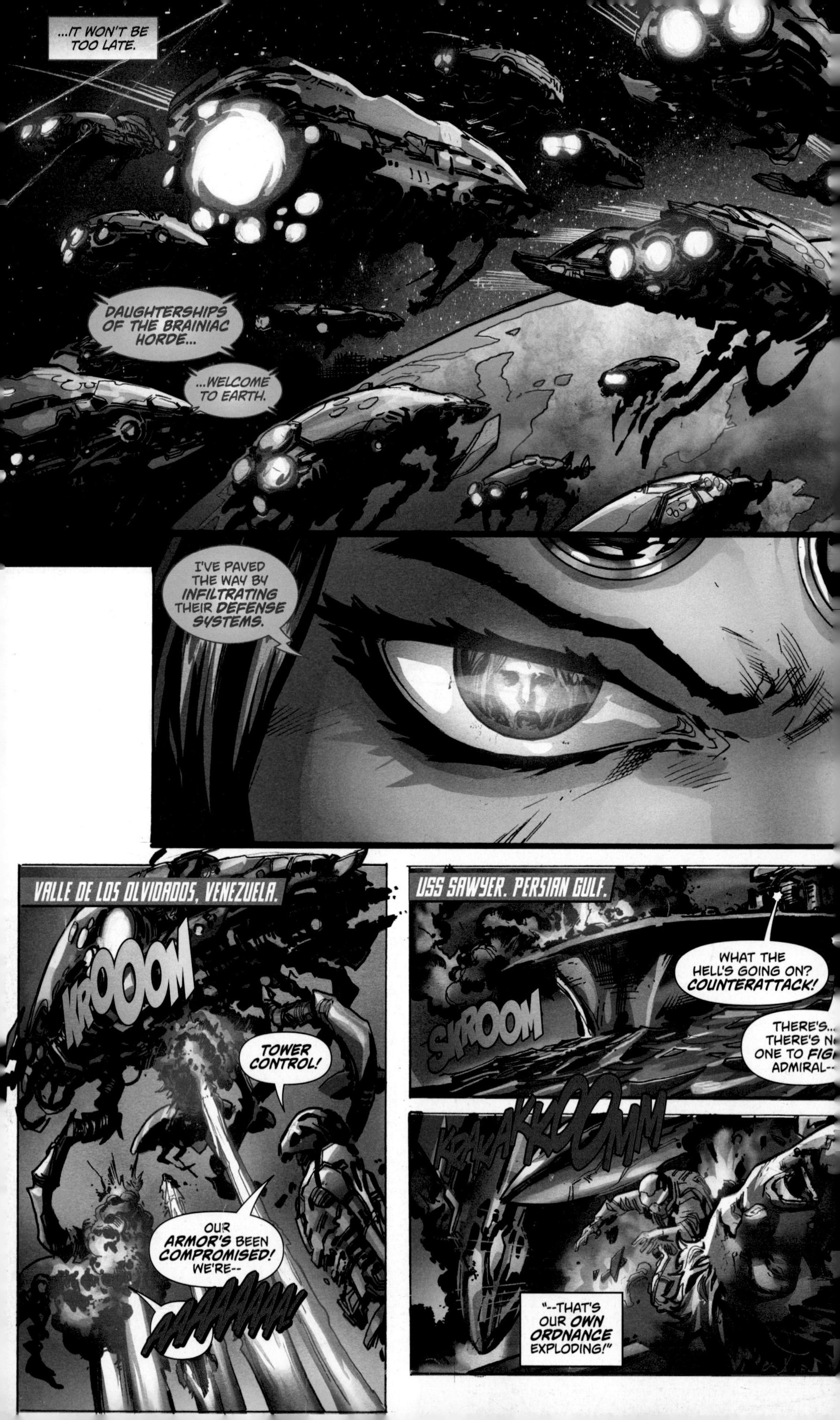
...IT WON'T BE TOO LATE.
DAUGHTERSHIPS OF THE BRAINIAC HORDE...
...WELCOME TO EARTH.
I'VE PAVED THE WAY BY INFILTRATING THEIR DEFENSE SYSTEMS.
VALLE DE LOS OLVIDADOS, VENEZUELA.
KROOOM
TOWER CONTROL!
OUR ARMOR'S BEEN COMPROMISED! WE'RE--
AAAAAAAA!
USS SAWYER. PERSIAN GULF.
WHAT THE HELL'S GOING ON? COUNTERATTACK!
SKROOM
THERE'S... THERE'S N ONE TO FIG ADMIRAL--
KRAKAKKOOMM
"--THAT'S OUR OWN ORDNANCE EXPLODING!"

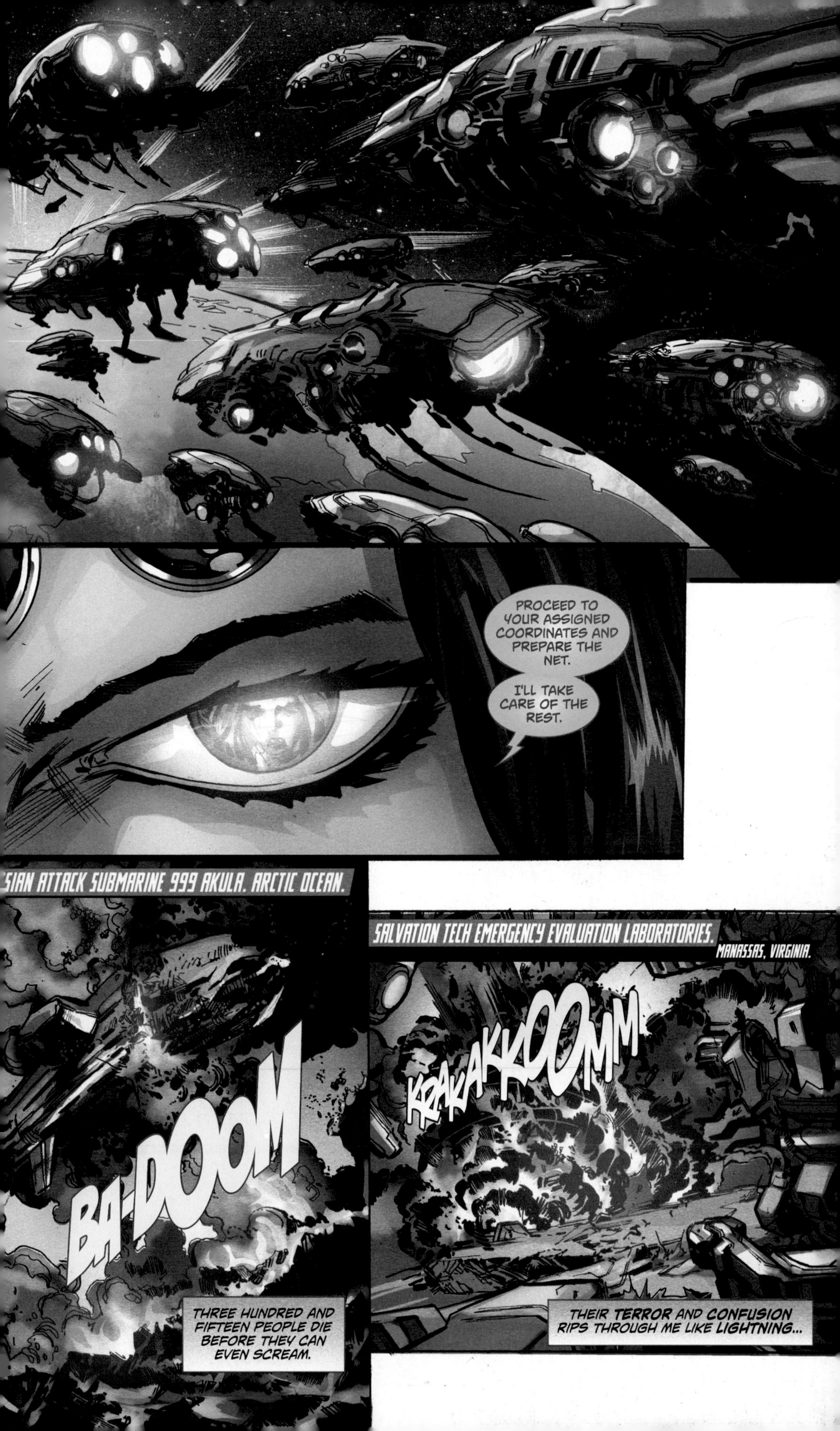
PROCEED TO YOUR ASSIGNED COORDINATES AND PREPARE THE NET.
I'LL TAKE CARE OF THE REST.
SIAN ATTACK SUBMARINE 999 AKULA. ARCTIC OCEAN.
BA-DOOM
THREE HUNDRED AND FIFTEEN PEOPLE DIE BEFORE THEY CAN EVEN SCREAM.
SALVATION TECH EMERGENCY EVALUATION LABORATORIES.
MANASSAS, VIRGINIA.
KRAKAKKOOMM
THEIR TERROR AND CONFUSION RIPS THROUGH ME LIKE LIGHTNING...

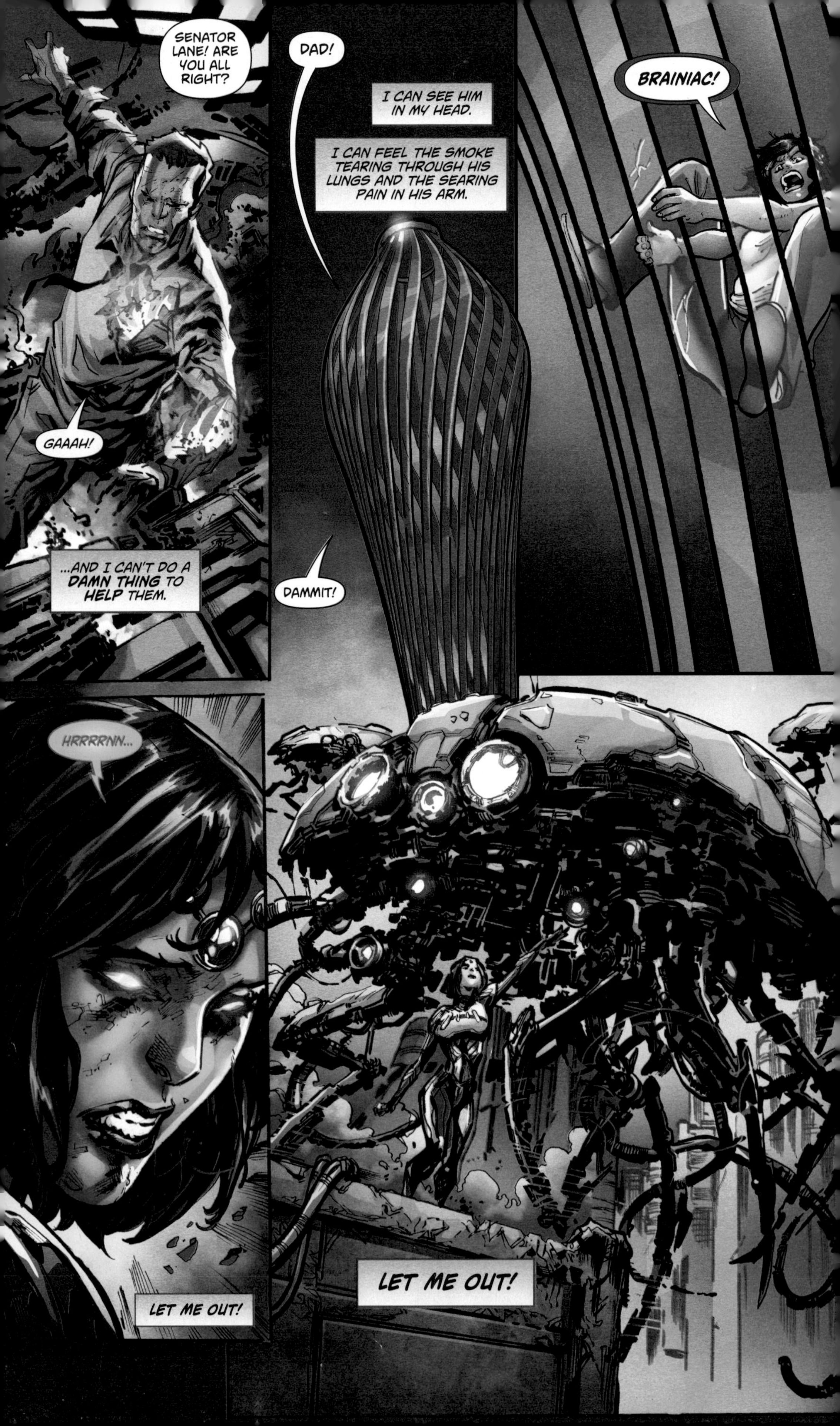
SENATOR LANE! ARE YOU ALL RIGHT?
GAAAH!
...AND I CAN'T DO A DAMN THING TO HELP THEM.
DAD!
I CAN SEE HIM IN MY HEAD.
I CAN FEEL THE SMOKE TEARING THROUGH HIS LUNGS AND THE SEARING PAIN IN HIS ARM.
DAMMIT!
BRAINIAC!
HRRRRNN...
LET ME OUT!
LET ME OUT!

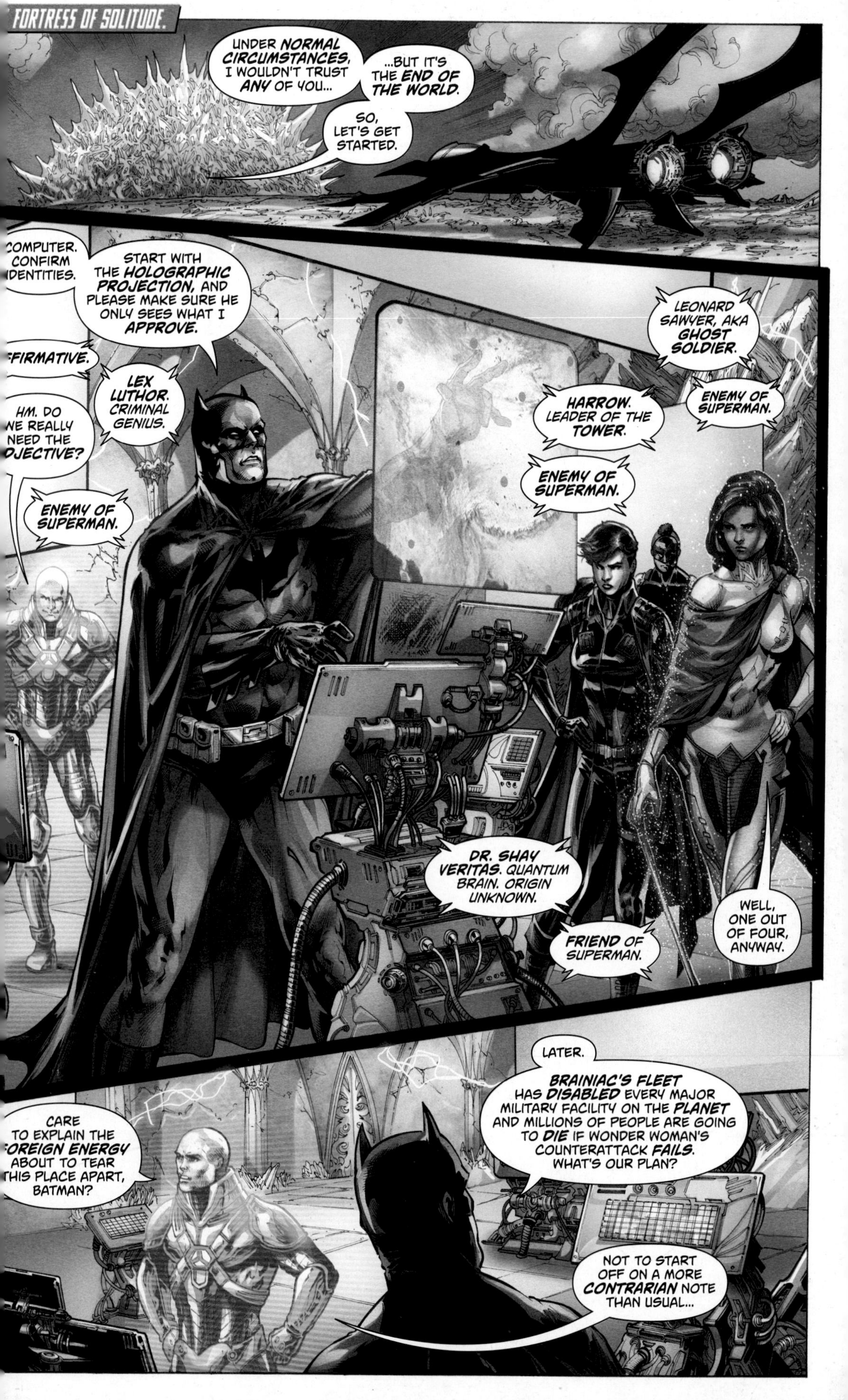
FORTRESS OF SOLITUDE.
UNDER NORMAL CIRCUMSTANCES, I WOULDN'T TRUST ANY OF YOU...
...BUT IT'S THE END OF THE WORLD.
SO, LET'S GET STARTED.
COMPUTER. CONFIRM IDENTITIES.
START WITH THE HOLOGRAPHIC PROJECTION, AND PLEASE MAKE SURE HE ONLY SEES WHAT I APPROVE.
FFIRMATIVE.
LEX LUTHOR. CRIMINAL GENIUS.
HM. DO WE REALLY NEED THE OBJECTIVE?
ENEMY OF SUPERMAN.
HARROW. LEADER OF THE TOWER.
ENEMY OF SUPERMAN.
LEONARD SAWYER, AKA GHOST SOLDIER.
ENEMY OF SUPERMAN.
DR. SHAY VERITAS. QUANTUM BRAIN. ORIGIN UNKNOWN.
FRIEND OF SUPERMAN.
WELL, ONE OUT OF FOUR, ANYWAY.
CARE TO EXPLAIN THE FOREIGN ENERGY ABOUT TO TEAR THIS PLACE APART, BATMAN?
LATER.
BRAINIAC'S FLEET HAS DISABLED EVERY MAJOR MILITARY FACILITY ON THE PLANET AND MILLIONS OF PEOPLE ARE GOING TO DIE IF WONDER WOMAN'S COUNTERATTACK FAILS. WHAT'S OUR PLAN?
NOT TO START OFF ON A MORE CONTRARIAN NOTE THAN USUAL...

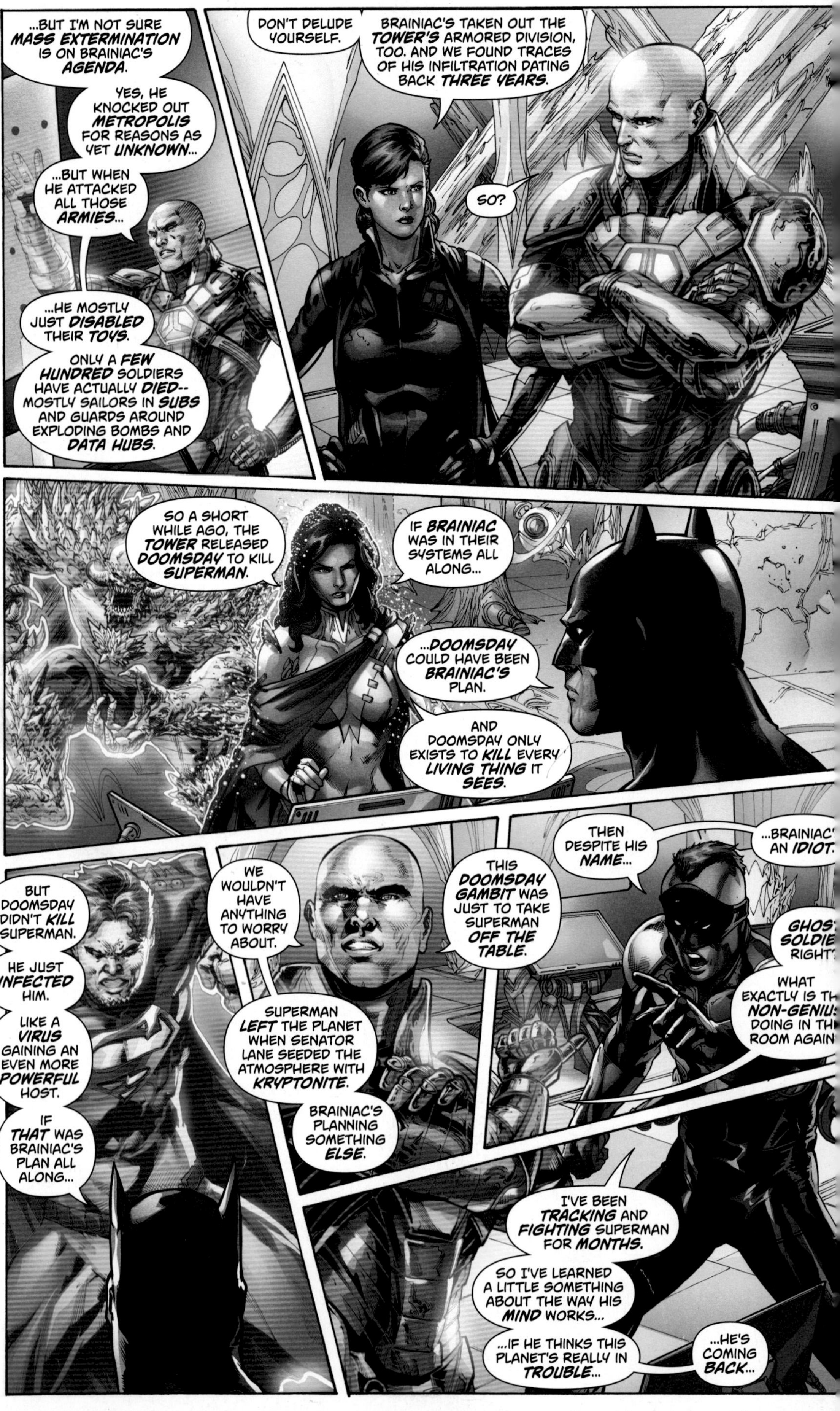
...BUT I'M NOT SURE MASS EXTERMINATION IS ON BRAINIAC'S AGENDA.
YES, HE KNOCKED OUT METROPOLIS FOR REASONS AS YET UNKNOWN...
...BUT WHEN HE ATTACKED ALL THOSE ARMIES...
...HE MOSTLY JUST DISABLED THEIR TOYS.
ONLY A FEW HUNDRED SOLDIERS HAVE ACTUALLY DIED-- MOSTLY SAILORS IN SUBS AND GUARDS AROUND EXPLODING BOMBS AND DATA HUBS.
DON'T DELUDE YOURSELF.
BRAINIAC'S TAKEN OUT THE TOWER'S ARMORED DIVISION, TOO. AND WE FOUND TRACES OF HIS INFILTRATION DATING BACK THREE YEARS.
SO?
SO A SHORT WHILE AGO, THE TOWER RELEASED DOOMSDAY TO KILL SUPERMAN.
IF BRAINIAC WAS IN THEIR SYSTEMS ALL ALONG...
...DOOMSDAY COULD HAVE BEEN BRAINIAC'S PLAN.
AND DOOMSDAY ONLY EXISTS TO KILL EVERY LIVING THING IT SEES.
BUT DOOMSDAY DIDN'T KILL SUPERMAN.
HE JUST INFECTED HIM.
LIKE A VIRUS GAINING AN EVEN MORE POWERFUL HOST.
IF THAT WAS BRAINIAC'S PLAN ALL ALONG...
WE WOULDN'T HAVE ANYTHING TO WORRY ABOUT.
SUPERMAN LEFT THE PLANET WHEN SENATOR LANE SEEDED THE ATMOSPHERE WITH KRYPTONITE.
BRAINIAC'S PLANNING SOMETHING ELSE.
THIS DOOMSDAY GAMBIT WAS JUST TO TAKE SUPERMAN OFF THE TABLE.
THEN DESPITE HIS NAME...
...BRAINIAC' AN IDIOT.
GHOS SOLDIE RIGHT
WHAT EXACTLY IS TH NON-GENIU DOING IN TH ROOM AGAIN
I'VE BEEN TRACKING AND FIGHTING SUPERMAN FOR MONTHS.
SO I'VE LEARNED A LITTLE SOMETHING ABOUT THE WAY HIS MIND WORKS...
...IF HE THINKS THIS PLANET'S REALLY IN TROUBLE...
...HE'S COMING BACK...

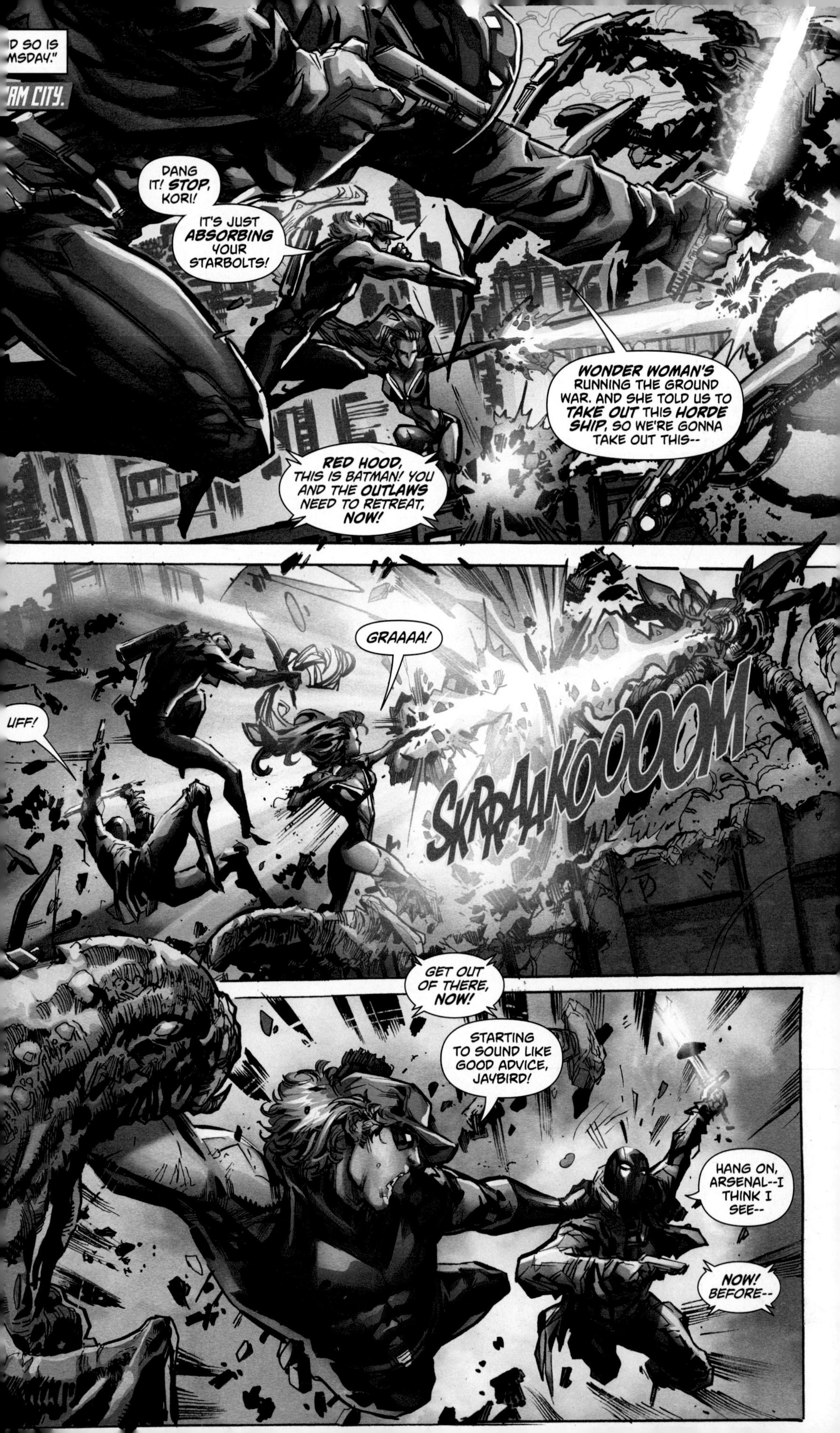

D SO IS
MSDAY."
AM CITY.
DANG IT! STOP, KORI!
IT'S JUST ABSORBING YOUR STARBOLTS!
WONDER WOMAN'S RUNNING THE GROUND WAR. AND SHE TOLD US TO TAKE OUT THIS HORDE SHIP, SO WE'RE GONNA TAKE OUT THIS--
RED HOOD, THIS IS BATMAN! YOU AND THE OUTLAWS NEED TO RETREAT, NOW!
GRAAAA!
UFF!
SKRRAAKOOOOM
GET OUT OF THERE, NOW!
STARTING TO SOUND LIKE GOOD ADVICE, JAYBIRD!
HANG ON, ARSENAL--I THINK I SEE--
NOW! BEFORE--

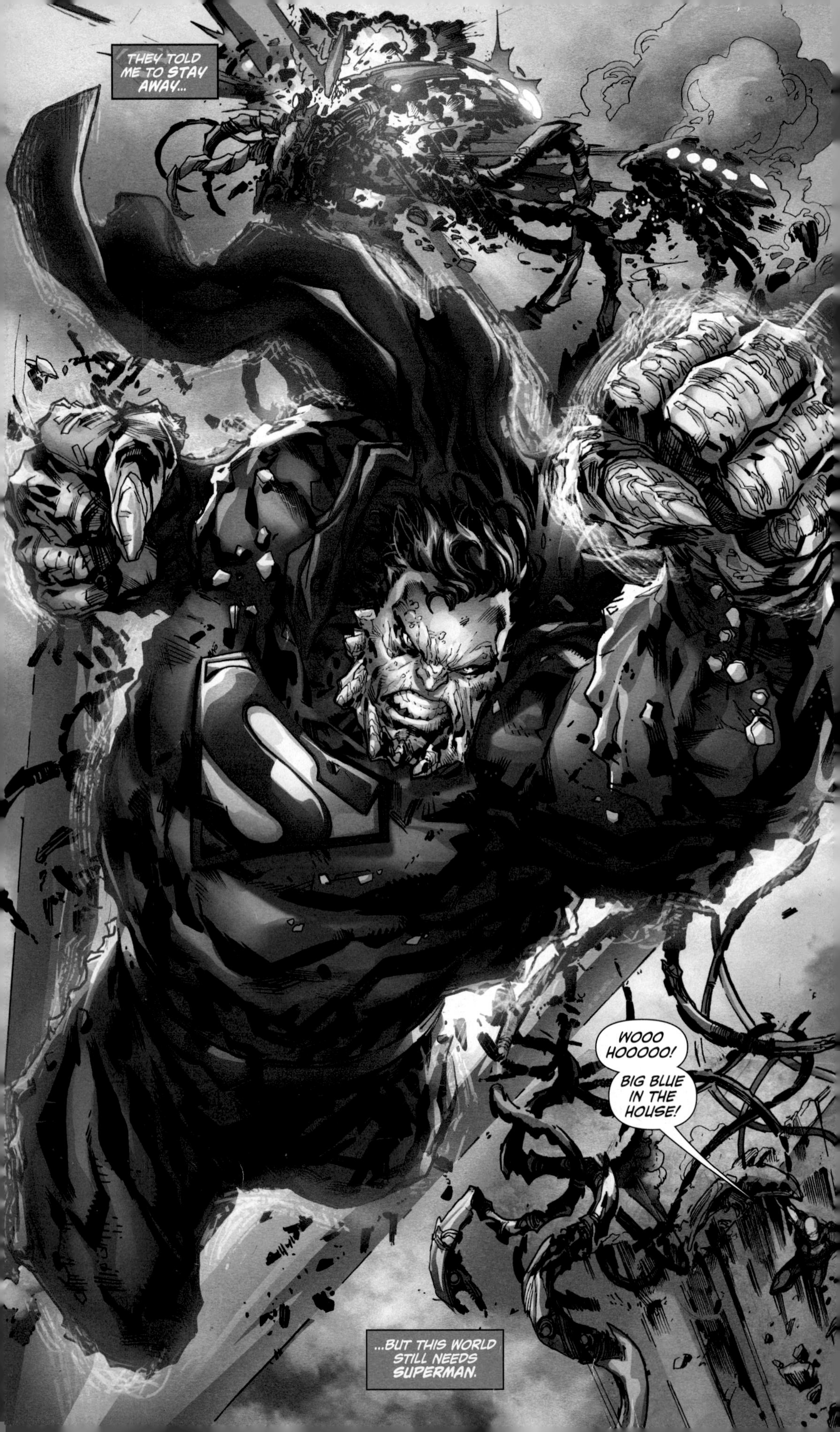
THEY TOLD ME TO STAY AWAY...
WOOO HOOOOO!
BIG BLUE IN THE HOUSE!
...BUT THIS WORLD STILL NEEDS SUPERMAN.

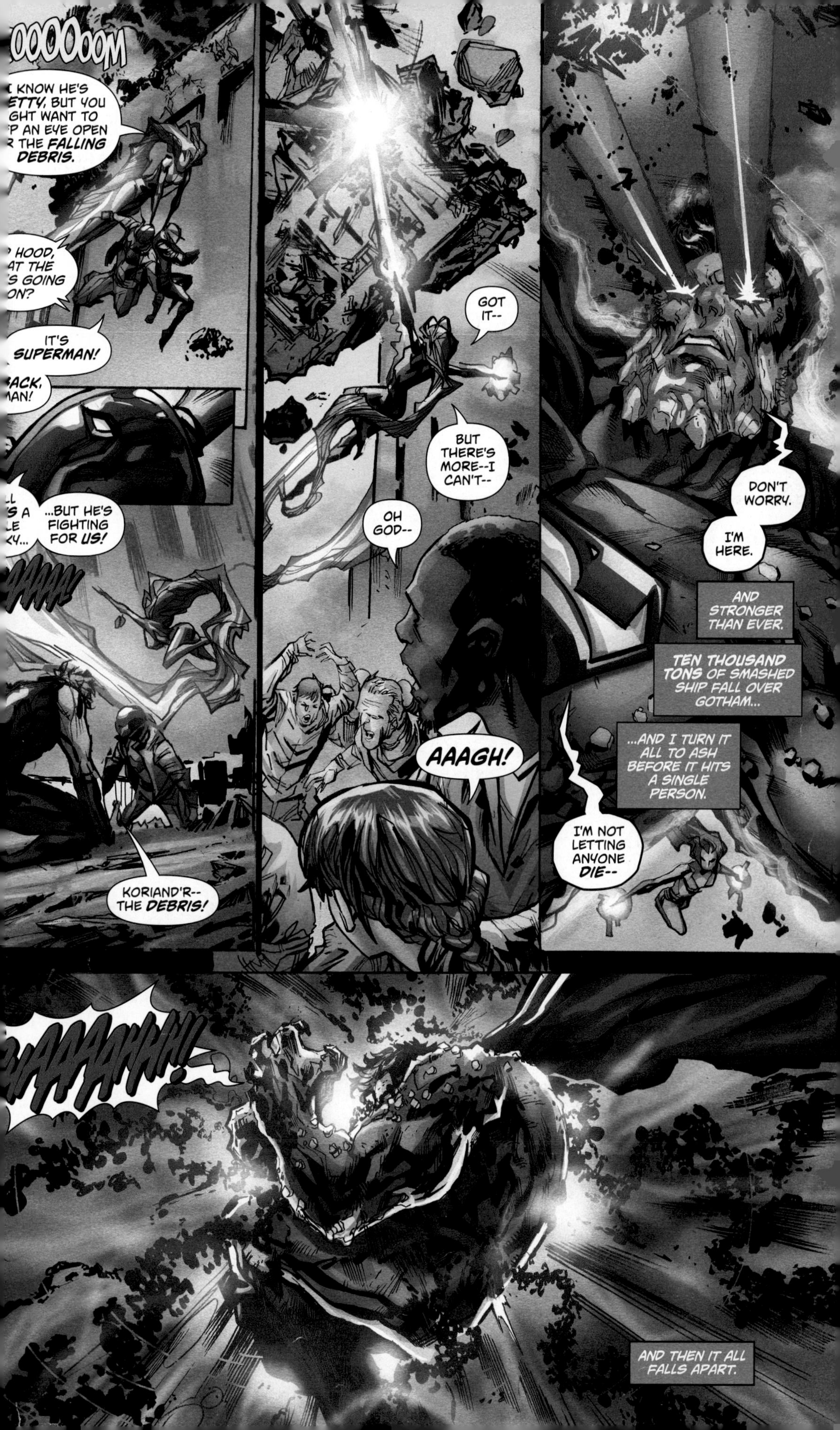

OOOOOOOM
I KNOW HE'S ETTY, BUT YOU GHT WANT TO P AN EYE OPEN R THE FALLING DEBRIS.
P HOOD, AT THE 'S GOING ON?
IT'S SUPERMAN!
BACK, MAN!
...BUT HE'S FIGHTING FOR US!
KORIAND'R-- THE DEBRIS!
GOT IT--
BUT THERE'S MORE--I CAN'T--
OH GOD--
AAAGH!
DON'T WORRY.
I'M HERE.
AND STRONGER THAN EVER.
TEN THOUSAND TONS OF SMASHED SHIP FALL OVER GOTHAM...
...AND I TURN IT ALL TO ASH BEFORE IT HITS A SINGLE PERSON.
I'M NOT LETTING ANYONE DIE--
AND THEN IT ALL FALLS APART.

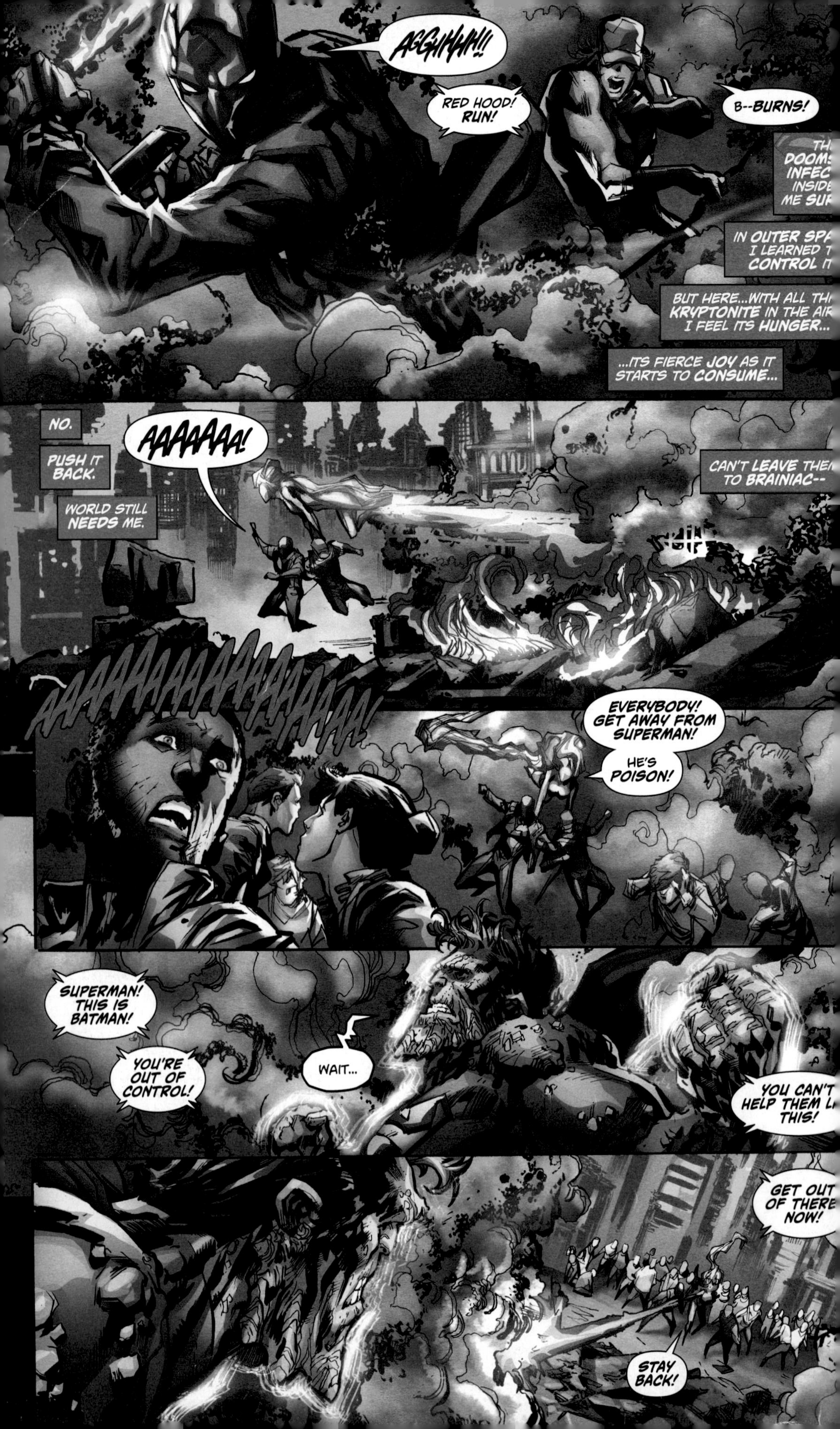
AGGHHH!!
RED HOOD! RUN!
B--BURNS!
TH DOOMS INFEC INSIDE ME SUR
IN OUTER SPA I LEARNED T CONTROL IT
BUT HERE...WITH ALL THI KRYPTONITE IN THE AIR I FEEL ITS HUNGER...
...ITS FIERCE JOY AS IT STARTS TO CONSUME...
NO.
PUSH IT BACK.
WORLD STILL NEEDS ME.
AAAAAAA!
CAN'T LEAVE THEM TO BRAINIAC--
AAAAAAAAAAAAAAAAAAA!
EVERYBODY! GET AWAY FROM SUPERMAN!
HE'S POISON!
SUPERMAN! THIS IS BATMAN!
YOU'RE OUT OF CONTROL!
WAIT...
YOU CAN'T HELP THEM LI THIS!
GET OUT OF THERE NOW!
STAY BACK!

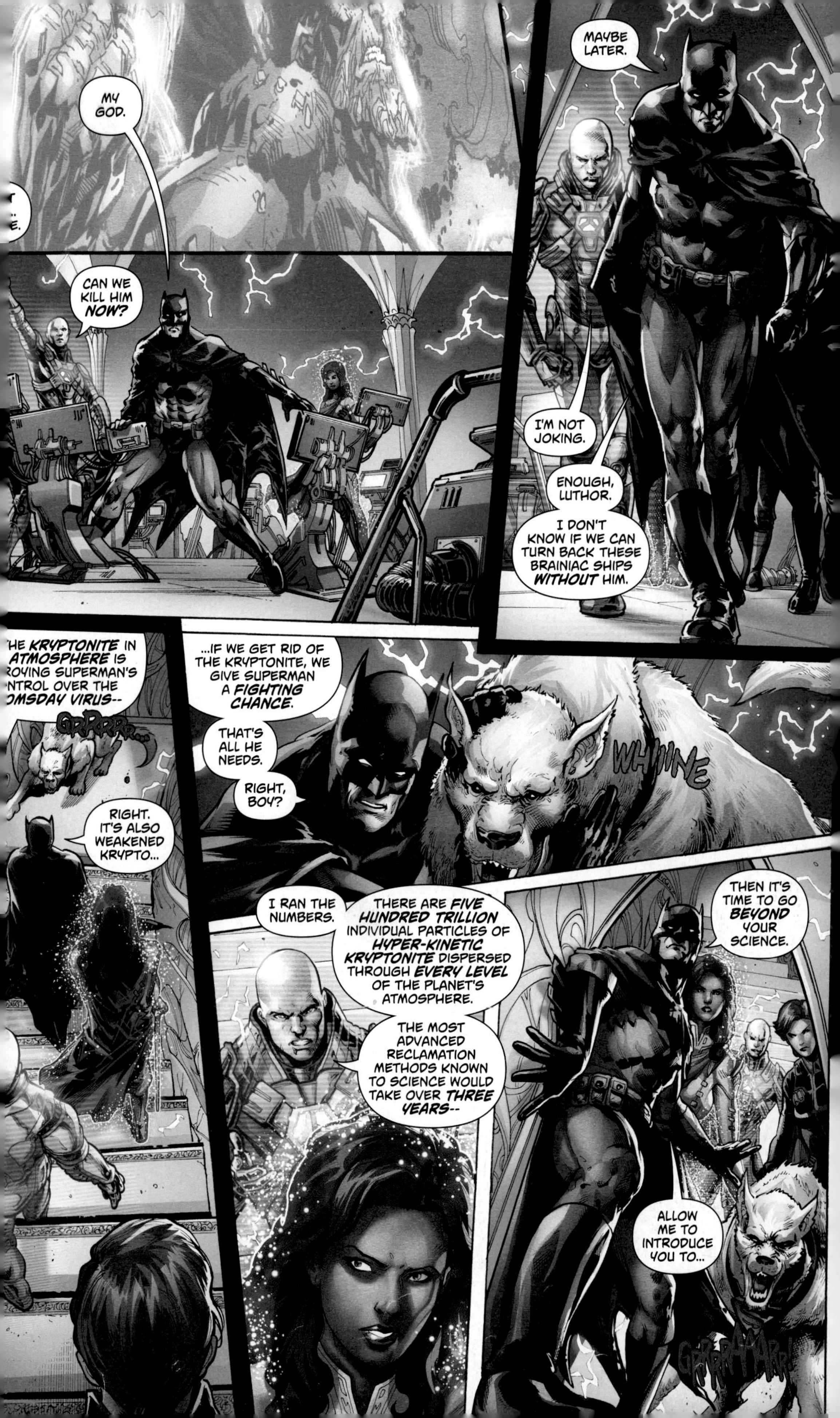
MY GOD.
CAN WE KILL HIM NOW?
MAYBE LATER.
I'M NOT JOKING.
ENOUGH, LUTHOR.
I DON'T KNOW IF WE CAN TURN BACK THESE BRAINIAC SHIPS WITHOUT HIM.
ATMOSPHERE IS
ROYING SUPERMAN'S
NTROL OVER THE
OMSDAY VIRUS--
GRRRRR...
RIGHT. IT'S ALSO WEAKENED KRYPTO...
...IF WE GET RID OF THE KRYPTONITE, WE GIVE SUPERMAN A FIGHTING CHANCE.
THAT'S ALL HE NEEDS.
RIGHT, BOY?
WHIIINE
I RAN THE NUMBERS.
THERE ARE FIVE HUNDRED TRILLION INDIVIDUAL PARTICLES OF HYPER-KINETIC KRYPTONITE DISPERSED THROUGH EVERY LEVEL OF THE PLANET'S ATMOSPHERE.
THE MOST ADVANCED RECLAMATION METHODS KNOWN TO SCIENCE WOULD TAKE OVER THREE YEARS--
THEN IT'S TIME TO GO BEYOND YOUR SCIENCE.
ALLOW ME TO INTRODUCE YOU TO...
GRRRAAARR!

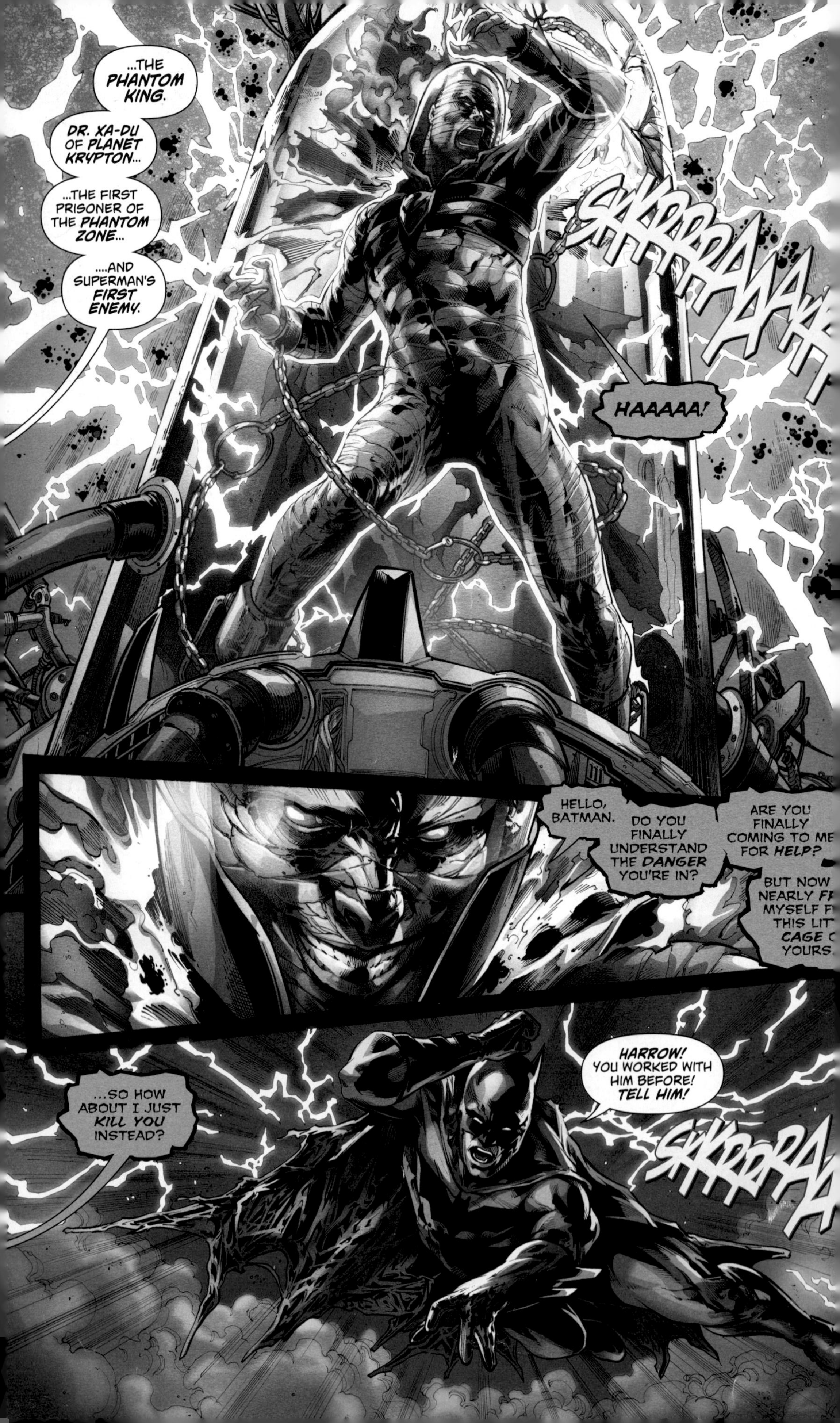

...THE PHANTOM KING.
DR. XA-DU OF PLANET KRYPTON...
...THE FIRST PRISONER OF THE PHANTOM ZONE...
....AND SUPERMAN'S FIRST ENEMY.
SKRRRAAAKK
HAAAAA!
HELLO, BATMAN.
DO YOU FINALLY UNDERSTAND THE DANGER YOU'RE IN?
ARE YOU FINALLY COMING TO ME FOR HELP?
...SO HOW ABOUT I JUST KILL YOU INSTEAD?
HARROW! YOU WORKED WITH HIM BEFORE! TELL HIM!
SKRRRAA

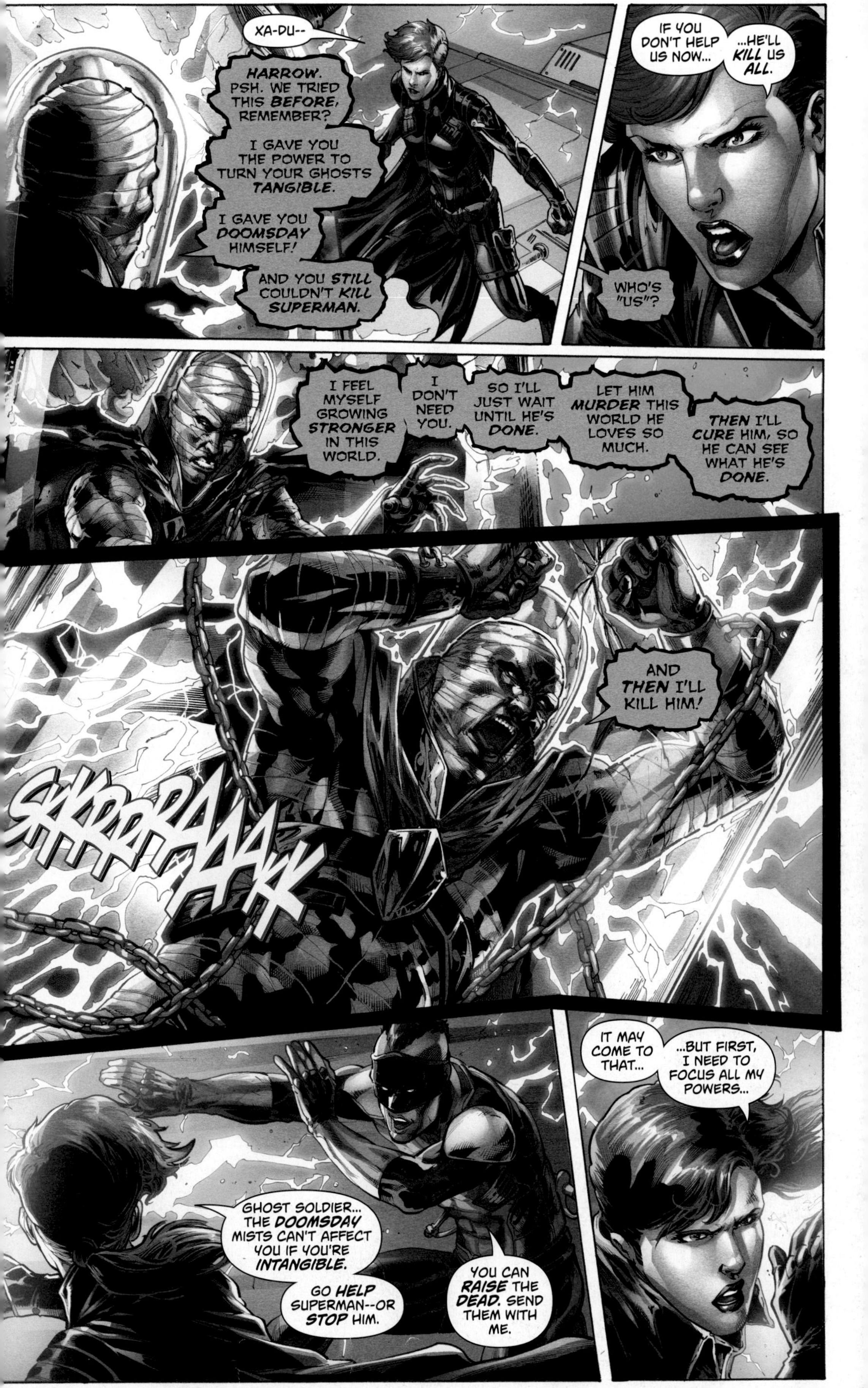
XA-DU--
HARROW. PSH. WE TRIED THIS BEFORE, REMEMBER?
I GAVE YOU THE POWER TO TURN YOUR GHOSTS TANGIBLE.
I GAVE YOU DOOMSDAY HIMSELF!
AND YOU STILL COULDN'T KILL SUPERMAN.
IF YOU DON'T HELP US NOW...
...HE'LL KILL US ALL.
WHO'S "US"?
I FEEL MYSELF GROWING STRONGER IN THIS WORLD.
I DON'T NEED YOU.
SO I'LL JUST WAIT UNTIL HE'S DONE.
LET HIM MURDER THIS WORLD HE LOVES SO MUCH.
THEN I'LL CURE HIM, SO HE CAN SEE WHAT HE'S DONE.
AND THEN I'LL KILL HIM!
SKRRRAAAKK
GHOST SOLDIER... THE DOOMSDAY MISTS CAN'T AFFECT YOU IF YOU'RE INTANGIBLE.
GO HELP SUPERMAN--OR STOP HIM.
YOU CAN RAISE THE DEAD. SEND THEM WITH ME.
IT MAY COME TO THAT...
...BUT FIRST, I NEED TO FOCUS ALL MY POWERS...

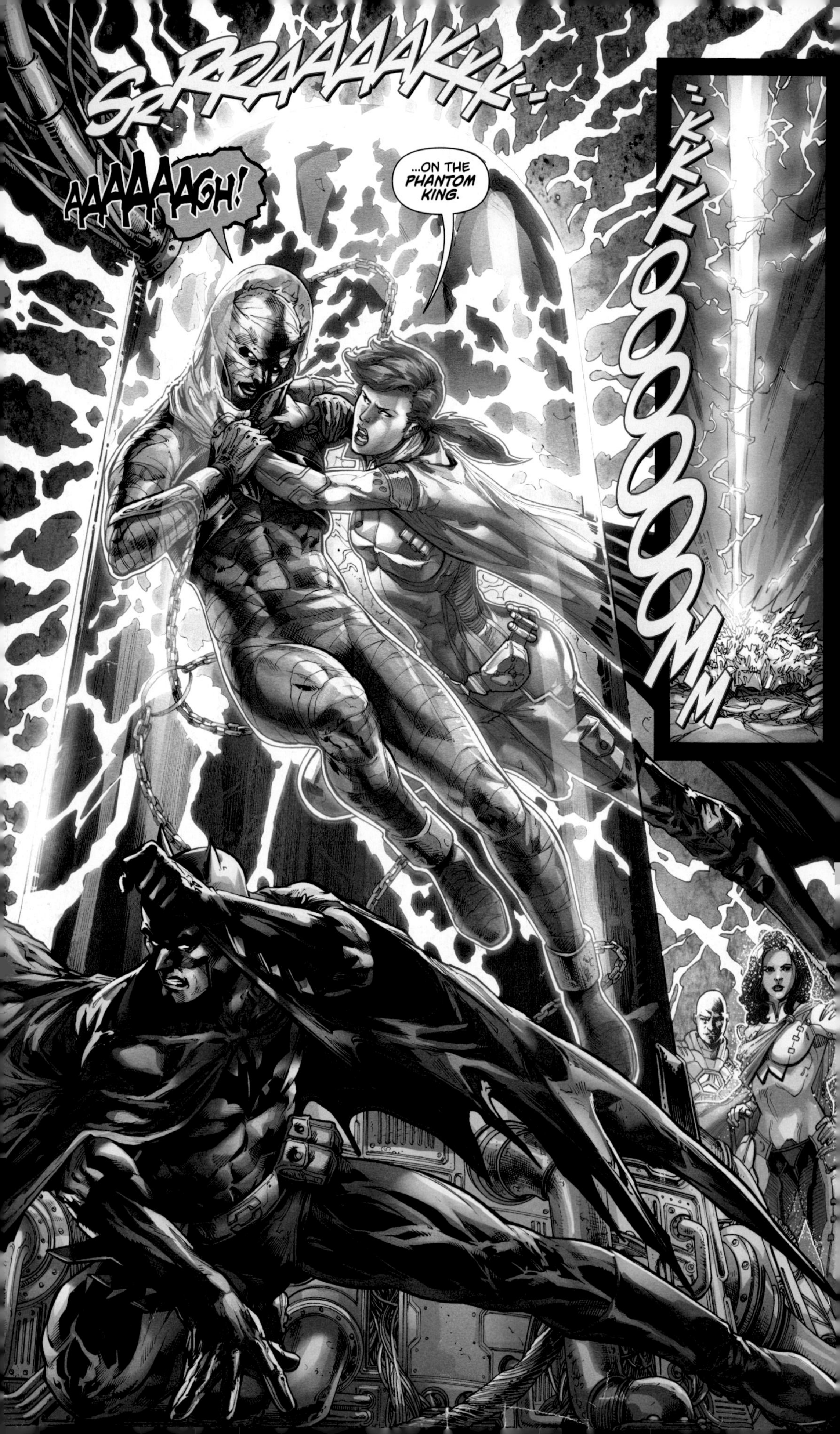

SRRRAAAAKKK--
AAAAAAGH!
...ON THE PHANTOM KING.
--KKKOOOOOOOMM

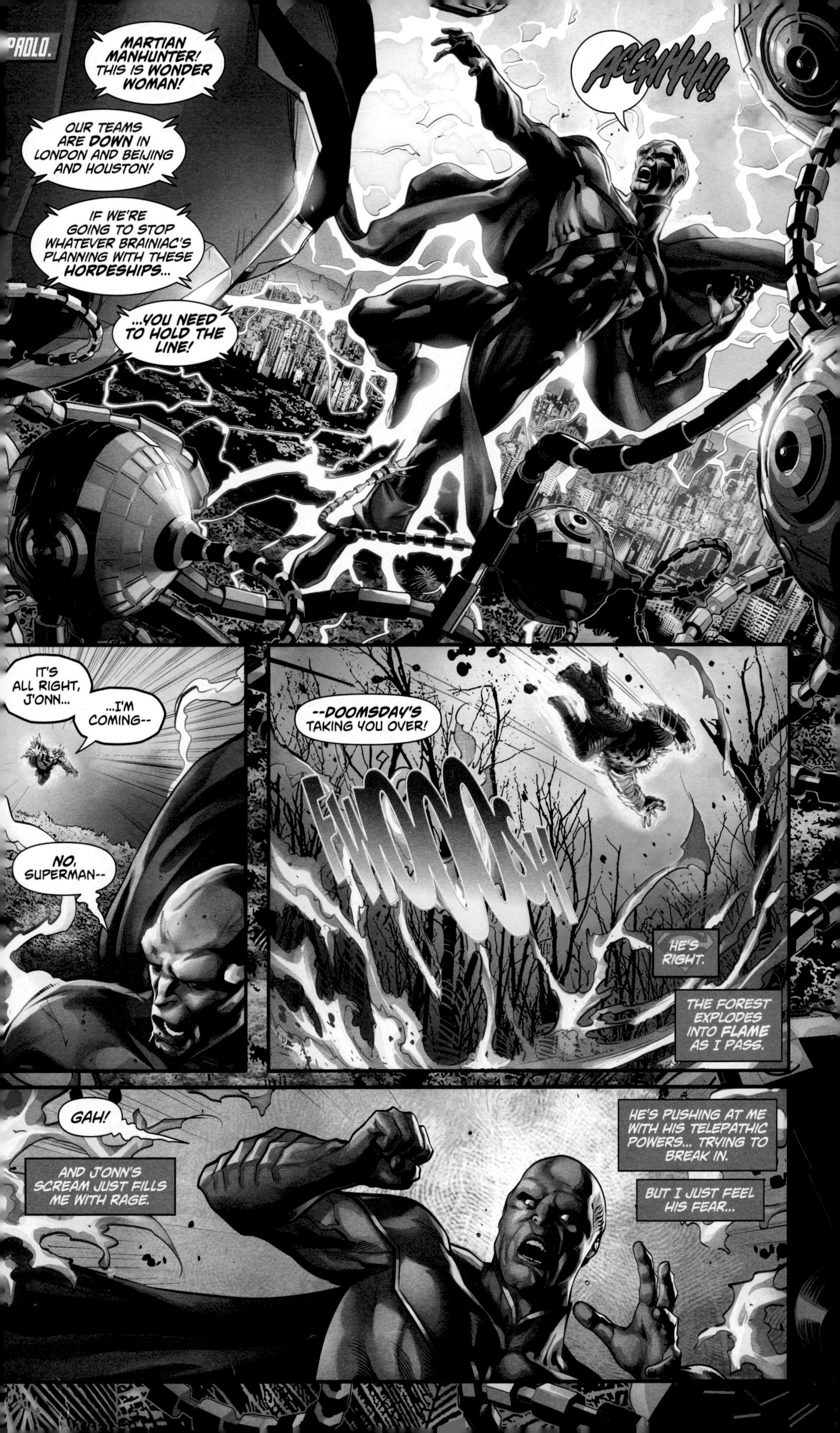
PAOLO.
MARTIAN MANHUNTER! THIS IS WONDER WOMAN!
OUR TEAMS ARE DOWN IN LONDON AND BEIJING AND HOUSTON!
IF WE'RE GOING TO STOP WHATEVER BRAINIAC'S PLANNING WITH THESE HORDESHIPS...
...YOU NEED TO HOLD THE LINE!
AGGHHHH!!
IT'S ALL RIGHT, J'ONN...
...I'M COMING--
NO, SUPERMAN--
--DOOMSDAY'S TAKING YOU OVER!
FWOOOOSH
HE'S RIGHT.
THE FOREST EXPLODES INTO FLAME AS I PASS.
GAH!
AND J'ONN'S SCREAM JUST FILLS ME WITH RAGE.
HE'S PUSHING AT ME WITH HIS TELEPATHIC POWERS... TRYING TO BREAK IN.
BUT I JUST FEEL HIS FEAR...

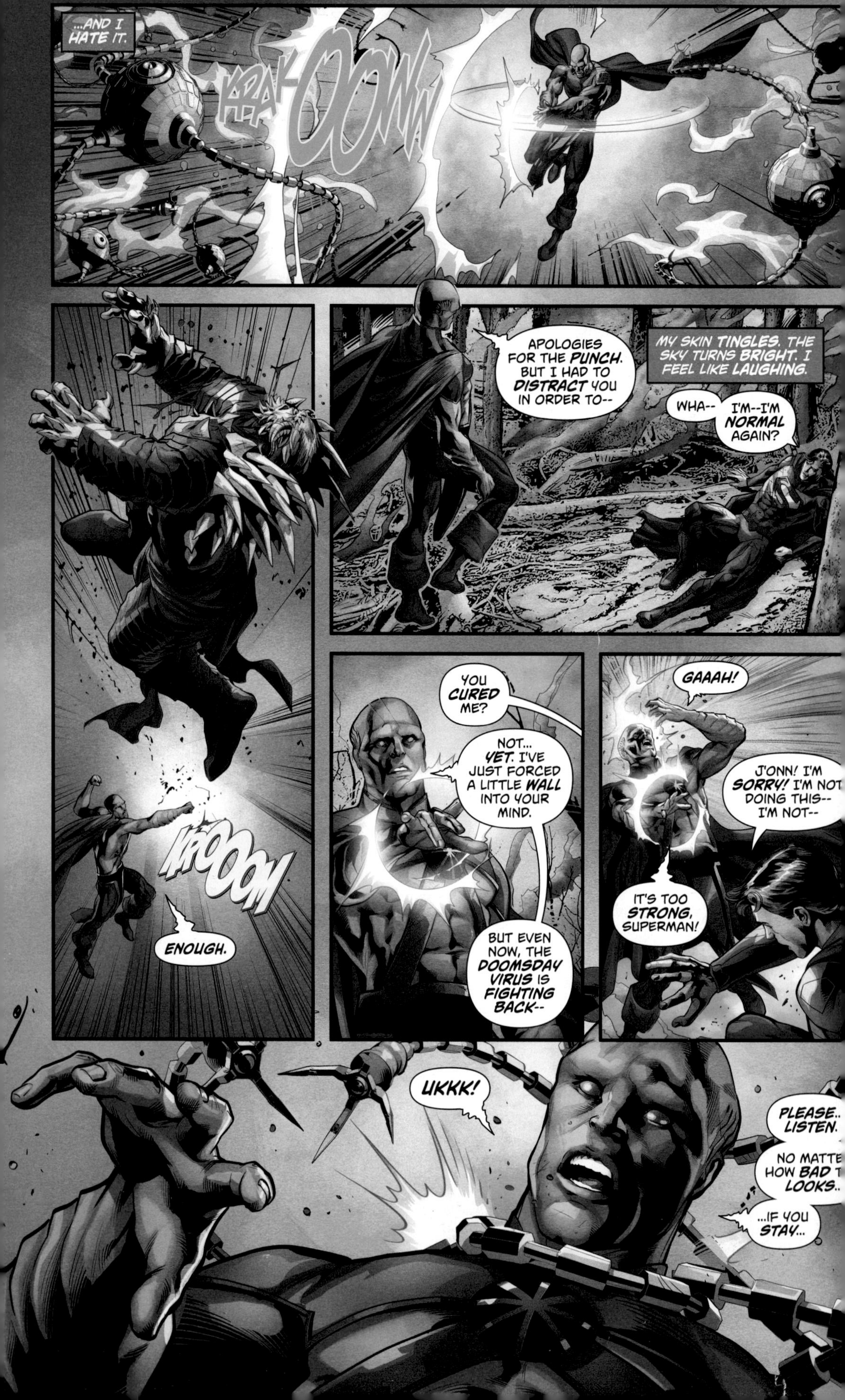

...AND I HATE IT.
KRAKOOOWW
APOLOGIES FOR THE PUNCH. BUT I HAD TO DISTRACT YOU IN ORDER TO--
MY SKIN TINGLES. THE SKY TURNS BRIGHT. I FEEL LIKE LAUGHING.
WHA--
I'M--I'M NORMAL AGAIN?
KROOOM
ENOUGH.
YOU CURED ME?
NOT... YET. I'VE JUST FORCED A LITTLE WALL INTO YOUR MIND.
BUT EVEN NOW, THE DOOMSDAY VIRUS IS FIGHTING BACK--
GAAAH!
J'ONN! I'M SORRY! I'M NOT DOING THIS-- I'M NOT--
IT'S TOO STRONG, SUPERMAN!
UKKK!
PLEASE... LISTEN.
NO MATTE HOW BAD LOOKS...
...IF YOU STAY...

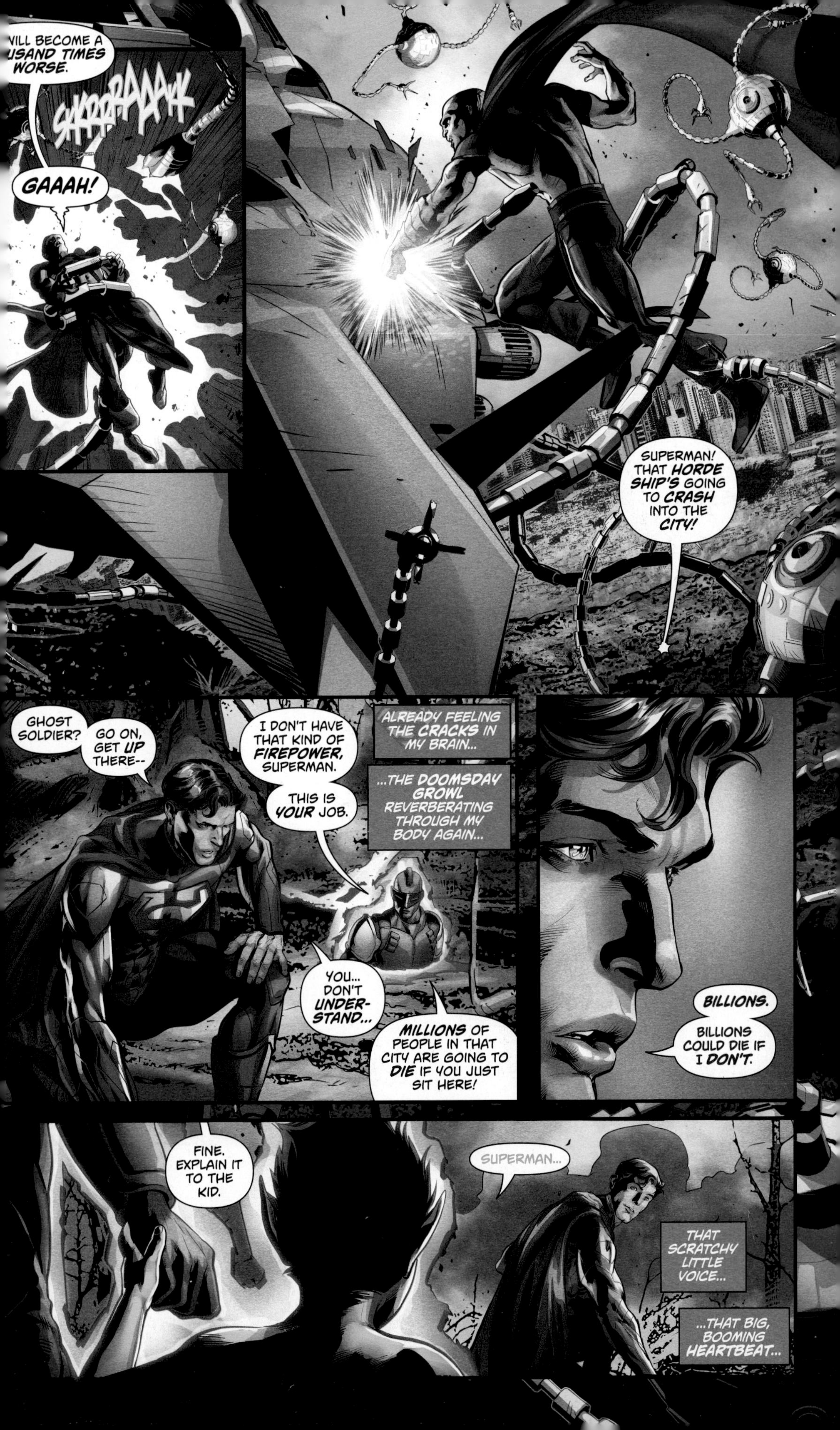

WILL BECOME A
USAND TIMES
WORSE.
SKRRRAAKK
GAAAH!
SUPERMAN! THAT HORDE SHIP'S GOING TO CRASH INTO THE CITY!
GHOST SOLDIER?
GO ON, GET UP THERE--
I DON'T HAVE THAT KIND OF FIREPOWER, SUPERMAN.
THIS IS YOUR JOB.
ALREADY FEELING THE CRACKS IN MY BRAIN...
...THE DOOMSDAY GROWL REVERBERATING THROUGH MY BODY AGAIN...
YOU... DON'T UNDER-STAND...
MILLIONS OF PEOPLE IN THAT CITY ARE GOING TO DIE IF YOU JUST SIT HERE!
BILLIONS.
BILLIONS COULD DIE IF I DON'T.
FINE. EXPLAIN IT TO THE KID.
SUPERMAN...
THAT SCRATCHY LITTLE VOICE...
...THAT BIG, BOOMING HEARTBEAT...

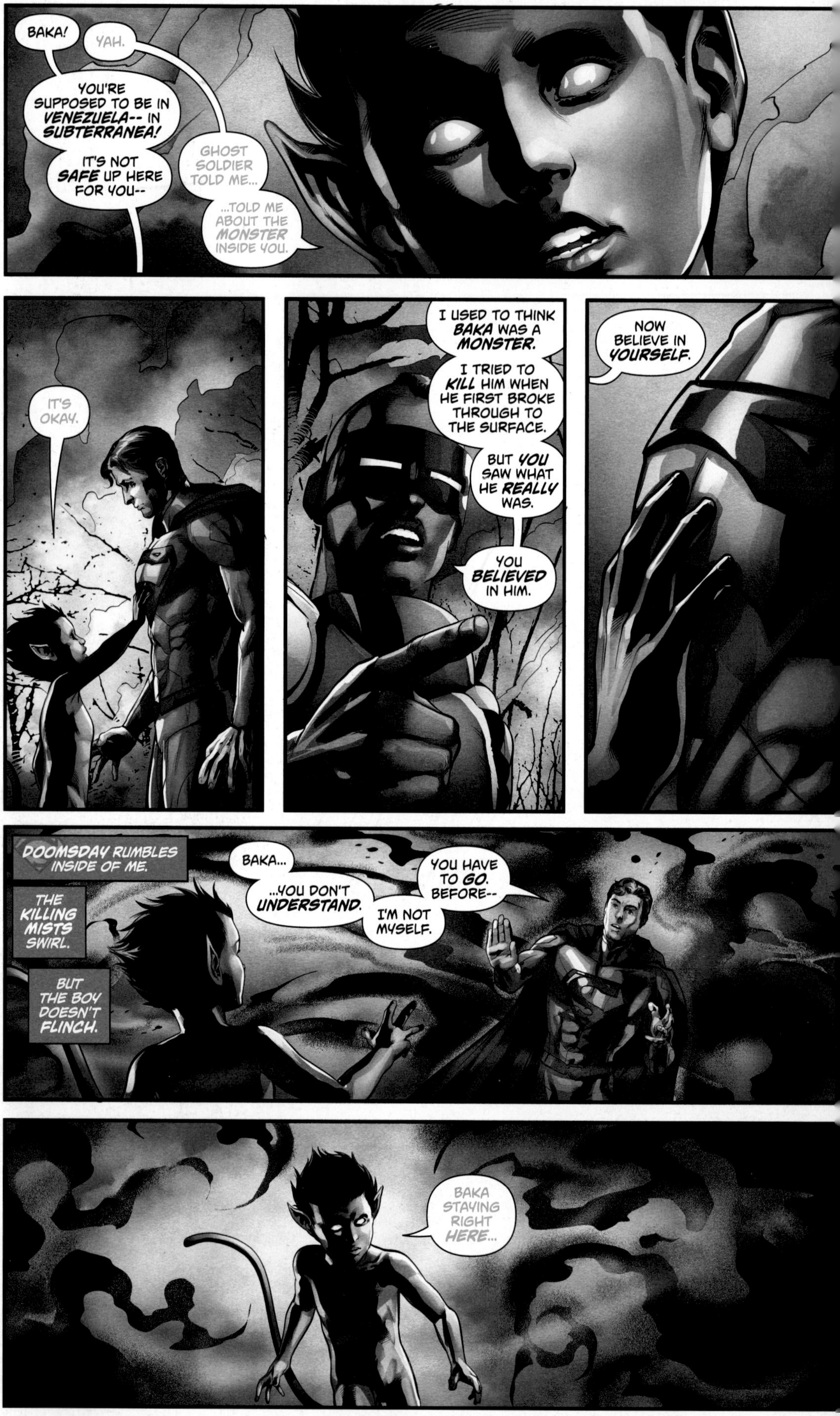
BAKA!
YAH.
YOU'RE SUPPOSED TO BE IN VENEZUELA-- IN SUBTERRANEA!
IT'S NOT SAFE UP HERE FOR YOU--
GHOST SOLDIER TOLD ME...
...TOLD ME ABOUT THE MONSTER INSIDE YOU.
IT'S OKAY.
I USED TO THINK BAKA WAS A MONSTER.
I TRIED TO KILL HIM WHEN HE FIRST BROKE THROUGH TO THE SURFACE.
BUT YOU SAW WHAT HE REALLY WAS.
YOU BELIEVED IN HIM.
NOW BELIEVE IN YOURSELF.
DOOMSDAY RUMBLES INSIDE OF ME.
THE KILLING MISTS SWIRL.
BUT THE BOY DOESN'T FLINCH.
BAKA...
...YOU DON'T UNDERSTAND.
I'M NOT MYSELF.
YOU HAVE TO GO. BEFORE--
BAKA STAYING RIGHT HERE...

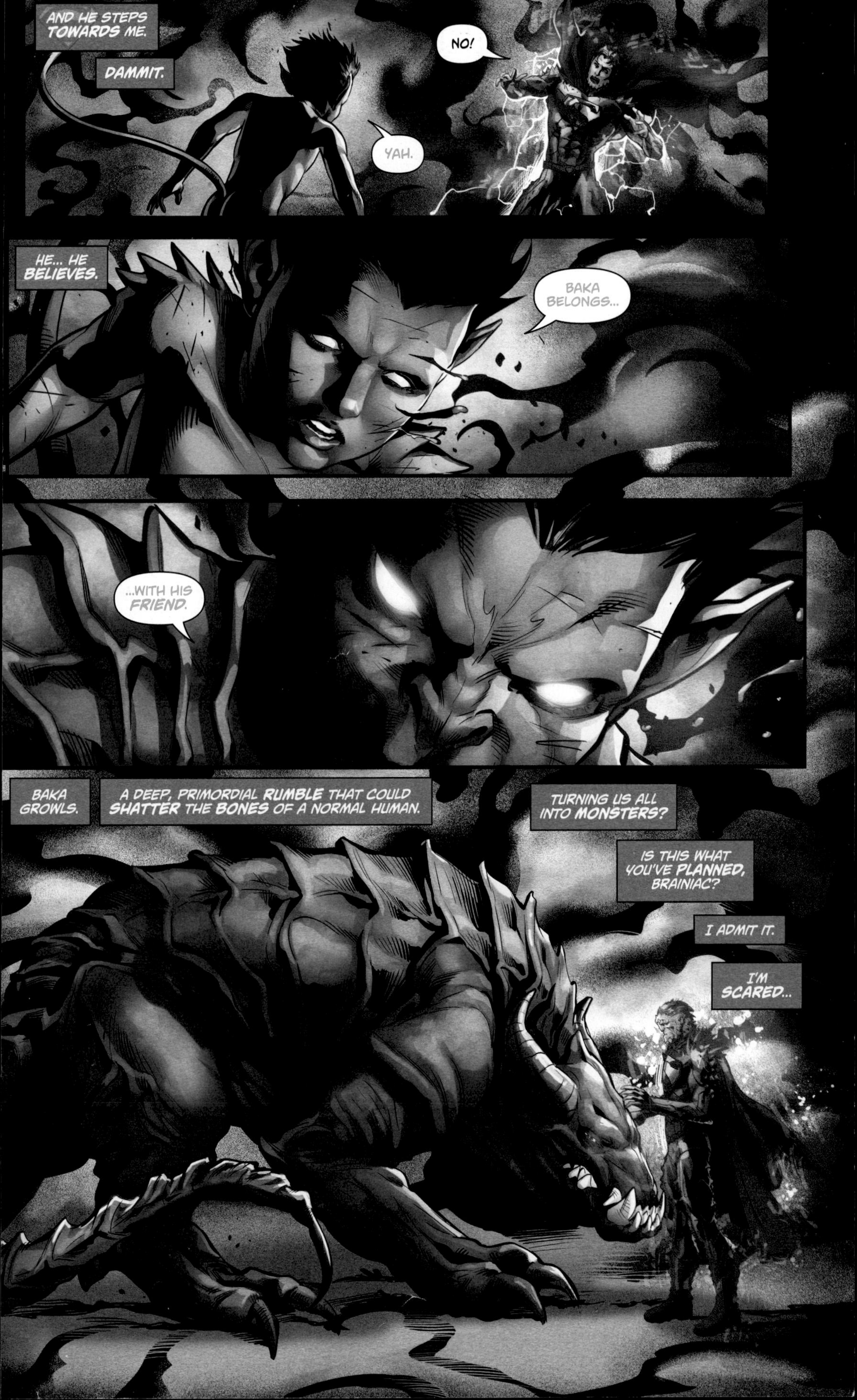
AND HE STEPS TOWARDS ME.
DAMMIT.
NO!
YAH.
HE... HE BELIEVES.
BAKA BELONGS...
...WITH HIS FRIEND.
BAKA GROWLS.
A DEEP, PRIMORDIAL RUMBLE THAT COULD SHATTER THE BONES OF A NORMAL HUMAN.
TURNING US ALL INTO MONSTERS?
IS THIS WHAT YOU'VE PLANNED, BRAINIAC?
I ADMIT IT.
I'M SCARED...

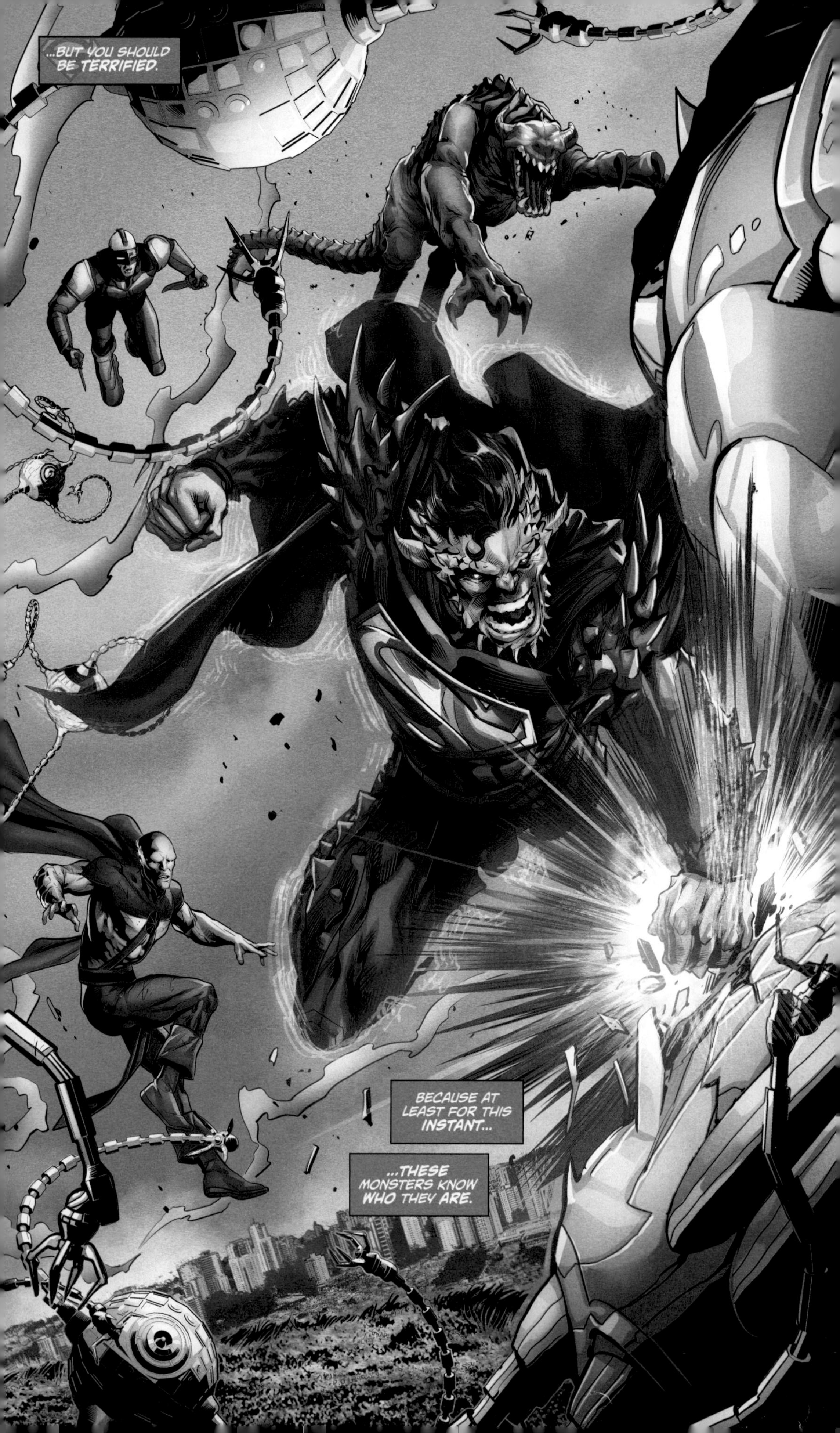
...BUT YOU SHOULD BE TERRIFIED.
BECAUSE AT LEAST FOR THIS INSTANT...
...THESE MONSTERS KNOW WHO THEY ARE.

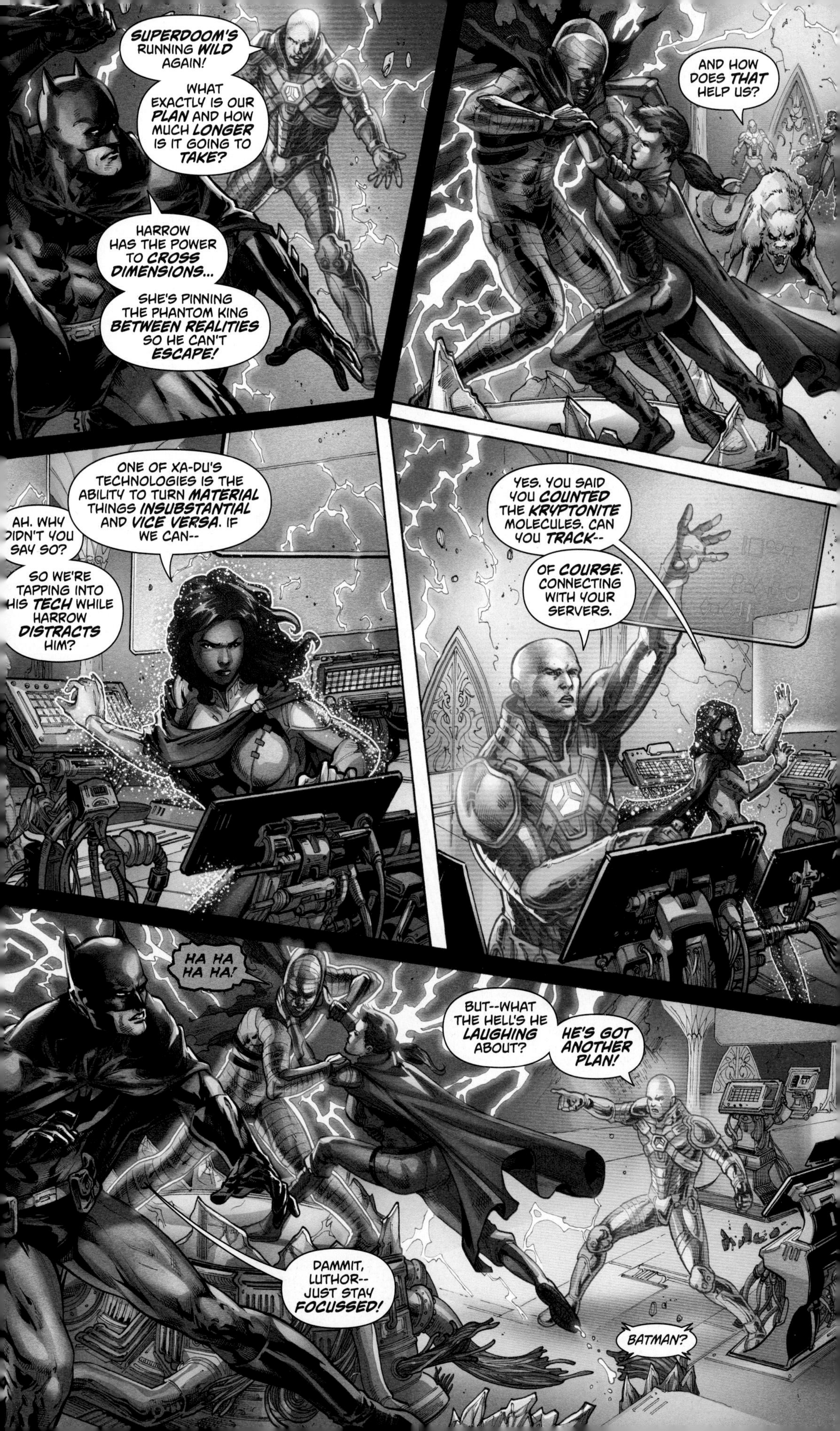
SUPERDOOM'S RUNNING WILD AGAIN!
WHAT EXACTLY IS OUR PLAN AND HOW MUCH LONGER IS IT GOING TO TAKE?
HARROW HAS THE POWER TO CROSS DIMENSIONS...
SHE'S PINNING THE PHANTOM KING BETWEEN REALITIES SO HE CAN'T ESCAPE!
AND HOW DOES THAT HELP US?
ONE OF XA-DU'S TECHNOLOGIES IS THE ABILITY TO TURN MATERIAL THINGS INSUBSTANTIAL AND VICE VERSA. IF WE CAN--
AH. WHY DIDN'T YOU SAY SO?
SO WE'RE TAPPING INTO HIS TECH WHILE HARROW DISTRACTS HIM?
YES. YOU SAID YOU COUNTED THE KRYPTONITE MOLECULES. CAN YOU TRACK--
OF COURSE. CONNECTING WITH YOUR SERVERS.
HA HA HA HA!
BUT--WHAT THE HELL'S HE LAUGHING ABOUT?
HE'S GOT ANOTHER PLAN!
DAMMIT, LUTHOR-- JUST STAY FOCUSSED!
BATMAN?

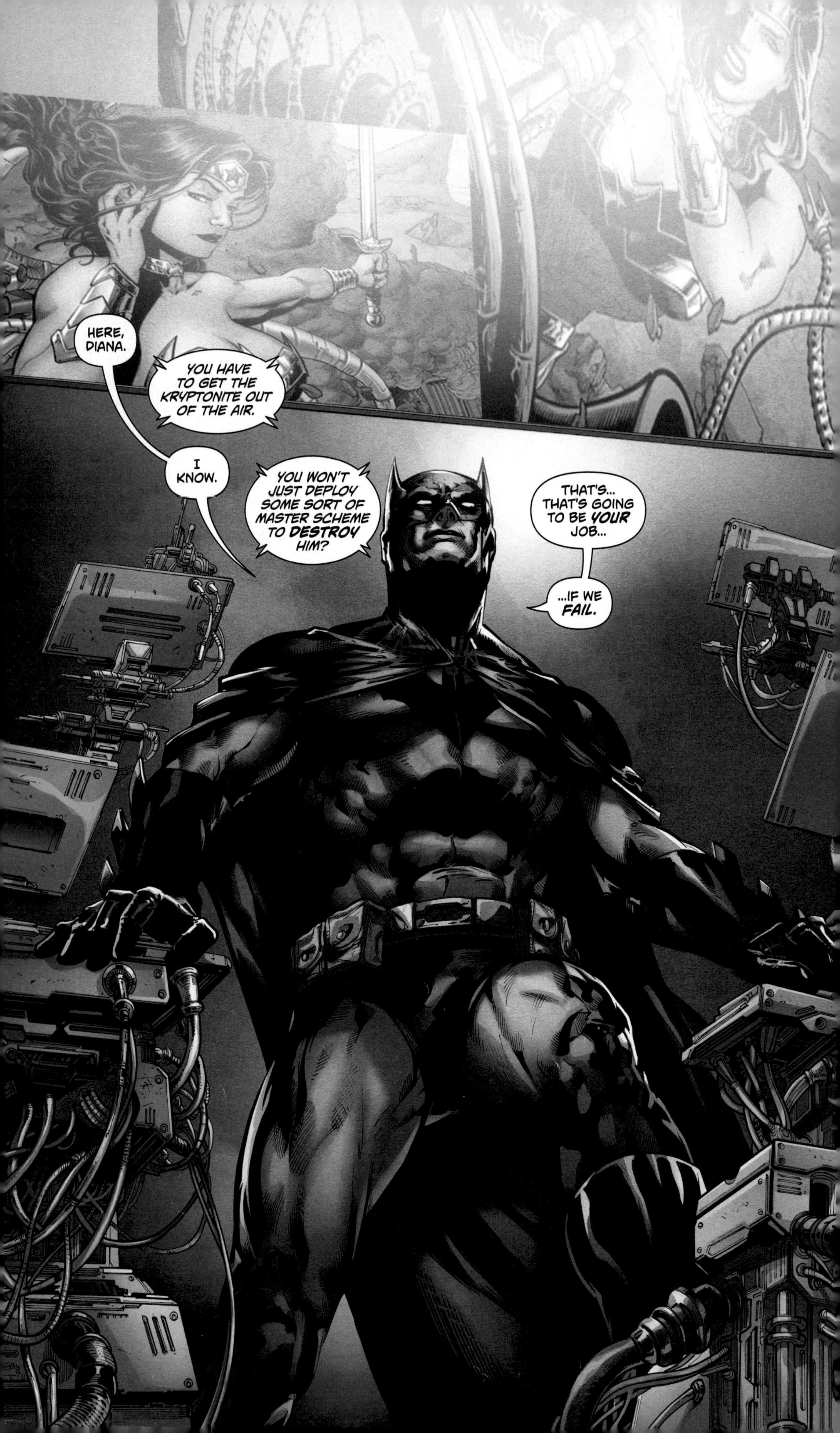
HERE, DIANA.
YOU HAVE TO GET THE KRYPTONITE OUT OF THE AIR.
I KNOW.
YOU WON'T JUST DEPLOY SOME SORT OF MASTER SCHEME TO **DESTROY** HIM?
THAT'S... THAT'S GOING TO BE **YOUR** JOB...
...IF WE **FAIL.**

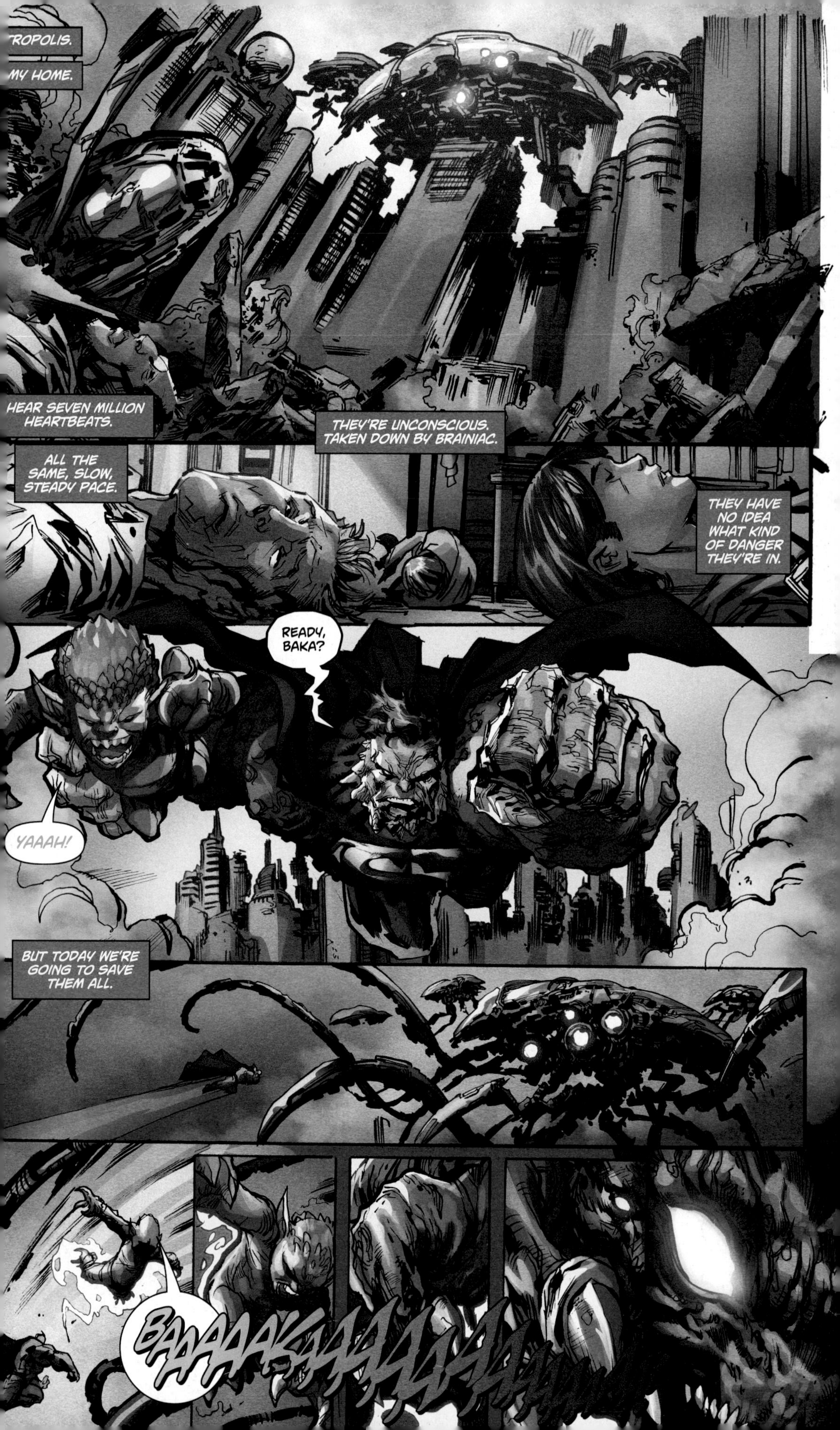

TROPOLIS.
MY HOME.
HEAR SEVEN MILLION HEARTBEATS.
THEY'RE UNCONSCIOUS. TAKEN DOWN BY BRAINIAC.
ALL THE SAME, SLOW, STEADY PACE.
THEY HAVE NO IDEA WHAT KIND OF DANGER THEY'RE IN.
READY, BAKA?
YAAAH!
BUT TODAY WE'RE GOING TO SAVE THEM ALL.
BAAAAKAAAAA

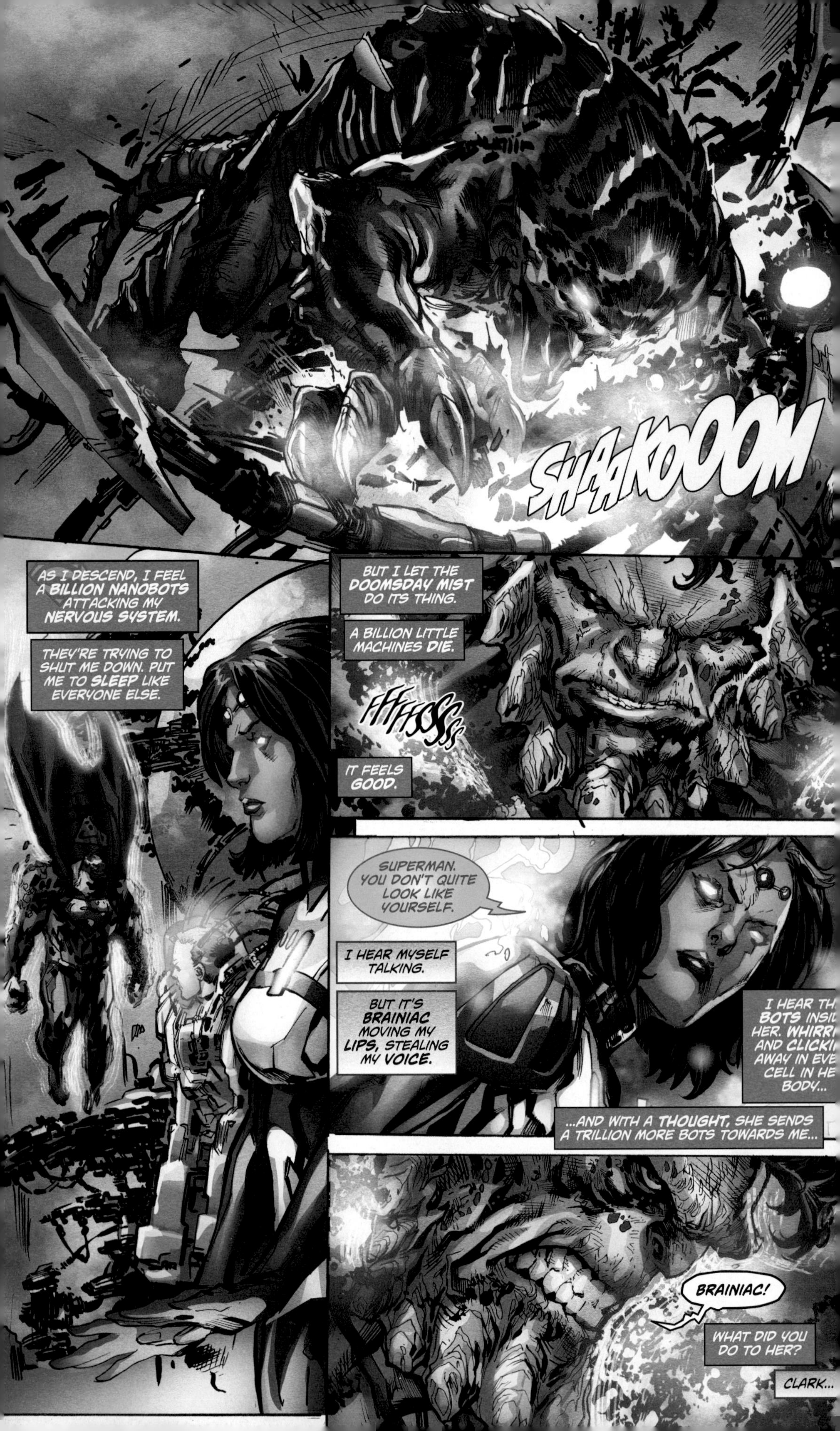
SHAAKOOOM
AS I DESCEND, I FEEL A BILLION NANOBOTS ATTACKING MY NERVOUS SYSTEM.
THEY'RE TRYING TO SHUT ME DOWN. PUT ME TO SLEEP LIKE EVERYONE ELSE.
BUT I LET THE DOOMSDAY MIST DO ITS THING.
A BILLION LITTLE MACHINES DIE.
FFFFFSSSSSS
IT FEELS GOOD.
SUPERMAN. YOU DON'T QUITE LOOK LIKE YOURSELF.
I HEAR MYSELF TALKING.
BUT IT'S BRAINIAC MOVING MY LIPS, STEALING MY VOICE.
I HEAR TH BOTS INSI HER. WHIRRI AND CLICKI AWAY IN EVE CELL IN HE BODY...
...AND WITH A THOUGHT, SHE SENDS A TRILLION MORE BOTS TOWARDS ME...
BRAINIAC!
WHAT DID YOU DO TO HER?
CLARK...

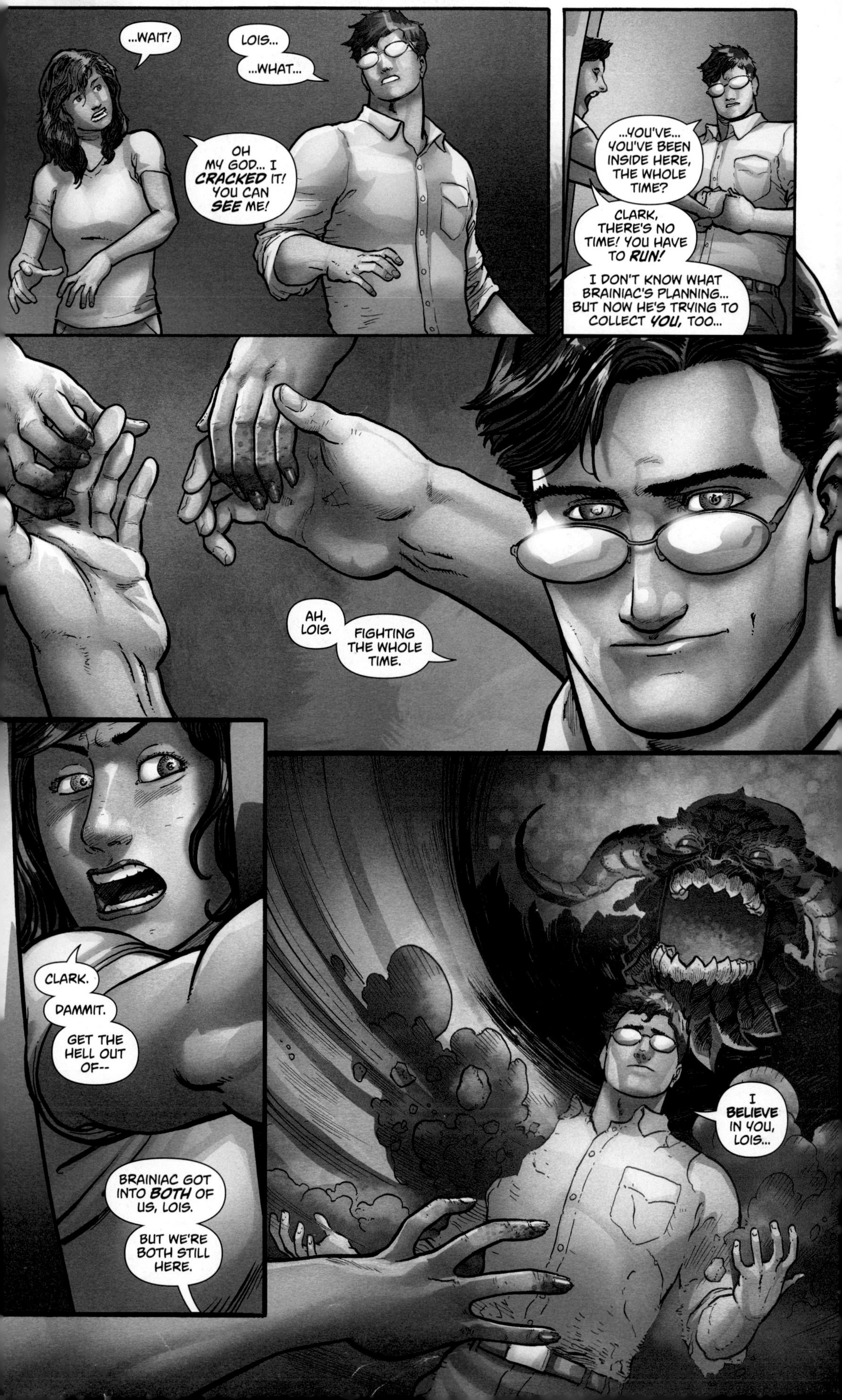
...WAIT!
LOIS...
...WHAT...
OH MY GOD... I CRACKED IT! YOU CAN SEE ME!
...YOU'VE... YOU'VE BEEN INSIDE HERE, THE WHOLE TIME?
CLARK, THERE'S NO TIME! YOU HAVE TO RUN!
I DON'T KNOW WHAT BRAINIAC'S PLANNING... BUT NOW HE'S TRYING TO COLLECT YOU, TOO...
AH, LOIS.
FIGHTING THE WHOLE TIME.
CLARK.
DAMMIT.
GET THE HELL OUT OF--
BRAINIAC GOT INTO BOTH OF US, LOIS.
BUT WE'RE BOTH STILL HERE.
I BELIEVE IN YOU, LOIS...

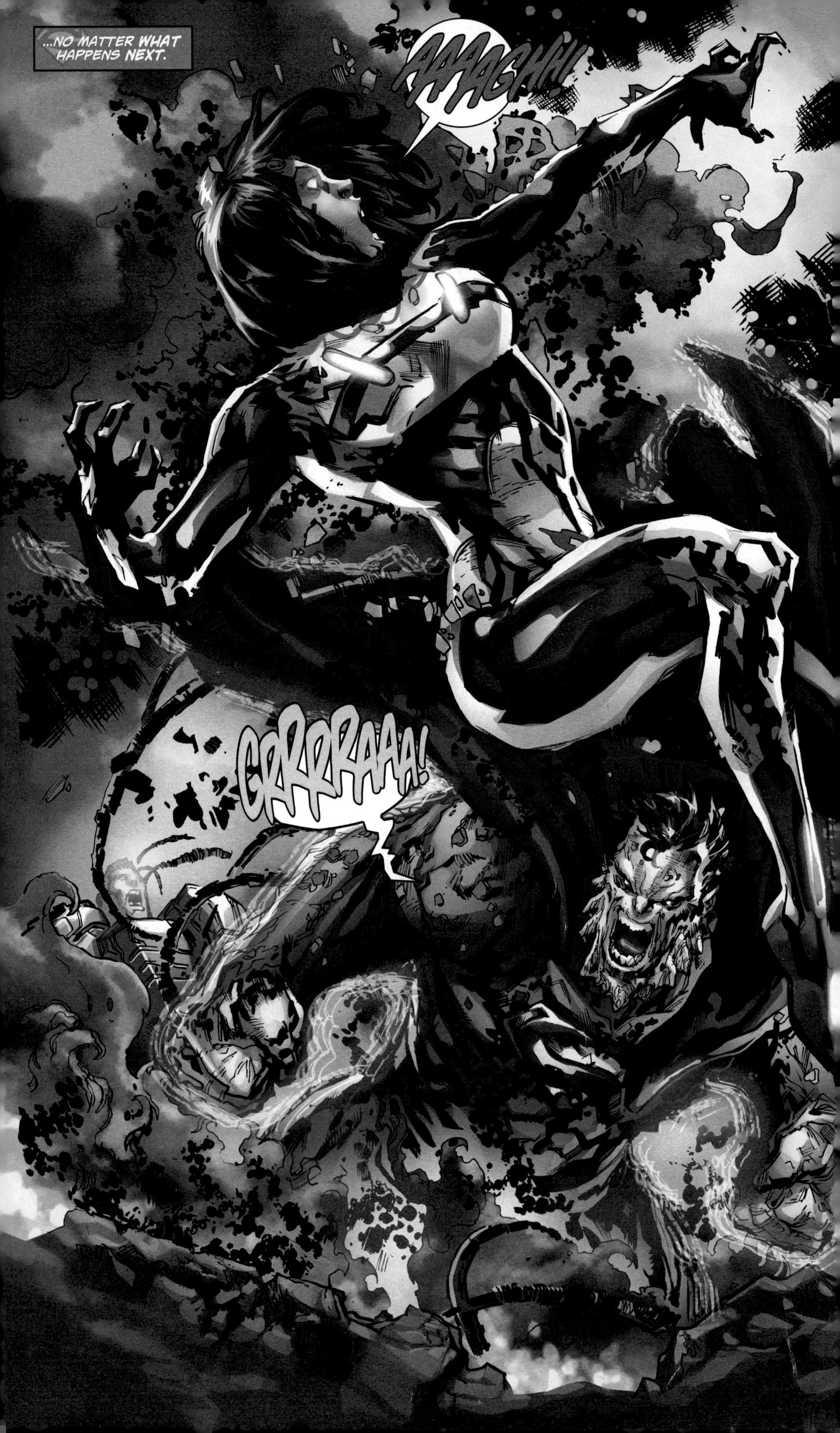
...NO MATTER WHAT HAPPENS NEXT.
AAAAGHH!
GRRRRAAA!

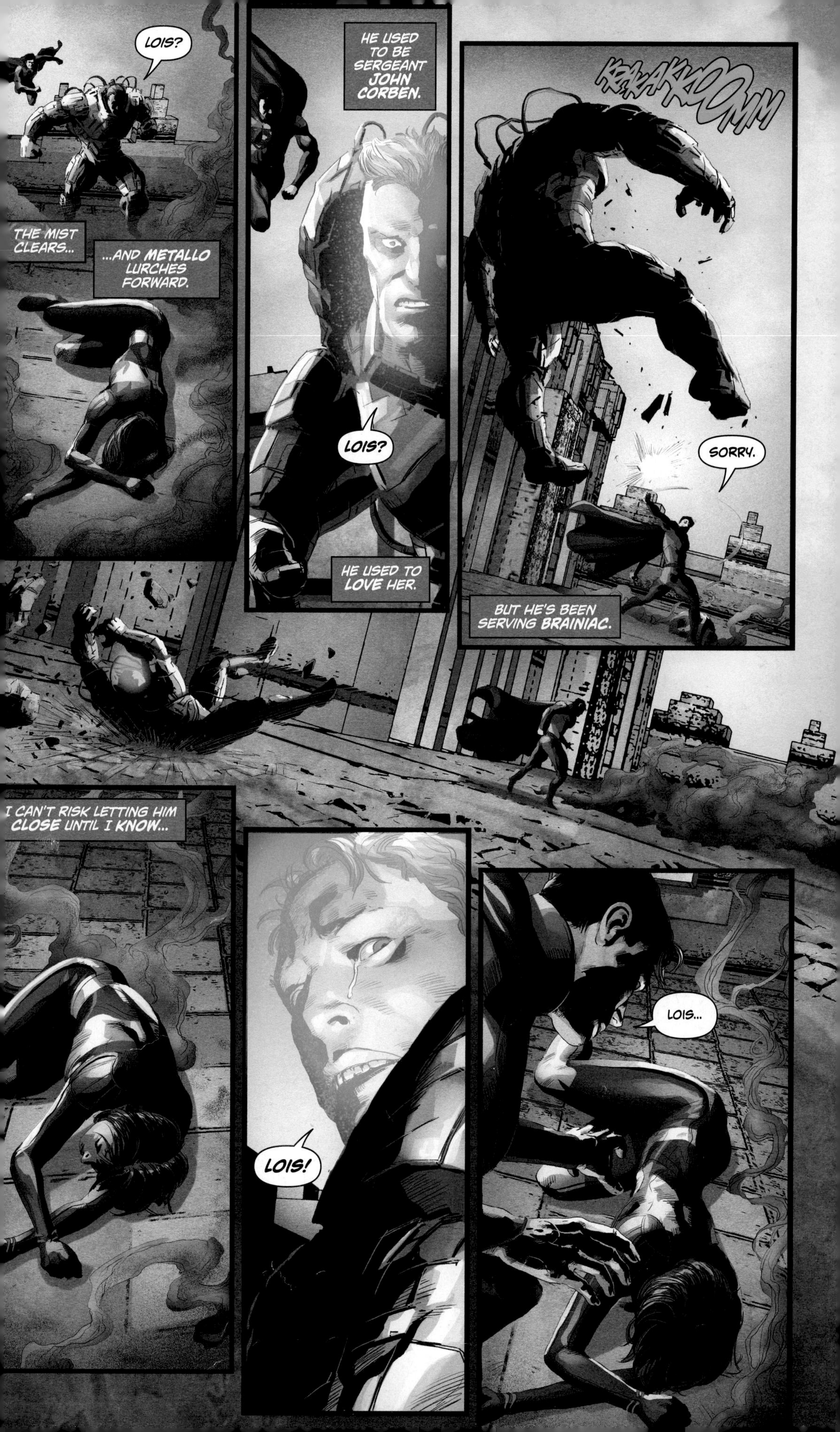
LOIS?
THE MIST CLEARS...
...AND METALLO LURCHES FORWARD.
HE USED TO BE SERGEANT JOHN CORBEN.
LOIS?
HE USED TO LOVE HER.
KRAKAKAKOOMM
SORRY.
BUT HE'S BEEN SERVING BRAINIAC.
I CAN'T RISK LETTING HIM CLOSE UNTIL I KNOW...
LOIS!
LOIS...

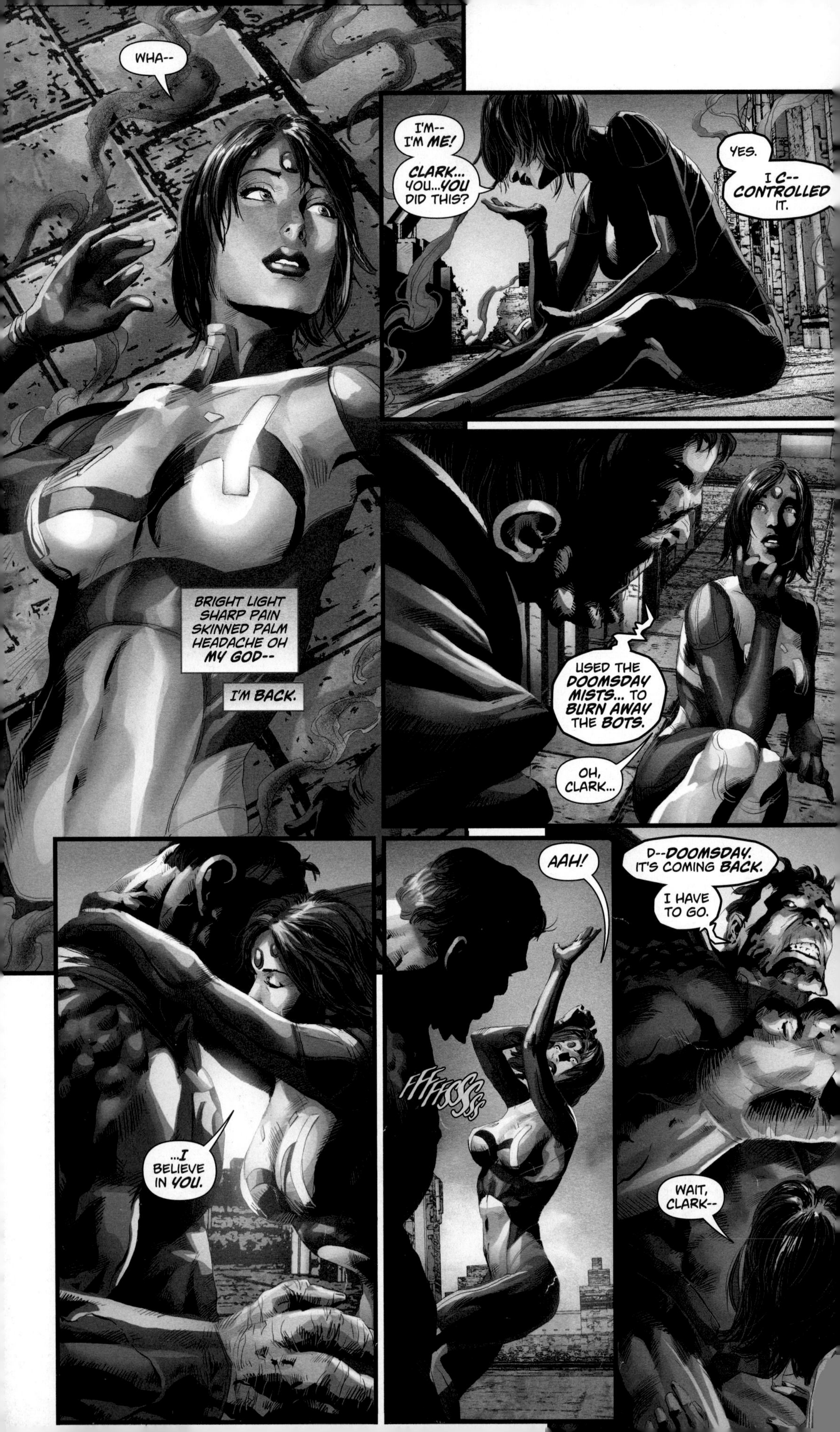
WHA--
BRIGHT LIGHT SHARP PAIN SKINNED PALM HEADACHE OH MY GOD--
I'M BACK.
I'M-- I'M ME!
CLARK... YOU...YOU DID THIS?
YES.
I C-- CONTROLLED IT.
USED THE DOOMSDAY MISTS... TO BURN AWAY THE BOTS.
OH, CLARK...
...I BELIEVE IN YOU.
AAH!
FFFFSSSSS
D--DOOMSDAY. IT'S COMING BACK.
I HAVE TO GO.
WAIT, CLARK--

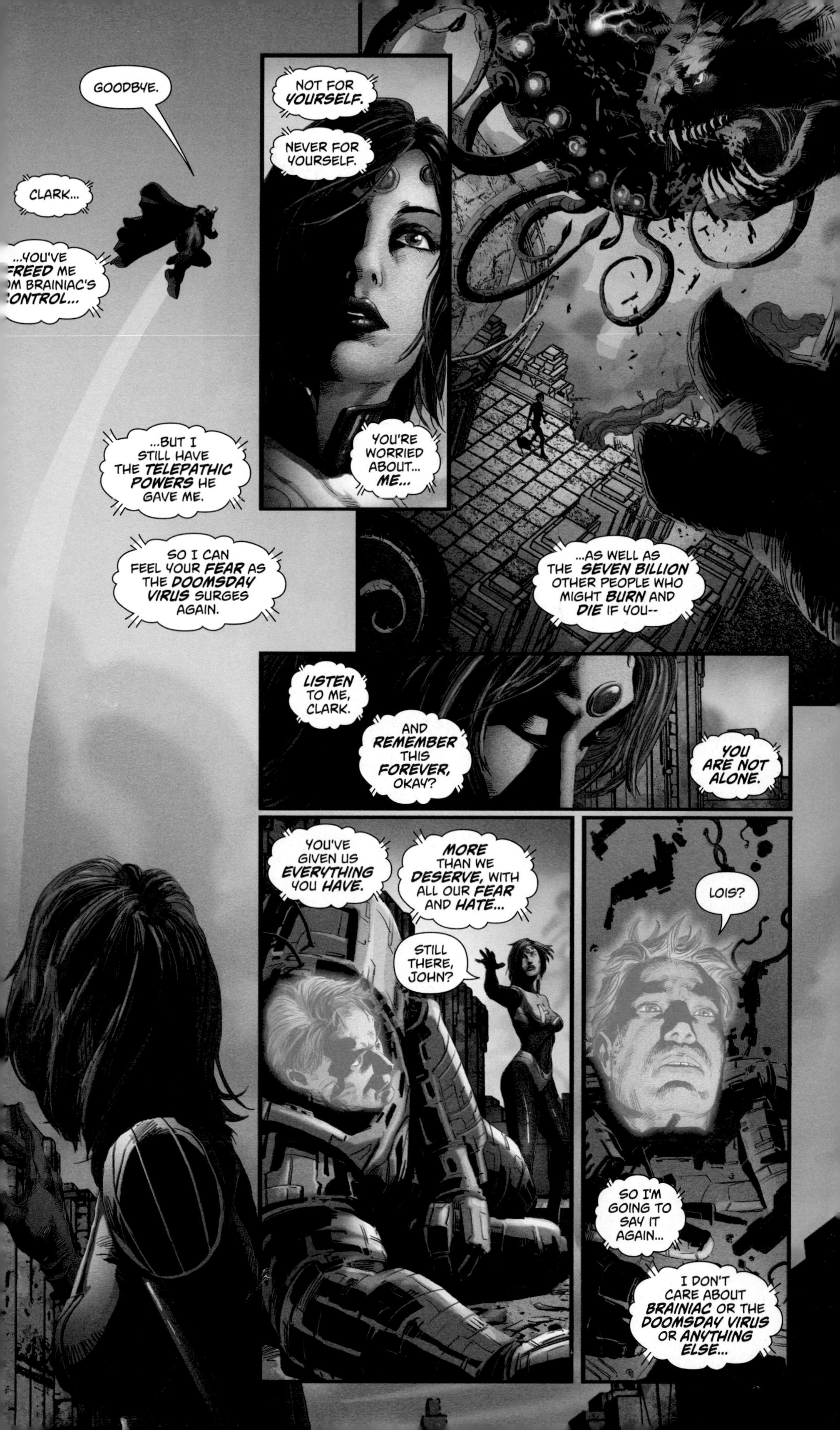
GOODBYE.
CLARK...
...YOU'VE FREED ME OM BRAINIAC'S CONTROL...
NOT FOR YOURSELF.
NEVER FOR YOURSELF.
YOU'RE WORRIED ABOUT... ME...
...BUT I STILL HAVE THE TELEPATHIC POWERS HE GAVE ME.
SO I CAN FEEL YOUR FEAR AS THE DOOMSDAY VIRUS SURGES AGAIN.
...AS WELL AS THE SEVEN BILLION OTHER PEOPLE WHO MIGHT BURN AND DIE IF YOU--
LISTEN TO ME, CLARK.
AND REMEMBER THIS FOREVER, OKAY?
YOU ARE NOT ALONE.
YOU'VE GIVEN US EVERYTHING YOU HAVE.
MORE THAN WE DESERVE, WITH ALL OUR FEAR AND HATE...
STILL THERE, JOHN?
LOIS?
SO I'M GOING TO SAY IT AGAIN...
I DON'T CARE ABOUT BRAINIAC OR THE DOOMSDAY VIRUS OR ANYTHING ELSE...

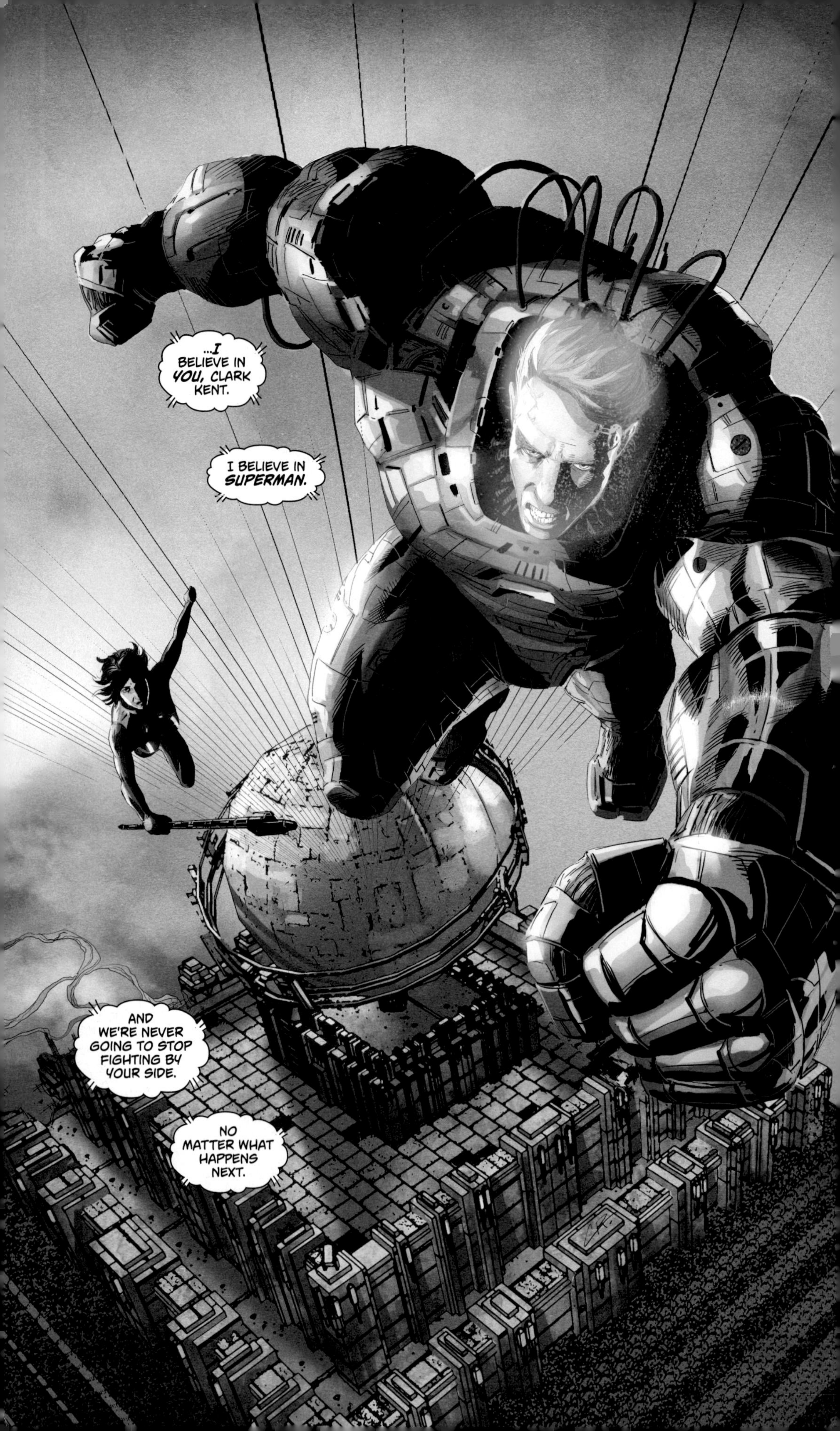
...I BELIEVE IN YOU, CLARK KENT.
I BELIEVE IN SUPERMAN.
AND WE'RE NEVER GOING TO STOP FIGHTING BY YOUR SIDE.
NO MATTER WHAT HAPPENS NEXT.

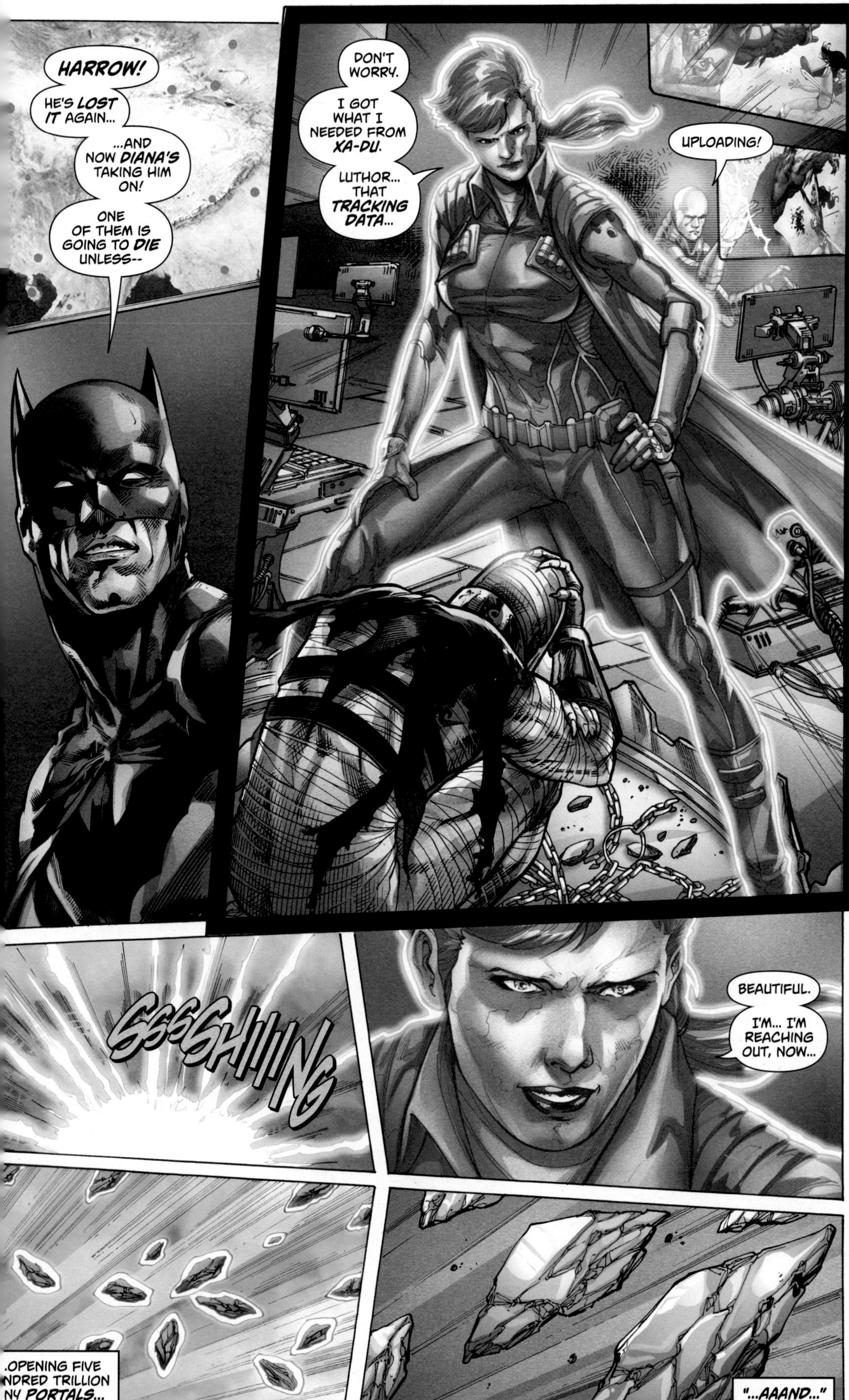
HARROW!
HE'S LOST IT AGAIN...
...AND NOW DIANA'S TAKING HIM ON!
ONE OF THEM IS GOING TO DIE UNLESS--
DON'T WORRY.
I GOT WHAT I NEEDED FROM XA-DU.
LUTHOR... THAT TRACKING DATA...
UPLOADING!
SSSSHIIIING
BEAUTIFUL.
I'M... I'M REACHING OUT, NOW...
...OPENING FIVE
...NDRED TRILLION
...NY PORTALS...
"...AAAND..."

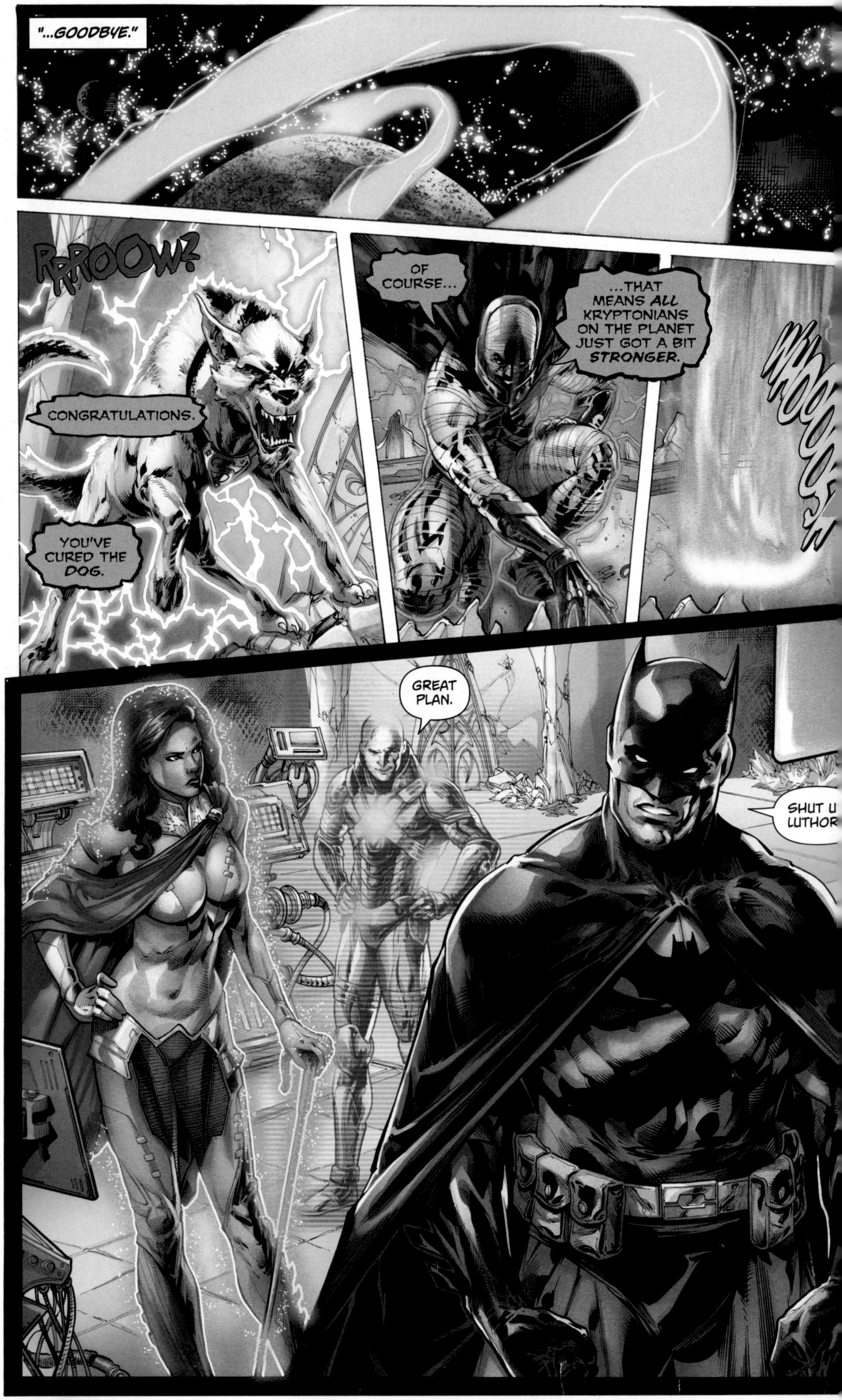

"...GOODBYE."
RRROOW?
CONGRATULATIONS.
YOU'VE CURED THE DOG.
OF COURSE...
...THAT MEANS ALL KRYPTONIANS ON THE PLANET JUST GOT A BIT STRONGER.
WHOOOOSH
GREAT PLAN.
SHUT U LUTHOR

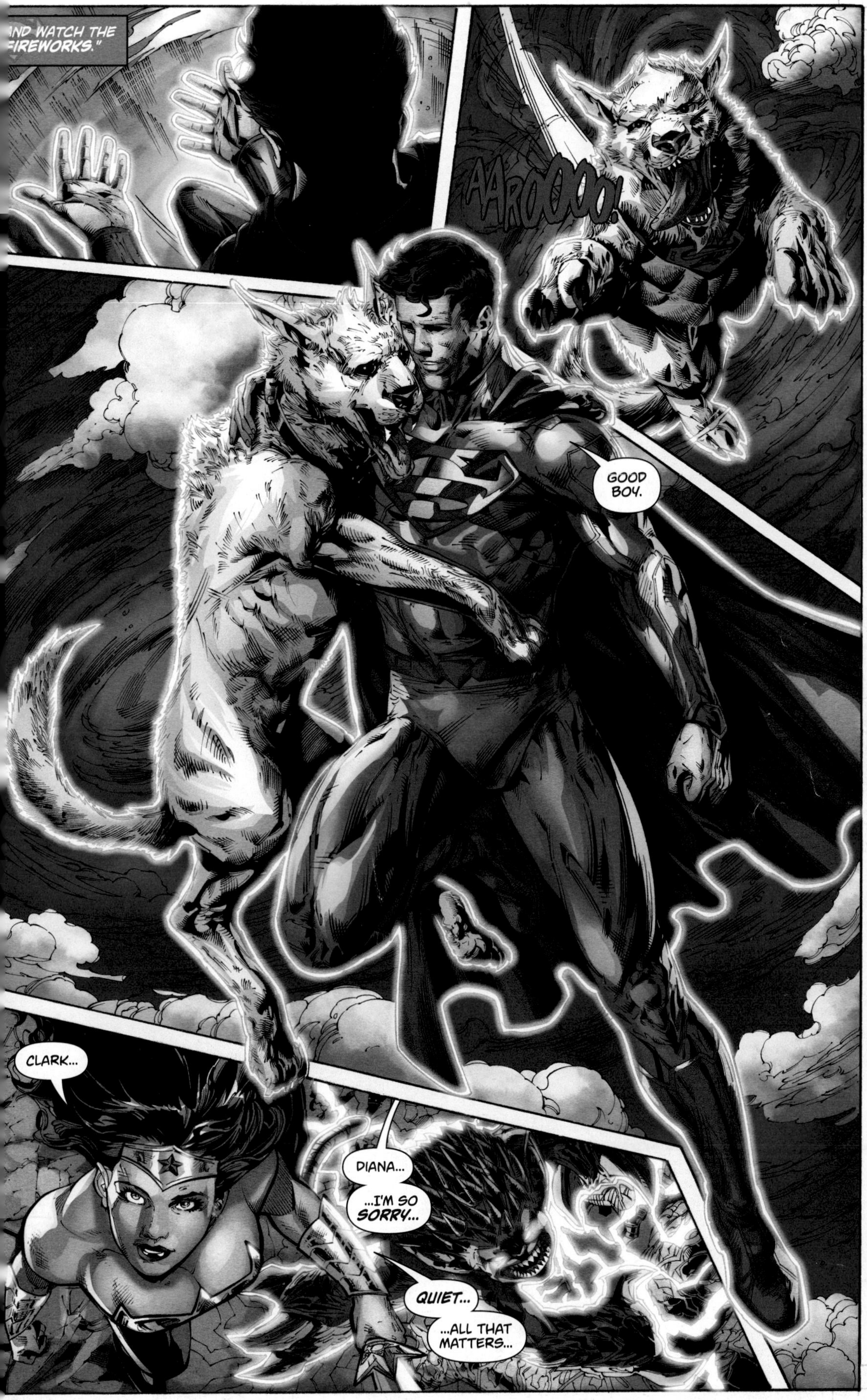

AND WATCH THE FIREWORKS."
AAROOOOO!
GOOD BOY.
CLARK...
DIANA...
...I'M SO SORRY...
QUIET...
...ALL THAT MATTERS...

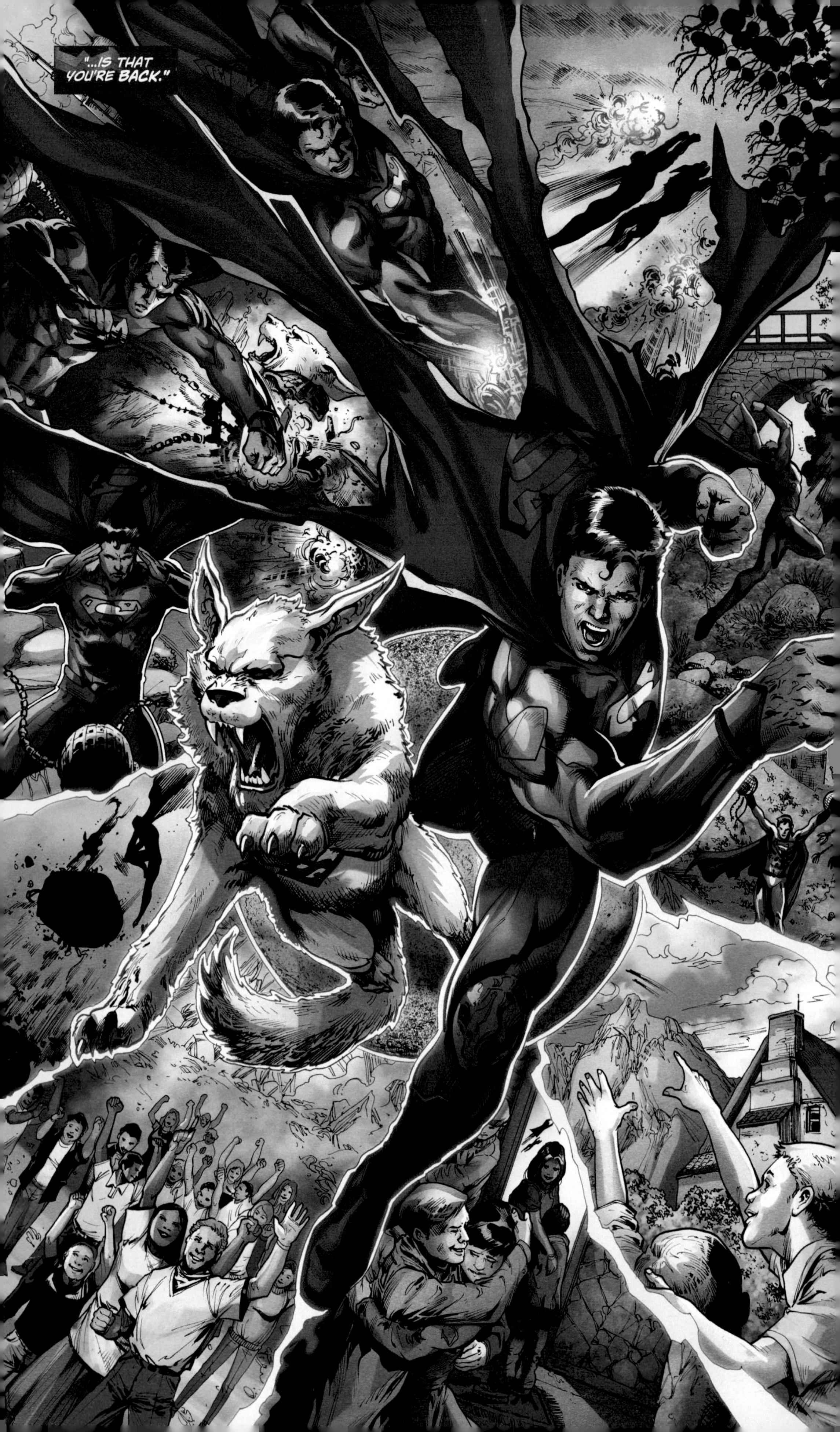
"...IS THAT YOU'RE BACK."

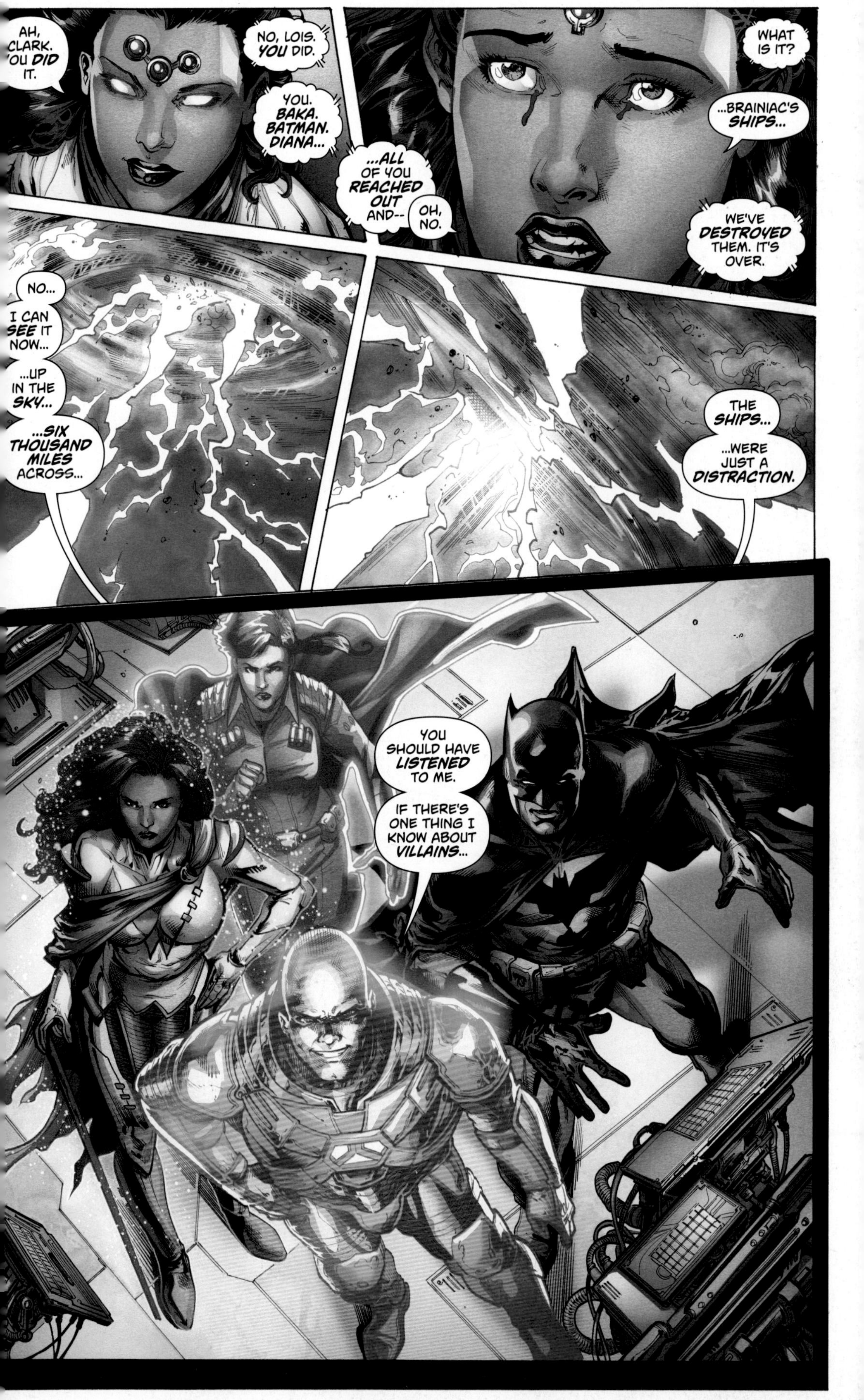

AH, CLARK. 'OU DID IT.
NO, LOIS. YOU DID.
YOU. BAKA. BATMAN. DIANA...
...ALL OF YOU REACHED OUT AND--
OH, NO.
WHAT IS IT?
...BRAINIAC'S SHIPS...
WE'VE DESTROYED THEM. IT'S OVER.
NO...
I CAN SEE IT NOW...
...UP IN THE SKY...
...SIX THOUSAND MILES ACROSS...
THE SHIPS...
...WERE JUST A DISTRACTION.
YOU SHOULD HAVE LISTENED TO ME.
IF THERE'S ONE THING I KNOW ABOUT VILLAINS...

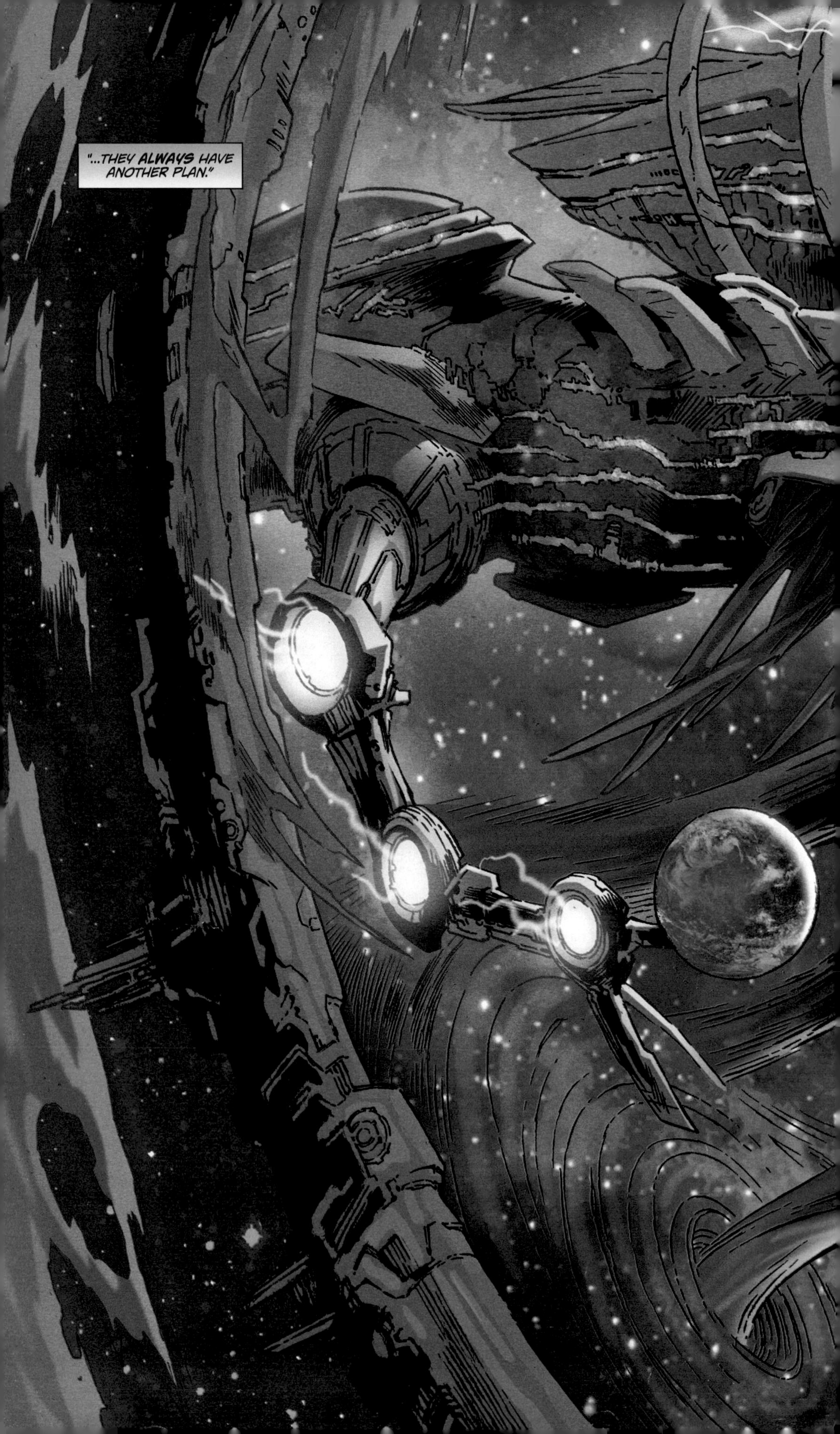
"...THEY ALWAYS HAVE ANOTHER PLAN."

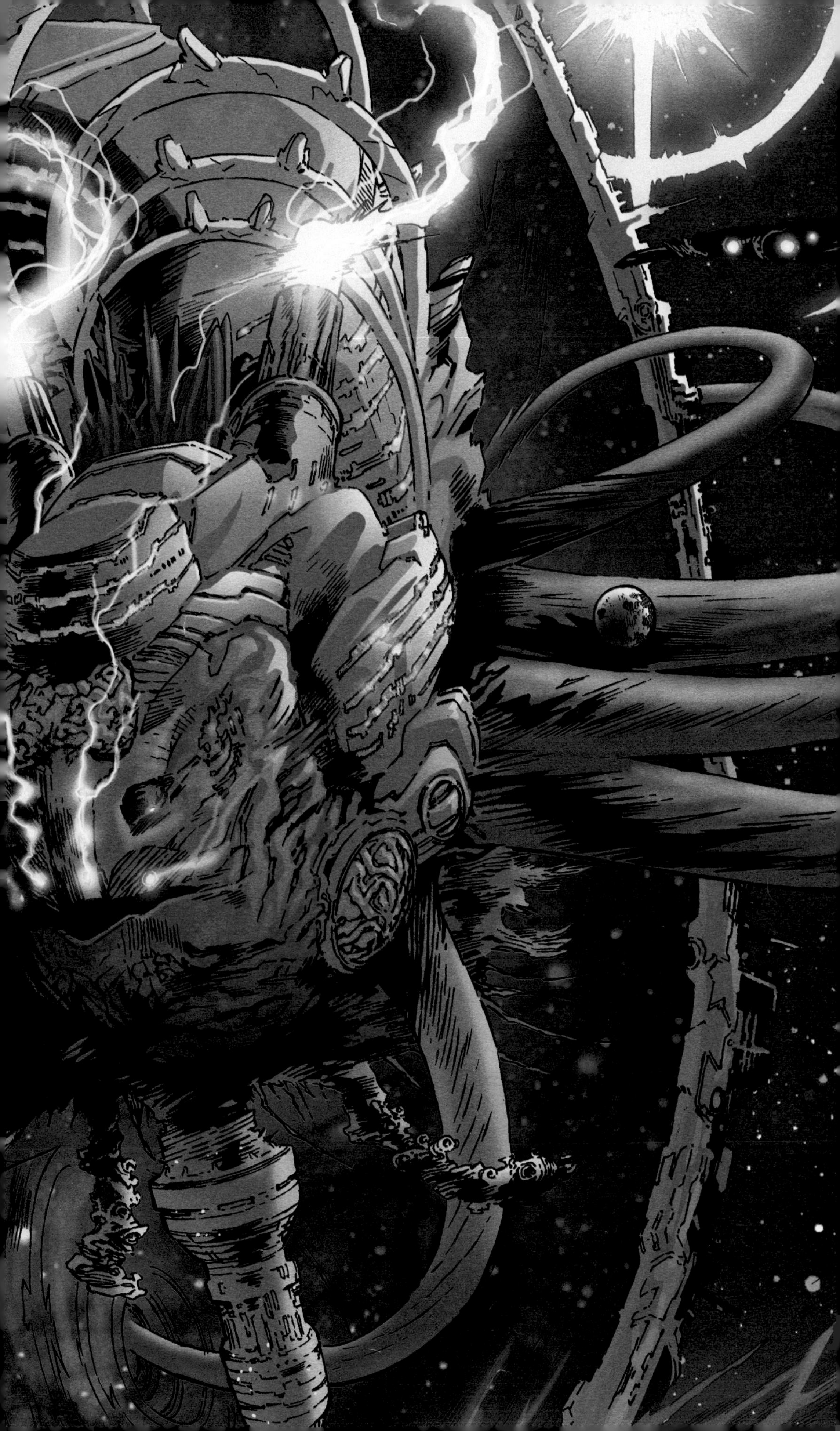

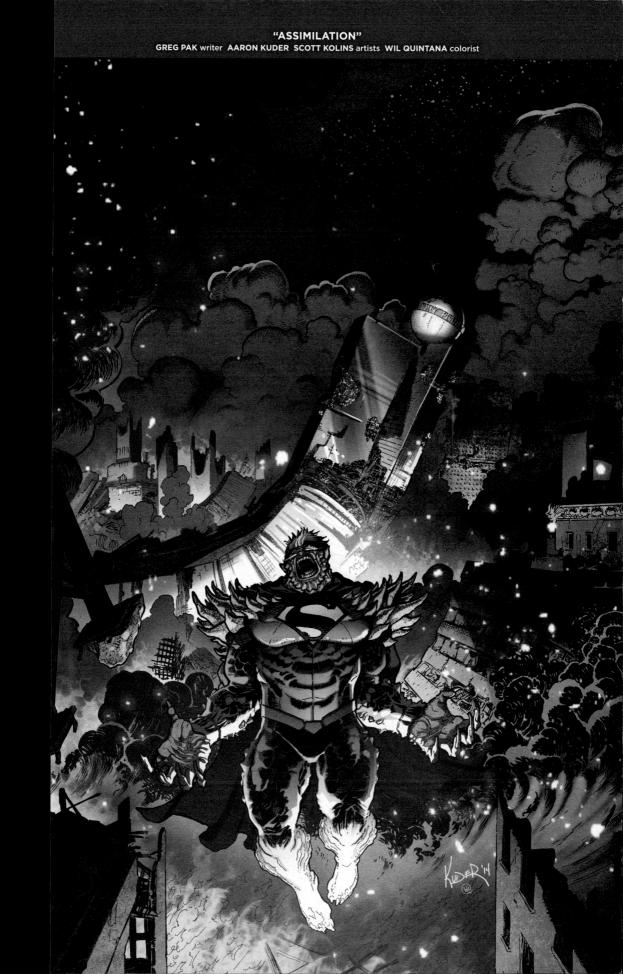

"ASSIMILATION"
GREG PAK writer AARON KUDER SCOTT KOLINS artists WIL QUINTANA colorist

WORLD   U.S.   METROPOLIS   BUSINESS   OPINION   SPORTS   ARTS   STYLE   VIDE

August 06,

Daily Planet

DAILY PLANET

PANIC IN THE SKY

BY LOIS LANE

The world is still here today. For how much longer I can't say.

Earth was invaded a few hours ago by a fleet of ships, now being referred to as nodes, seeking to link up together here on Earth as they disabled all of the planet's defenses. In command of this armada is what strangely appears to be a Cyborg version of Superman. The Justice League and many others responded to the threat quickly, but their ultimate goal was just that—to be a diversionary tactic allowing a stargate to be built and let what seems to be a planet sized starship through.

We cannot lose hope yet. Superman has returned. Batman and a group that

Artis Rendering : Po

included Lex Luthor have managed to get rid of the Kryptonite in the atmosphere, allowing the Man of Steel to shed his Doomsday persona and become more himself. My unwitting role in this as a pawn of the true mastermind behind this, Brainiac has been severed. But nothing

has changed for Smallvill Metropolis where its citize still remain in comas.

There are still many that stand against this new danger. We have to just no stop believing in them. Th next move is the enemies.

X   Slideshow - Superdoom's Path of Destruction

404 Error
404 Error
404 Error

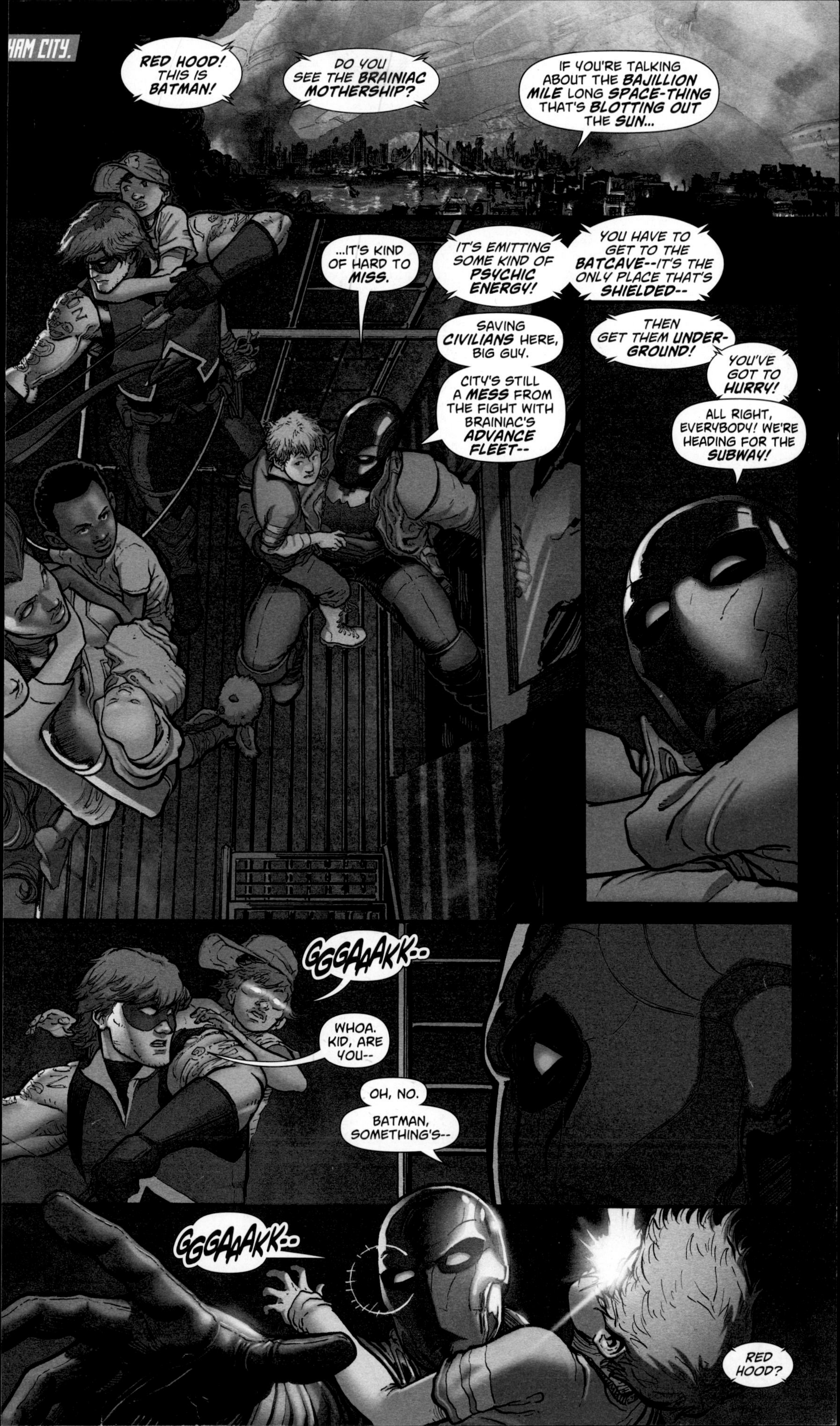
HAM CITY.
RED HOOD! THIS IS BATMAN!
DO YOU SEE THE BRAINIAC MOTHERSHIP?
IF YOU'RE TALKING ABOUT THE BAJILLION MILE LONG SPACE-THING THAT'S BLOTTING OUT THE SUN...
...IT'S KIND OF HARD TO MISS.
IT'S EMITTING SOME KIND OF PSYCHIC ENERGY!
YOU HAVE TO GET TO THE BATCAVE--IT'S THE ONLY PLACE THAT'S SHIELDED--
SAVING CIVILIANS HERE, BIG GUY.
CITY'S STILL A MESS FROM THE FIGHT WITH BRAINIAC'S ADVANCE FLEET--
THEN GET THEM UNDER-GROUND!
YOU'VE GOT TO HURRY!
ALL RIGHT, EVERYBODY! WE'RE HEADING FOR THE SUBWAY!
GGGAAAKK--
WHOA. KID, ARE YOU--
OH, NO.
BATMAN, SOMETHING'S--
GGGAAAKK--
RED HOOD?

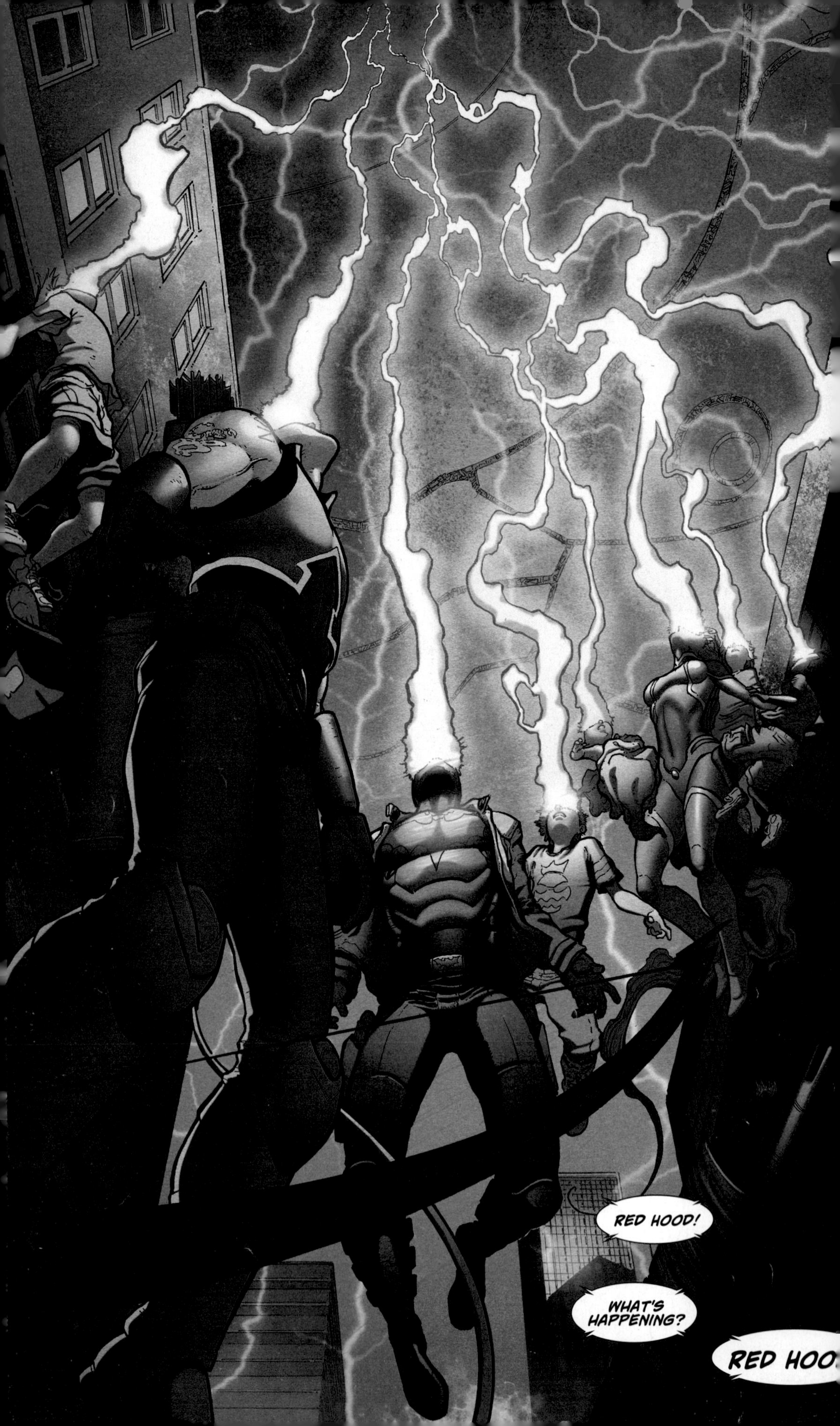

RED HOOD!
WHAT'S HAPPENING?
RED HOO

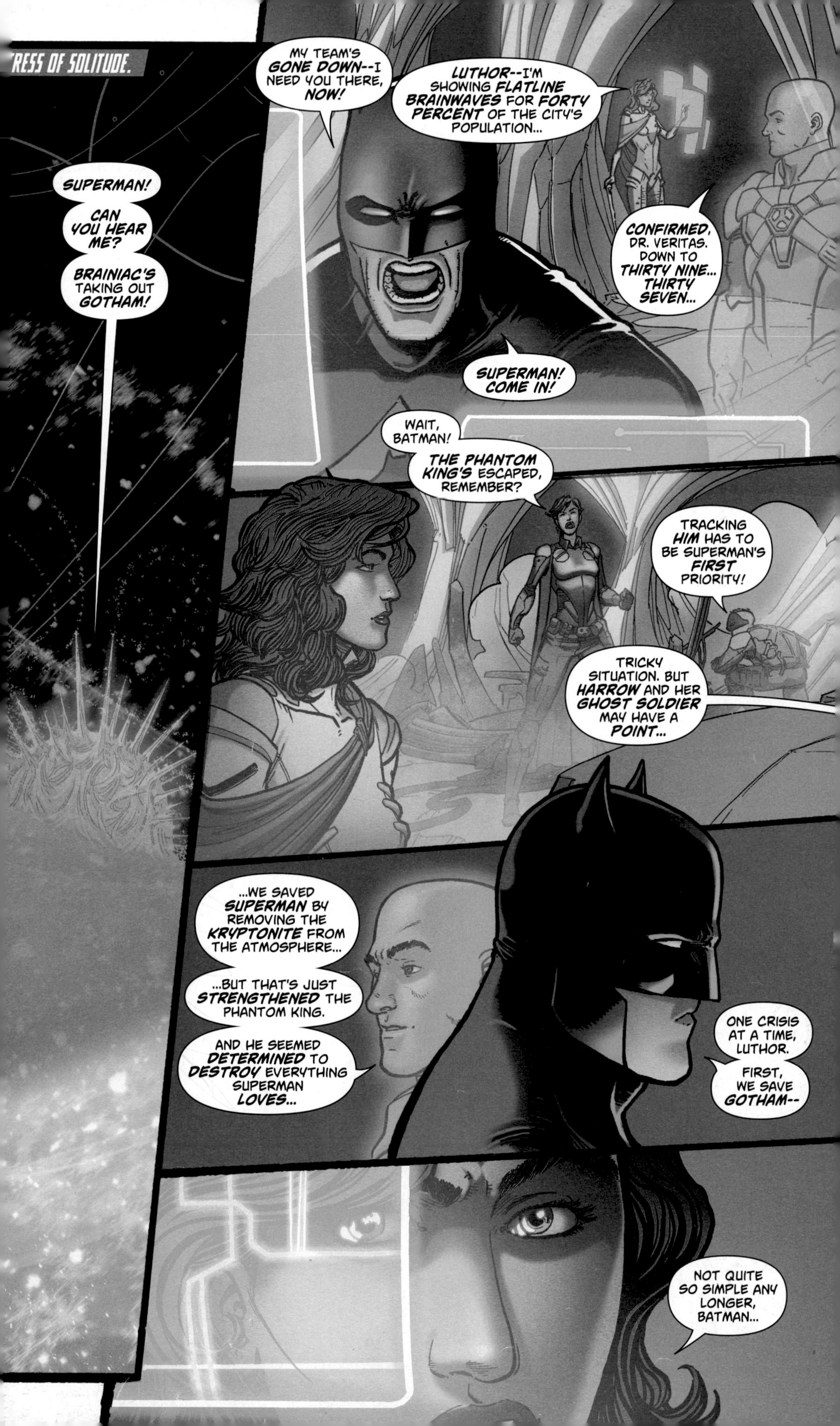

RESS OF SOLITUDE.
MY TEAM'S GONE DOWN--I NEED YOU THERE, NOW!
LUTHOR--I'M SHOWING FLATLINE BRAINWAVES FOR FORTY PERCENT OF THE CITY'S POPULATION...
CONFIRMED, DR. VERITAS. DOWN TO THIRTY NINE... THIRTY SEVEN...
SUPERMAN!
CAN YOU HEAR ME?
BRAINIAC'S TAKING OUT GOTHAM!
SUPERMAN! COME IN!
WAIT, BATMAN!
THE PHANTOM KING'S ESCAPED, REMEMBER?
TRACKING HIM HAS TO BE SUPERMAN'S FIRST PRIORITY!
TRICKY SITUATION. BUT HARROW AND HER GHOST SOLDIER MAY HAVE A POINT...
...WE SAVED SUPERMAN BY REMOVING THE KRYPTONITE FROM THE ATMOSPHERE...
...BUT THAT'S JUST STRENGTHENED THE PHANTOM KING.
AND HE SEEMED DETERMINED TO DESTROY EVERYTHING SUPERMAN LOVES...
ONE CRISIS AT A TIME, LUTHOR.
FIRST, WE SAVE GOTHAM--
NOT QUITE SO SIMPLE ANY LONGER, BATMAN...

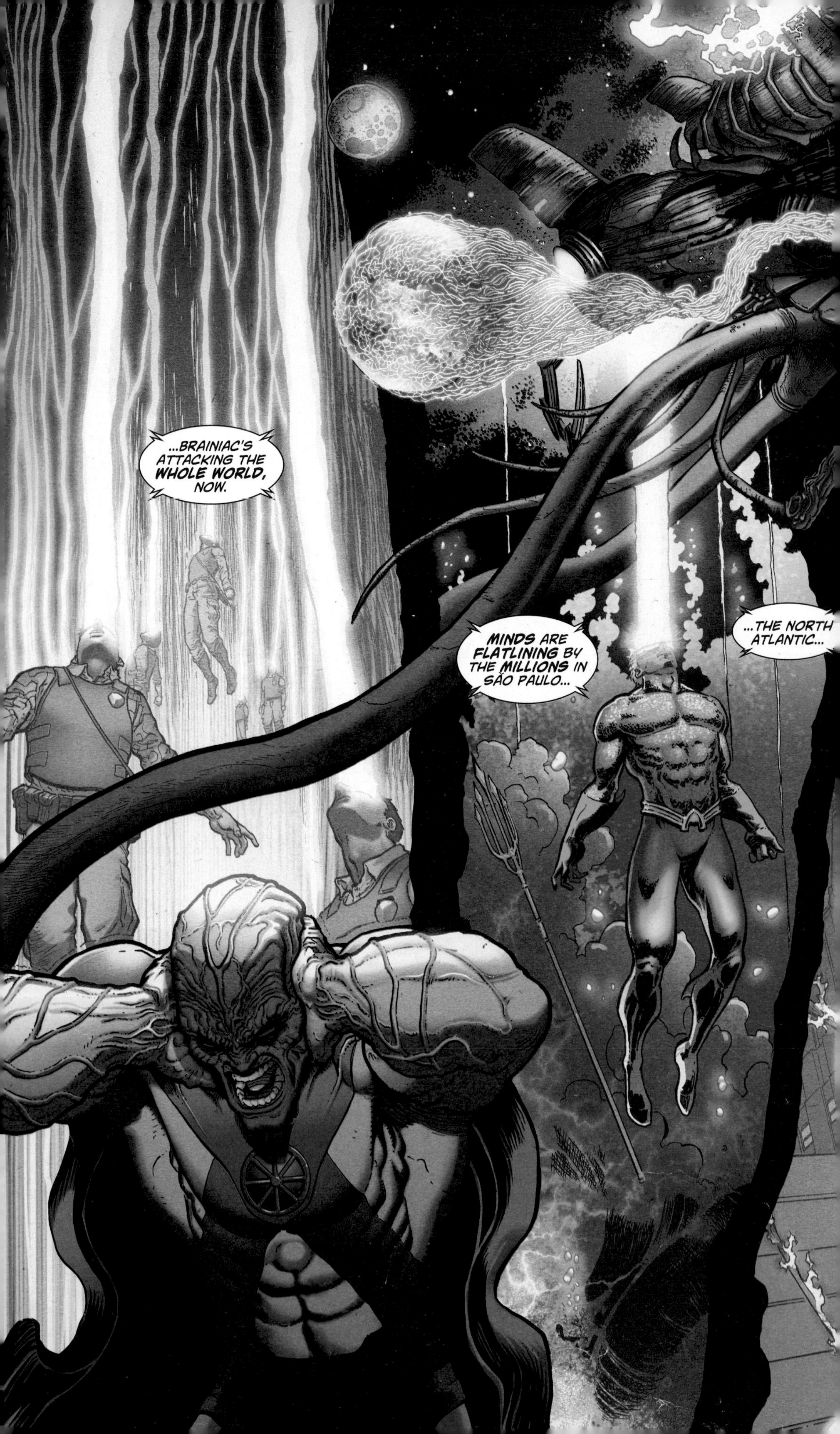
...BRAINIAC'S ATTACKING THE WHOLE WORLD, NOW.
MINDS ARE FLATLINING BY THE MILLIONS IN SÃO PAULO...
...THE NORTH ATLANTIC...

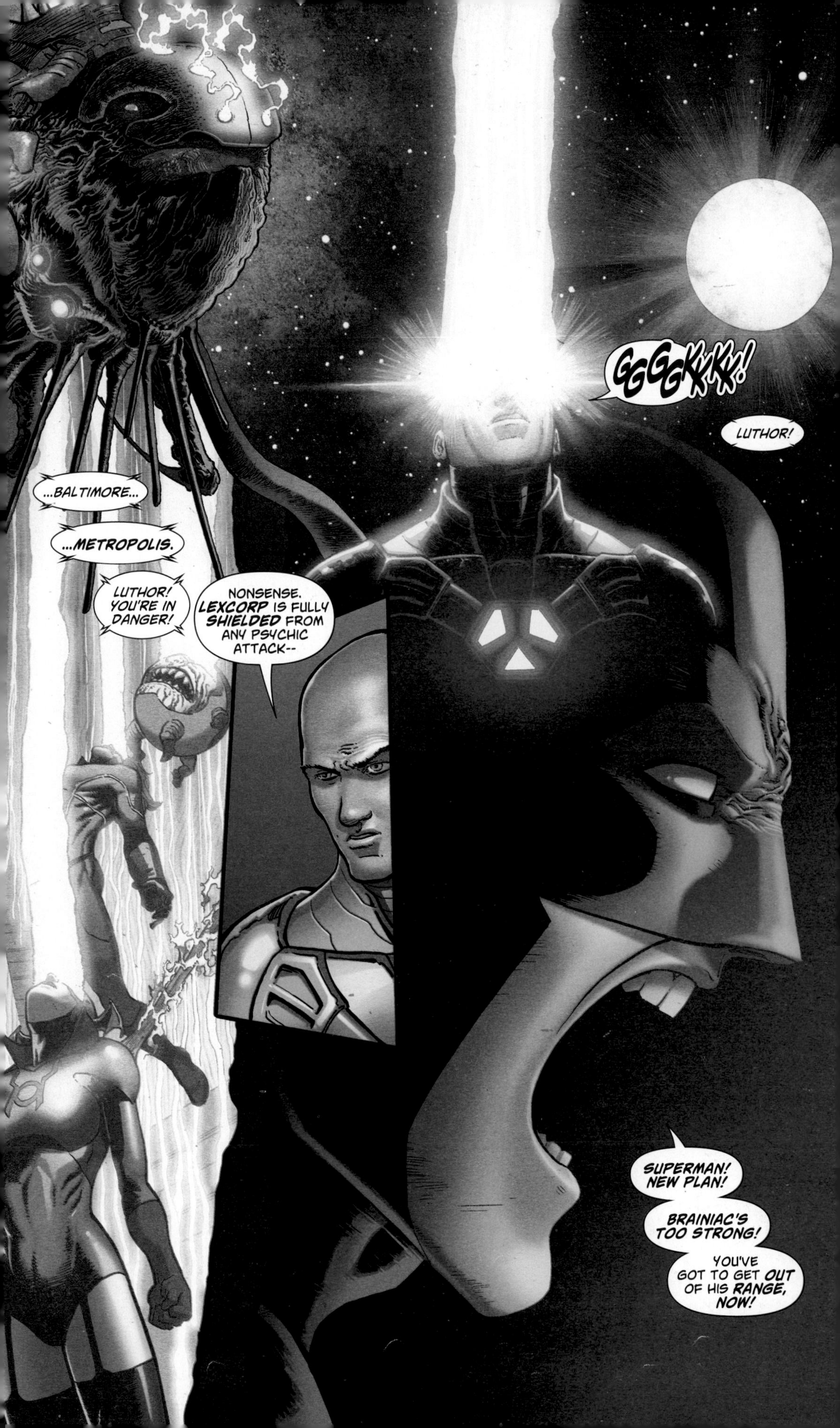
GGGGKKKKK!
LUTHOR!
...BALTIMORE...
...METROPOLIS.
LUTHOR! YOU'RE IN DANGER!
NONSENSE. LEXCORP IS FULLY SHIELDED FROM ANY PSYCHIC ATTACK--
SUPERMAN! NEW PLAN!
BRAINIAC'S TOO STRONG!
YOU'VE GOT TO GET OUT OF HIS RANGE, NOW!

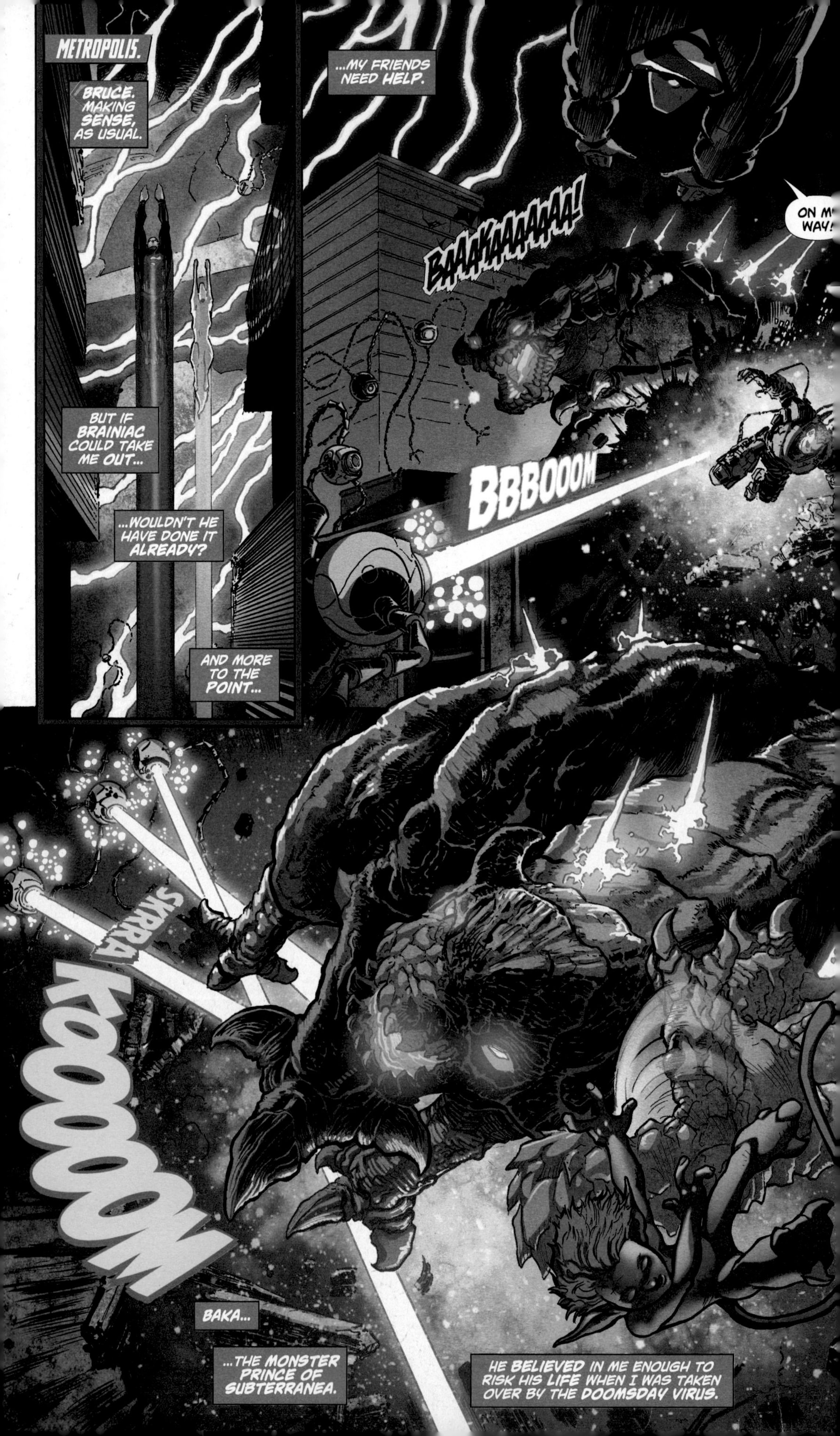
METROPOLIS.
BRUCE. MAKING SENSE, AS USUAL.
BUT IF BRAINIAC COULD TAKE ME OUT...
...WOULDN'T HE HAVE DONE IT ALREADY?
AND MORE TO THE POINT...
...MY FRIENDS NEED HELP.
BAAAKAAAAAAA!
ON MY WAY!
BBBOOOM
SKRRA
KOOOOOM
BAKA...
...THE MONSTER PRINCE OF SUBTERRANEA.
HE BELIEVED IN ME ENOUGH TO RISK HIS LIFE WHEN I WAS TAKEN OVER BY THE DOOMSDAY VIRUS.

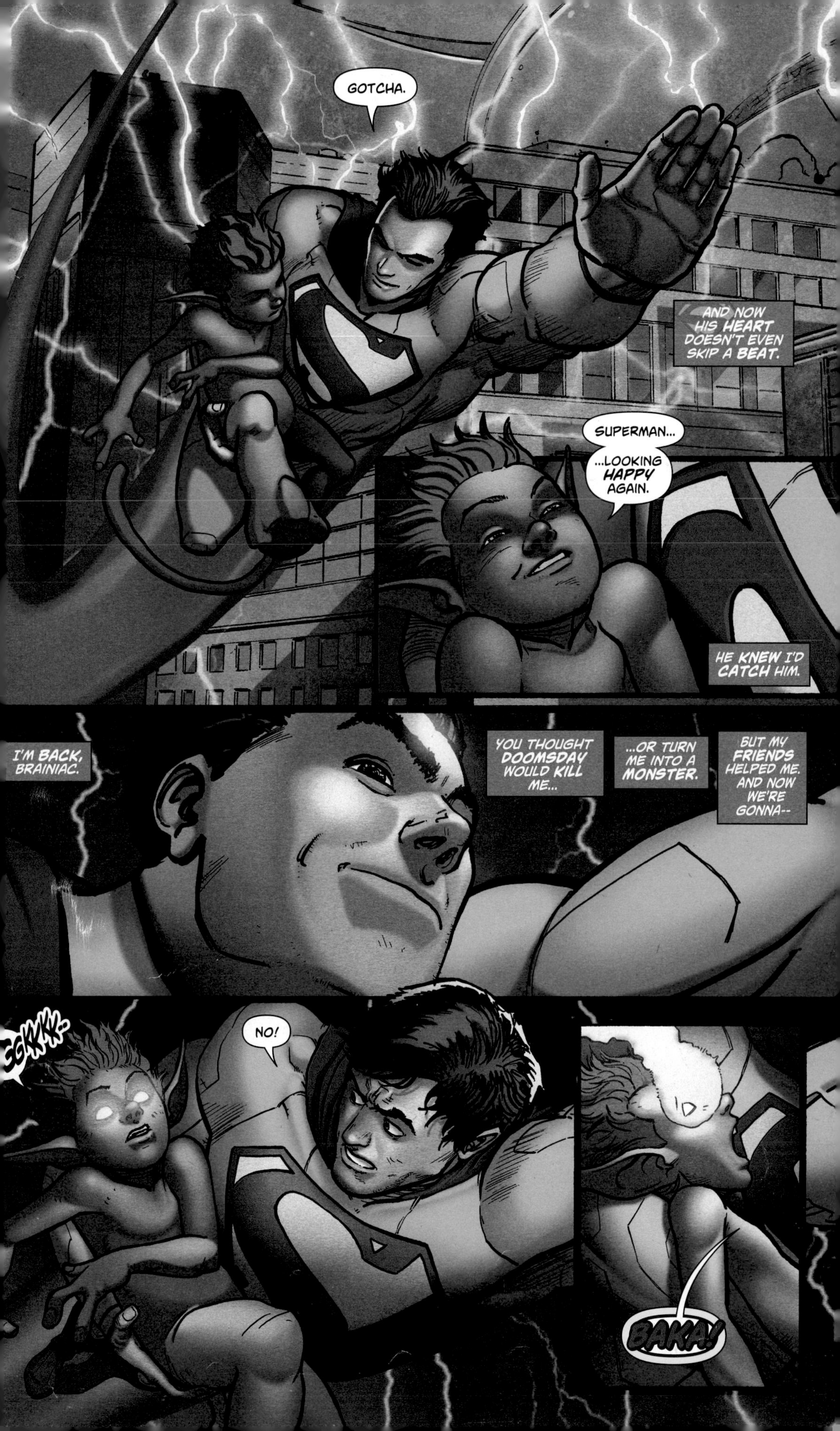
GOTCHA.
AND NOW HIS HEART DOESN'T EVEN SKIP A BEAT.
SUPERMAN...
...LOOKING HAPPY AGAIN.
HE KNEW I'D CATCH HIM.
I'M BACK, BRAINIAC.
YOU THOUGHT DOOMSDAY WOULD KILL ME...
...OR TURN ME INTO A MONSTER.
BUT MY FRIENDS HELPED ME. AND NOW WE'RE GONNA--
NO!
BAKA!

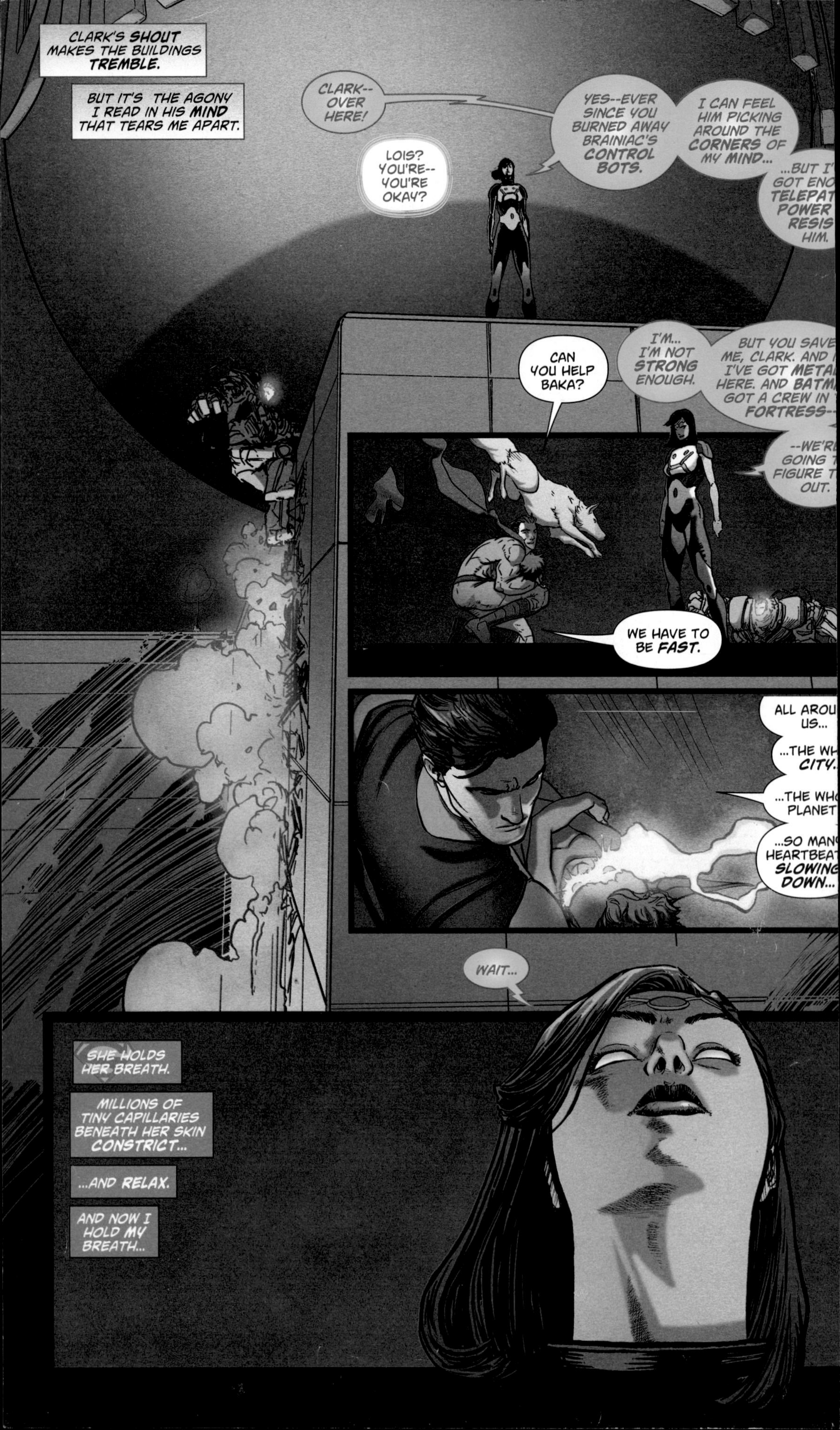

CLARK'S SHOUT MAKES THE BUILDINGS TREMBLE.
BUT IT'S THE AGONY I READ IN HIS MIND THAT TEARS ME APART.
CLARK-- OVER HERE!
LOIS? YOU'RE-- YOU'RE OKAY?
YES--EVER SINCE YOU BURNED AWAY BRAINIAC'S CONTROL BOTS.
I CAN FEEL HIM PICKING AROUND THE CORNERS OF MY MIND...
...BUT I'
GOT ENO
TELEPAT
POWER
RESIS
HIM.
CAN YOU HELP BAKA?
I'M... I'M NOT STRONG ENOUGH.
BUT YOU SAVE
ME, CLARK. AND I
I'VE GOT META
HERE. AND BATM
GOT A CREW IN T
FORTRESS--
--WE'R
GOING T
FIGURE T
OUT.
WE HAVE TO BE FAST.
ALL AROU
US...
...THE WH
CITY.
...THE WH
PLANET
...SO MAN
HEARTBEAT
SLOWING
DOWN...
WAIT...
SHE HOLDS HER BREATH.
MILLIONS OF TINY CAPILLARIES BENEATH HER SKIN CONSTRICT...
...AND RELAX.
AND NOW I HOLD MY BREATH...

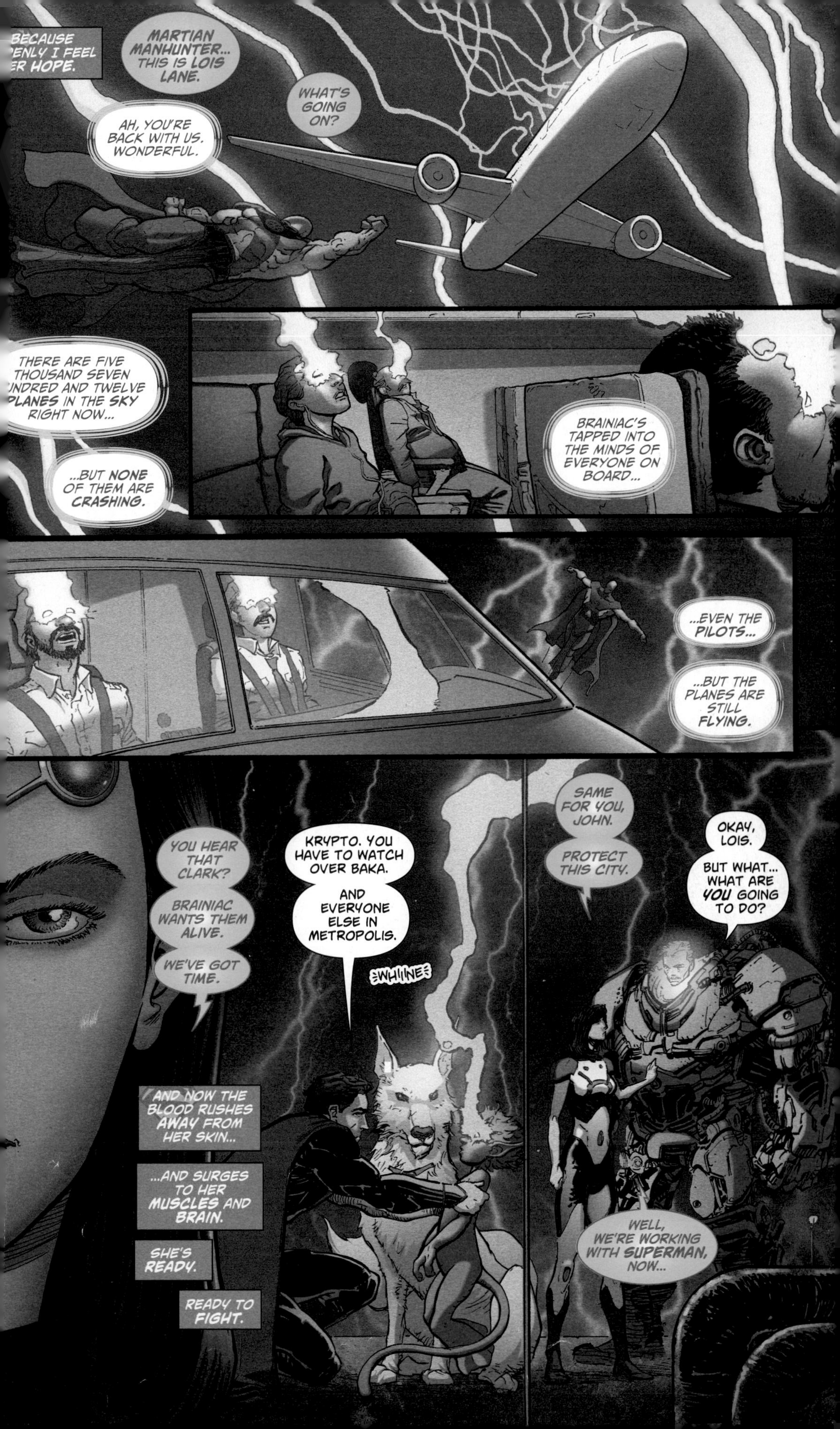
BECAUSE
PENLY I FEEL
ER HOPE.
MARTIAN MANHUNTER... THIS IS LOIS LANE.
WHAT'S GOING ON?
AH, YOU'RE BACK WITH US. WONDERFUL.
THERE ARE FIVE THOUSAND SEVEN
UNDRED AND TWELVE
PLANES IN THE SKY RIGHT NOW...
...BUT NONE OF THEM ARE CRASHING.
BRAINIAC'S TAPPED INTO THE MINDS OF EVERYONE ON BOARD...
...EVEN THE PILOTS...
...BUT THE PLANES ARE STILL FLYING.
YOU HEAR THAT CLARK?
BRAINIAC WANTS THEM ALIVE.
WE'VE GOT TIME.
AND NOW THE BLOOD RUSHES AWAY FROM HER SKIN...
...AND SURGES TO HER MUSCLES AND BRAIN.
SHE'S READY.
READY TO FIGHT.
KRYPTO. YOU HAVE TO WATCH OVER BAKA.
AND EVERYONE ELSE IN METROPOLIS.
WHIINE
SAME FOR YOU, JOHN.
PROTECT THIS CITY.
OKAY, LOIS.
BUT WHAT... WHAT ARE YOU GOING TO DO?
WELL, WE'RE WORKING WITH SUPERMAN, NOW...

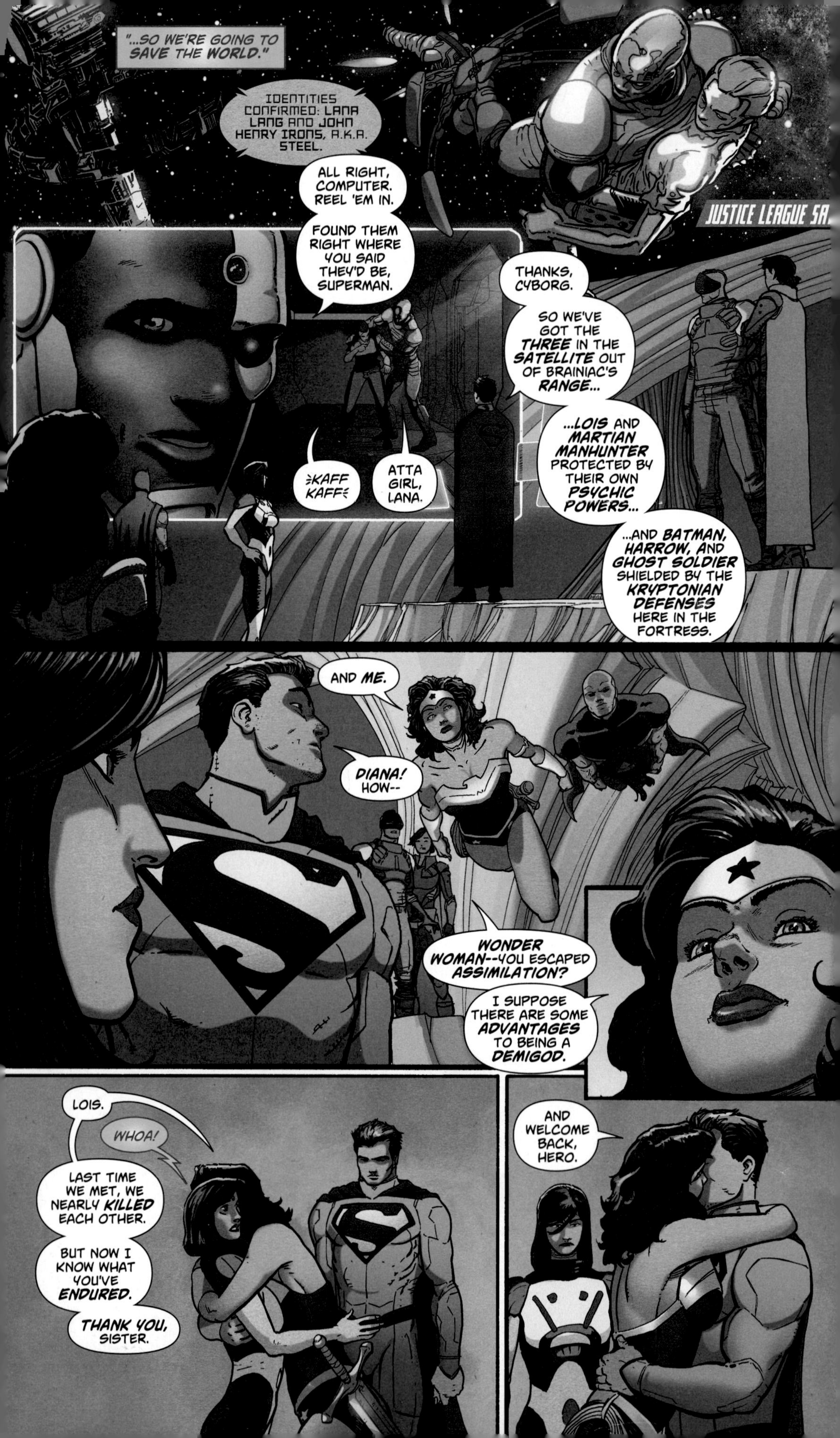
"...SO WE'RE GOING TO SAVE THE WORLD."
IDENTITIES CONFIRMED: LANA LANG AND JOHN HENRY IRONS, A.K.A. STEEL.
ALL RIGHT, COMPUTER. REEL 'EM IN.
FOUND THEM RIGHT WHERE YOU SAID THEY'D BE, SUPERMAN.
THANKS, CYBORG.
SO WE'VE GOT THE THREE IN THE SATELLITE OUT OF BRAINIAC'S RANGE...
KAFF KAFF
ATTA GIRL, LANA.
...LOIS AND MARTIAN MANHUNTER PROTECTED BY THEIR OWN PSYCHIC POWERS...
...AND BATMAN, HARROW, AND GHOST SOLDIER SHIELDED BY THE KRYPTONIAN DEFENSES HERE IN THE FORTRESS.
AND ME.
DIANA! HOW--
WONDER WOMAN--YOU ESCAPED ASSIMILATION?
I SUPPOSE THERE ARE SOME ADVANTAGES TO BEING A DEMIGOD.
LOIS.
WHOA!
LAST TIME WE MET, WE NEARLY KILLED EACH OTHER.
BUT NOW I KNOW WHAT YOU'VE ENDURED.
THANK YOU, SISTER.
AND WELCOME BACK, HERO.

HEY, GUYS! LANA LANG, HERE!

'M GETTING A OOK AT THIS NEW DATA...

AND I THINK BRAINIAC'S ETWORKING ALL THESE BRAINS!

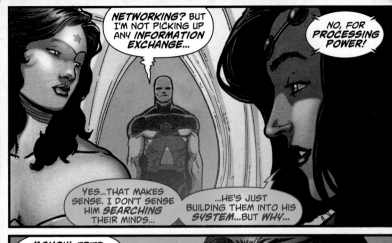

NETWORKING? BUT I'M NOT PICKING UP ANY *INFORMATION EXCHANGE*...

NO, FOR *PROCESSING POWER!*

YES...THAT MAKES SENSE. I DON'T SENSE HIM *SEARCHING* THEIR MINDS...

...HE'S JUST BUILDING THEM INTO HIS *SYSTEM*...BUT *WHY*...

MONGUL TRIED SOMETHING LIKE THIS A WHILE BACK.

TAPPED INTO MILLIONS OF BRAINS, TRIED TO TURN THE EARTH INTO A MASSIVE PSYCHIC *WEAPON*.

WE HAD TO THROW HIM INTO THE *PHANTOM ZONE* TO STOP HIM.

GUESSING THE *MOTHERSHIP'S* A LITTLE TO *BIG* FOR *THAT* SOLUTION.

BUT WE'VE GOT TO TAKE IT *DOWN*.

HARROW CAN *SUMMON* THE *DEAD*. WE CAN STAY *INTANGIBLE* UNTIL THE LAST MINUTE, WHICH SHOULD HELP US FROM GETTING *ASSIMILATED*.

JUST POINT US TO THE SHIP'S *SOFT SPOT* AND--

EVE ME, OVE TO K ALL OF 'INIAC'S OYS.

BUT RIGHT NOW, *SEVEN BILLION MINDS* ARE LINKED TO THAT MOTHERSHIP.

I...I DON'T KNOW WHAT'LL HAPPEN TO THEM IF WE JUST *SMASH* IT.

HRNN...

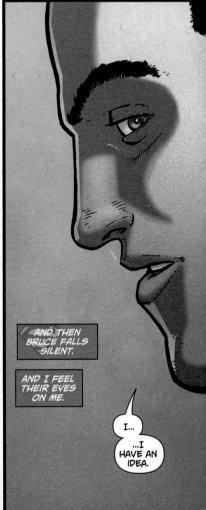

AND THEN *BRUCE* FALLS *SILENT*.

AND I FEEL THEIR EYES ON ME.

I...

...I HAVE AN IDEA.

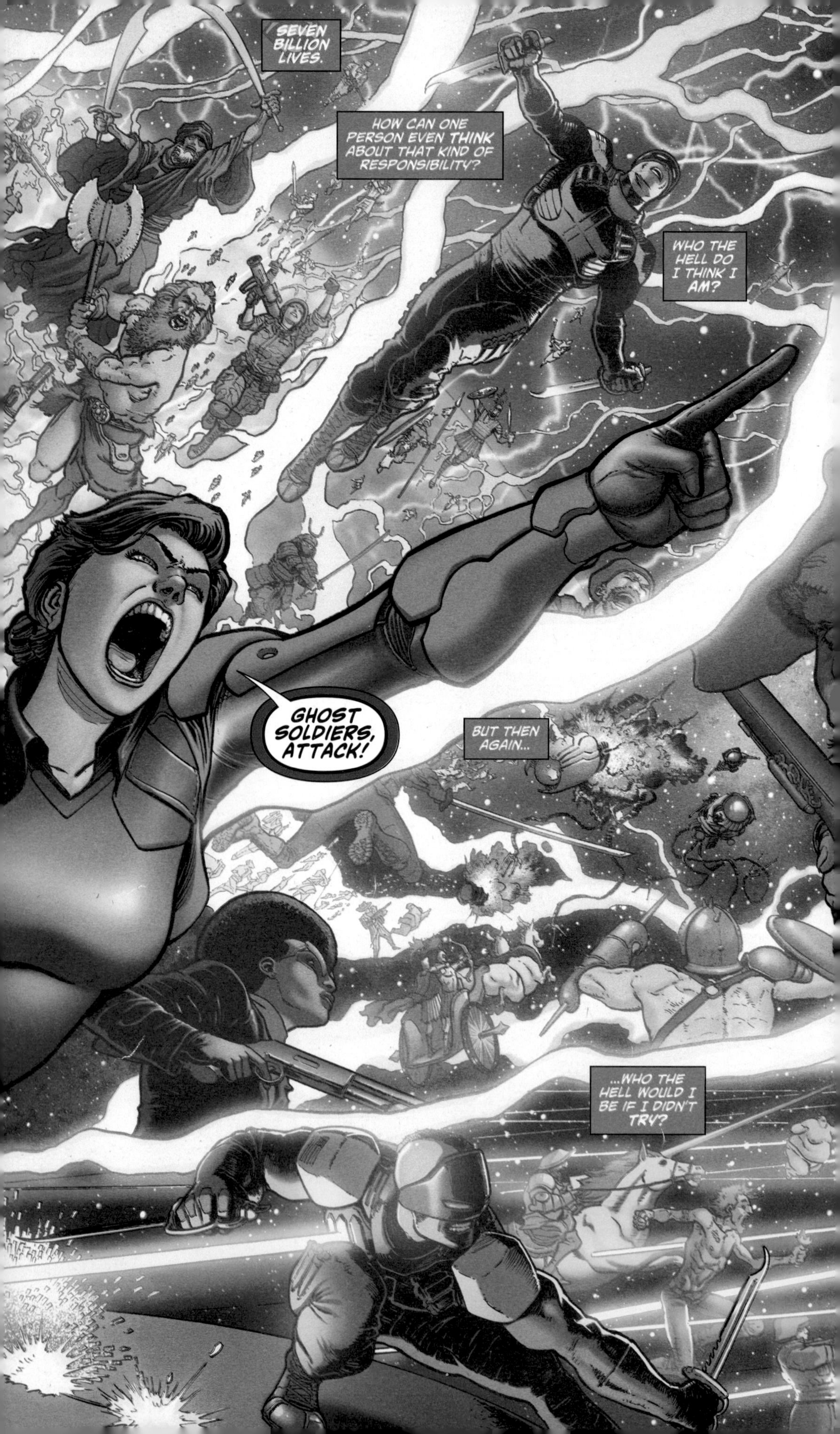
SEVEN BILLION LIVES.
HOW CAN ONE PERSON EVEN THINK ABOUT THAT KIND OF RESPONSIBILITY?
WHO THE HELL DO I THINK I AM?
GHOST SOLDIERS, ATTACK!
BUT THEN AGAIN...
...WHO THE HELL WOULD I BE IF I DIDN'T TRY?

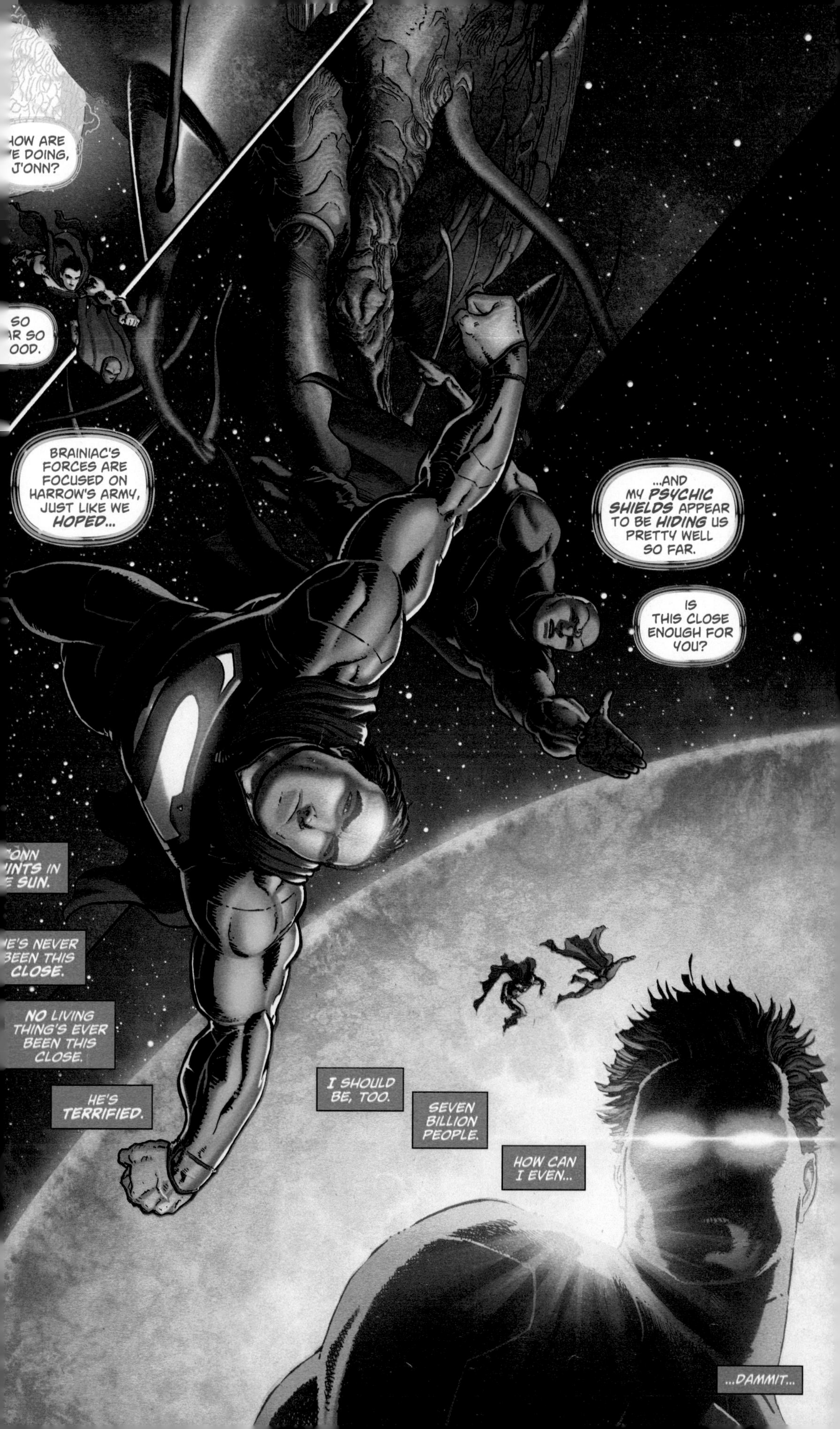
HOW ARE
WE DOING,
J'ONN?
SO
FAR SO
GOOD.
BRAINIAC'S FORCES ARE FOCUSED ON HARROW'S ARMY, JUST LIKE WE HOPED...
...AND MY PSYCHIC SHIELDS APPEAR TO BE HIDING US PRETTY WELL SO FAR.
IS THIS CLOSE ENOUGH FOR YOU?
J'ONN SQUINTS IN THE SUN.
HE'S NEVER BEEN THIS CLOSE.
NO LIVING THING'S EVER BEEN THIS CLOSE.
HE'S TERRIFIED.
I SHOULD BE, TOO.
SEVEN BILLION PEOPLE.
HOW CAN I EVEN...
...DAMMIT...

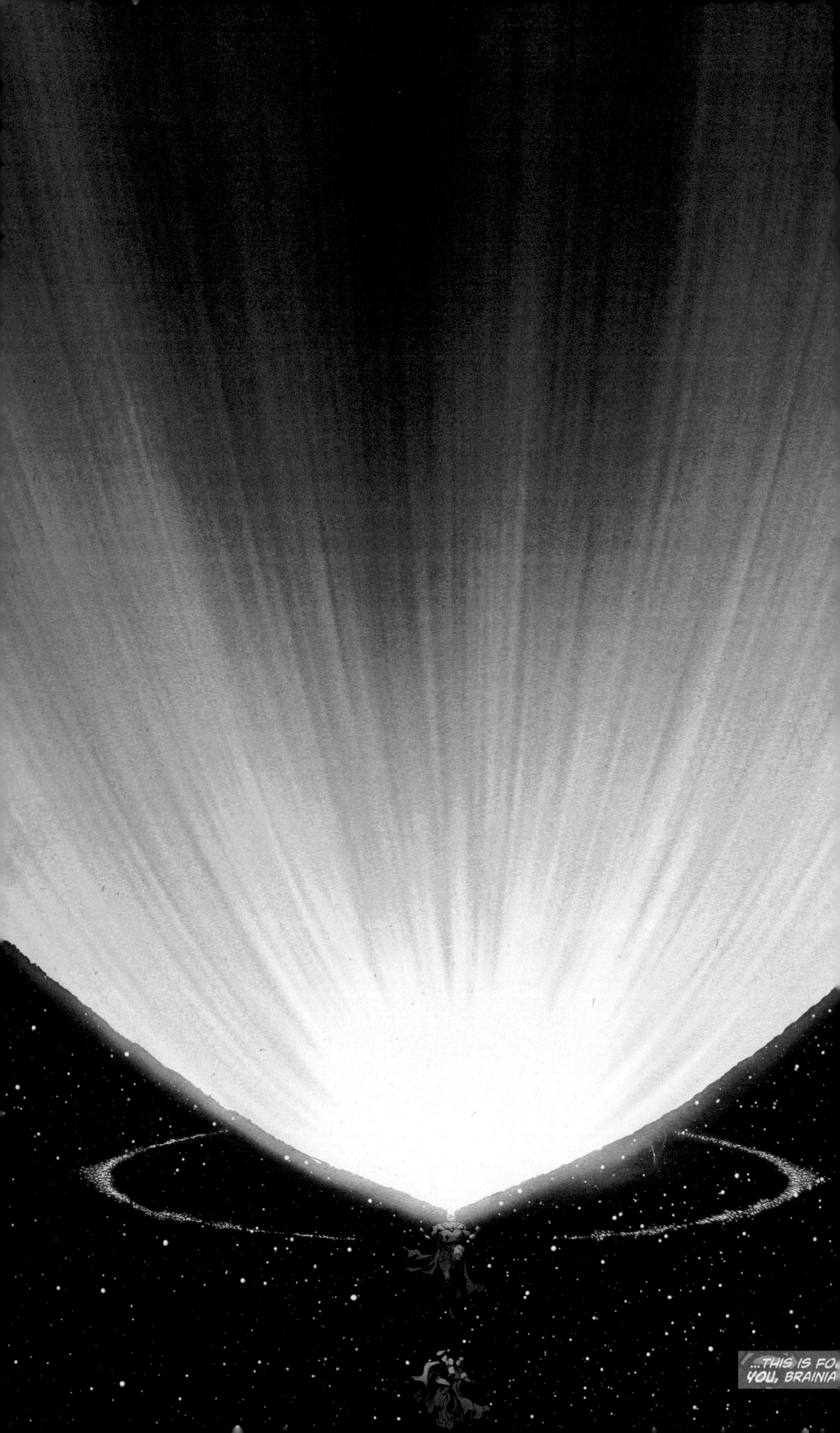

...THIS IS FOR
YOU, BRAINIA

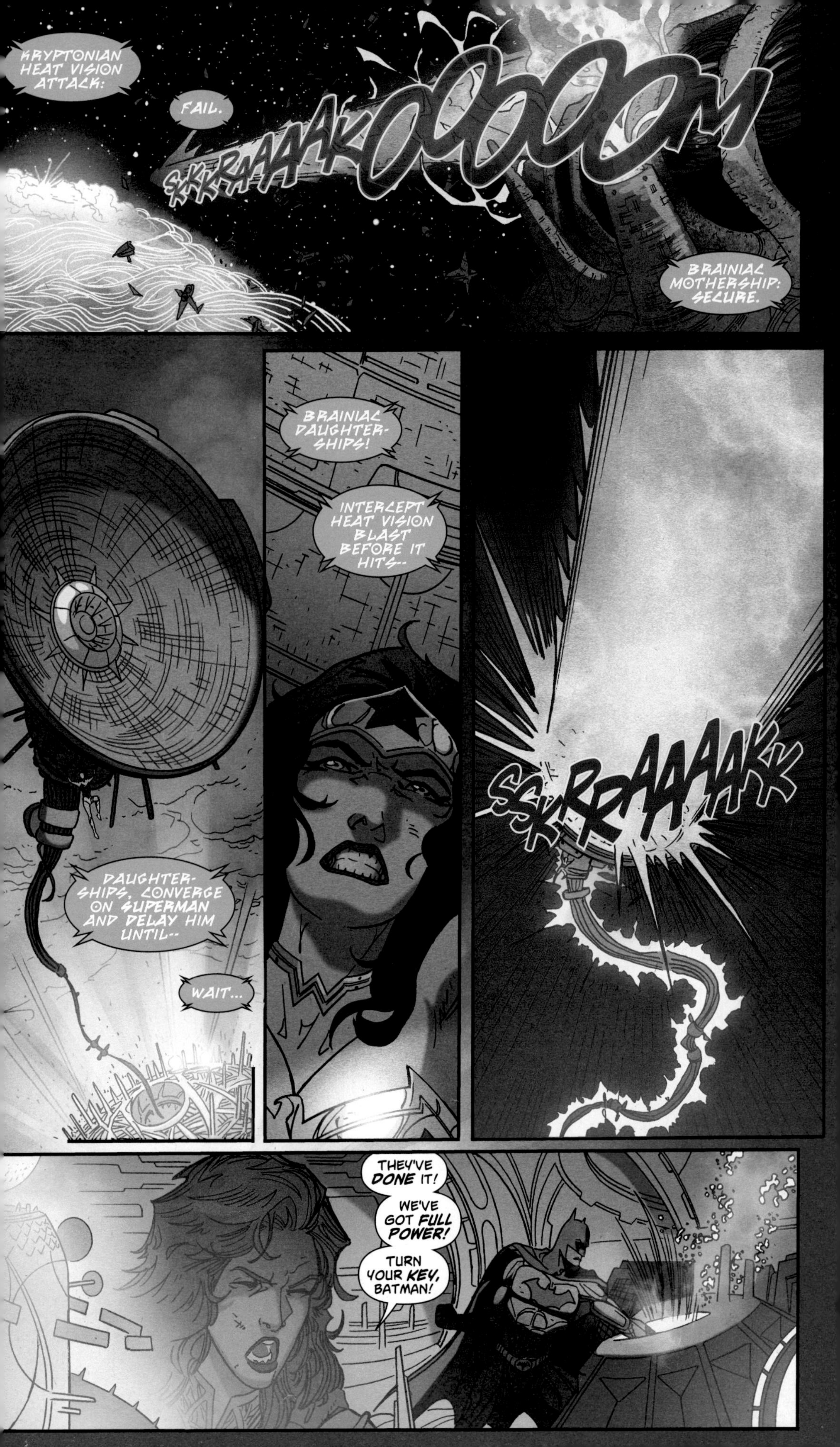
KRYPTONIAN HEAT VISION ATTACK:
FAIL.
SKKRAAAAKOOOOOOM
BRAINIAC MOTHERSHIP: SECURE.
BRAINIAC DAUGHTER-SHIPS!
INTERCEPT HEAT VISION BLAST BEFORE IT HITS--
DAUGHTER-SHIPS, CONVERGE ON SUPERMAN AND DELAY HIM UNTIL--
WAIT...
SSKRRAAAAKK
THEY'VE DONE IT!
WE'VE GOT FULL POWER!
TURN YOUR KEY, BATMAN!

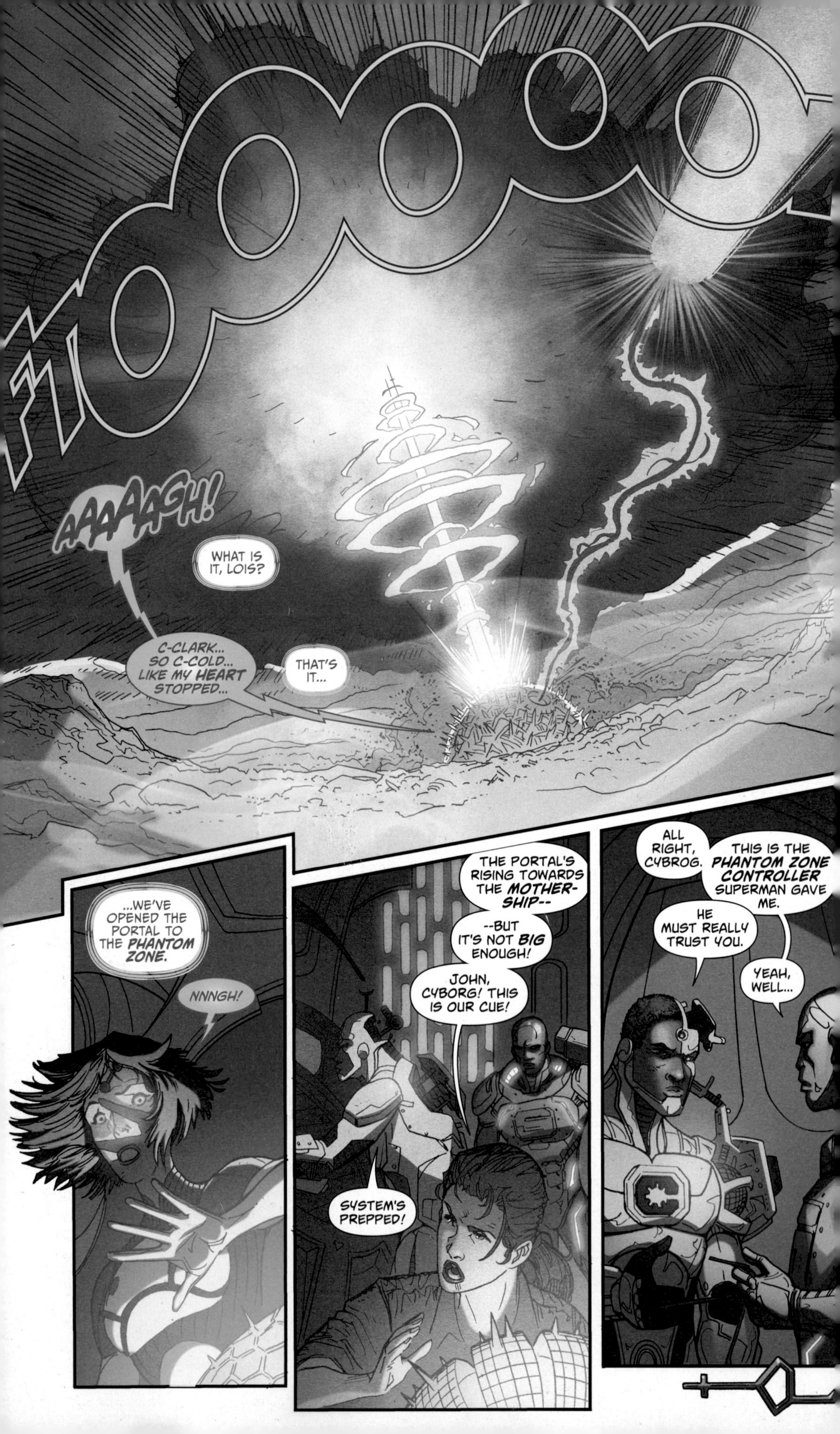
ZOOOOOOM
AAAAAGH!
WHAT IS IT, LOIS?
C-CLARK... SO C-COLD... LIKE MY HEART STOPPED...
THAT'S IT...
...WE'VE OPENED THE PORTAL TO THE PHANTOM ZONE.
NNNGH!
THE PORTAL'S RISING TOWARDS THE MOTHER-SHIP--
--BUT IT'S NOT BIG ENOUGH!
JOHN, CYBORG! THIS IS OUR CUE!
SYSTEM'S PREPPED!
ALL RIGHT, CYBROG.
THIS IS THE PHANTOM ZONE CONTROLLER SUPERMAN GAVE ME.
HE MUST REALLY TRUST YOU.
YEAH, WELL...

...NOW I GUESS
'S TIME FOR US
O TRUST HIM."
SECONDARY PHANTOM ENERGY SOURCE DETECTED!
CONVERGING WITH PRIMARY PORTAL!
MOTHERSHIP TRAJECTORY SHIFTING!
SHAY.
PLEASE TELL ME SOMETHING GOOD.
HAPPY TO OBLIGE, SUPERMAN.
IT'S WORKING.
WE'RE GOING TO PULL BOTH THE MOTHER-SHIP...
...AND THE ENTIRE PLANET...
...INTO THE PHANTOM ZONE...
...A PLACE WITHOUT TIME...
...IN ORDER TO BUY THE TIME WE NEED TO SAVE EVERYONE.
INTRIGUING...

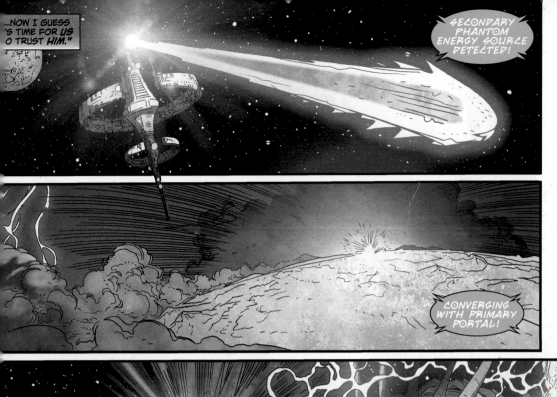

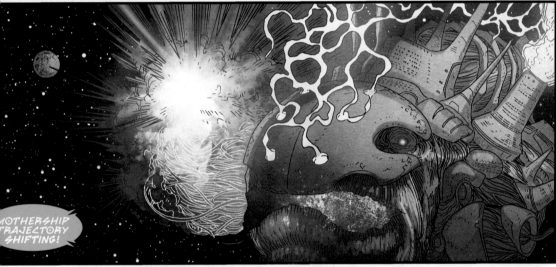

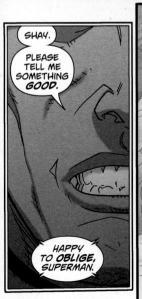

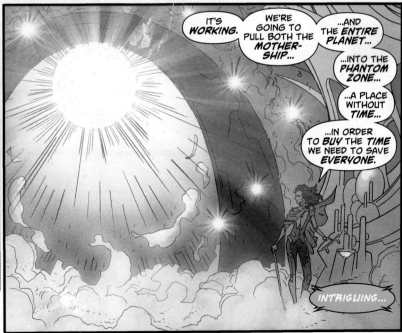

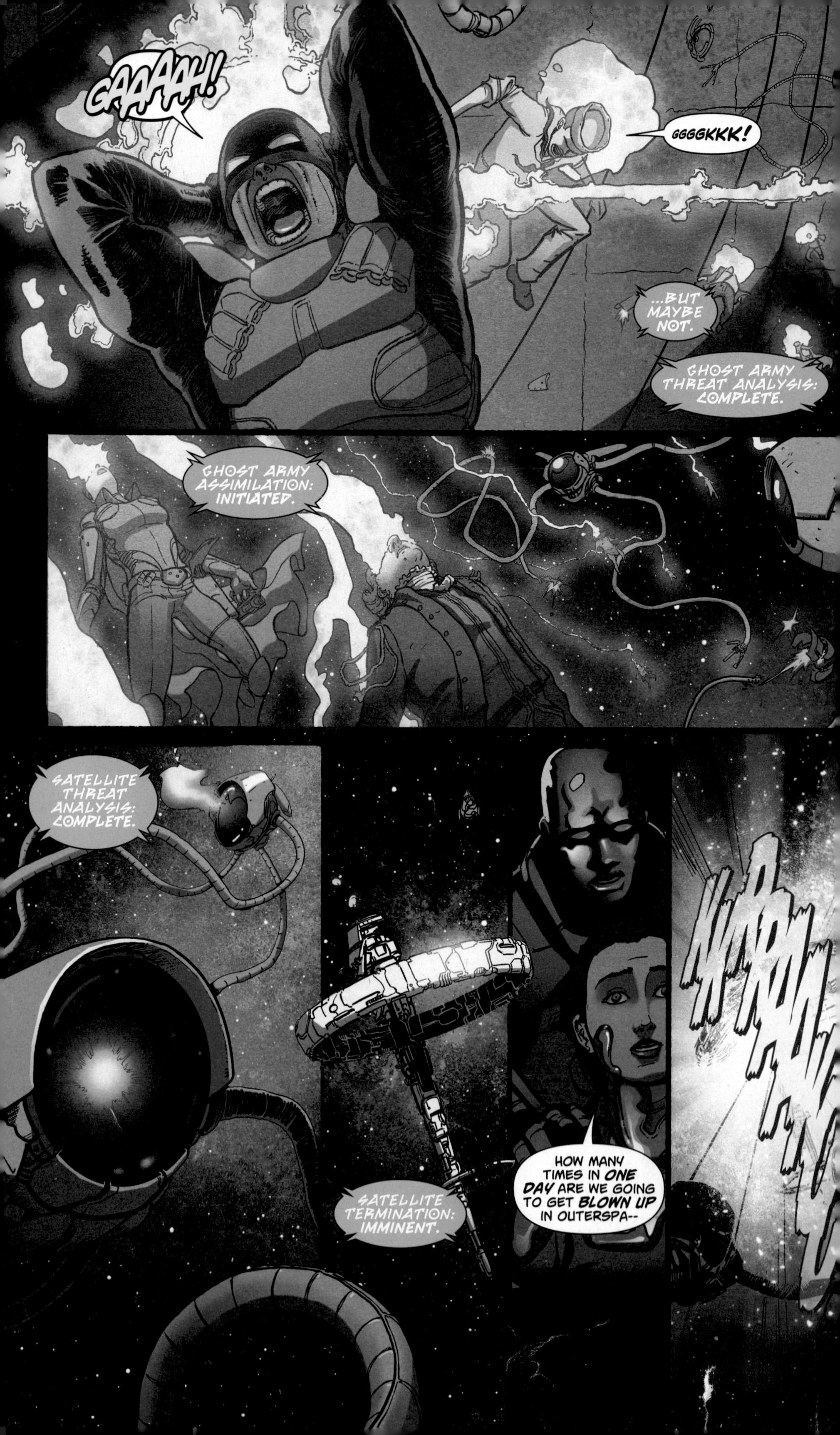
GAAAAH!
GGGGKKK!
...BUT MAYBE NOT.
GHOST ARMY THREAT ANALYSIS: COMPLETE.
GHOST ARMY ASSIMILATION: INITIATED.
SATELLITE THREAT ANALYSIS: COMPLETE.
SATELLITE TERMINATION: IMMINENT.
HOW MANY TIMES IN ONE DAY ARE WE GOING TO GET BLOWN UP IN OUTERSPA--

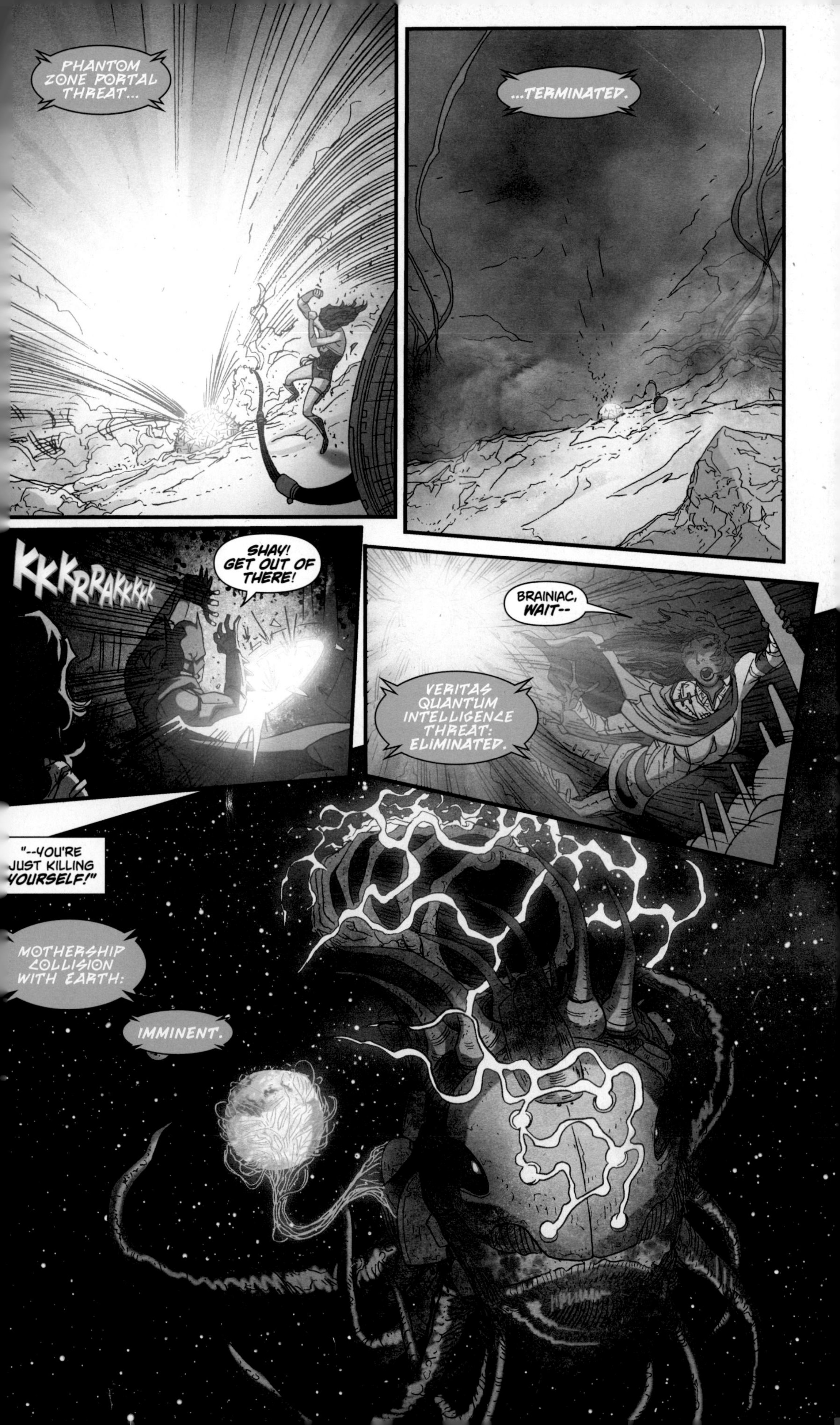
PHANTOM ZONE PORTAL THREAT...
...TERMINATED.
KKKRRAKKKKK
SHAY! GET OUT OF THERE!
BRAINIAC, WAIT--
VERITAS QUANTUM INTELLIGENCE THREAT: ELIMINATED.
"--YOU'RE JUST KILLING YOURSELF!"
MOTHERSHIP COLLISION WITH EARTH:
IMMINENT.

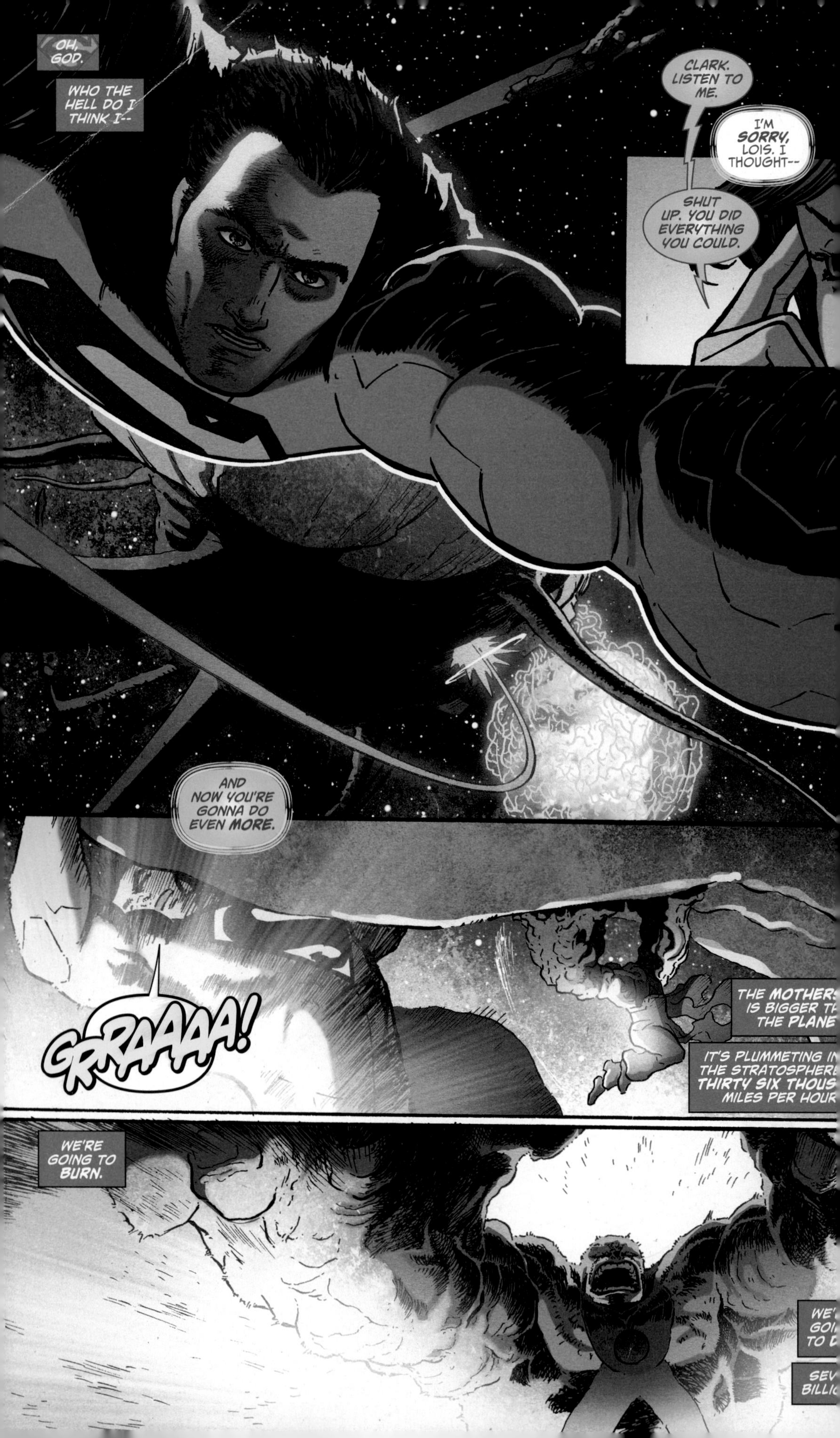
OH, GOD.
WHO THE HELL DO I THINK I--
CLARK. LISTEN TO ME.
I'M SORRY, LOIS. I THOUGHT--
SHUT UP. YOU DID EVERYTHING YOU COULD.
AND NOW YOU'RE GONNA DO EVEN MORE.
GRRAAAA!
WE'RE GOING TO BURN.

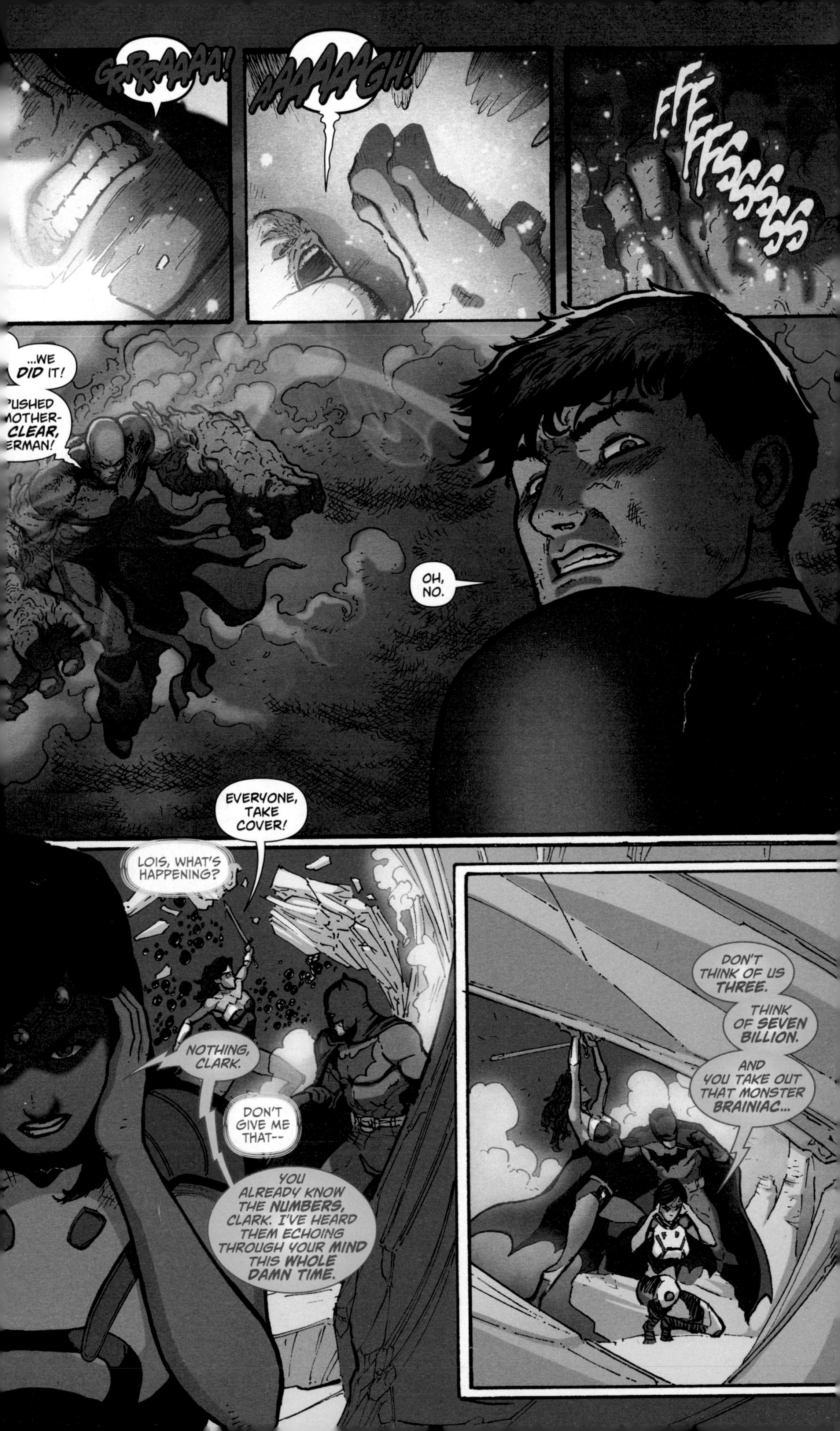

GRRRAAAA!
AAAAAAGH!
FFFFFSSSSSS
...WE DID IT!
PUSHED MOTHER- CLEAR, ERMAN!
OH, NO.
EVERYONE, TAKE COVER!
LOIS, WHAT'S HAPPENING?
NOTHING, CLARK.
DON'T GIVE ME THAT--
YOU ALREADY KNOW THE NUMBERS, CLARK. I'VE HEARD THEM ECHOING THROUGH YOUR MIND THIS WHOLE DAMN TIME.
DON'T THINK OF US THREE.
THINK OF SEVEN BILLION.
AND YOU TAKE OUT THAT MONSTER BRAINIAC...

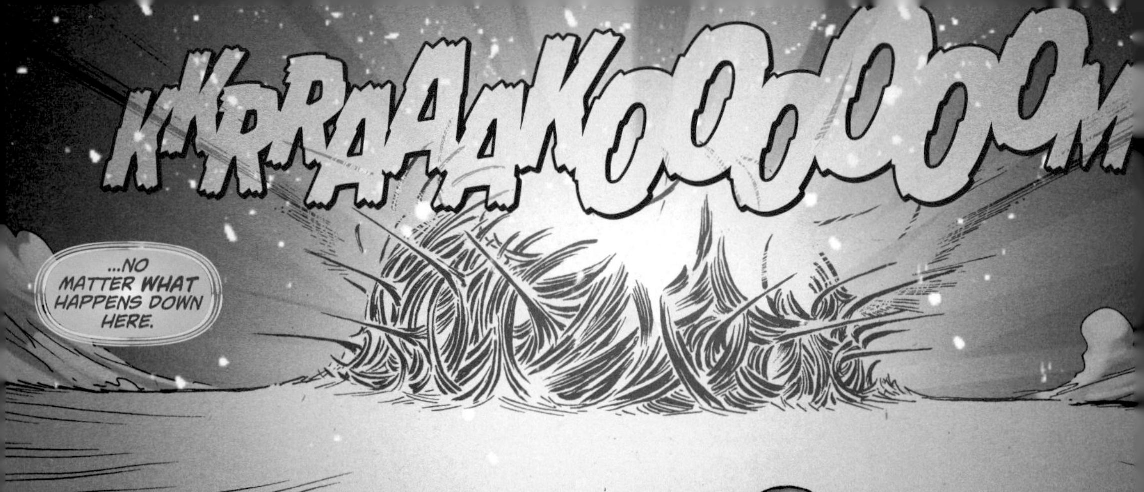
KKRRAAAKOOOOOOM
...NO MATTER WHAT HAPPENS DOWN HERE.

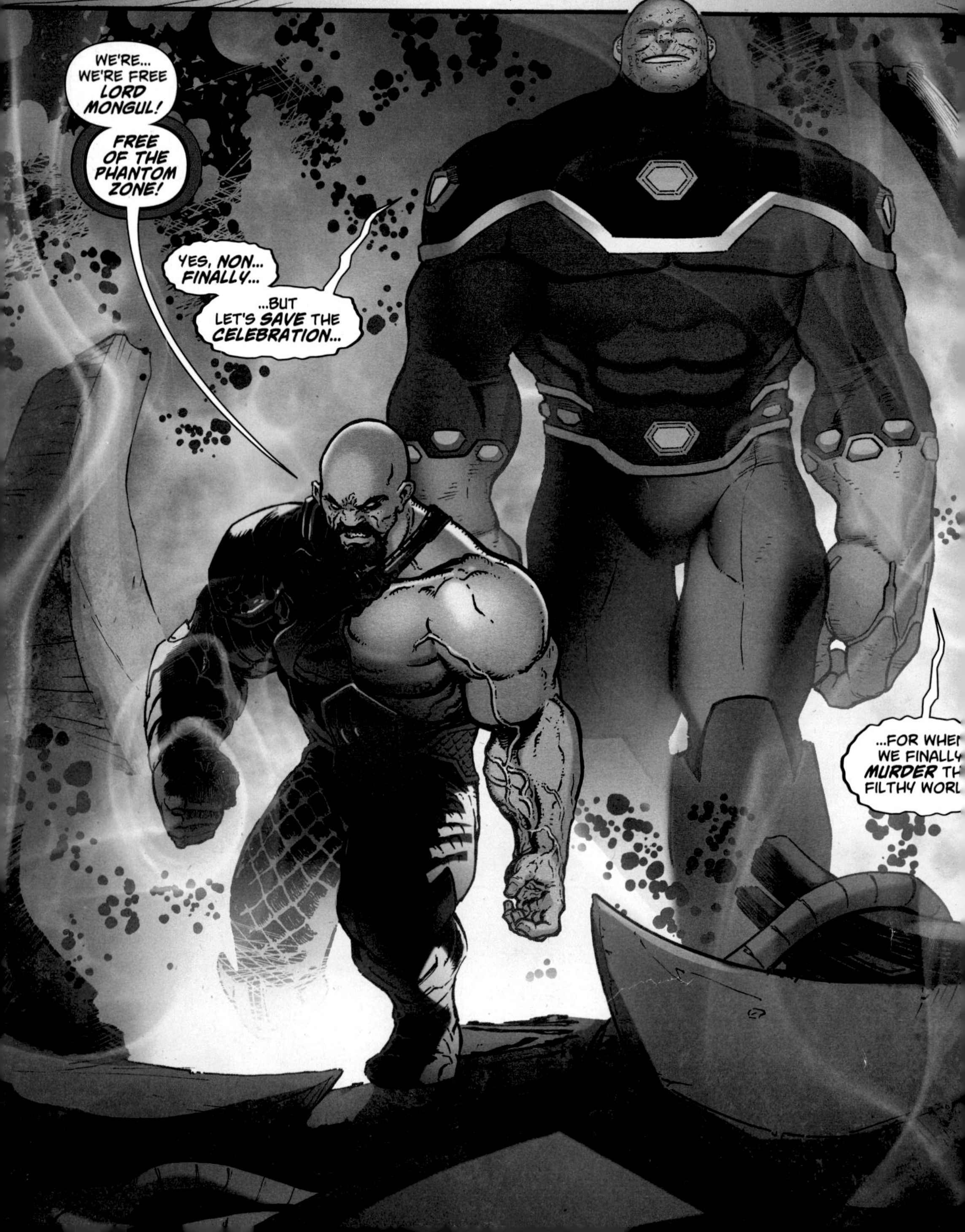
WE'RE... WE'RE FREE LORD MONGUL!
FREE OF THE PHANTOM ZONE!
YES, NON... FINALLY...
...BUT LET'S SAVE THE CELEBRATION...
...FOR WHE
WE FINALLY
MURDER TH
FILTHY WORL

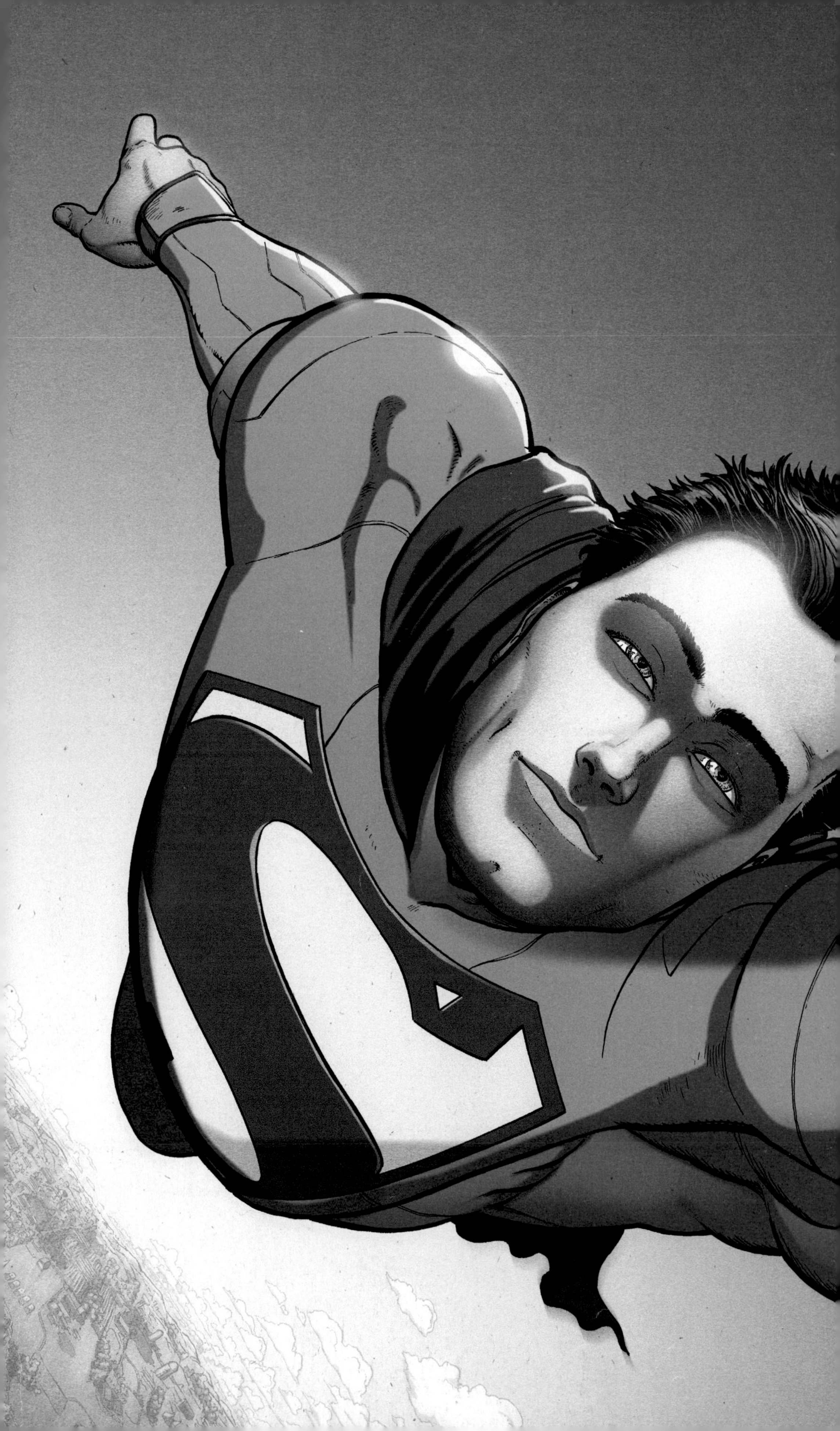

"AFTER DOOMED"

GREG PAK writer **SCOTT KOLINS VICENTE CIFUENTES** artists **WIL QUINTANA** colorist

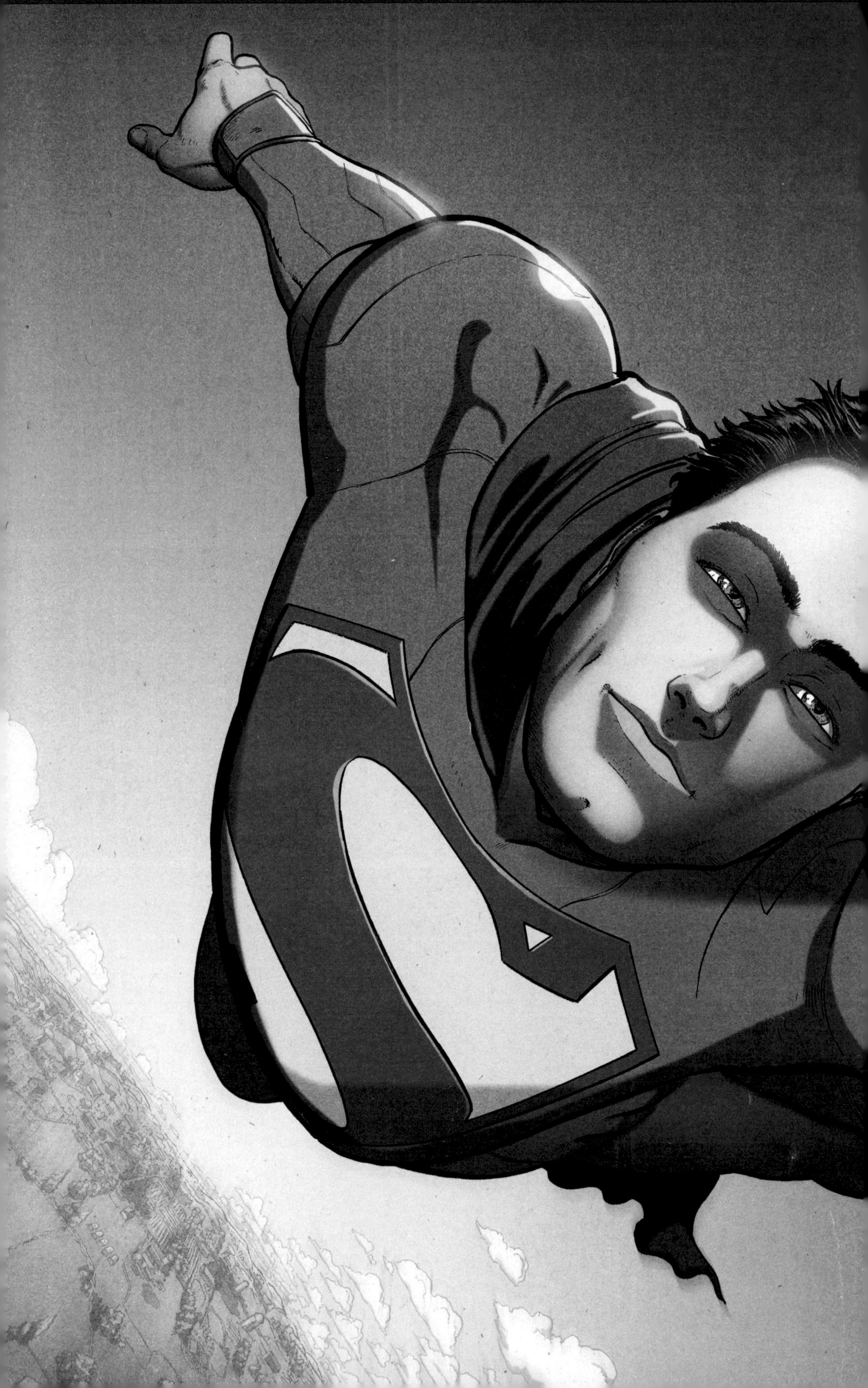

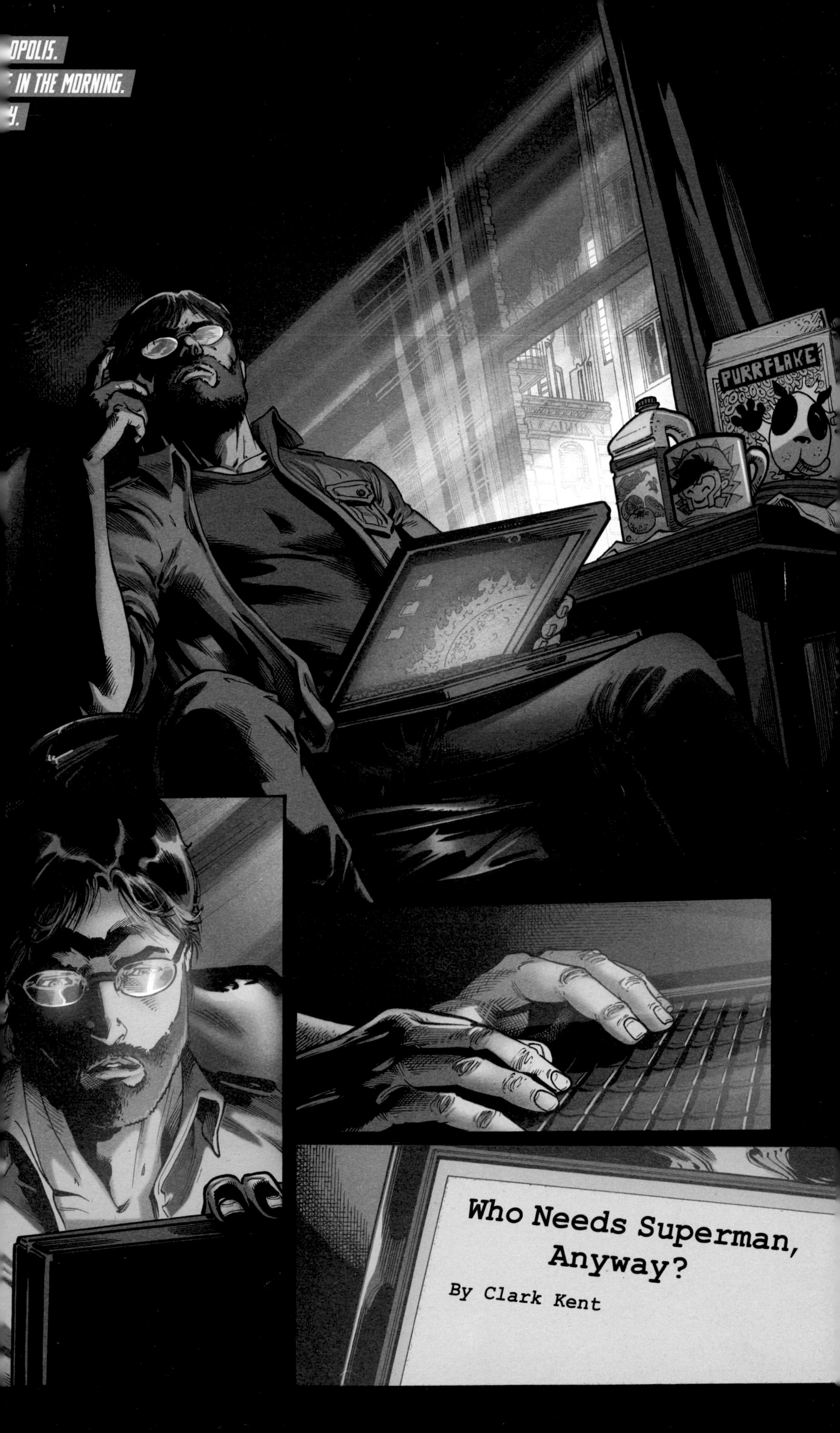
OPOLIS.
IN THE MORNING.
Y.
PURRFLAKE
Who Needs Superman, Anyway?
By Clark Kent

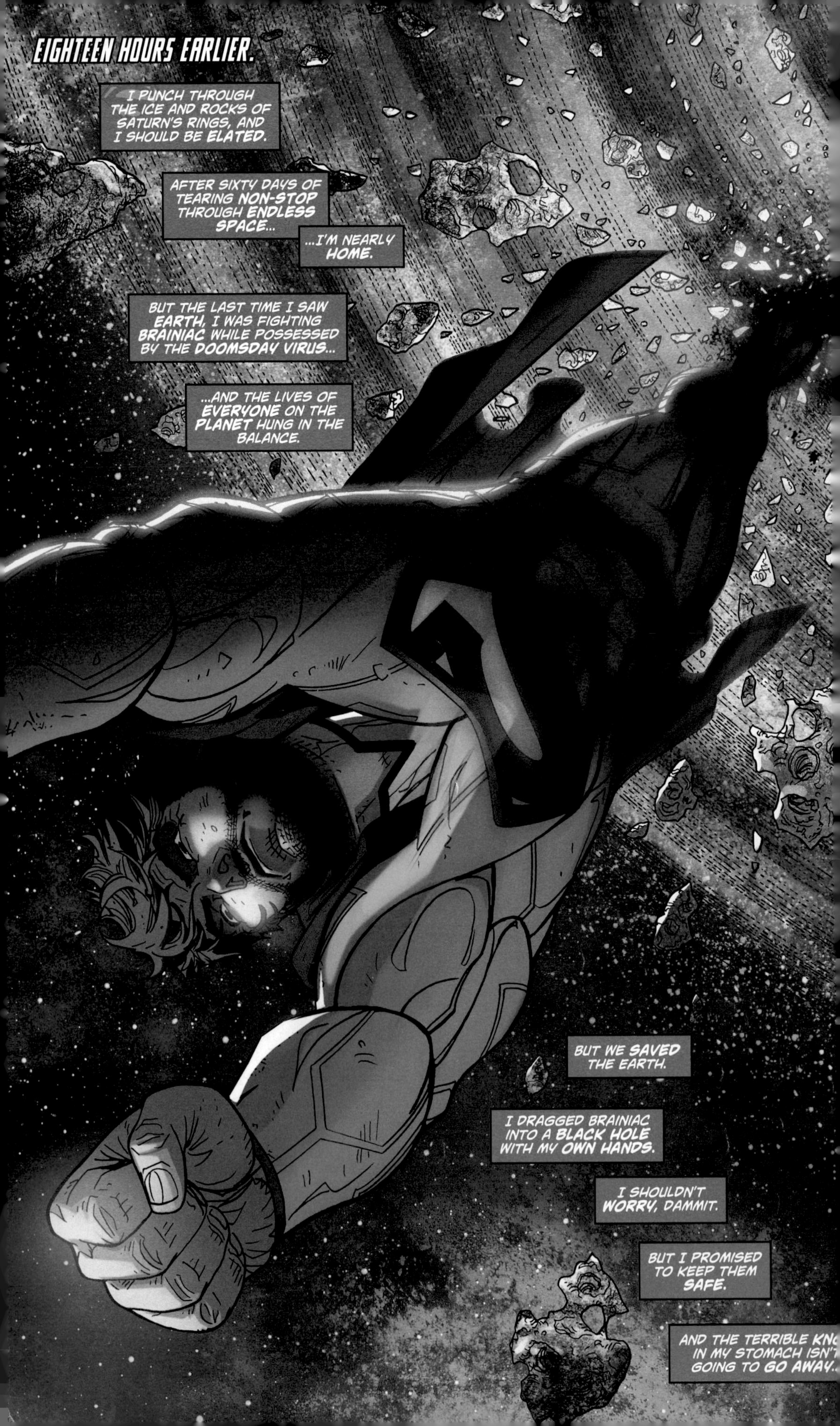
EIGHTEEN HOURS EARLIER.
I PUNCH THROUGH THE ICE AND ROCKS OF SATURN'S RINGS, AND I SHOULD BE ELATED.
AFTER SIXTY DAYS OF TEARING NON-STOP THROUGH ENDLESS SPACE...
...I'M NEARLY HOME.
BUT THE LAST TIME I SAW EARTH, I WAS FIGHTING BRAINIAC WHILE POSSESSED BY THE DOOMSDAY VIRUS...
...AND THE LIVES OF EVERYONE ON THE PLANET HUNG IN THE BALANCE.
BUT WE SAVED THE EARTH.
I DRAGGED BRAINIAC INTO A BLACK HOLE WITH MY OWN HANDS.
I SHOULDN'T WORRY, DAMMIT.
BUT I PROMISED TO KEEP THEM SAFE.
AND THE TERRIBLE KNO IN MY STOMACH ISN'T GOING TO GO AWAY.

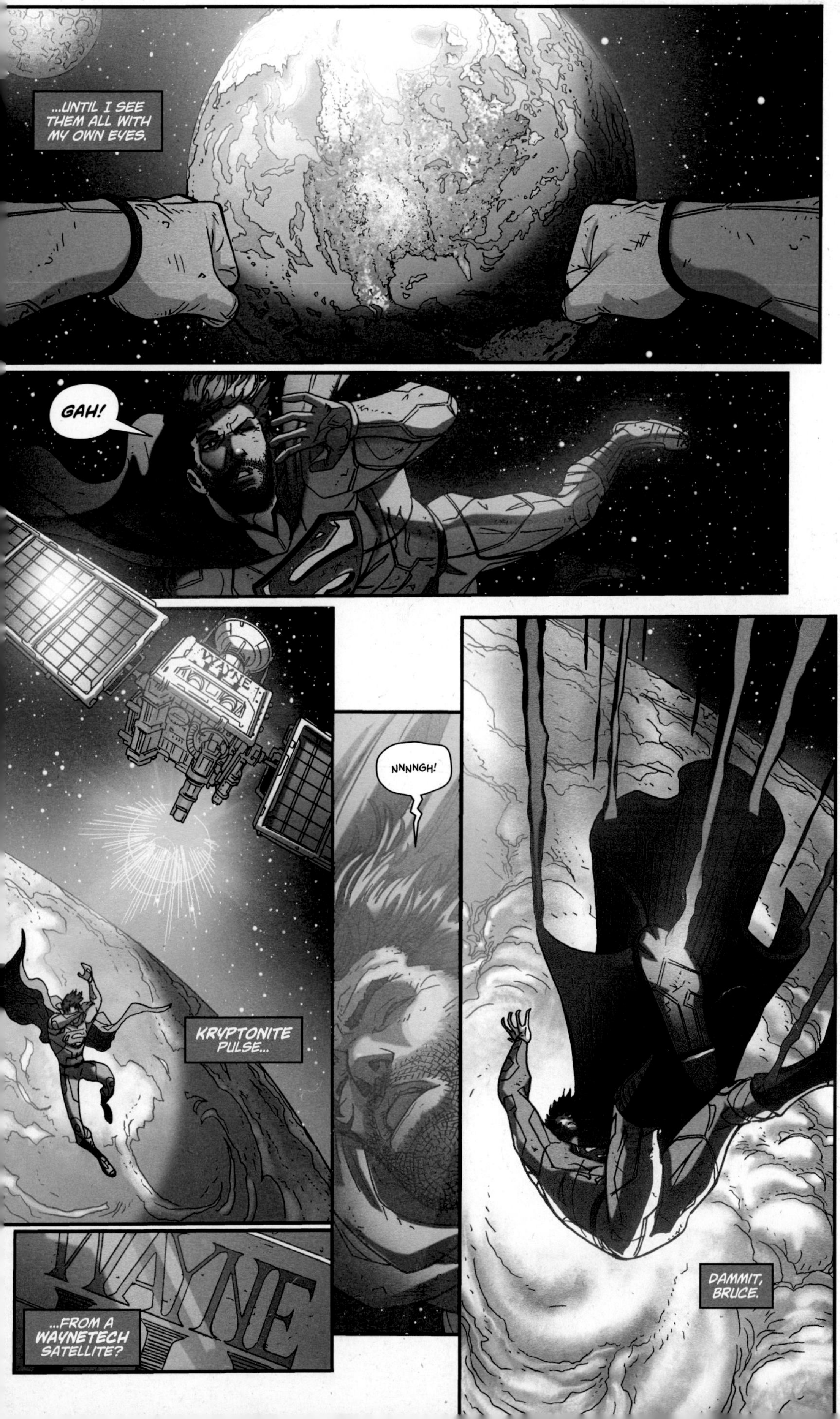
...UNTIL I SEE THEM ALL WITH MY OWN EYES.
GAH!
WAYNE
KRYPTONITE PULSE...
WAYNE
...FROM A WAYNETECH SATELLITE?
NNNNGH!
DAMMIT, BRUCE.

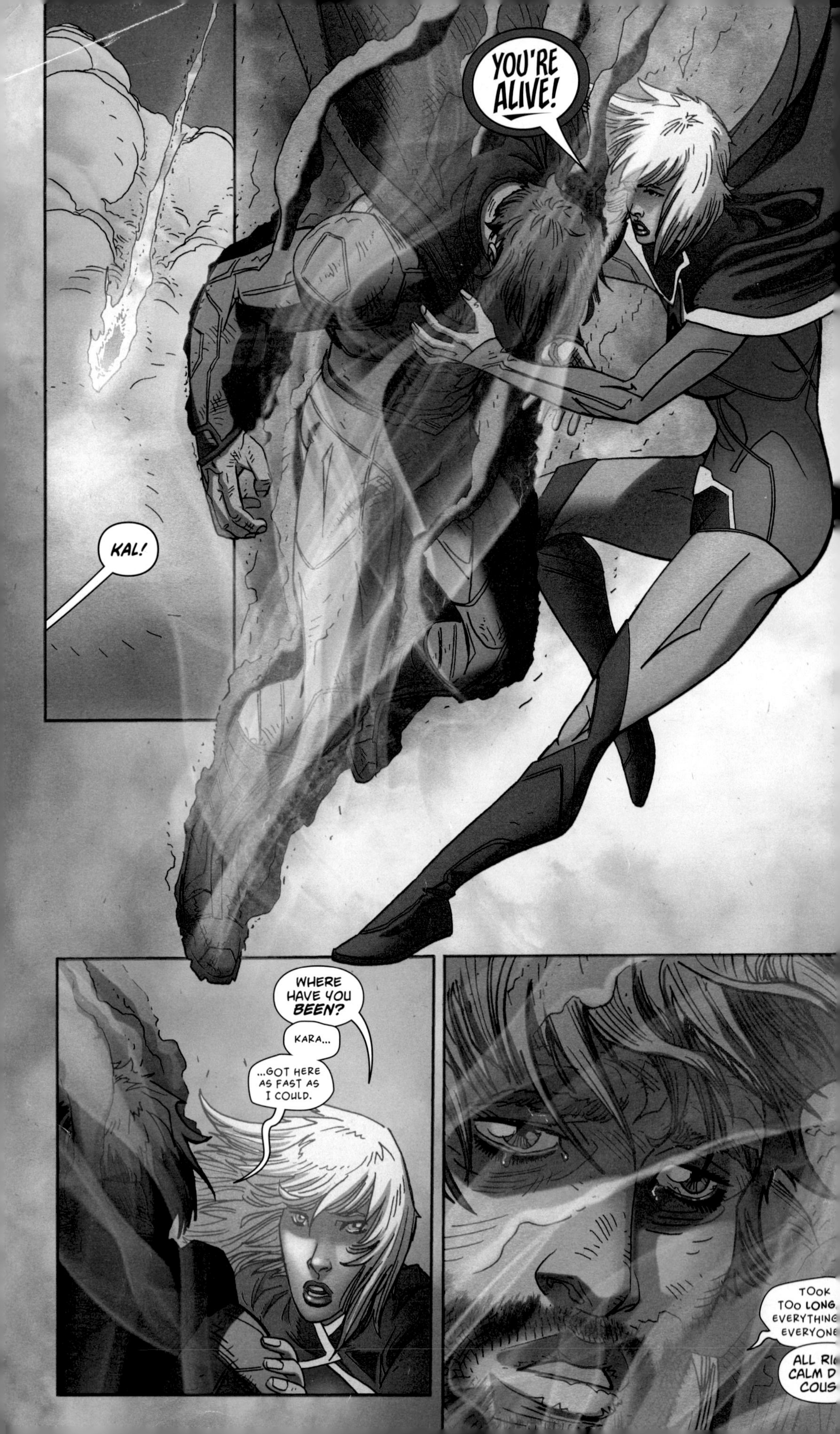
YOU'RE ALIVE!
KAL!
WHERE HAVE YOU BEEN?
KARA...
...GOT HERE AS FAST AS I COULD.
TOOK TOO LONG. EVERYTHING EVERYONE
ALL RI CALM D COUS

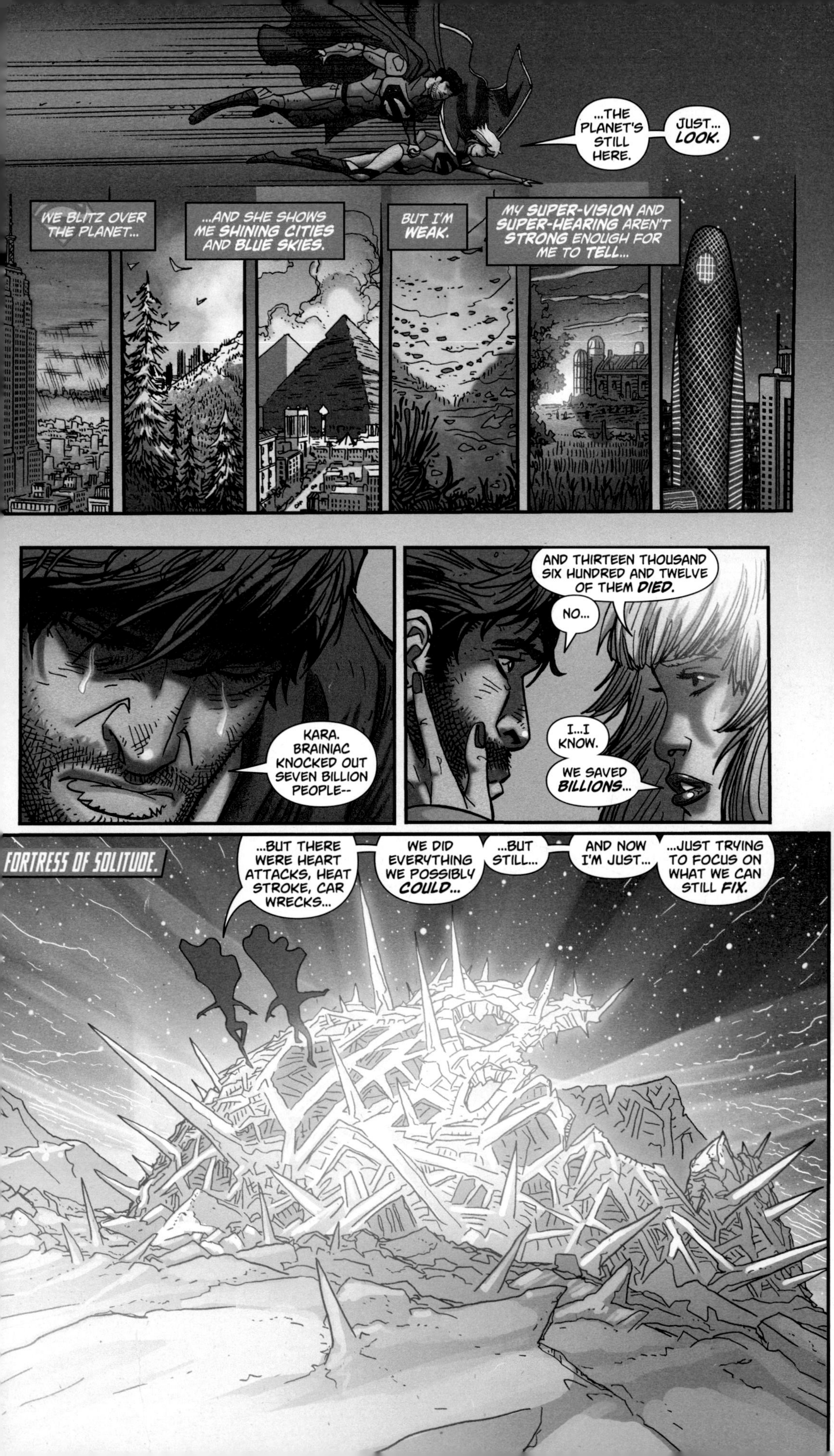
...THE PLANET'S STILL HERE.
JUST... LOOK.
WE BLITZ OVER THE PLANET...
...AND SHE SHOWS ME SHINING CITIES AND BLUE SKIES.
BUT I'M WEAK.
MY SUPER-VISION AND SUPER-HEARING AREN'T STRONG ENOUGH FOR ME TO TELL...
KARA. BRAINIAC KNOCKED OUT SEVEN BILLION PEOPLE--
AND THIRTEEN THOUSAND SIX HUNDRED AND TWELVE OF THEM DIED.
NO...
I...I KNOW.
WE SAVED BILLIONS...
FORTRESS OF SOLITUDE.
...BUT THERE WERE HEART ATTACKS, HEAT STROKE, CAR WRECKS...
WE DID EVERYTHING WE POSSIBLY COULD...
...BUT STILL...
AND NOW I'M JUST...
...JUST TRYING TO FOCUS ON WHAT WE CAN STILL FIX.

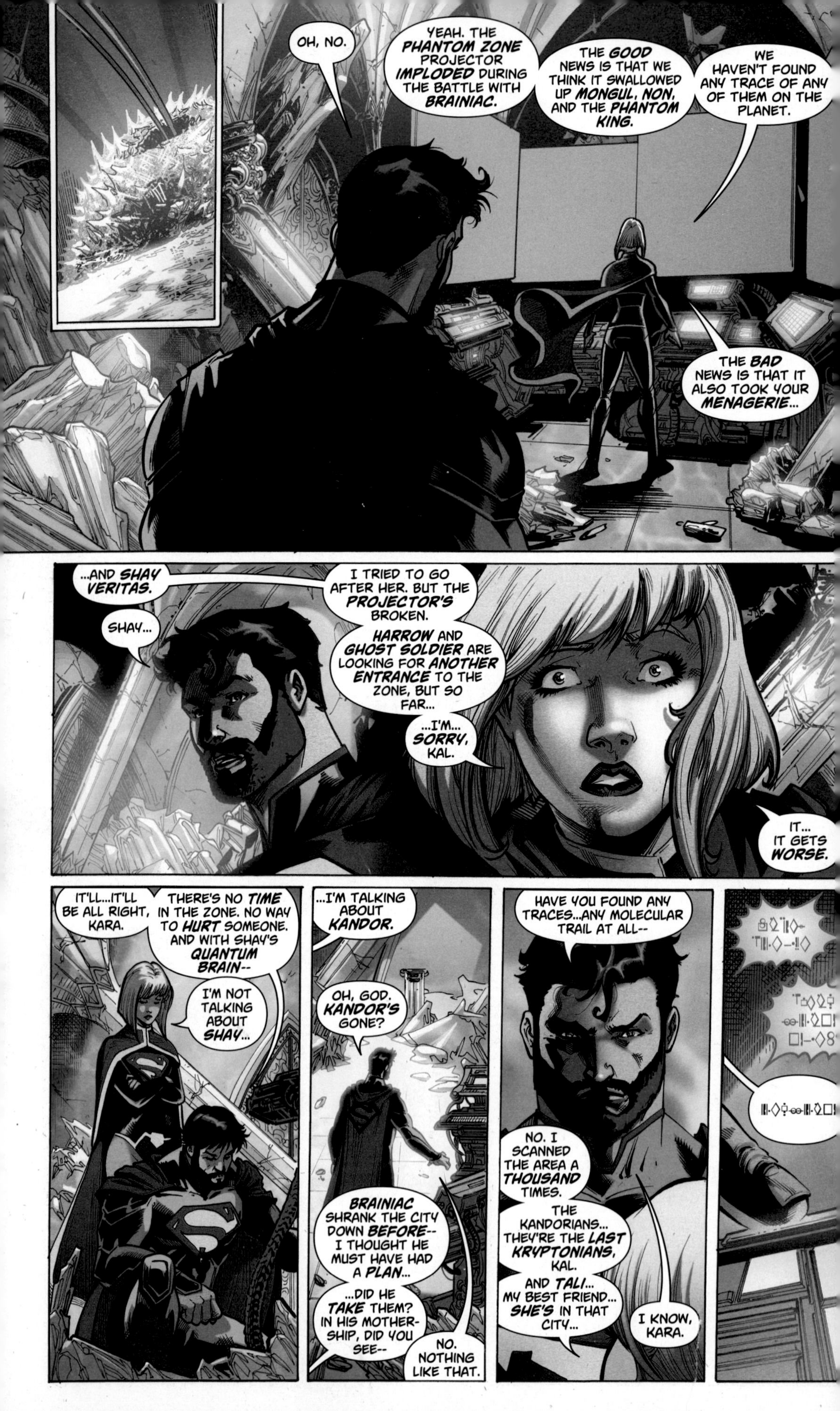

OH, NO.
YEAH. THE PHANTOM ZONE PROJECTOR IMPLODED DURING THE BATTLE WITH BRAINIAC.
THE GOOD NEWS IS THAT WE THINK IT SWALLOWED UP MONGUL, NON, AND THE PHANTOM KING.
WE HAVEN'T FOUND ANY TRACE OF ANY OF THEM ON THE PLANET.
THE BAD NEWS IS THAT IT ALSO TOOK YOUR MENAGERIE...
...AND SHAY VERITAS.
SHAY...
I TRIED TO GO AFTER HER. BUT THE PROJECTOR'S BROKEN.
HARROW AND GHOST SOLDIER ARE LOOKING FOR ANOTHER ENTRANCE TO THE ZONE, BUT SO FAR...
...I'M... SORRY, KAL.
IT... IT GETS WORSE.
IT'LL...IT'LL BE ALL RIGHT, KARA.
THERE'S NO TIME IN THE ZONE. NO WAY TO HURT SOMEONE. AND WITH SHAY'S QUANTUM BRAIN--
I'M NOT TALKING ABOUT SHAY...
...I'M TALKING ABOUT KANDOR.
OH, GOD. KANDOR'S GONE?
BRAINIAC SHRANK THE CITY DOWN BEFORE-- I THOUGHT HE MUST HAVE HAD A PLAN...
...DID HE TAKE THEM? IN HIS MOTHER-SHIP, DID YOU SEE--
NO. NOTHING LIKE THAT.
HAVE YOU FOUND ANY TRACES...ANY MOLECULAR TRAIL AT ALL--
NO. I SCANNED THE AREA A THOUSAND TIMES.
THE KANDORIANS... THEY'RE THE LAST KRYPTONIANS, KAL.
AND TALI... MY BEST FRIEND... SHE'S IN THAT CITY...
I KNOW, KARA.

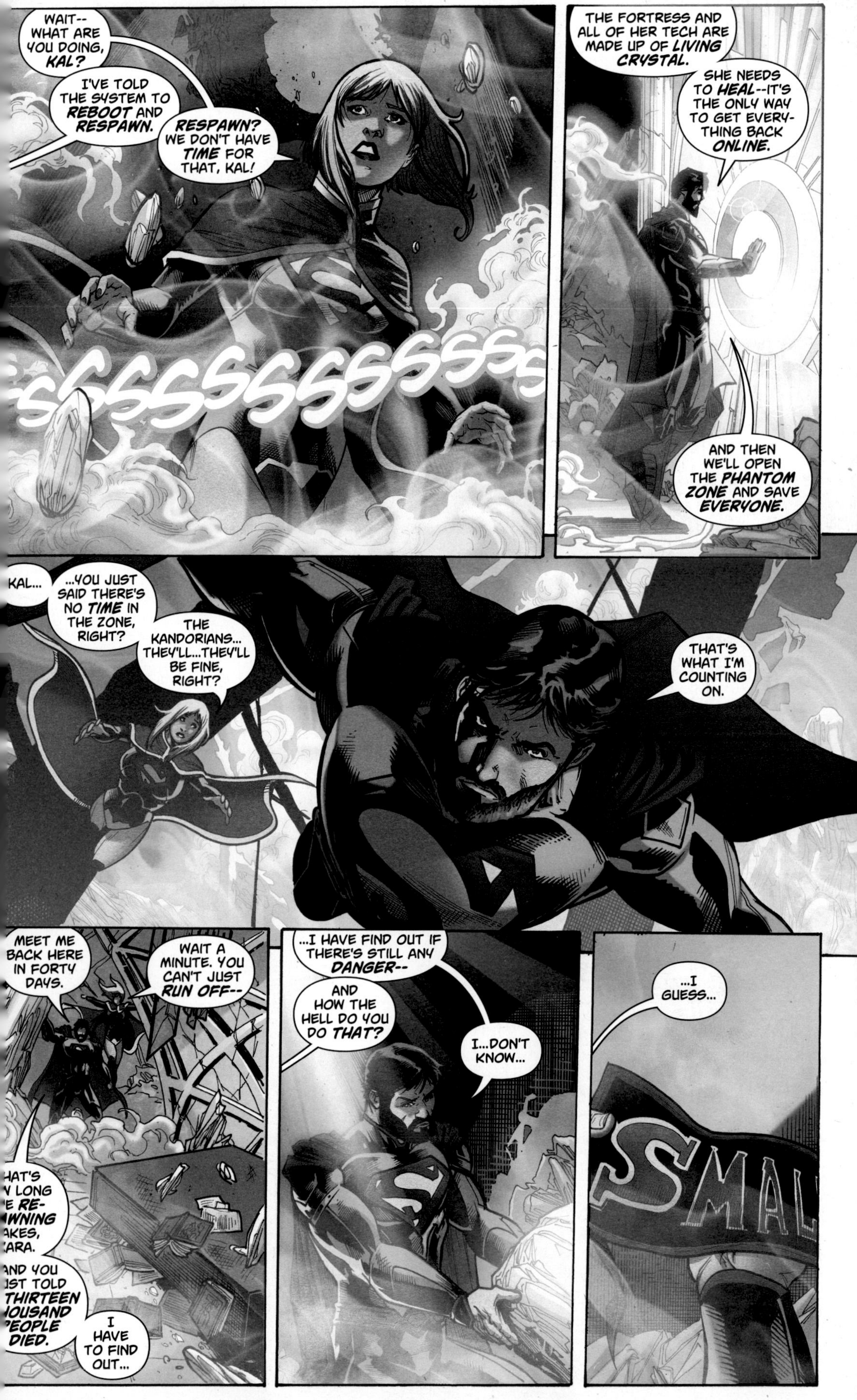
WAIT-- WHAT ARE YOU DOING, KAL?
I'VE TOLD THE SYSTEM TO REBOOT AND RESPAWN.
RESPAWN? WE DON'T HAVE TIME FOR THAT, KAL!
SSSSSSSSSSSSSS
THE FORTRESS AND ALL OF HER TECH ARE MADE UP OF LIVING CRYSTAL.
SHE NEEDS TO HEAL--IT'S THE ONLY WAY TO GET EVERY-THING BACK ONLINE.
AND THEN WE'LL OPEN THE PHANTOM ZONE AND SAVE EVERYONE.
KAL...
...YOU JUST SAID THERE'S NO TIME IN THE ZONE, RIGHT?
THE KANDORIANS... THEY'LL...THEY'LL BE FINE, RIGHT?
THAT'S WHAT I'M COUNTING ON.
MEET ME BACK HERE IN FORTY DAYS.
WAIT A MINUTE. YOU CAN'T JUST RUN OFF--
HAT'S W LONG E RE-WNING AKES, ARA.
AND YOU ST TOLD THIRTEEN HOUSAND PEOPLE DIED.
I HAVE TO FIND OUT...
...I HAVE FIND OUT IF THERE'S STILL ANY DANGER--
AND HOW THE HELL DO YOU DO THAT?
I...DON'T KNOW...
...I GUESS...
SMAL

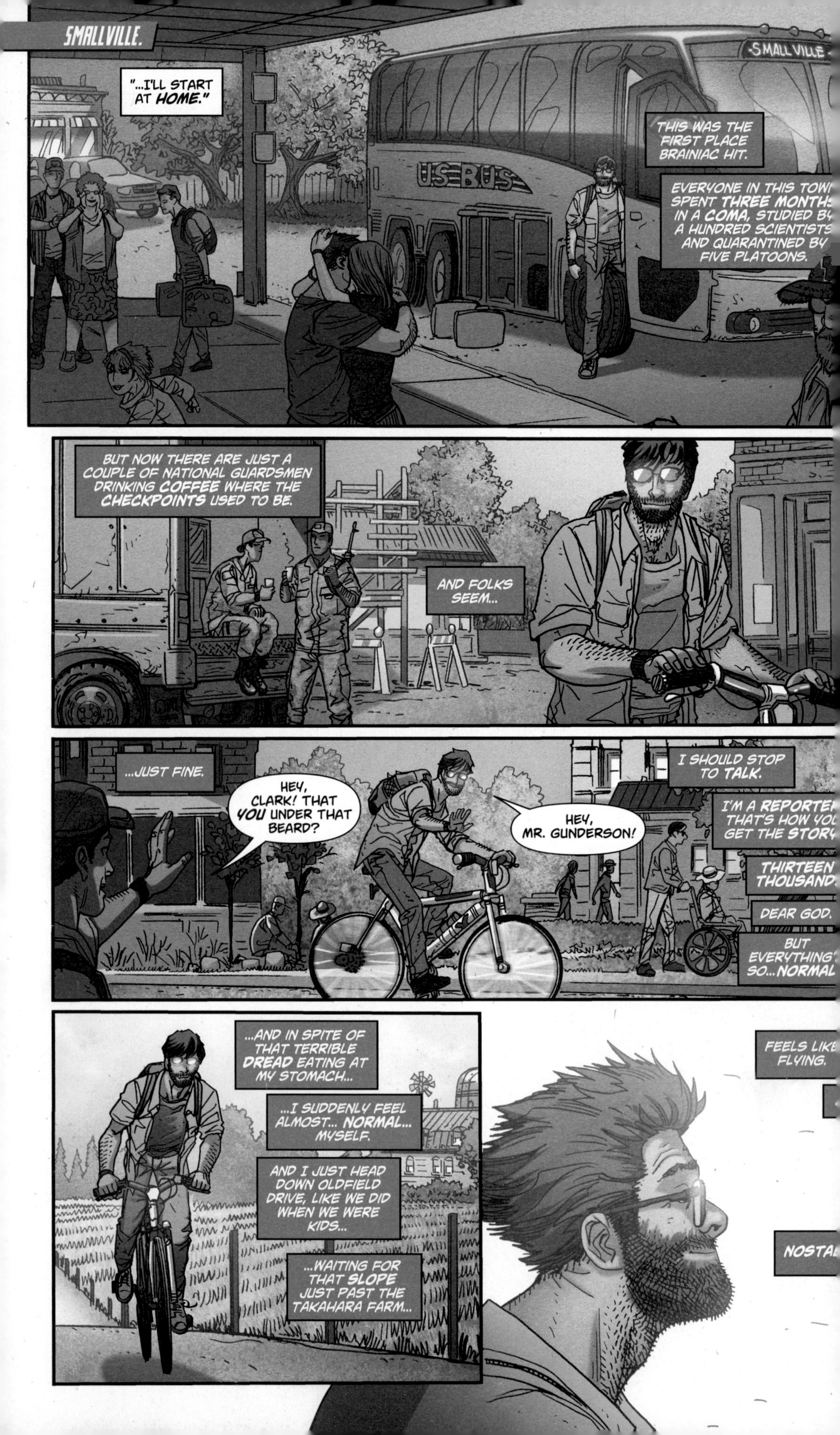

SMALLVILLE.
"...I'LL START AT HOME."
-SMALLVILLE
US BUS
THIS WAS THE FIRST PLACE BRAINIAC HIT.
EVERYONE IN THIS TOWN SPENT THREE MONTHS IN A COMA, STUDIED BY A HUNDRED SCIENTISTS AND QUARANTINED BY FIVE PLATOONS.
BUT NOW THERE ARE JUST A COUPLE OF NATIONAL GUARDSMEN DRINKING COFFEE WHERE THE CHECKPOINTS USED TO BE.
AND FOLKS SEEM...
...JUST FINE.
HEY, CLARK! THAT YOU UNDER THAT BEARD?
HEY, MR. GUNDERSON!
I SHOULD STOP TO TALK.
I'M A REPORTER THAT'S HOW YOU GET THE STORY
THIRTEEN THOUSAND.
DEAR GOD.
BUT EVERYTHING'S SO...NORMAL
...AND IN SPITE OF THAT TERRIBLE DREAD EATING AT MY STOMACH...
...I SUDDENLY FEEL ALMOST... NORMAL... MYSELF.
AND I JUST HEAD DOWN OLDFIELD DRIVE, LIKE WE DID WHEN WE WERE KIDS...
...WAITING FOR THAT SLOPE JUST PAST THE TAKAHARA FARM...
FEELS LIKE FLYING.
NOSTA

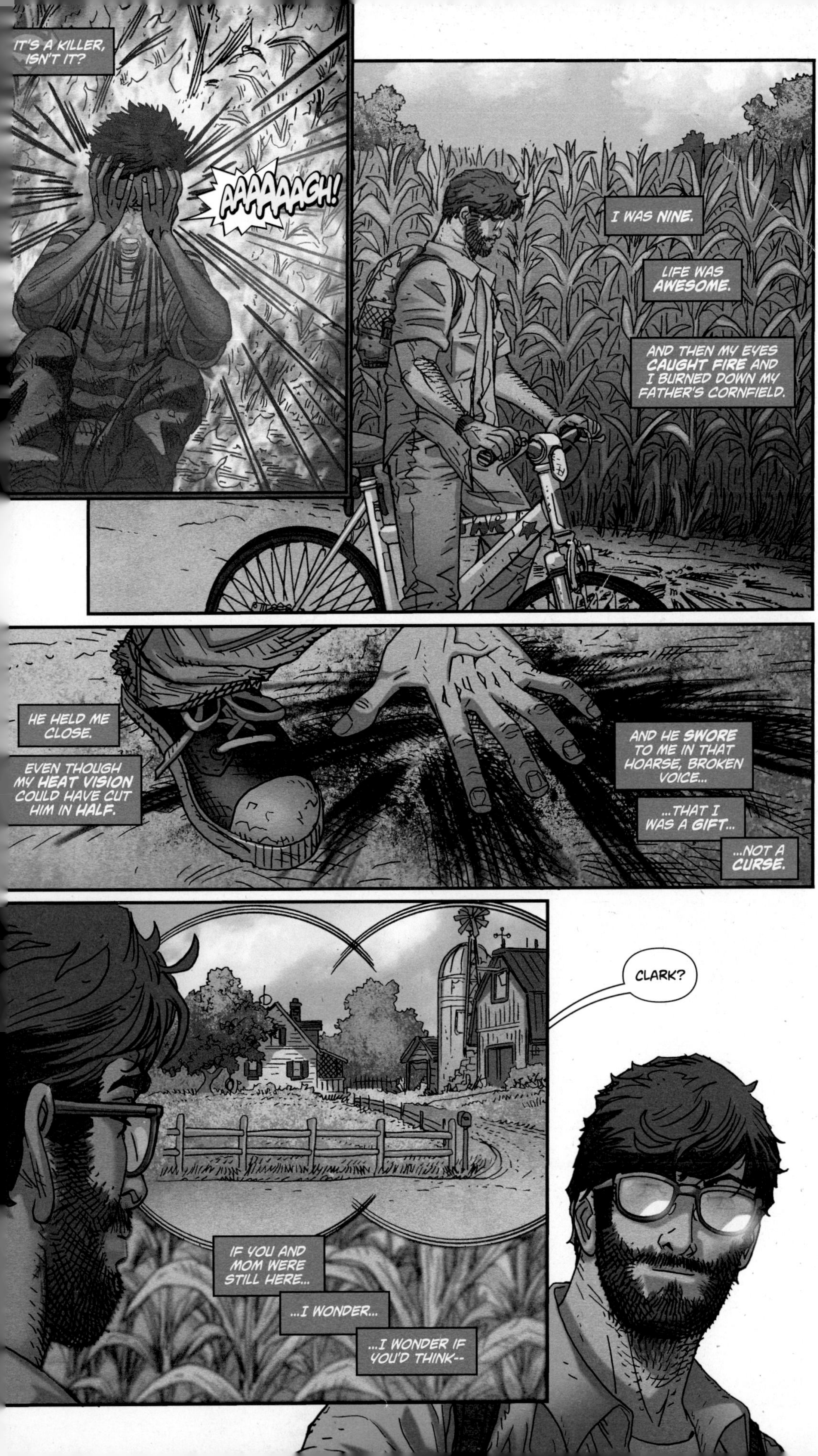

IT'S A KILLER, ISN'T IT?
AAAAAAGH!
I WAS NINE.
LIFE WAS AWESOME.
AND THEN MY EYES CAUGHT FIRE AND I BURNED DOWN MY FATHER'S CORNFIELD.
HE HELD ME CLOSE.
EVEN THOUGH MY HEAT VISION COULD HAVE CUT HIM IN HALF.
AND HE SWORE TO ME IN THAT HOARSE, BROKEN VOICE...
...THAT I WAS A GIFT...
...NOT A CURSE.
IF YOU AND MOM WERE STILL HERE...
...I WONDER...
...I WONDER IF YOU'D THINK--
CLARK?

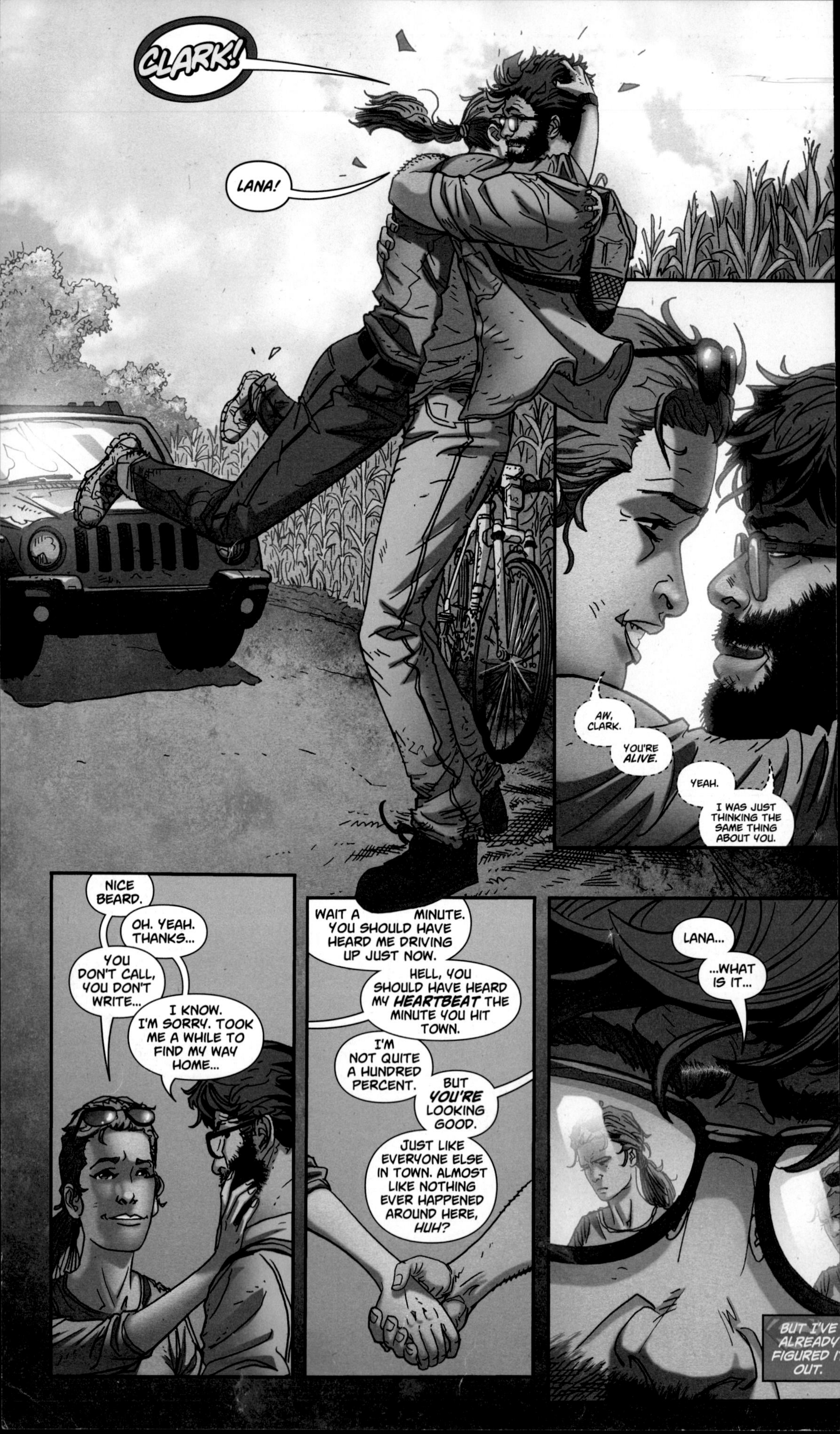

CLARK!
LANA!
AW, CLARK.
YOU'RE *ALIVE*.
YEAH.
I WAS JUST THINKING THE SAME THING ABOUT YOU.
NICE BEARD.
OH. YEAH. THANKS...
YOU DON'T CALL, YOU DON'T WRITE...
I KNOW. I'M SORRY. TOOK ME A WHILE TO FIND MY WAY HOME...
WAIT A MINUTE. YOU SHOULD HAVE HEARD ME DRIVING UP JUST NOW.
HELL, YOU SHOULD HAVE HEARD MY *HEARTBEAT* THE MINUTE YOU HIT TOWN.
I'M NOT QUITE A HUNDRED PERCENT.
BUT *YOU'RE* LOOKING GOOD.
JUST LIKE EVERYONE ELSE IN TOWN. ALMOST LIKE NOTHING EVER HAPPENED AROUND HERE, *HUH?*
LANA...
...WHAT IS IT...

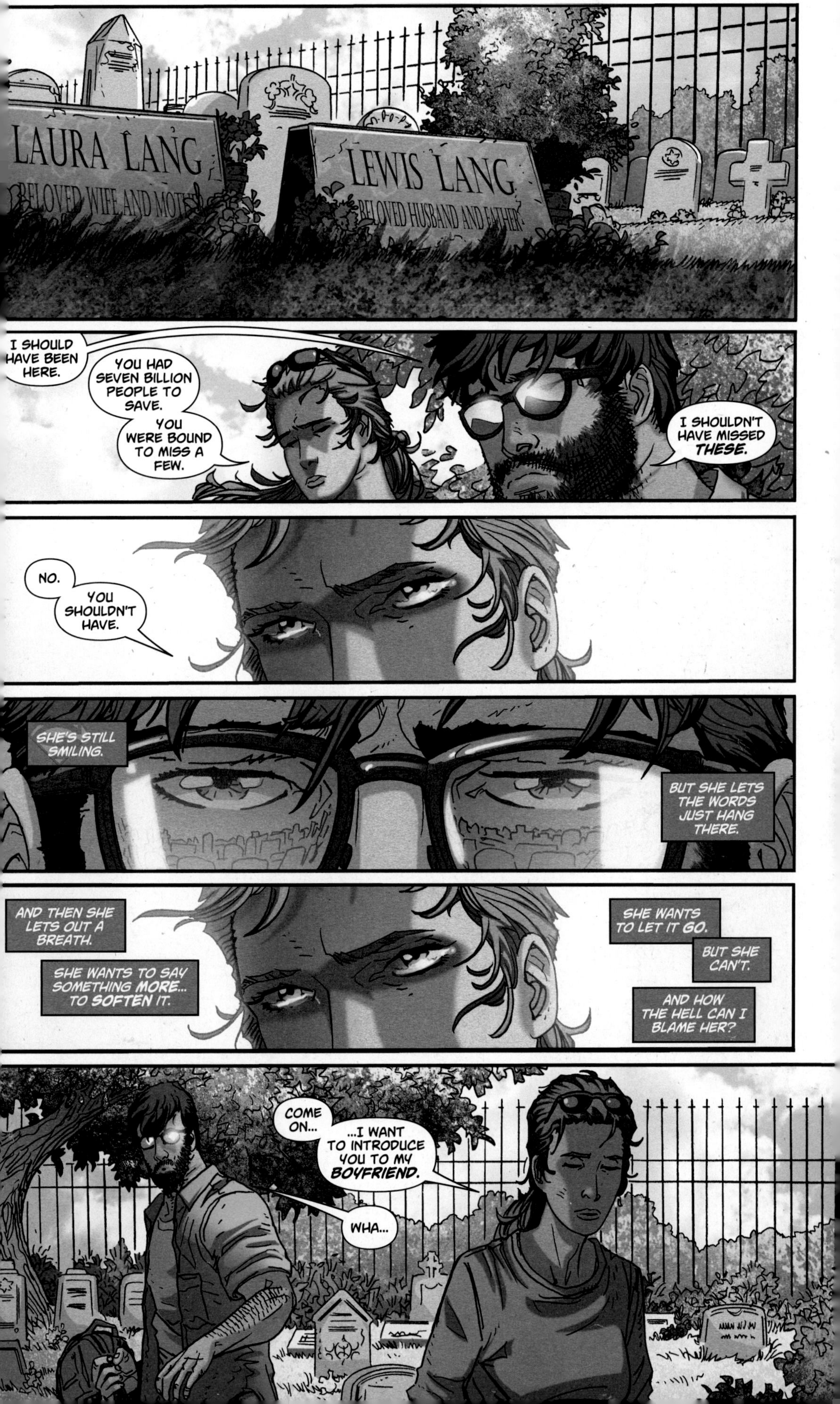

LAURA LANG
BELOVED WIFE AND MOTH
LEWIS LANG
BELOVED HUSBAND AND FATHER
I SHOULD HAVE BEEN HERE.
YOU HAD SEVEN BILLION PEOPLE TO SAVE.
YOU WERE BOUND TO MISS A FEW.
I SHOULDN'T HAVE MISSED THESE.
NO.
YOU SHOULDN'T HAVE.
SHE'S STILL SMILING.
BUT SHE LETS THE WORDS JUST HANG THERE.
AND THEN SHE LETS OUT A BREATH.
SHE WANTS TO SAY SOMETHING MORE... TO SOFTEN IT.
SHE WANTS TO LET IT GO.
BUT SHE CAN'T.
AND HOW THE HELL CAN I BLAME HER?
COME ON...
...I WANT TO INTRODUCE YOU TO MY BOYFRIEND.
WHA...

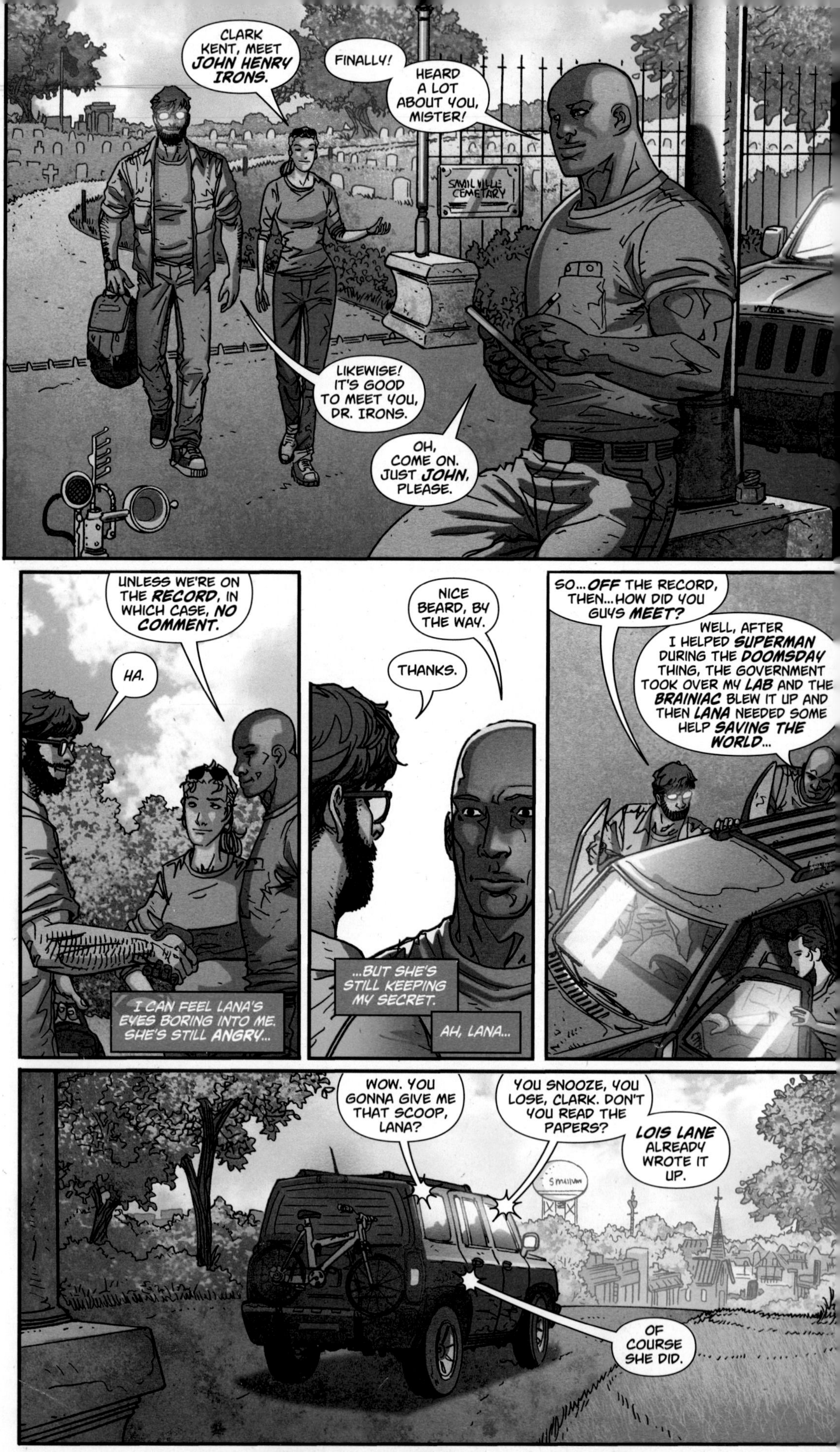
CLARK KENT, MEET JOHN HENRY IRONS.
FINALLY!
HEARD A LOT ABOUT YOU, MISTER!
SMALLVILLE CEMETARY
LIKEWISE! IT'S GOOD TO MEET YOU, DR. IRONS.
OH, COME ON. JUST JOHN, PLEASE.
UNLESS WE'RE ON THE RECORD, IN WHICH CASE, NO COMMENT.
HA.
I CAN FEEL LANA'S EYES BORING INTO ME. SHE'S STILL ANGRY...
NICE BEARD, BY THE WAY.
THANKS.
...BUT SHE'S STILL KEEPING MY SECRET.
AH, LANA...
SO...OFF THE RECORD, THEN...HOW DID YOU GUYS MEET?
WELL, AFTER I HELPED SUPERMAN DURING THE DOOMSDAY THING, THE GOVERNMENT TOOK OVER MY LAB AND THE BRAINIAC BLEW IT UP AND THEN LANA NEEDED SOME HELP SAVING THE WORLD...
WOW. YOU GONNA GIVE ME THAT SCOOP, LANA?
YOU SNOOZE, YOU LOSE, CLARK. DON'T YOU READ THE PAPERS?
LOIS LANE ALREADY WROTE IT UP.
OF COURSE SHE DID.

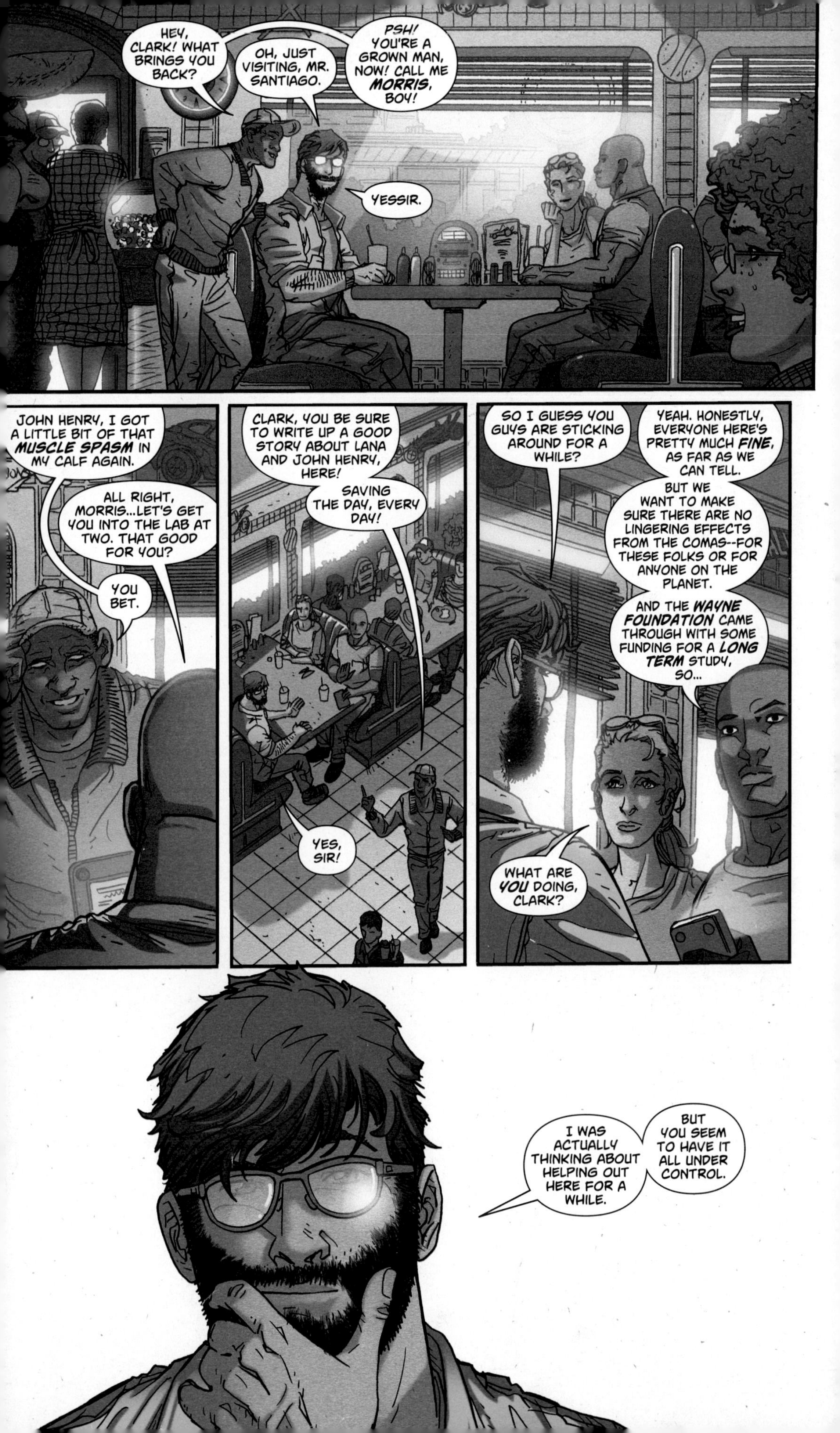
HEY, CLARK! WHAT BRINGS YOU BACK?
OH, JUST VISITING, MR. SANTIAGO.
PSH! YOU'RE A GROWN MAN, NOW! CALL ME MORRIS, BOY!
YESSIR.
JOHN HENRY, I GOT A LITTLE BIT OF THAT MUSCLE SPASM IN MY CALF AGAIN.
ALL RIGHT, MORRIS...LET'S GET YOU INTO THE LAB AT TWO. THAT GOOD FOR YOU?
YOU BET.
CLARK, YOU BE SURE TO WRITE UP A GOOD STORY ABOUT LANA AND JOHN HENRY, HERE!
SAVING THE DAY, EVERY DAY!
YES, SIR!
SO I GUESS YOU GUYS ARE STICKING AROUND FOR A WHILE?
YEAH. HONESTLY, EVERYONE HERE'S PRETTY MUCH FINE, AS FAR AS WE CAN TELL.
BUT WE WANT TO MAKE SURE THERE ARE NO LINGERING EFFECTS FROM THE COMAS--FOR THESE FOLKS OR FOR ANYONE ON THE PLANET.
AND THE WAYNE FOUNDATION CAME THROUGH WITH SOME FUNDING FOR A LONG TERM STUDY, SO...
WHAT ARE YOU DOING, CLARK?
I WAS ACTUALLY THINKING ABOUT HELPING OUT HERE FOR A WHILE.
BUT YOU SEEM TO HAVE IT ALL UNDER CONTROL.

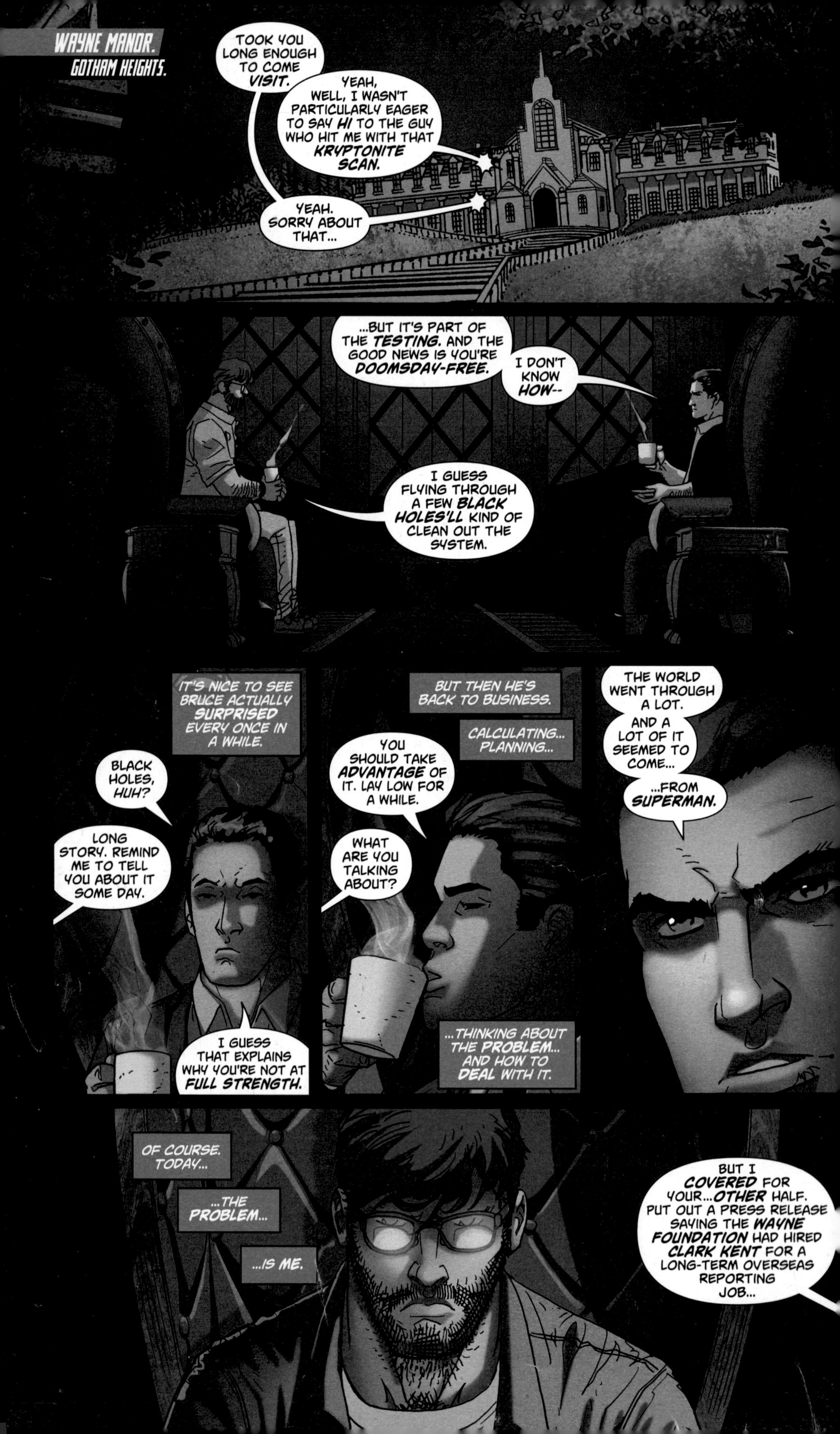
WAYNE MANOR.
GOTHAM HEIGHTS.
TOOK YOU LONG ENOUGH TO COME VISIT.
YEAH, WELL, I WASN'T PARTICULARLY EAGER TO SAY HI TO THE GUY WHO HIT ME WITH THAT KRYPTONITE SCAN.
YEAH. SORRY ABOUT THAT...
...BUT IT'S PART OF THE TESTING. AND THE GOOD NEWS IS YOU'RE DOOMSDAY-FREE.
I DON'T KNOW HOW--
I GUESS FLYING THROUGH A FEW BLACK HOLES'LL KIND OF CLEAN OUT THE SYSTEM.
IT'S NICE TO SEE BRUCE ACTUALLY SURPRISED EVERY ONCE IN A WHILE.
BLACK HOLES, HUH?
LONG STORY. REMIND ME TO TELL YOU ABOUT IT SOME DAY.
I GUESS THAT EXPLAINS WHY YOU'RE NOT AT FULL STRENGTH.
BUT THEN HE'S BACK TO BUSINESS.
CALCULATING... PLANNING...
YOU SHOULD TAKE ADVANTAGE OF IT. LAY LOW FOR A WHILE.
WHAT ARE YOU TALKING ABOUT?
...THINKING ABOUT THE PROBLEM... AND HOW TO DEAL WITH IT.
THE WORLD WENT THROUGH A LOT.
AND A LOT OF IT SEEMED TO COME...
...FROM SUPERMAN.
OF COURSE. TODAY...
...THE PROBLEM...
...IS ME.
BUT I COVERED FOR YOUR...OTHER HALF. PUT OUT A PRESS RELEASE SAYING THE WAYNE FOUNDATION HAD HIRED CLARK KENT FOR A LONG-TERM OVERSEAS REPORTING JOB...

"...SO GO HOME, CLARK.

"GO HOME...

"...AND GIVE IT SOME *TIME*."

...TROPOLIS.

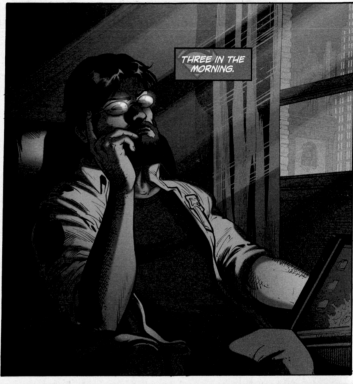

THREE IN THE MORNING.

Who Needs Superman, Anyway?

By Clark Kent

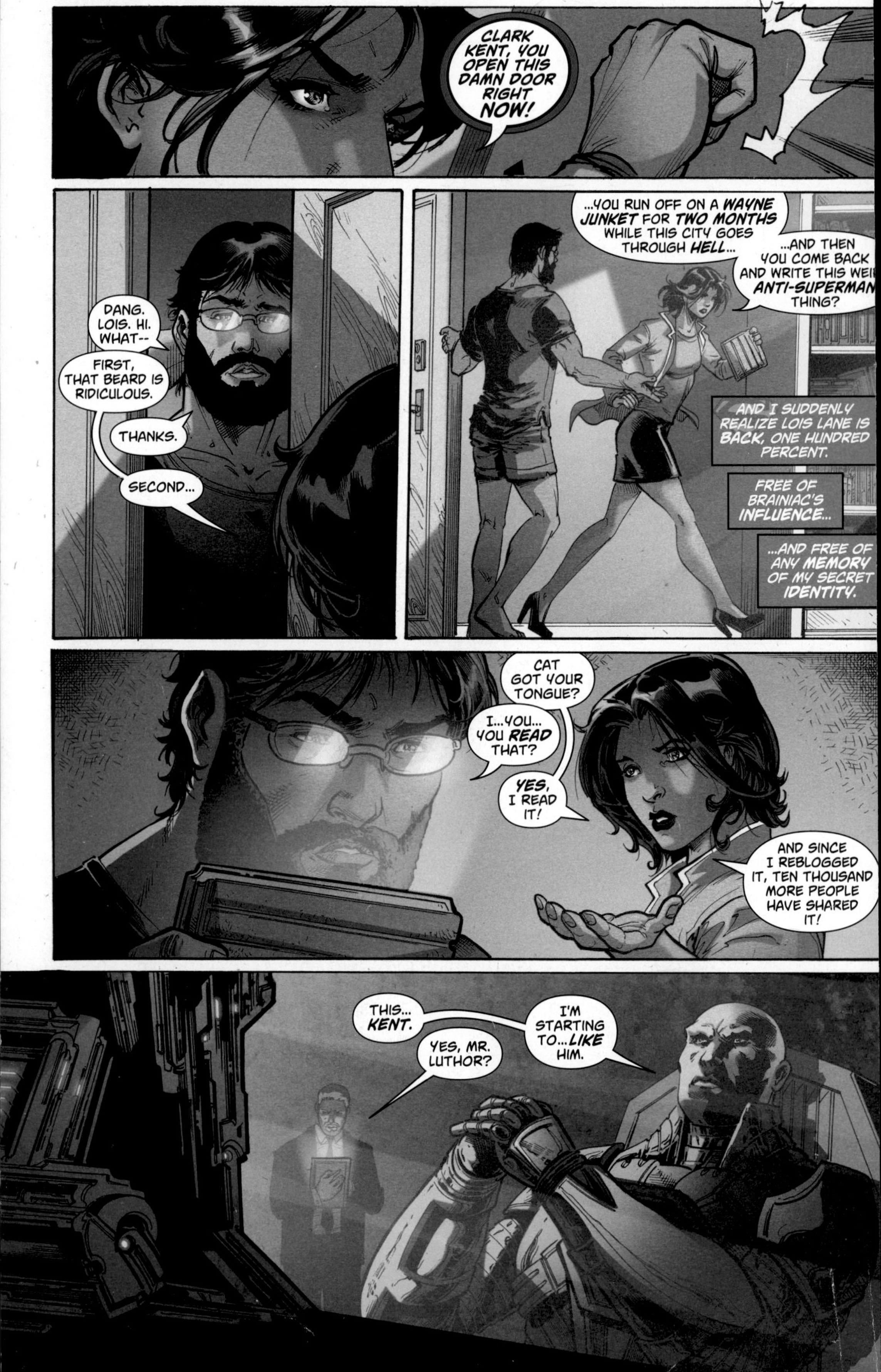
CLARK KENT, YOU OPEN THIS DAMN DOOR RIGHT NOW!
DANG. LOIS. HI. WHAT--
FIRST, THAT BEARD IS RIDICULOUS.
THANKS.
SECOND...
...YOU RUN OFF ON A WAYNE JUNKET FOR TWO MONTHS WHILE THIS CITY GOES THROUGH HELL...
...AND THEN YOU COME BACK AND WRITE THIS WEI ANTI-SUPERMAN THING?
AND I SUDDENLY REALIZE LOIS LANE IS BACK, ONE HUNDRED PERCENT.
FREE OF BRAINIAC'S INFLUENCE...
...AND FREE OF ANY MEMORY OF MY SECRET IDENTITY.
CAT GOT YOUR TONGUE?
I...YOU... YOU READ THAT?
YES, I READ IT!
AND SINCE I REBLOGGED IT, TEN THOUSAND MORE PEOPLE HAVE SHARED IT!
THIS... KENT.
YES, MR. LUTHOR?
I'M STARTING TO...LIKE HIM.

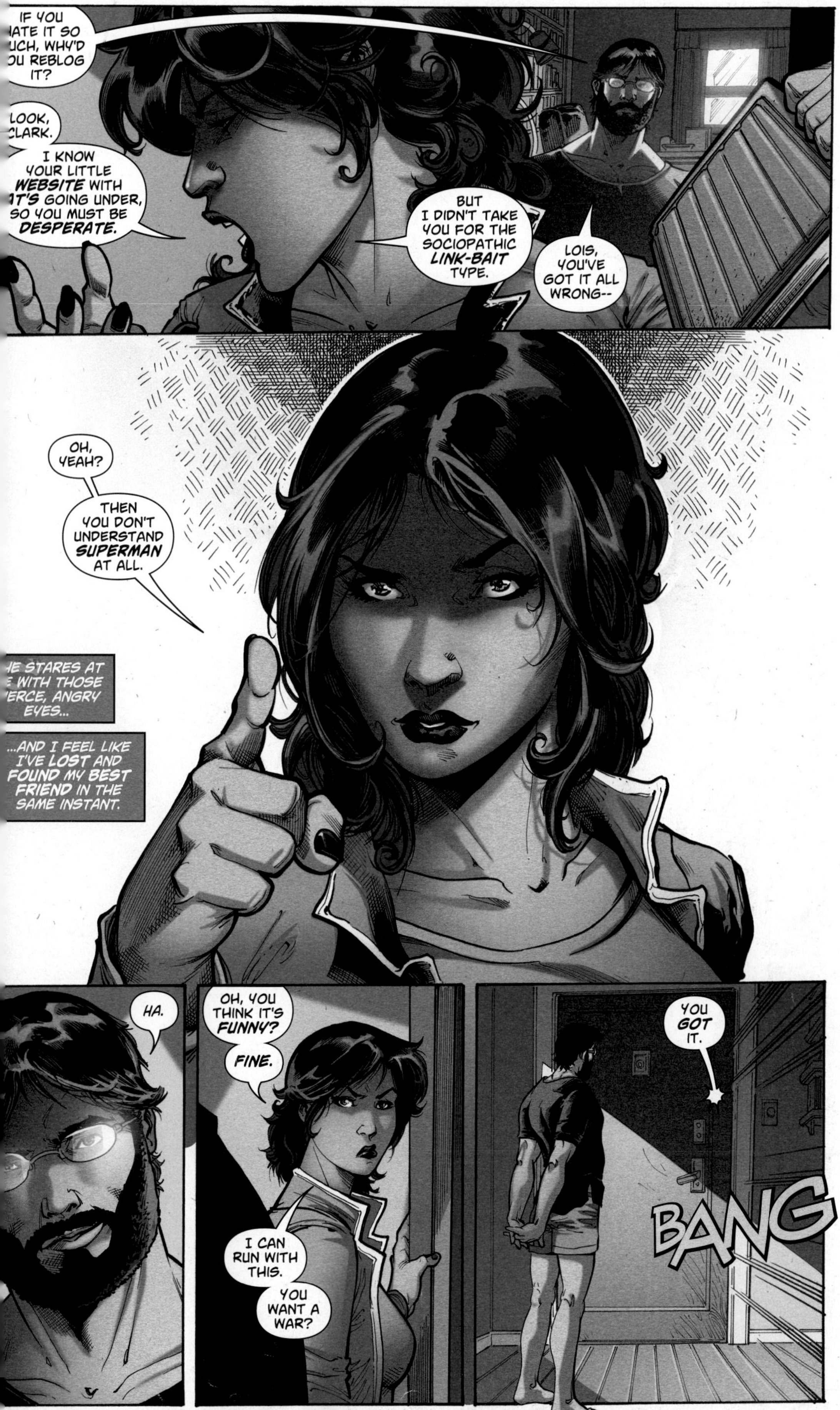

IF YOU
HATE IT SO
UCH, WHY'D
OU REBLOG
IT?
LOOK,
CLARK.
I KNOW
YOUR LITTLE
WEBSITE WITH
IT'S GOING UNDER,
SO YOU MUST BE
DESPERATE.
BUT
I DIDN'T TAKE
YOU FOR THE
SOCIOPATHIC
LINK-BAIT
TYPE.
LOIS,
YOU'VE
GOT IT ALL
WRONG--
OH,
YEAH?
THEN
YOU DON'T
UNDERSTAND
SUPERMAN
AT ALL.
HE STARES AT
E WITH THOSE
ERCE, ANGRY
EYES...
...AND I FEEL LIKE
I'VE LOST AND
FOUND MY BEST
FRIEND IN THE
SAME INSTANT.
HA.
OH, YOU
THINK IT'S
FUNNY?
FINE.
I CAN
RUN WITH
THIS.
YOU
WANT A
WAR?
YOU
GOT
IT.
BANG

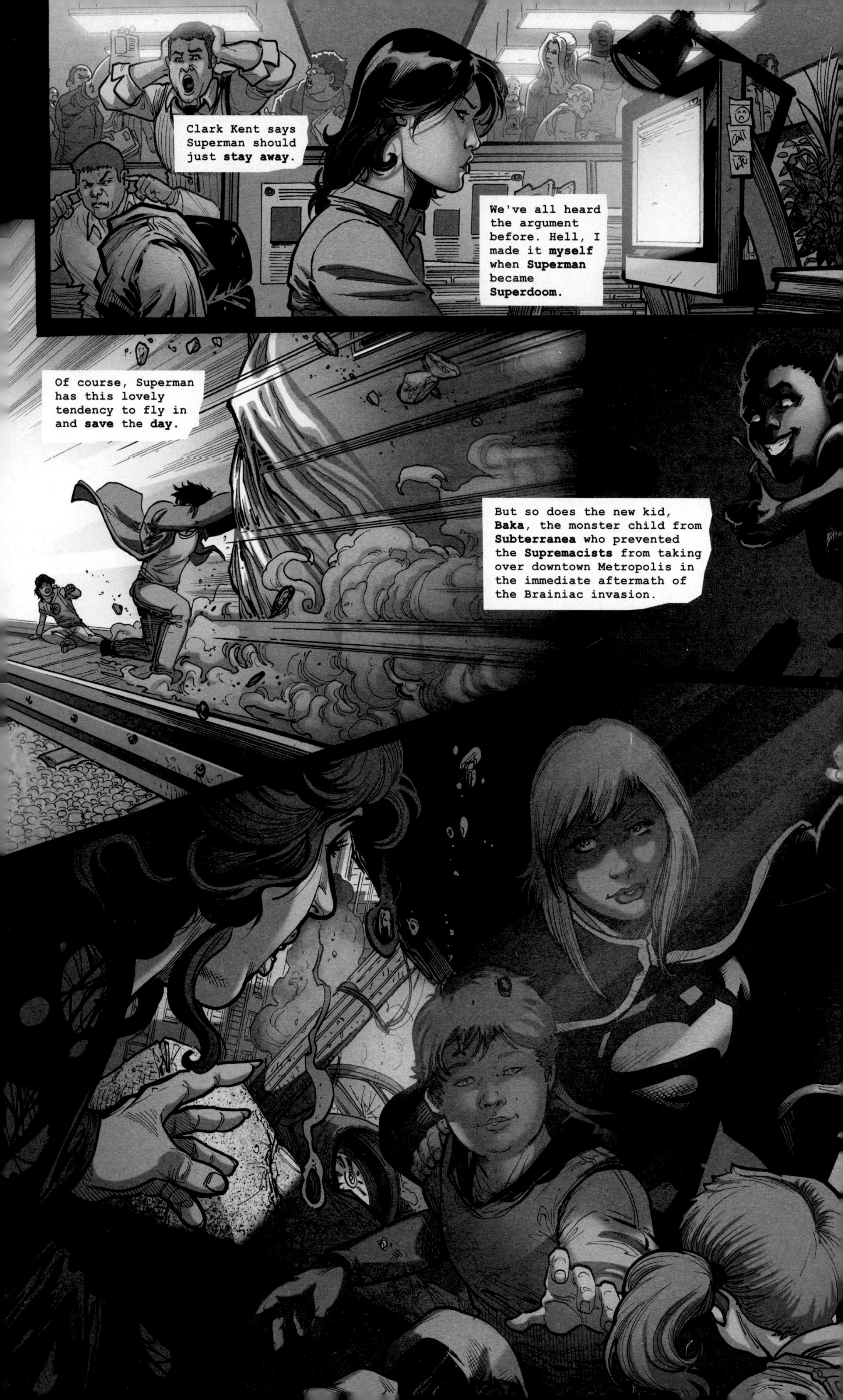
Clark Kent says Superman should just **stay away**.
We've all heard the argument before. Hell, I made it **myself** when **Superman** became **Superdoom**.
Of course, Superman has this lovely tendency to fly in and **save** the **day**.
But so does the new kid, **Baka**, the monster child from **Subterranea** who prevented the **Supremacists** from taking over downtown Metropolis in the immediate aftermath of the Brainiac invasion.

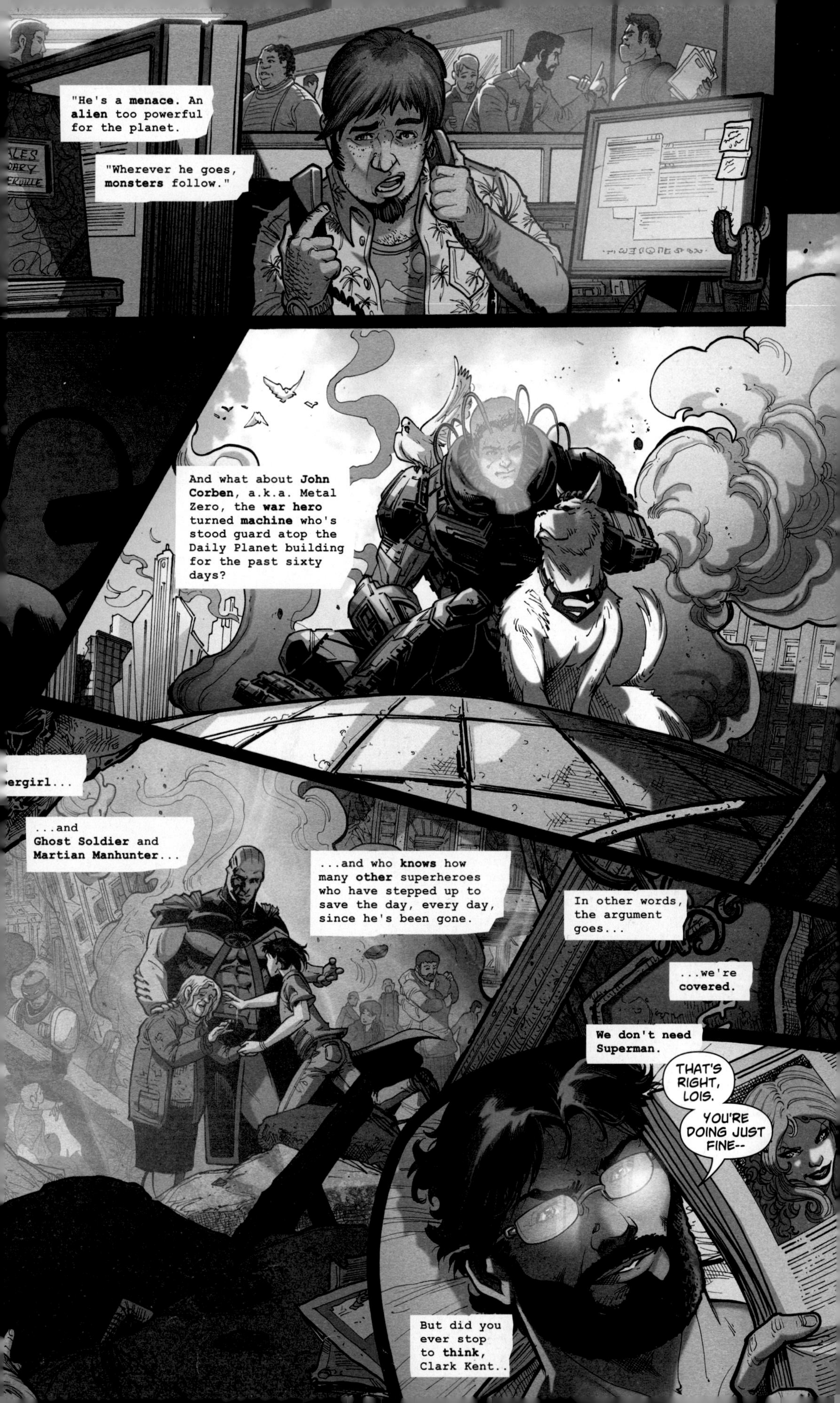

"He's a menace. An alien too powerful for the planet.
"Wherever he goes, monsters follow."
And what about John Corben, a.k.a. Metal Zero, the war hero turned machine who's stood guard atop the Daily Planet building for the past sixty days?
ergirl...
...and Ghost Soldier and Martian Manhunter...
...and who knows how many other superheroes who have stepped up to save the day, every day, since he's been gone.
In other words, the argument goes...
...we're covered.
We don't need Superman.
THAT'S RIGHT, LOIS.
YOU'RE DOING JUST FINE--
But did you ever stop to think, Clark Kent..

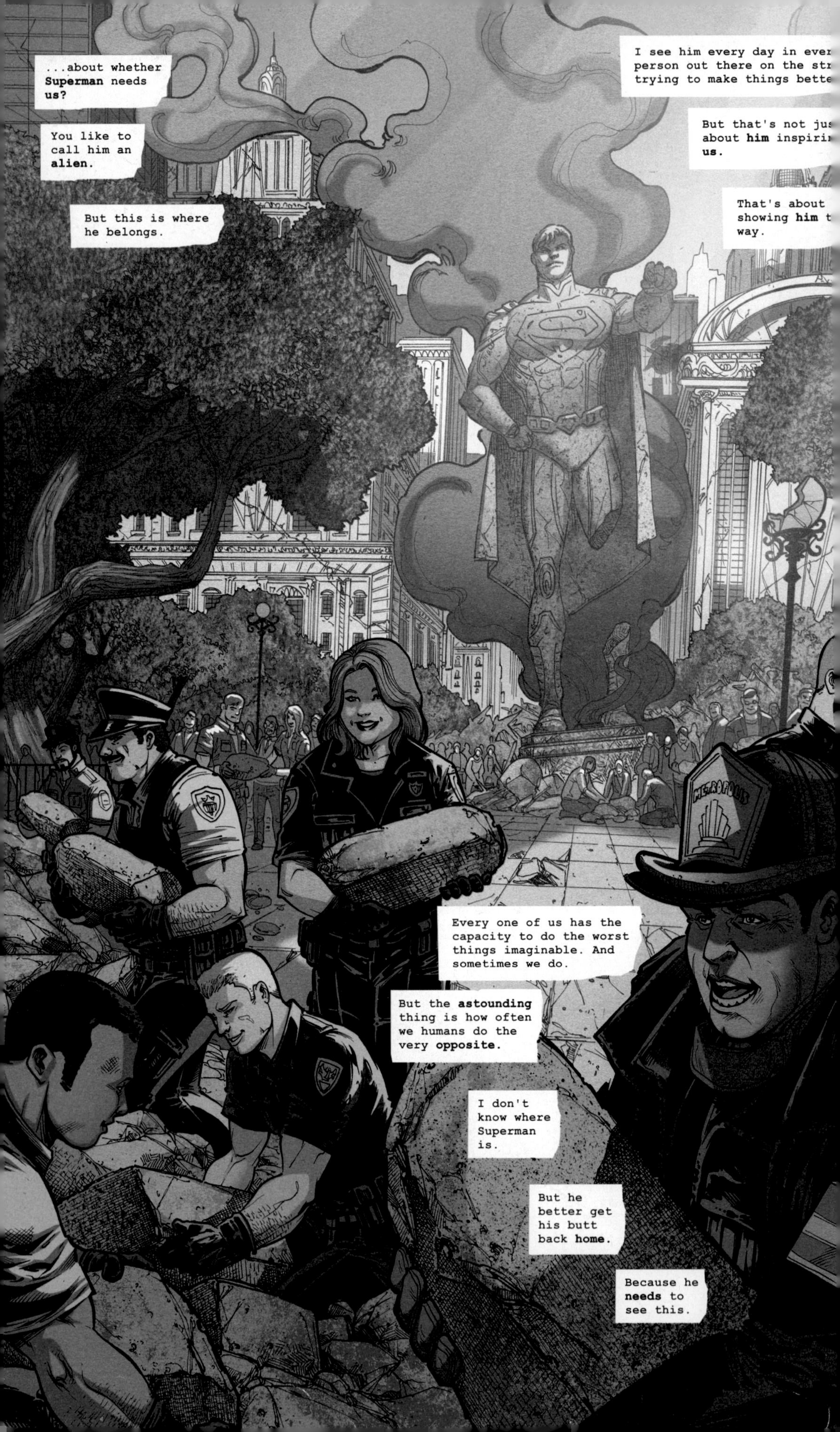

...about whether **Superman** needs **us?**
You like to call him an **alien.**
But this is where he belongs.
I see him every day in ever person out there on the str trying to make things bette
But that's not jus about **him** inspiri **us.**
That's about showing **him** t way.
Every one of us has the capacity to do the worst things imaginable. And sometimes we do.
But the **astounding** thing is how often we humans do the very **opposite.**
I don't know where Superman is.
But he better get his butt back **home.**
Because he **needs** to see this.
METROPOLIS

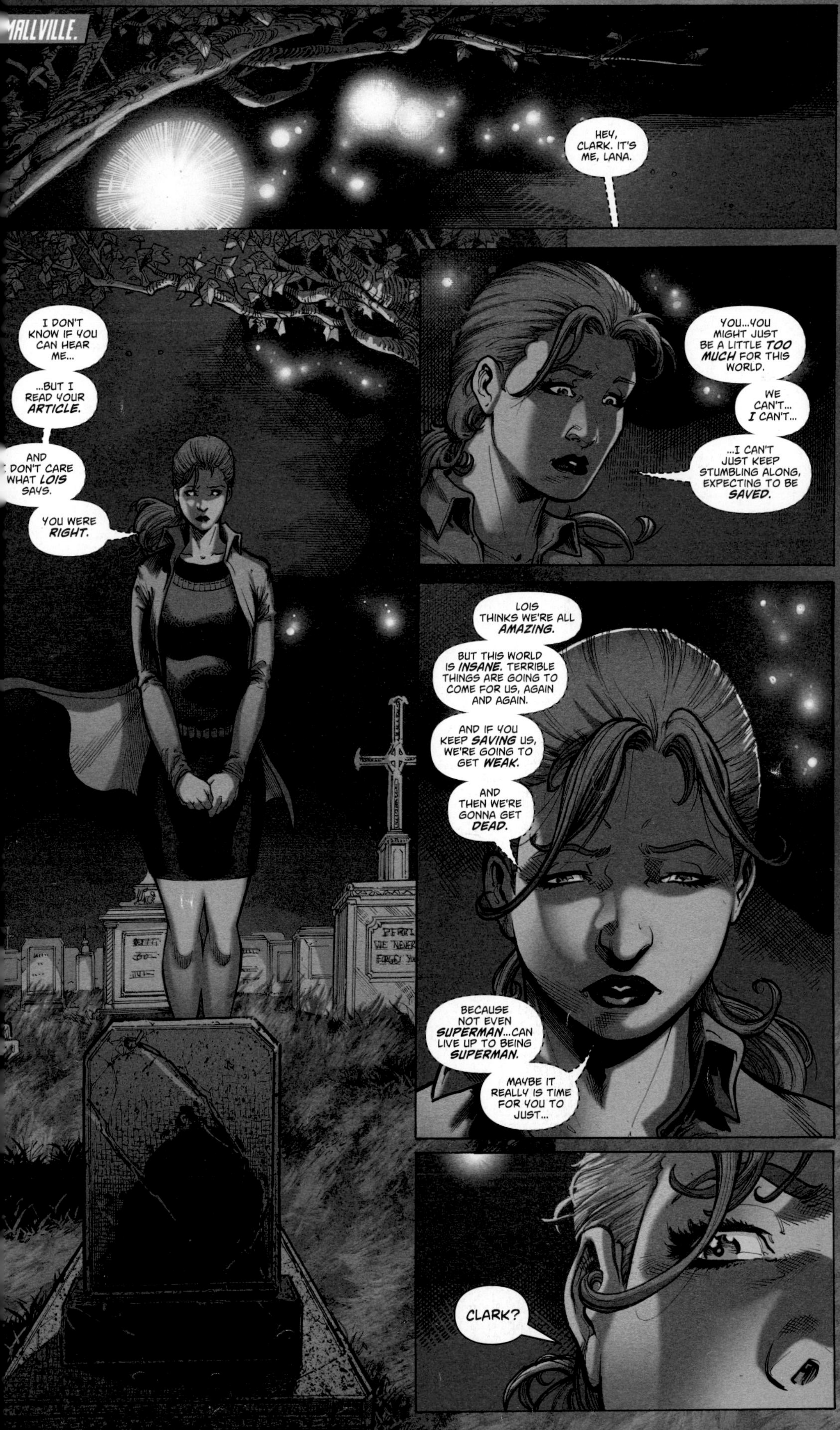
MALLVILLE.
HEY, CLARK. IT'S ME, LANA.
I DON'T KNOW IF YOU CAN HEAR ME...
...BUT I READ YOUR ARTICLE.
AND I DON'T CARE WHAT LOIS SAYS.
YOU WERE RIGHT.
YOU...YOU MIGHT JUST BE A LITTLE TOO MUCH FOR THIS WORLD.
WE CAN'T... I CAN'T...
...I CAN'T JUST KEEP STUMBLING ALONG, EXPECTING TO BE SAVED.
LOIS THINKS WE'RE ALL AMAZING.
BUT THIS WORLD IS INSANE. TERRIBLE THINGS ARE GOING TO COME FOR US, AGAIN AND AGAIN.
AND IF YOU KEEP SAVING US, WE'RE GOING TO GET WEAK.
AND THEN WE'RE GONNA GET DEAD.
BECAUSE NOT EVEN SUPERMAN...CAN LIVE UP TO BEING SUPERMAN.
MAYBE IT REALLY IS TIME FOR YOU TO JUST...
CLARK?

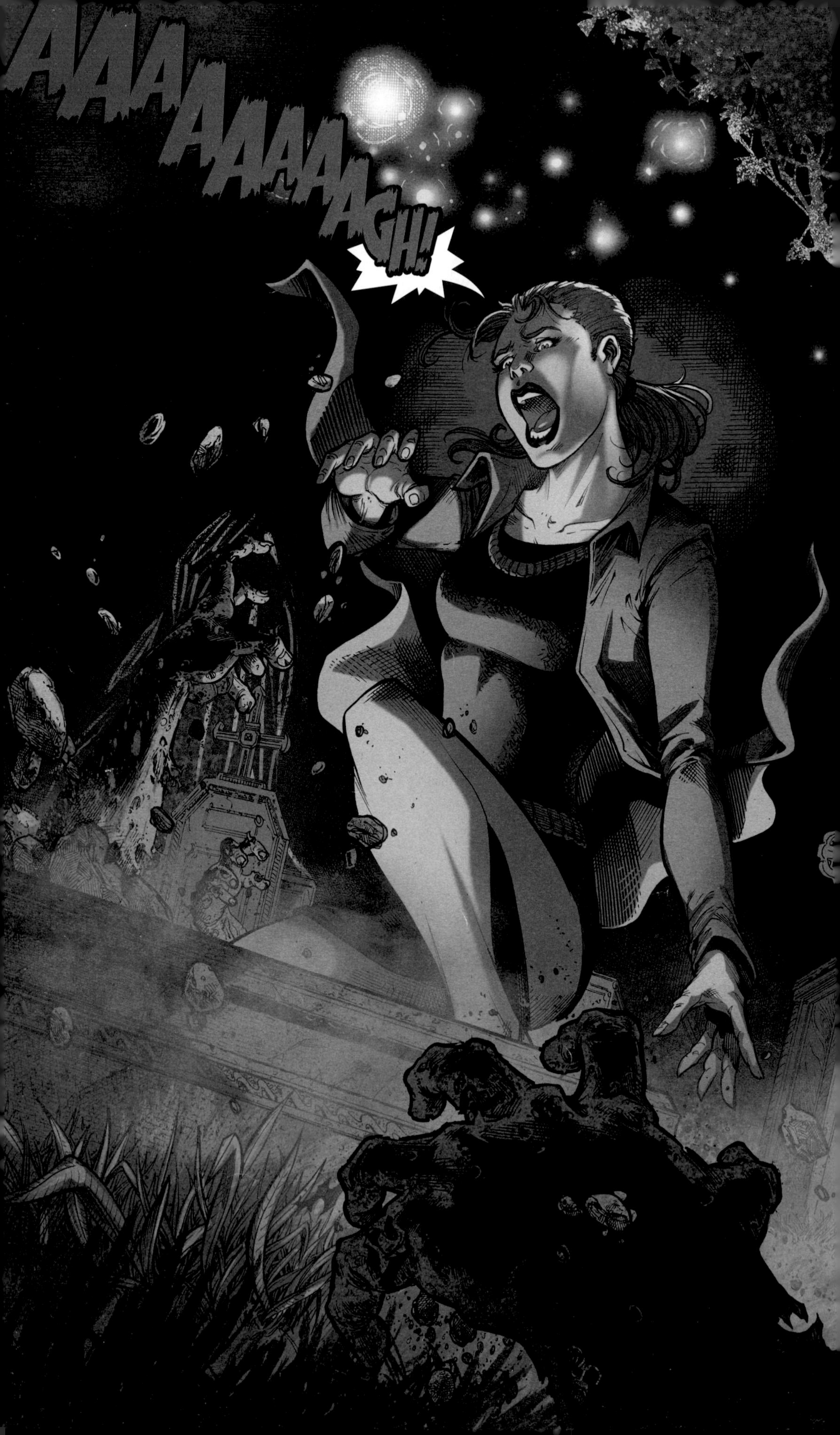
AAAAAAAAAAAGH!!

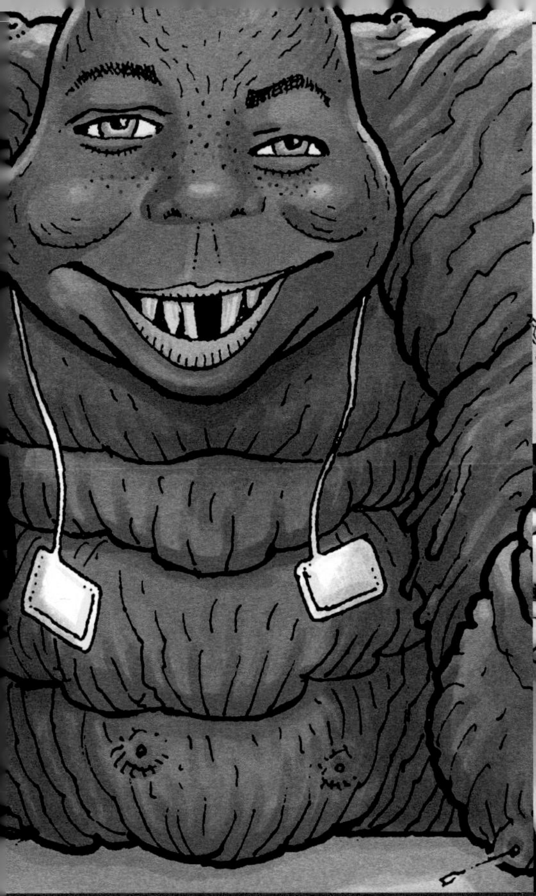

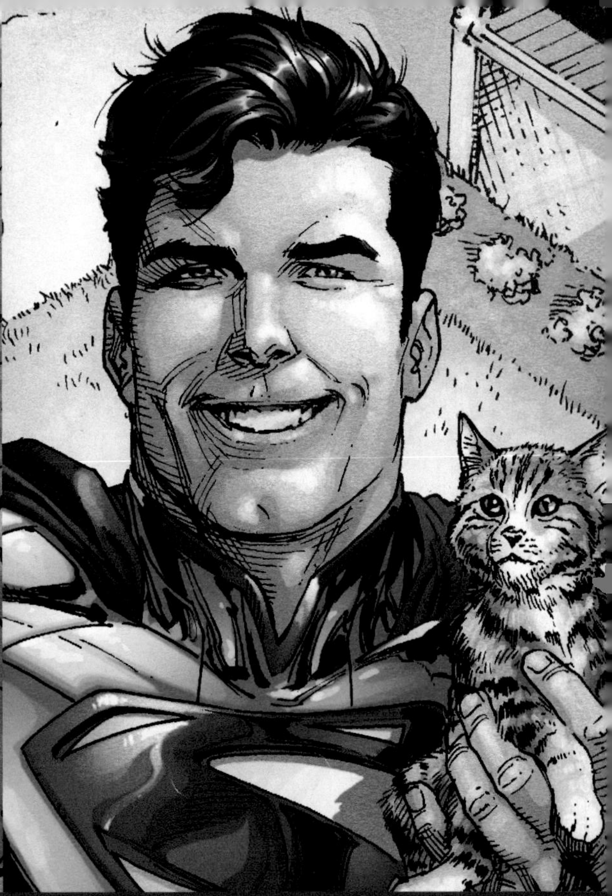

VARIANT COVER GALLERY

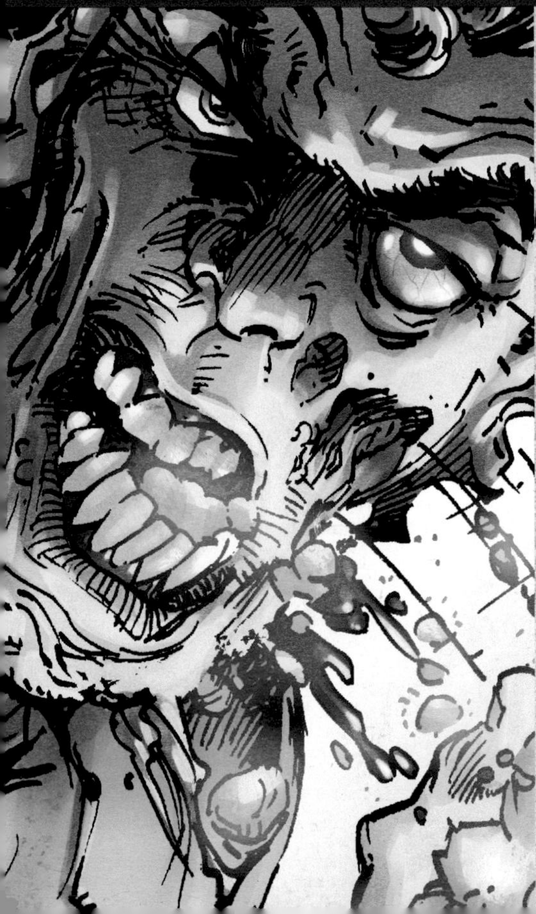

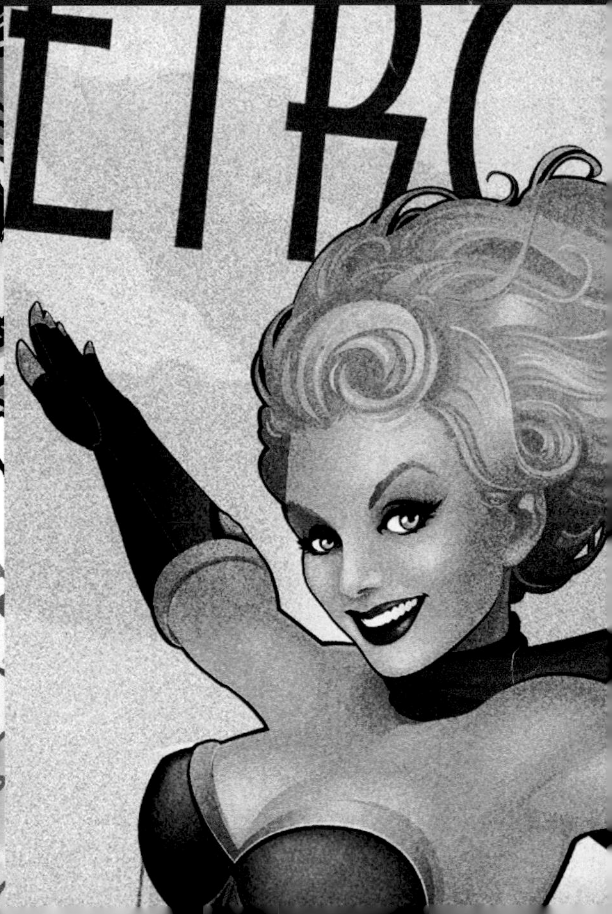

ACTION COMICS #30
MAD VARIANT COVER BY AL JAFFEE

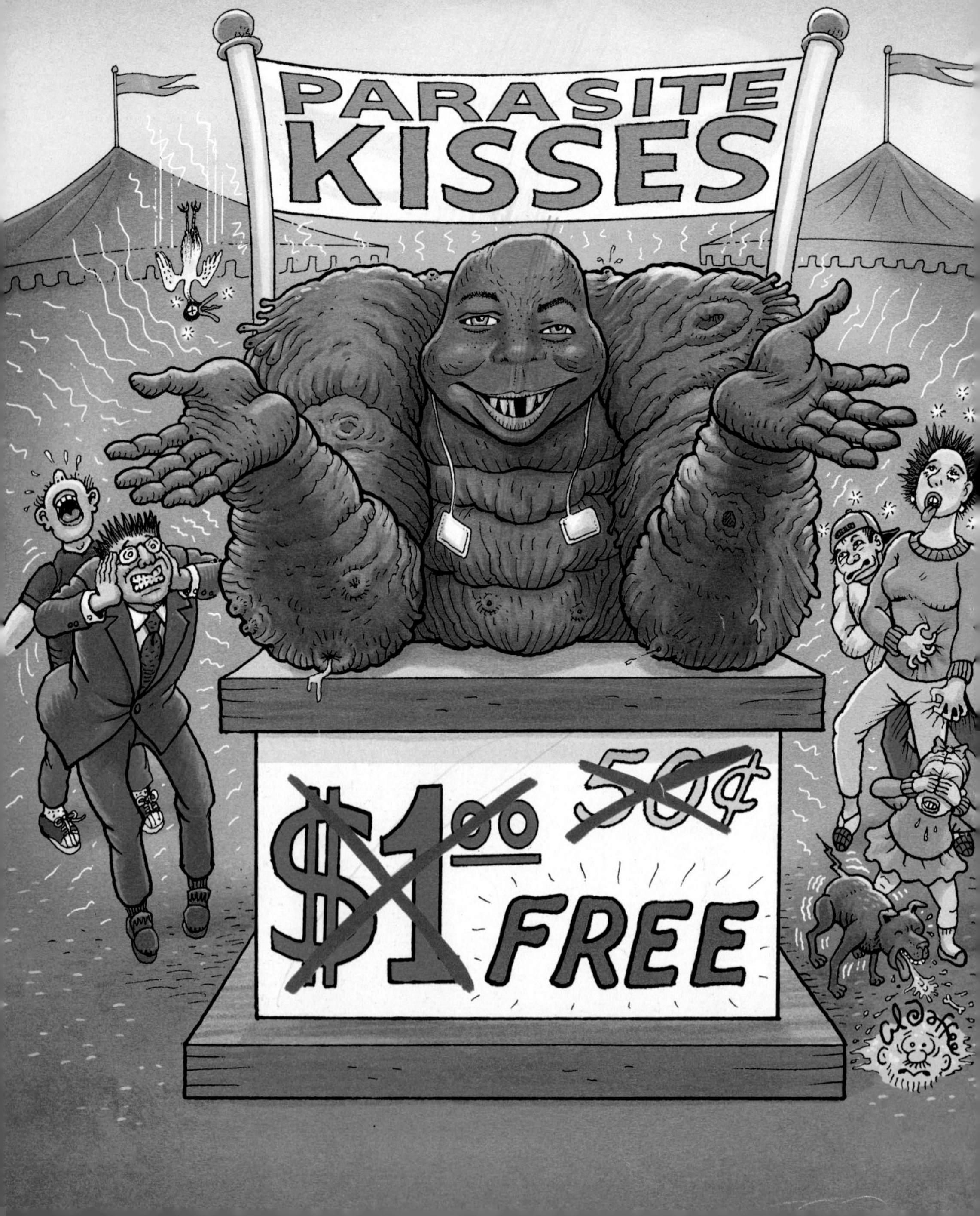
PARASITE KISSES
$1.00
50¢
FREE
al jaffee

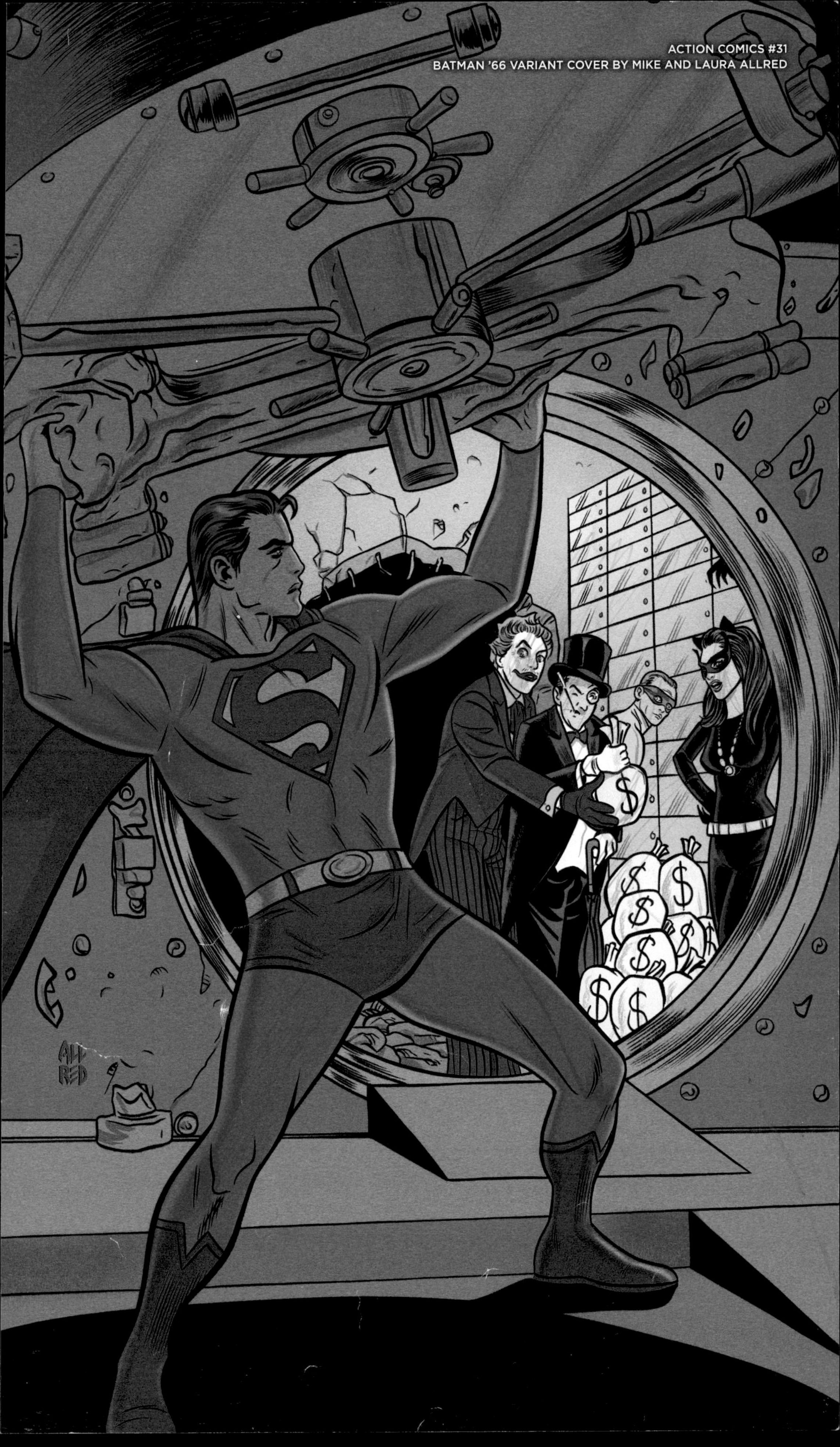
ALL
RED

ACTION COMICS #31
BATMAN '66 VARIANT COVER BY MIKE AND LAURA ALLRED

ACTION COMICS #32
BOMBSHELL VARIANT COVER BY ANT LUCIA

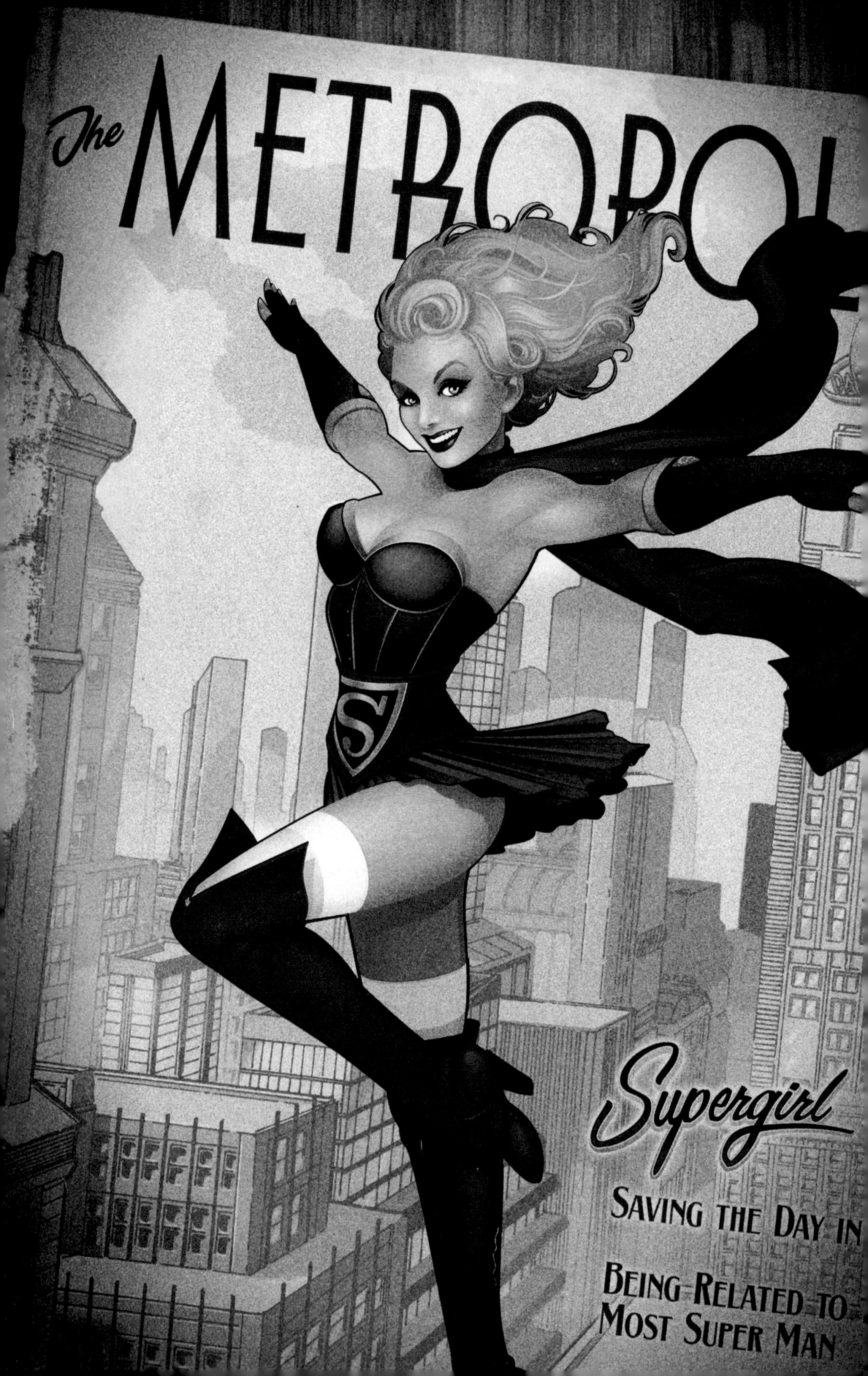

ACTION COMICS #33
BATMAN 75TH ANNIVERSARY VARIANT COVER BY KEVIN NOWLAN

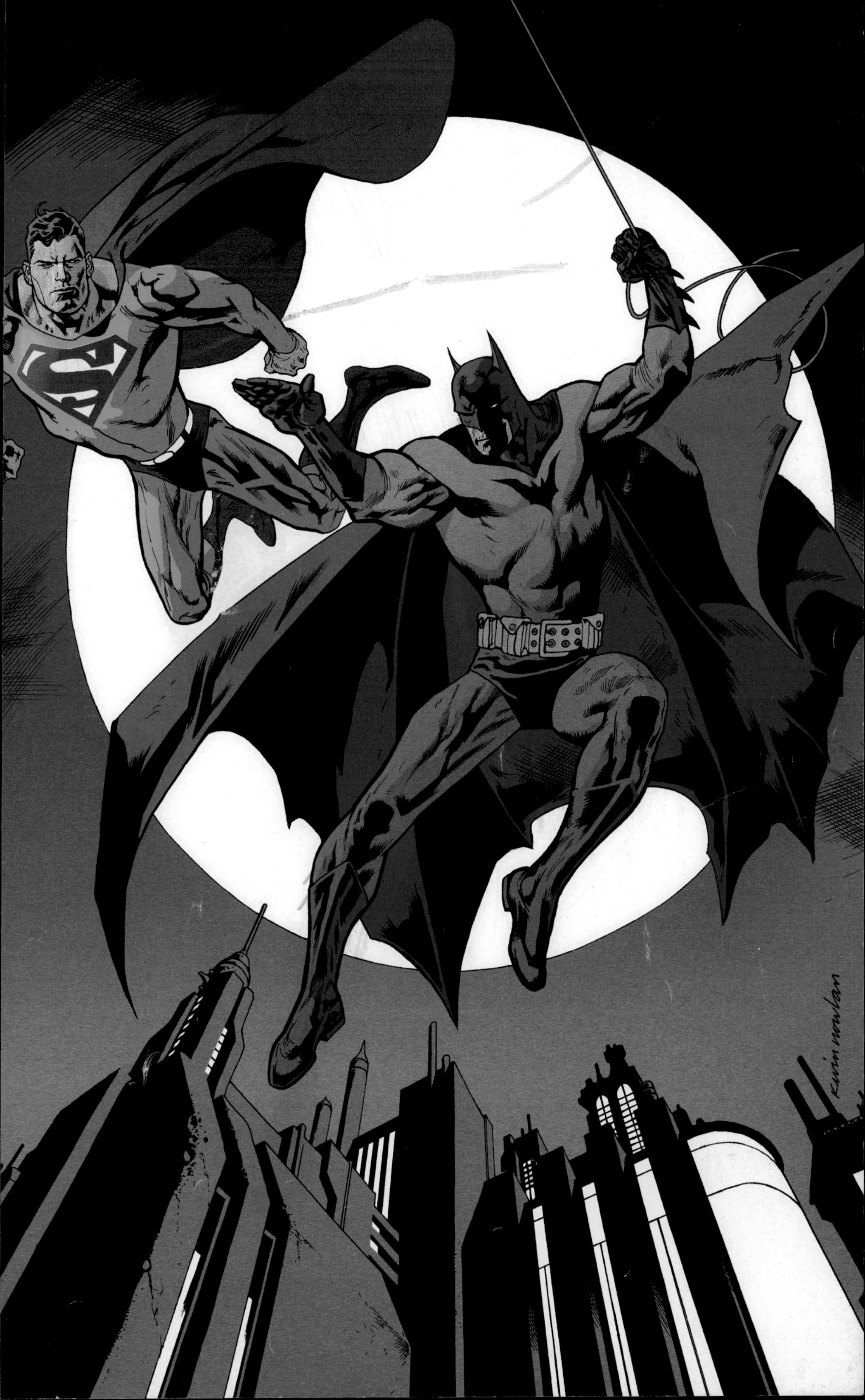
Kevin Nowlan

ACTION COMICS #34
SELFIE VARIANT COVER BY GARY FRANK AND BRAD ANDERSON

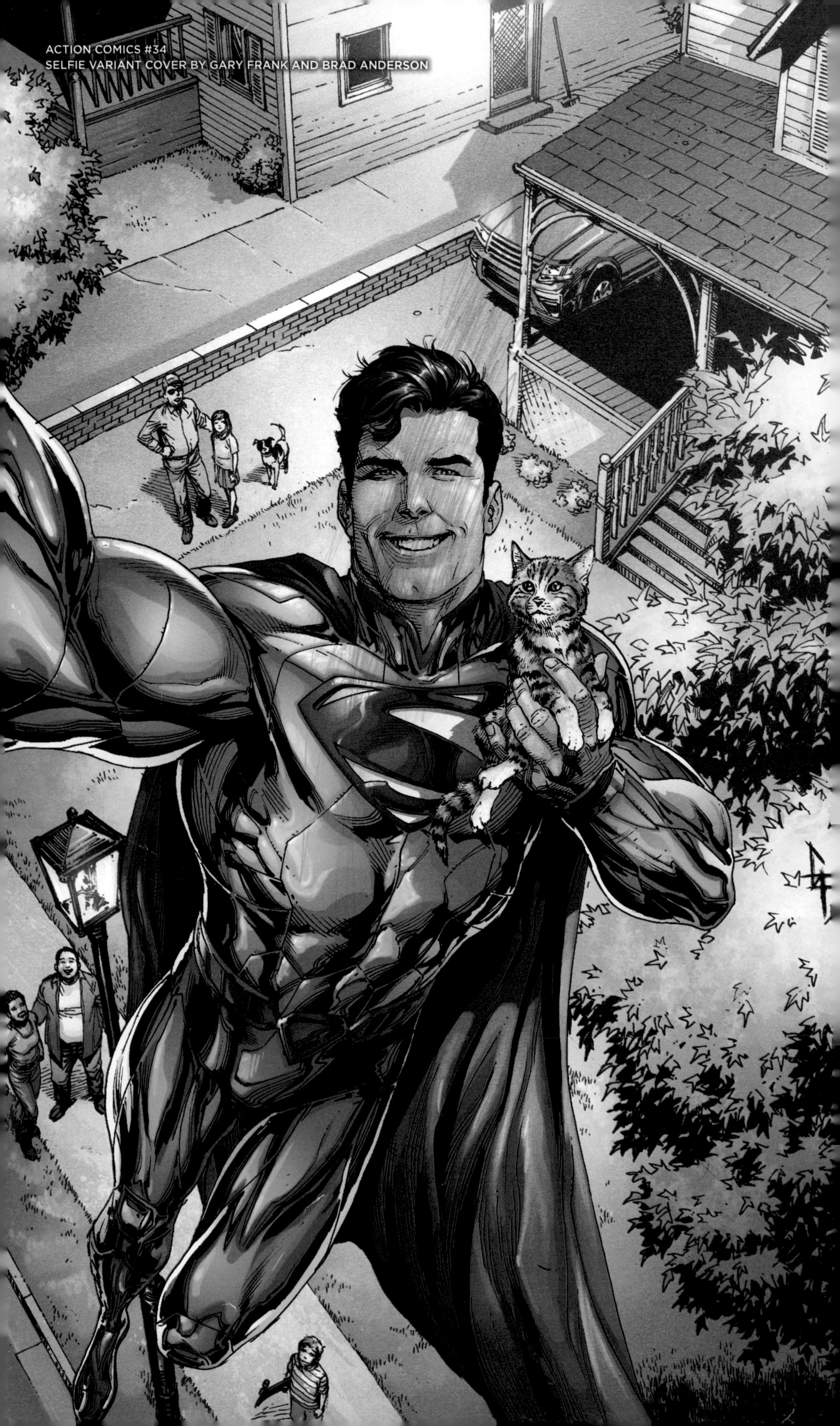

ACTION COMICS #35
MONSTERS OF THE MONTH VARIANT COVER BY NEAL ADAMS AND ALEX SINCLAIR

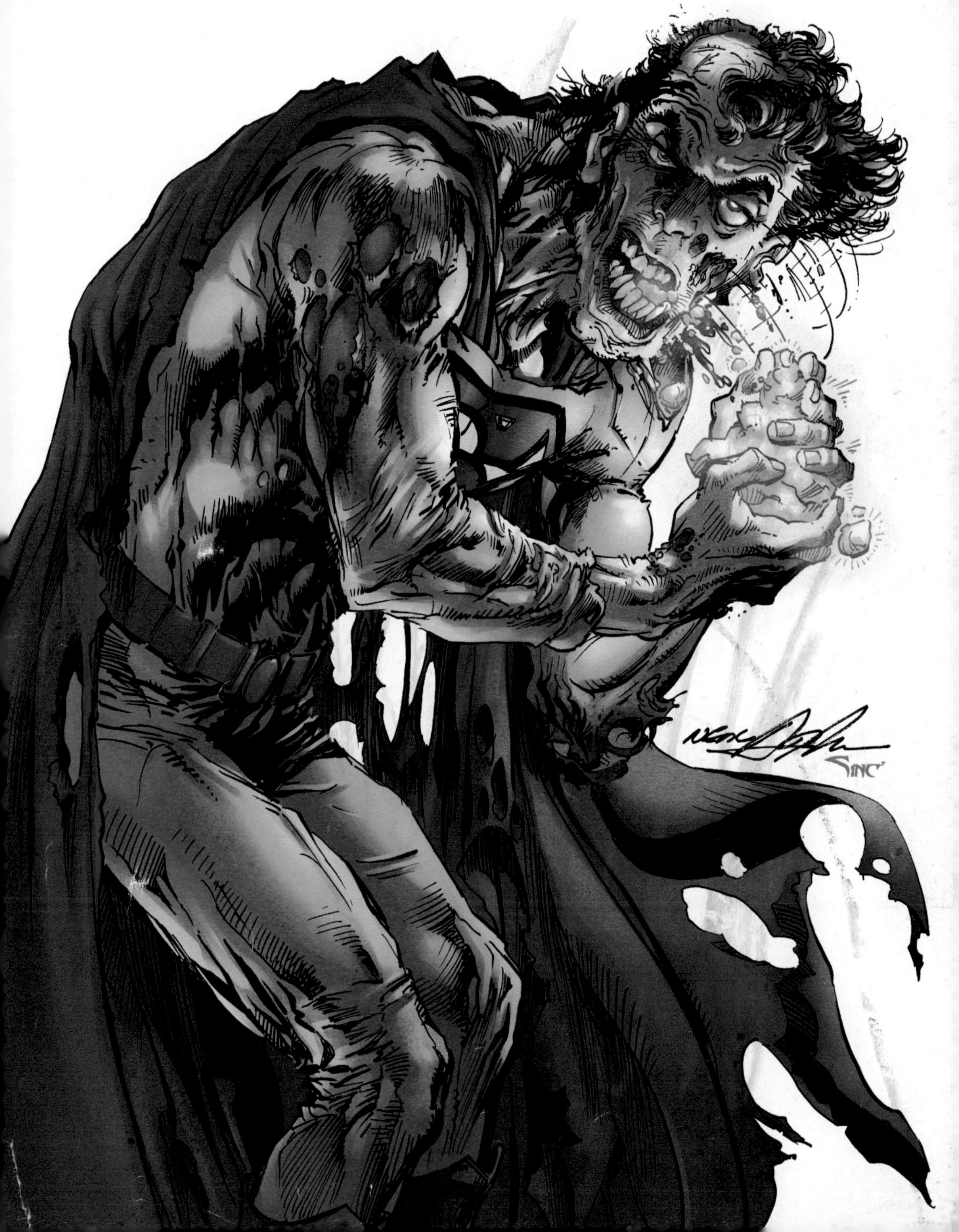

DC COMICS™

START AT THE BEGINNING

SUPERMAN: ACTION
COMICS VOLUME 1
SUPERMAN AND THE MEN OF STEE

SUPERMAN:
ACTION COMICS
VOL. 2: BULLETPROOF

with GRANT
MORRISON and RAGS
MORALES

SUPERMAN: ACTION
COMICS VOL. 3: AT
THE END OF DAYS

with GRANT
MORRISON and RAGS
MORALES

SUPERBOY VOL. 1:
INCUBATION

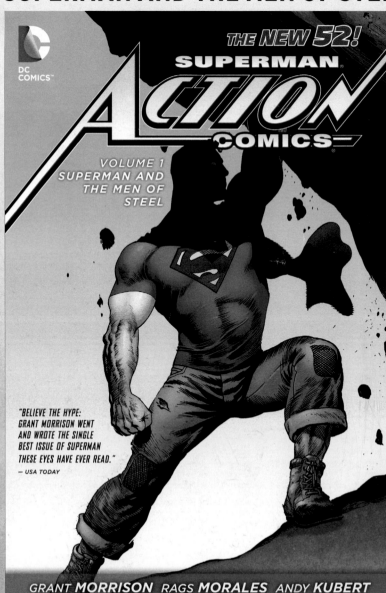

START AT THE BEGINNING!

SUPERMAN VOLUME 1: WHAT PRICE TOMORROW?

UPERMAN VOL. 2: SECRETS & LIES

UPERMAN VOL. 3: URY AT WORLD'S END

SUPERMAN: H'EL ON EARTH

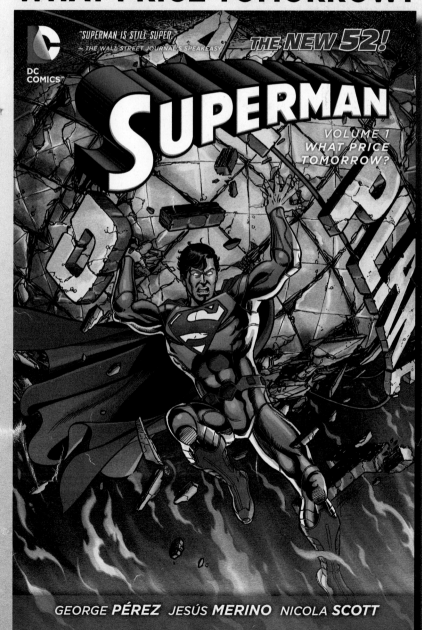

GEORGE **PÉREZ** JESÚS **MERINO** NICOLA **SCOTT**

DC COMICS™

"Writer Geoff Johns and artist Jim Lee toss you–and heroes–into the action from the very start and don't pu the brakes. DC's über-creative team craft an inviting worl those who are trying out a comic for the first time. Lee's stunning."—USA TO

"A fun ride."–

START AT THE BEGINNING

JUSTICE LEAGUE
VOLUME 1: ORIGIN
GEOFF JOHNS and JIM LEE

JUSTICE LEAGUE
VOL. 2: THE VILLAIN'S
JOURNEY

JUSTICE LEAGUE
VOL. 3: THRONE OF
ATLANTIS

JUSTICE LEAGUE
OF AMERICA VOL. 1:
WORLD'S MOST
DANGEROUS